THE MYTH
OF SANTA FE

THE MYTH
OF SANTA FE

CREATING A MODERN REGIONAL TRADITION

CHRIS WILSON

UNIVERSITY OF NEW MEXICO PRESS
ALBUQUERQUE
1997

Third paperbound printing, 1999

Library of Congress Cataloging-in-Publication Data

Wilson, Chris, 1951-
 The myth of Santa Fe : creating a modern regional tradition / Chris Wilson. — 1st ed.
 p. cm.
 Includes index.
 1. Santa Fe (N.M)—Civilization—20th century. 2. Regionalism—New Mexico—Santa
Fe—History—20th century. 3. Ethnicity—New Mexico—Santa Fe—History—20th century. 4. Tourist
trade—New Mexico—Santa Fe—History—20th century. I. Title.
 F804.S25W55 1996
 978.9'5605—dc20 95-50222
 CIP

Design: Mary Shapiro

The author wishes to thank the following publishers and publications for the opportunity to air some
of this material previously, and to adapt portions of those articles for publication here:
"The Spanish Pueblo Revival Defined, 1904-1921," *New Mexico Studies in the Fine Arts*, 7, © 1982 by
Regents of the University of New Mexico.
"Regionalism Redefined: The Impact of Modernism in New Mexico," *MASS* (Journal of the School of
Architecture, University of New Mexico, 1, © 1983 by Regents of the University of New Mexico.
"Santa Fe Architecture: The Lost Art of Picturesque Composition," *Artspace*, 10, no. 3, © 1986 by
Artspace, Inc.
"New Mexico Architecture in the Tradition of Romantic Reaction," *Artspace*, 13, no. 1, © 1988 by
Artspace, Inc.
"New Mexico in the Tradition of Romantic Reaction," in Nicholas C. Markovich, Wolgang F.E. Preiser,
and Fred G. Strum eds., *Pueblo Style and Regional Architecture*, (New York: Van Nostrand Reinhold),
© 1990 by Van Nostrand Reinhold.

CONTENTS

ACKNOWLEDGMENTS

As a resident of Albuquerque, my relation to Santa Fe is suspect from opposite points of view. For some National Endowment for the Humanities fellowship reviewers, research on the region in which one lives automatically raises the suspicion that one is a provincial partisan. Conversely, for certain cultivated Santa Feans, I have the impression, that residence in my sprawling, vulgar Sunbelt metropolis sixty-five miles to the southwest raises serious doubts about one's sensibilities and ability to say anything useful about their beloved city. While my affections for Santa Fe, its people and rich community life are deep, the perspective from Albuquerque has allowed me to cast a critical (and I hope constructive) eye on some of the city's traditions and pretensions. I do know that my work has benefitted equally from the support and encouragement of people from those opposite directions—from scholars scattered across the country, as well as from residents of the city. My heartfelt thanks go to these diverse individuals who helped me along the way.

This research began fifteen years ago at the University of New Mexico, where Bainbridge Bunting, Douglas George, Mary Grizzard, Christopher Mead and Charles Biebel served on my thesis committee. Mrs. Haskell, Mr. Martin, Mr. Davis, Thomas Gould, Michael Lesy, Vincent Scully and Michael Roemer made significant contributions to my earlier education. Among the many people who offered encouragement and research leads along the way were Harry Wiess, Tomas Atencio, Henry Glassie, J.J. Brody, William Tydeman, Henry Tobias, Carl Sheppard, Mary Jean Cook, Mary Ann Anders, Gabriel Melendez, John Dorst, Dell Upton, Jeff Bryan, Stan Hordes, Thomas Carter, Harry Moul, Paul Groth, Marta Weigle, Marc Treib, and Mario Montaño. Patty Pollock, Amy Shelhammer, Robert Sullivan and Arnold Valdez among other students at the University of New Mexico School of Architecture and Planning also contributed to the research. My thanks go also to the many Santa Fe residents who agreed to be interviewed for this book (and are cited in the footnotes), but most especially to José N. Trujillo.

Deserving particular mention are those who read and made valuable comments on any of the various generations of the manuscript: Felipe Gonzáles, Rina Swentzell,

Marc Simmons, Boyd C. Pratt, John Conron, Eileen Devereux, Barrett Price, David Kammer, Sylvia Rodríguez, Richard Longstreth, Charles Cutter, George Pearl, and John B. Jackson. Catherine Bishir, David Margolin, and Gwendolyn Wright, who each gave the draft a particularly close reading, especially helped to improve the clarity of the arguments and the quality of the writing. My many congenial collaborators at the University of New Mexico Press ranged from the director of the press, Beth Hadas, and editor for art and architecture Dana Asbury, to book designer Mary Shapiro, art director Tina Kachele, and marketing director Peter Moulson.

As any researcher knows, archivists are frequently instrumental in guiding one into the fruitful recesses of their collections. Among my many generous guides were Robert Torrez, Al Regensberg and Paul Saavedra at the State Archives and Records Center, Santa Fe; Emily Oakhill, Rockefeller Archive Center, North Tarrytown, New York; Rose Díaz, Stella de la Rego, Kathlene Ferris, Nancy Brown, and Jan Barnhart, Center for Southwest Research, University of New Mexico, Albuquerque; Orlando Romero, History Library, Museum of New Mexico, Santa Fe; Marilyn Ibach, Library of Congress, Washington D.C.; Mo Palmer, Albuquerque Museum; and, above all, Arthur Olivas and Richard Rudisell, Photo Archives, Museum of New Mexico, whose long labors assembling an unsurpassed collection of New Mexico images is reflected in the pages of this book. The Rockefeller Archive Center also generously provided a research travel grant to allow work with their collections. In addition to the numerous other institutions and individuals who provided single images, I would like to particularly acknowledge Sam Leyba, Jack Parsons, Robert Reck, Patrick Nagatani, Harry Fonseca, Nora Naranjo-Morris, Luis Jiménez, Anita Rodríguez, and Miguel Gandert, who provided examples of their art for reproduction.

My parents, Joanne Marie Hausser and Martin Lucien Wilson, imparted a deep interest in history to me. My warmest thanks go to them and to my wife, Kathryn Ann Williams (a Santa Fe expatriate), and my son, Luc Wilson, without whose support and patience with the long absences in my home office, this book could not have been completed.

For Kathryn and for Luc

THE MYTH
OF SANTA FE

INTRODUCTION: SOME PARADOXES OF MODERN CULTURAL IDENTITY

At first the 1988 motion picture *The Milagro Beanfield War* was difficult for many New Mexicans to swallow. Imagine the misgivings of local audiences as the movie opened to unfamiliar accordion music and an aged figure dressed in a serape and sombrero— a costume not worn in the region during this century, except perhaps by an Anglo tourist at a 1920s Santa Fe Fiesta. Here was a character in the stereotypic Oaxacan peasant costume worn by Marlon Brando at the beginning of *Viva Zapata!,* playing a Mexican variation of Tevye from *Fiddler on the Roof,* with the music from Fellini's *Amarcord* in the background.

John Nichols's novel about a Hispanic mountain village, on which the movie is based, had been a favorite in the area since it appeared in 1974. The book reveled in comic caricatures, to be sure. But its humor helped introduce the history and contemporary consequences of stolen land and water rights. Such was the fondness for the book that people eagerly anticipated the movie version of this true fiction of northern New Mexico because, for once, something of the actual local history and cultural dynamics would be presented to national audiences.

As the movie unfolded, the distinguished cast of Chicano, Hispanic, and Latino actors from Los Angeles, Texas, Mexico, Panama, and Brazil appeared in turn, each speaking a different variety of Spanish and English with a different Spanish (or Portuguese) accent. As a student of the region's architecture, I found the sets particularly jarring; made of lathe, styrofoam, and plaster, they simulated adobe houses with large patches of plaster fallen off—the standard Hollywood cliche of Mexican architecture. After a few minutes, though, the beautiful landscape and sunsets and the momentum of the plot pulled most viewers into the movie.[1]

Certainly Hollywood's depictions of other subcultures, from *The Grapes of Wrath, Norma Rae,* and *Dances with Wolves* to *The Waltons, Miami Vice,* and *Northern Exposure* are open to the same provincial nit-picking. On this count, *The Milagro Beanfield War* may be typical of its type; the soundtrack music so many New Mexicans found incongruous even won an Academy Award. This is not so much a criticism, then, as it is

the recognition that mass culture relentlessly projects its stereotypes onto distinctive, local cultures.

The images and metaphors applied to New Mexico over the years have been drawn from virtually every Native American and Latin source, from the American Southwest, Mexico, and South America, as well as from Spain, Italy, and the Holy Land. Don Quixote, Montezuma, Coronado, and Plains Indians in war bonnets have all made appearances set amid buildings patterned on California Missions, the Moorish Alhambra, and Pueblo villages, accompanied by everything from Mariachi music to Peruvian panpipes, Spanish rice to Texan fajitas.

The interplay of these tourist stereotypes with symbols of local ethnic identities and the less symbolically charged but no less distinctive details of contemporary life is complex and reciprocal. Not only are outside images projected onto Santa Fe, but the Museum of New Mexico and local businessmen and women have appropriated select details of Pueblo and Hispano cultures to promote tourism and foster civic identity. But these images can also retain a force of their own, beyond the power of commercial and government interests. In many instances, these stereotypes, at once idealized, romantic, and often implicitly denigrating, have been reclaimed by ethnic groups as weapons of resistance to cultural domination and tourist commodification.

This manipulation of historical and cultural symbolism began in earnest in 1912, the year statehood was granted. Following the arrival of the railroad in 1880, the city had rapidly modernized its appearance, even as it declined economically after being left off the main rail line. Santa Fe's Plan of 1912 sought to reverse this decline by remaking Santa Fe into an exotic tourist destination—a self-styled "City Different." In the teens, the Museum of New Mexico drew elements selectively from local building traditions to define the Santa Fe style. In time this revival echoed back into the vocabulary of local vernacular builders. The modern Santa Fe Fiesta, to mention another example, was established in 1919 under the direction of the Anglo-American museum staff. But within a generation, the Spanish-American community had taken control and reshaped it into

1. Promotional still for The Milagro Beanfield War, a Robert Redford/Moctesuma Esparza Production, Universal City Studios, 1987.

a historical allegory extolling Catholic virtues and contemporary ethnic identity. (Throughout this book I employ contemporaneous ethnic terminology: Spanish-American in the 1920's, for instance, but Hispanic in the 1980's to reflect changing terms.)

Just as outside stereotypes have been projected onto Santa Fe, so too has the city emerged as a cultural center in its own right, generating images that project outward across New Mexico and neighboring states to Santa Fe style restaurants and furniture stores around the country, and even to Hotel Santa Fe at Euro Disneyland, outside Paris. In a world infatuated with maintaining historical traditions and ethnic identities, Santa Fe has created an unusually successful illusion of authenticity.

Indeed the mobilization of history and cultural traditions in response to the rapid social changes of the past two centuries is one of the major phenomena of the modern world. As people left their rural and village-based traditions behind to seek industrial jobs in the booming cities, new traditions were created wholesale to take their place. This phenomenon, which historians refer to as the "invention of tradition," peaked in the United States between the Civil War and World War I, but continues with vigor to this day. Invented traditions rework serviceable fragments from our regional, family, and ethnic traditions, mixed with borrowings from other times and peoples, and leavened by pure invention. Paradoxically, invented traditions frequently are clothed in historical garb; they deny their modern origins, while claiming historical authenticity.[2]

During these past two centuries, the number of nation-states has grown from under twenty-five to nearly two hundred. Each required its own flag, symbols, holidays, and deified founding fathers. Monumental buildings and statues, allegorical murals, and world's fairs demonstrated the growing power of the state. The coronation of the British monarch, for instance, was elaborated into a major public ceremony during the nineteenth century; on the eve of the First World War, a mania for local historical pageants honoring pioneer settlers swept the United States and found a distinctively Southwestern expression in the Santa Fe Fiesta. Since the Second World War, social justice movements the world over have also found symbols to rally behind, such as

the Native American Mother Earth, and the mythic Chicano homeland, Aztlán. Entering the modern world of scientific rationalism and nation-states, history began to assume some of the functions of religious myth when it explained the origins of particular nations and groups, while also justifying the social order as something based on almost sacred historical precedent.

The romantic movement beginning at the end of the 1700s and its continuation in the Arts and Crafts movement the following century provided the aesthetics and methods for much tradition making. It championed preindustrial craftsmanship and rekindled interest in traditional music, costume, folklore, and custom. The novelist Sir Walter Scott, for instance, linked the romantic spirit with nationalism in the 1820s, when he orchestrated the adoption of the Highland kilt, clan tartans, and the bagpipe as symbols of modern Scottish identity. Historical romances from *Frankenstein, Robin Hood,* and *The Last of the Mohicans,* to *Treasure Island, Ben Hur,* and *Gone with the Wind* have made perfect fodder for Hollywood movie makers and captured the imaginations of audiences worldwide. The height of romantic historicism also saw new buildings dressed up as Gothic cathedrals, Georgian mansions, California missions, and Pueblo villages; while world's fairs and civic centers were cast as imperial Roman cities.

2. VIEW ACROSS THE WEST END OF THE MAIN BASIN, WORLD'S COLUMBIAN
EXPOSITION, CHICAGO, 1893. (PHOTOGRAPHER: C.D. ARNOLD)

Historic preservation and the romantic movement have gone hand in hand from the first. Indeed when modernism forbade historical styles in the 1940s, 1950s, and 1960s, the historic preservation movement helped keep the romantic historical impulse alive.

Urbanization and colonialism also bring groups of varying origins into closer contact. But while modern technology and economics might make people's day-to-day lives increasingly similar, paradoxically their perception of ethnic difference often increases. The elevation of selected traditional cultural details as symbols of group identity reaches a new level when ethnic music, celebrations, food, costumes, arts, and architecture are packaged as tourist commodities. As modern society compresses past differences, mass culture often pays lip service to the very folk and ethnic traditions that are being transformed.[3]

Our very notion of culture is bound up with this mid-nineteenth-century world of industrialization, urbanization, and colonialism. *Culture* first meant "what was most elevated, sensitive, essential, and precious—most uncommon in our society." This was culture with a capital *C,* what we still mean when we speak of the symphony as a cultural institution. Culture in this sense was the result of an evolutionary process culminating in European bourgeois society; it provided a bulwark against the vulgarity and incoherence of the industrial city.

Around 1900, however, anthropologists and progressive intellectuals began to use the plural *cultures* as a challenge to the Eurocentric attitudes bound up in the early sense of the word. This new usage reflected the emergence of cultural relativism— the notion that each culture is coherent and valid in its own terms. Although this is clearly less elitist and ethnocentric, the assumption that culture is a stabilizing influence carries over from the early definition. A culture was assumed to be "enduring, traditional, structural"; it is "a process of ordering, not disruption"; it "does not normally 'survive' abrupt disruptions."[4]

Anthropologists and folklorists who shared these assumptions typically denigrated cultural mixing and instead sought out the ever-shrinking number of isolated cultures, those that seemingly remained untainted by modern influences. A similar distaste for the messy complexity of history leads historic preservationists to remove alterations and additions from buildings to return them to their (often imagined) historic appearance. Ethnic boosters emphasize tradition, while anthropologists seek cultural authenticity, and preservationists value historic integrity.

These paradoxes intertwine. Invented traditions claim historic continuity. Groups of different origins grow more alike, while expressions of ethnic difference intensify. The notion of culture as something ordered and stable emerges from an era of profound change. The romantic and ethnic fixation on the survival of authentic cultural fragments diverts attention from the very modern dislocations that stimulated the desire for continuity and stability in the first place. A city that buries its utility lines the better to sustain a historical fantasy, such as Santa Fe, is utterly dependent on tourists, who owe their leisure to the prosperity of industrialization.

Is this nineteenth-century notion of enduring culture, then, really the most useful for understanding societies that, with only rare exceptions, have been drawn into global economic and communication networks? The migration from country to city and from continent to continent, mass media, the mixing of cultures, and the often significant degree of marriage between groups characterize the modern world. Individuals and communities faced with these unprecedented transformations have adopted the practice of reinventing their identities. To this way of thinking, culture has become an ongoing process of creating plausible fictions. Better to accept this situation and try to understand how societies and their symbols change than to continue to lament the passing of supposedly authentic traditional cultures.[5]

Santa Fe is an extreme and therefore instructive example of the invention of tradition and the on-going interaction of ethnic identity with tourist image making. The Santa Fe style of architecture, sometimes known as the Spanish Pueblo revival or simply the Pueblo style, emerged first and has continued to epitomize local identity. Since it was codified by the Museum of New Mexico between 1912 and 1916, this distinctive regional

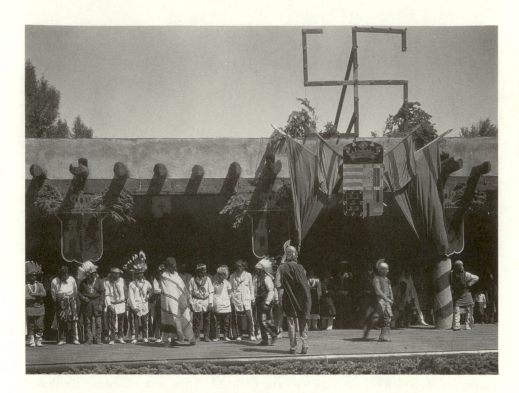

revival has provided a unifying civic identity for the city, a promotional image to attract tourists, and a romantic backdrop for Anglo-American newcomers. In the late teens, the museum staff embarked on a broader program of cultural tradition making, which encompassed the revival of Native American and Hispanic arts, the elaboration of the annual Santa Fe Fiesta into a public pageant, and the fostering of an art colony.

This constellation of arts and architectural revivals, public ceremony, romantic literature, and historic preservation together have created what I am calling the myth of Santa Fe. It is a myth in the pejorative sense of the word—a half-truth, something made up. But like invented traditions elsewhere, it is also a myth in the honorific sense of the word—something that provides a unifying vision of the city, its people, and their history, and that has fostered one of the most active art and myth-making centers in the United States.

Initiated to promote tourism, it has also provided a sense of coherence and continuity to a region in the midst of social and economic transformation. Central to this myth is the rhetoric of tricultural harmony; that is harmony among Native Americans, Hispanics, and Anglo-Americans. Despite this rhetoric of social tolerance, and despite the unifying image provided by ubiquitous adobe-colored stucco, the myth of Santa Fe obscures long-standing cultural and class frictions.

3. 1921 Santa Fe Fiesta pageant in front of Palace of the Governors, remodeled 1913. (T. Harmon Parkhurst)

While the basic patterns and content of the myth emerged by the early 1920s, it has continued to respond to broader socioeconomic currents in American society. The New Deal populists of the 1930s sought to balance the myth of Santa Fe between the economic necessity of tourism and the use of its symbols to promote more broadly conceived social objectives such as public education and local economic self-sufficiency. Progressive regionalism peaked again in the early 1970s, with the counterculture and the Chicano and environmental movements.

But in the 1980s, this balance tilted almost completely toward the manipulation of the myth as a tourism marketing image. Simultaneously Ronald Reagan led a reallocation of resources from social programs to the military and from the lower and middle classes to the wealthy. Some of those with conspicuous new wealth were attracted to the city by the upsurge of international publicity that projected Santa Fe as a Tahiti in the desert, bathed in rosy sunsets, and elevated it (or reduced it, depending on your point of view) to a chic style of interior design and a world-class tourist destination.

The magnitude of the subsequent boom (millions of tourist visitors and thousands of amenity migrants who came and stayed) was more than a city of sixty thousand could comfortably absorb. In effect the entire community began to be gentrified, as more and more native residents could no longer afford the city's cost of living. Local politicians led by Debbie Jaramillo, who won election as mayor in 1994, insisted that public policy address the negative side effects of the tourism boom.

Throughout this history, different ethnic groups and social classes have tended to control particular arts and cultural realms. Anglo-Americans have long dominated the architecture revival and historic preservation. Pueblo Indians, who benefit from the tourist market for their arts, have seen the myth as otherwise largely irrelevant, because it diverges so greatly from their world view. The Spanish-American elite reclaimed a portion of the myth through their control of the annual fiesta. And while the *mexicano* working class today continues an unbroken and largely unrecognized vernacular building tradition, the myth has been challenged by the Chicano retelling of history.

The shape of this book derives from an attempt to unravel the creation of the myth. The first three chapters, which make up Part One, give an overview of local history before 1912. This provides the background necessary for understanding the subsequent manipulation of that history, in particular the events, architectural elements, and ethnic traditions that would become fodder for the myth. Two interludes provide thematic cross-sections through our story. In the first, "Adobe Camouflage," the changing surface treatments of Santa Fe's buildings reveal broad shifts in cultural attitudes.

While Part One proceeds chronologically, the five chapters of Part Two look in depth at the creation of the myth in specific cultural realms. The groundbreaking definition of the architectural revival holds center stage in Chapter 4, the evolution of ethnic identities in Chapter 5, the creation of public celebrations in Chapter 6, the historic preservation movement in Chapter 7, and the more recent evolution of the architectural revival in Chapter 8.

The second interlude, "Coyote Consciousness," proposes a form of contemporary mythmaking to counteract the potentially destructive overemphasis of ethnic purity. The conclusion continues this speculation on the ways the residents of Santa Fe and those of us living elsewhere might better harness the mechanisms of modern tradition and mythmaking for the social health of our communities.

Throughout this second part of the book, the focus remains on the active construction of the myth of Santa Fe—which historical and cultural elements have been appropriated for tourist, civic, and ethnic purposes, and which aspects have been distorted or wholly repressed because of the unsettling questions they raise. These patterns of emphasis and omission reflect prevailing cultural, political, and economic forces, some of which are local, while others are national or international in scope.

This interpretation assumes that history is not something neutral or ever completely objective, but rather is a subjective retelling based on a selection and ordering of a small portion of the facts. History is not written for those who lived it and are now gone, but is constantly reshaped in terms meaningful to the living, unavoidably reflecting the concerns of the era in which it is written. It follows that this book is a selective interpretation of history, shaped by my sense of what questions are important and, to the extent that it may be found interesting or useful to others, by the issues and concerns of this era.[6]

I have tried in two ways to offer glimpses of the subjective apparatus of selection, distillation, and interpretation at work in this or any other volume of history. Chapter six presents a collection of historical descriptions and interpretations of public ceremonies—excerpts that not only conflict with each other, but sometimes contradict my narrative. These are designed to permit you, the reader, to form your own understanding of Santa Fe's fiesta. The speculations nearer the end of the book are in part an attempt to connect the lessons of history to contemporary social issues and future possibilities. But they also serve to bring my own concerns and biases more fully to the surface, the better to judge their effect on the entire book.

This is my framework for relating architecture and public ceremony to tourism and ethnic identity—and for connecting past to present and future. I avidly anticipate other historical interpretations and unforeseen social initiatives that engage these cultural forces to reshape Santa Fe.

11

PART ONE

SANTA FE BEFORE
IT BECAME A STYLE

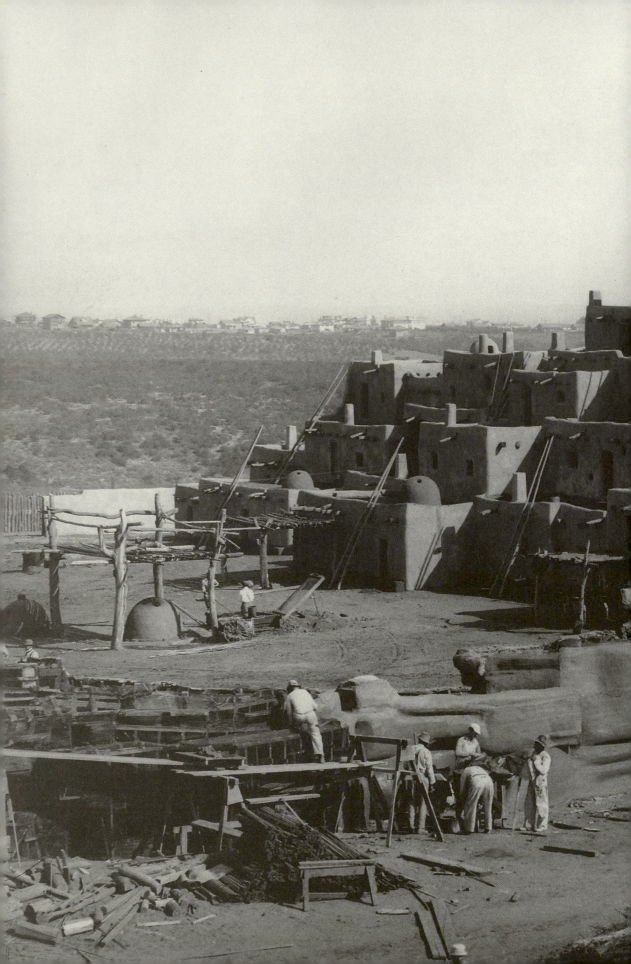

1

SPANISH AND
PUEBLO SANTA FE

Dressed in a padded doublet and stiff pleated collar, astride his parade saddle trimmed in embroidered blue velvet, the new governor, Don Pedro de Peralta, led a caravan of colonists up a tributary of the Rio Grande. Whether the firearms, metal tools, and adobe brick molds they carried in their carts or the town planning ordinances, Catholic faith, and habits of colonial government they carried in their minds would have the greater impact is difficult to say. When they reached a place the Tewa Pueblo Indians called *ogaponge,* "over at the shells by the water," near a modest Spanish herding camp, they halted. There in the spring of 1610, immediately north of the river, Peralta laid out a plaza for the new town of Santa Fe. So began a two-centuries-long encounter between official Spanish ideals, the frontier realities of a hard and arid land, and the distinctive Pueblo culture.

The Anasazi, ancestors of the Pueblo Indians, had occupied the Southwest for over a millennium before the arrival of the Spanish. The earliest evidence of human occupation in present-day Santa Fe consists of stone spear points and scraps of storage baskets left behind at the camps of hunter-gatherers. The arrival of agriculture from central Mexico about A.D. 500 made permanent settlements possible. Across northern New Mexico, the Anasazi began to build pit houses, clustered together above their irrigated fields (fig. 4).

They first dug a square pit, 12 to 14 feet on a side and 2 or 3 feet deep, then erected a four-post armature, which they covered with branches and grass and finally sealed with earthen plaster. Each house had a fire pit in the middle of the floor and a smoke hole in the roof, which doubled as an entrance. Soon they also built above-ground food storage rooms of stone laid in ample earthen mortar; and about 900, some people began to move into these above-ground structures.[1]

The largest, most sophisticated Anasazi villages were built between 1050 and 1300 at Chaco Canyon and Mesa Verde, 120 miles west and 160 miles northwest of Santa Fe, respectively. Builders sheathed these great communal buildings with intricate stone veneers. The largest contained five hundred rooms, stood five stories tall, and were planned in regular D-shaped and rectangular forms (fig. 5).

Their flat roofs consisted of horizontal log rafters covered (as the pit houses had been) with branches, brush, grass, and earth. The pit house evolved into a fully subterranean chamber known today as a kiva, used primarily for religious and social purposes. Santa Fe and the upper Rio Grande Valley stood at the margins of this classic Anasazi world. Members of the culture living along the Santa Fe River only began farming and building pit houses about 1000. [2]

People began leaving Chaco Canyon about 1175, and by 1300 Mesa Verde also was abandoned. It is unclear whether soil depletion, drought, and arroyo cutting (resulting in a drop of the water table) or social and religious factionalism caused this exodus. There is no evidence, however, of abandonment caused by warfare. These Anasazi migrated west and south to the contemporary Hopi, Zuni, and Acoma Pueblos and east into the Rio Grande Valley. Along the Santa Fe River, they joined with the indigenous population to build large villages during what archaeologists term the Coalition Period of 1175 to 1325. Instead of finished stone masonry, the newcomers reverted to coarse stone rubble construction, or hand-shaped, "puddled adobe" walls of successive courses of mud, 12 to 16 inches high. Each of the six Santa Fe area pueblos (the largest stood a block north of the current Santa Fe plaza) had two hundred or so rooms grouped around one or two small plazas. Kivas were incorporated into the room blocks or excavated in the plazas, their flat roofs level with the ground. All six were abandoned by 1425. A century later, the ancestors of the present-day Navajos and Apaches appeared on the northeastern frontier of the Anasazi world, after migrating south from Canada. When Spanish explorers arrived from the south in 1540, they found the Anasazi living in seventy-five villages spread across northern New Mexico and northeastern Arizona, inhabited by some hundred thousand people.[3]

These earthen villages resembled Spanish adobe architecture to such an extent that the Spanish called them by their word for village, *pueblo,* a term which in time they also applied to the inhabitants (fig. 6). Although all Pueblo Indians shared a common

4. ARTIST'S RECONSTRUCTION OF A PIT HOUSE FROM THE FOUR CORNERS AREA WITH SIDE CUT AWAY, ABOUT A.D. 600. (ROBERT EASTON)

5. ARTIST'S RECONSTRUCTION OF PUEBLO BONITO, CHACO CANYON, EARLY 1100S. SUSTAINED BUILDING CAMPAIGN OF THIS AND OTHER LARGE, ANASAZI VILLAGES INDICATE HIGHLY ORGANIZED SOCIETIES. (LLOYD K. TOWNSEND)

tradition of agriculture, architecture, and basic cosmology, they spoke several different languages. Pueblo villages stood two to five stories tall, had fifty to five hundred rooms each, and were arranged around community plazas and ceremonial kivas. Storage rooms on the ground floor were entered not by doors but by ladders up onto the roofs and down again through small hatches. The living quarters on the upper levels, however, often had doors opening out onto the roofs of the lower levels. "The second terrace is all surrounded with lanes which enable one to circle the whole pueblo," marveled one early Spanish chronicler.[4]

SPANISH COLONIZATION

Spanish explorers and colonists carried the same cultural baggage into the Anasazi world that would transform all New World societies: horses, sheep, and cattle; firearms, metal tools, and the printed word; typhoid, measles, and smallpox. They also brought a highly developed colonial bureaucracy, a formal set of town planning ordinances, a social class system, and the Catholic faith. At Santa Fe and in the surrounding kingdom hopefully christened *New* Mexico, the Spanish colonial ideals of plaza-centered towns, courtyard houses, and mission complexes were reshaped through isolation, meager resources, and interaction with Pueblo Indians to form a regional variation of Spanish-Mexican culture.

6. TAOS PUEBLO, NORTH BUILDING, 1880. ROOF TERRACES FUNCTIONED AS OUTDOOR LIVING SPACE. (JOHN K. HILLERS)

Francisco Vásquez de Coronado led the first Spanish foray into the Southwest in the early 1540s. He sought easy riches like those taken from the Aztecs and Incas, but finding none, soon departed. After Coronado closed the first wave of conquest in the New World, the Spanish concentrated on the extraction of mineral wealth. Beginning in 1546 with the founding of Zacatecas, 300 miles north of Mexico City, silver mines were worked by Black and Native American slaves. The determined fifty-year resistance of local Indians is commonly known as the Chichimeca Wars.

Rumors of British colonization on the northern frontier, coupled with renewed dreams of mineral wealth, and the prospect of a docile Pueblo labor force, brought attention back to New Mexico. Juan de Oñate, son of a wealthy founding citizen of Zacatecas, was selected in 1595 to head a new expedition. Oñate had fought in the Chichimeca Wars in his youth and was thoroughly familiar with mining and the slave trade. He pledged to finance the expedition, and over the next three years he recruited 12 Franciscan friars and 129 soldiers; together with their families, servants, slaves, and Mexican Indian auxiliaries, they totaled over 600 people.[5]

On reaching New Mexico in 1598, Oñate established an outpost near the present-day pueblo of San Juan, 30 miles north of Santa Fe. The Spanish occupied the partially deserted Pueblo village of Yunque, renaming it San Gabriel. Like Coronado before them, Oñate and his men dreamed of fabled cities of gold and supported their forays across the Southwest and out onto the Great Plains with supplies extracted from the Pueblo villages. When Acoma Pueblo, 50 miles west of the Rio Grande, was slow to yield cornmeal to one reconnaissance party, a skirmish erupted, in which thirteen Spaniards were killed. Oñate dispatched seventy soldiers with artillery to lay siege to Acoma, located defensively atop a 350-foot-high mesa. In three days of pitched battle, the Spanish bombarded the village and set it afire, killing approximately eight hundred Acomas. Nearly six hundred prisoners were marched to Santo Domingo Pueblo on the Rio Grande, to receive judgement from Oñate. Those under twelve were distributed as servants to the missionaries and soldiers, those older were given

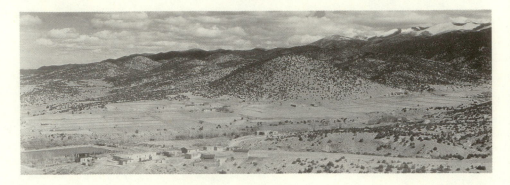

twenty years of servitude, while the twenty-four men over twenty-five years of age were also sentenced to have a foot chopped off. These mutilations were carried out at various Rio Grande pueblos, as an object lesson of the futility of resistance. Two Hopi men captured at Acoma each lost their right hand and were sent home bearing the same message.[6]

When the quest for mineral wealth was again unsuccessful, most of Oñate's men deserted back to Mexico. Others settled near Pueblo villages that Oñate granted them as *encomiendas,* an arrangement that entitled the Spaniard to annual tribute from the Indians in return for protection and instruction in Christian culture. When Oñate resigned his commission as governor in 1607, the viceroy in Mexico City was reluctant to send aid and reinforcements to sustain the colony. But rather than abandon the Indians already converted by the Franciscans, the Spanish crown decided to subsidize the colony.[7]

Oñate's replacement, Pedro de Peralta, was instructed to start afresh by founding a new capital, which he did by establishing Santa Fe in 1610. "Until the above mentioned Villa shall have been founded and inhabited nothing else shall be attended to," the viceroy instructed Peralta, "the Governor is requested not to allow or permit any order to be given allowing anyone to move to another place." Peralta's instructions clearly echoed the town planning ordinances of the Laws of the Indies. Compiled in 1573 by King Philip II of Spain, the Laws codified seventy years of Spanish town planning experience in the Americas and drew from a variety of European sources: Roman and Renaissance planning theory from Vitruvius to Alberti, monastic complexes and military encampments, and the siege towns built during the reconquest of Spain from the Moors. The Laws of the Indies provided specific, practical instructions for maintaining friendly relations with natives, selecting a town site, laying out a grid of streets with a central plaza, locating a church and government buildings on the plaza, and distributing town lots and farming lands to the colonists. In effect for over 250 years, from 1573 to 1821, the Laws shaped virtually every city in the Spanish

7. SANTA FE RIVER VALLEY ABOVE THE TOWN, AND SANGRE DE CRISTO MOUNTAINS, ABOUT 1935. THE SETTING OF SANTA FE MUCH AS IT WOULD HAVE APPEARED TO EARLY SETTLERS. (T. HARMON PARKHURST)

~ISOMETRIC DRAWING~
~of~
·SAN·ESTEBAN·DEL·REY·
·OLD·SPANISH·MISSION·
~at~
·ACOMA·PUEBLO·
·NEW·MEXICO·

domain. On the isolated, underfinanced northern frontier, however, these dictates were imperfectly realized.[8]

When Oñate occupied Yunque and renamed it San Gabriel, in 1598, he had ignored the injunction, repeated three times in the Laws, to "select the site to build a town and capital without damage to the Indians for having occupied the area."[9] This was a major concern, since the conversion of Indians was the crown's stated motivation for expansion in the New World. Spanish towns were also to be defensible and permanent in appearance so that the Indians would be impressed with their intention to stay. Each male settler received farmland, as well as a town lot, where he was expected to build a house and dwell. Unlike Oñate's fortune seekers at San Gabriel, Peralta's colonists established a permanent new community at Santa Fe. The location selected for the new capital epitomized the Laws' selection criteria: the town must be "in an elevated and healthful location; with means of fortification; fertile soil with plenty of land for farming and pasturage; have fuel, timber and resources; fresh water, a native population."[10]

While Santa Fe would be the sole permanent Spanish community during the 1600s, the Franciscans also built nearly fifty mission complexes at Indian pueblos (fig. 8). The Spanish Colonial mission form (a church and an attached residential courtyard)

8. SAN ESTEBAN MISSION, ACOMA PUEBLO, BUILT 1629-1644, BIRD'S EYE VIEW, 1934. (DUDLEY T. SMITH, HISTORIC AMERICAN BUILDING SURVEY—HABS)

developed during the first wave of conversions in the Valley of Mexico during the 1500s and was carried north to New Mexico in the following century by Franciscan friars. The courtyard complex, known as a *convento*, resembled other large Spanish residences with its single file of rooms arranged around three or four sides of an open rectangle; sometimes the church provided one side. Each room opened onto a porch ringing the courtyard. Here the Franciscans not only lived and proselytized but also transmitted Spanish culture and technology, for the *convento* typically contained not only living quarters but also a school, workshops, a small orchard, and a garden.[11]

Pueblo Indians under Franciscan direction constructed simple flat- roofed, single-nave churches out of adobe or unfinished stone set in earthen mortar—a convergence of Pueblo and Spanish folk-building technologies. At the head of these long, dark church naves, light flooded the altar from a transverse clerestory window inserted where the ceiling stepped up two to four feet just before the sanctuary. This ingenious local invention translated the Baroque transept dome into the simple New Mexican building technology. The shift from the multidirectional light of the dome to the unidirectional clerestory window required a departure from the European preference for western-facing facades with altars toward the Holy Land. New Mexican church facades instead faced east or southeast to take advantage of light from the clerestory window during morning mass. While this light streaming in from above symbolized the presence of the Holy Spirit for the Franciscans, the lighting scheme and orientation also appealed to the Pueblo building crews, who oriented their own kivas along a sacred southeast axis, toward the rising sun.[12]

REVOLT AND RECONQUEST

Pueblo Indians faced hard years under the Spanish. Famine, warfare (both with the Spanish and with nomadic Indians emboldened by the acquisition of horses), and epidemics of measles, typhoid, influenza, and smallpox reduced the Pueblo population from some one hundred thousand to twenty thousand during the first eighty years of Spanish rule. The burden of tribute in food, blankets, and labor levied by the governor, settlers, and missionaries rose as the Pueblo population fell. Although the clergy sheltered the Pueblos from some demands and abuses, they also banned native ceremonies, burned confiscated sacred objects, and occasionally executed native religious leaders.[13]

In August of 1680, the Pueblos united together for the first time to drive out the Spanish. In attacks against isolated missions and ranches, they killed twenty-one friars and approximately four hundred of the twenty-five hundred Spanish settlers. The Spanish survivors fled to Santa Fe, where they took refuge in the compound formed by the Palace of the Governors and other *casas reales*, before escaping south 400 miles to Guadalupe del Norte, present-day Juárez, Mexico.[14]

Tano-speaking Pueblo Indians from the Galisteo basin, south of the city, occupied Santa Fe along with a few Tewa-speakers from the Española Valley, to the north. When the Spanish returned twelve years later, Santa Fe had been transformed into a communal village of three- and four-story dwellings arranged around two plazas, with a ceremonial kiva at the center of each. This community of fifteen hundred was fortified against the Spanish return with round towers at each of the four corners and a single entrance guarded by a heavy wooden gate, trenches, embankments, and a semicircular tower.[15]

The new Spanish governor, Diego de Vargas, returned in 1692 with fifty Spanish soldiers, fifty Indian auxiliaries, and two artillery pieces. After a brief siege, Vargas forced the Pueblos to erect a cross in their main plaza. He entered the village, knelt and kissed the cross, and required the Pueblo leaders to do the same as a sign of obedience to their Catholic God and Spanish king. These events are known locally today as the peaceful reconquest of Santa Fe.[16]

Vargas then returned south to marshal additional allies, settlers, and resources for a permanent colony. Prerevolt Spanish families that had languished for thirteen years at Guadalupe del Norte were augmented by thirteen Franciscans, a few gentlemen soldiers from Spain, thirty-seven families from the Valley of Mexico, and others recruited from the silver-mining district around Zacatecas. Altogether a caravan of eight hundred people and fifteen hundred head of livestock set out with Vargas on the journey north, in October of 1693. Beginning so late in the year without adequate provisions for the winter, they clearly expected to be housed and fed in the Pueblo village at Santa Fe. The wary Indians, for their part, allowed only a few *mestizos* of mixed Pueblo-Spanish ancestry to move in with them, while the other colonists pitched their tents at a distance from the village. Vargas did, however, bluff the Pueblos into sharing their stores of corn by saying that more soldiers were on the way. As the weather turned bitter, and twenty-one of their number died of exposure, the Spanish became desperate.

On December 29th, reenforced by allies from nearby Pecos Pueblo, Vargas attacked the village. In a two-day battle, the Spanish emerged victorious, with only one dead. Two of the nine Indian dead had committed suicide to avoid capture, including the Pueblo leader, whom the Spanish called Governor José. Many of the inhabitants had slipped away before the battle, but the four hundred who surrendered were sentenced to ten years of servitude. Another seventy, captured in room-to-room searches after the battle, were taken out behind the village and executed. The next three years saw intermittent conflict across the Kingdom of New Mexico: sieges, mass flight to avoid Spanish rule, minor revolts, and swift retribution.[17]

CASTA HIERARCHY

Anasazi and later Pueblo villages frequently were composed of people of different origins. Two groups distinct in material culture (referred to as the New and the Old Bonitians by archaeologists) lived side by side at Pueblo Bonito in Chaco Canyon. During the thirteenth-century Coalition Period, the indigenous population along the upper Rio Grande was joined by immigrants from Chaco Canyon and Mesa Verde. In historic times, to mention a few well-known examples, Tanos and Tewas occupied Santa

Fe together after the 1680 revolt; a group of Tanos from the Rio Grande came to live with the Hopis; the few remaining families of Pecos Pueblo moved to Jemez Pueblo in 1838; and in 1880, a conservative faction from Laguna moved to Isleta.[18]

The Spanish experience with mixed populations, beginning during the reconquest of Spain from the Moors and the subsequent conquest of the New World, provided the system of social and ethnic categorization used in Santa Fe, where people from Europe, Africa, and North America (including Native Americans from central Mexico, the Pueblo villages, and surrounding nomadic bands) lived together. This Spanish system classed people by *casta*, which equated social class with racial ancestry and, to a degree, ethnic identity. Although dozens of terms were developed to describe the innumerable mixtures of ancestry that emerged in the New World, only a handful of these were ever widely used: *español* (Spanish), *indio* (Indian), *mestizo* (mixed Spanish-Indian), *mulato* (Spanish-Black), *zambo* (Indian-Black), *coyote* (dark-skinned mestizo), and *castizo* (light-skinned mestizo). Social status under these *castas* was loosely linked to facial features and skin color. "The whiter one's skin, the greater was one's claim to the honor and precedence Spaniards expected and received," writes social historian Rámon Gutiérrez. "The darker a person's skin, the closer one was presumed to be to the physical labor of slaves and tributary Indians."[19]

While the first wave of Spanish colonists to arrive in New Mexico during the 1590s included many Spaniards, the second wave during the reconquest of the 1690s reflected the general *mestizaje* (racial mixing) throughout New Spain. Just over half of the 210 soldier-settlers who accompanied Juan de Oñate in 1598–1600 were born in Spain, another quarter in New Spain, and the rest were of scattered or undetermined origin. Only 13 of the approximately 130 soldiers who arrived in 1598 brought wives; many took native women as partners. The largest surviving categorization of New Mexican colonists by casta covers the 128 people recruited by Vargas from the northern mining towns, especially Zacatecas, in 1694 and 1695. Of these people, 47 percent were classified as *mestizo*, 29 percent *español* (only a quarter of these born in Spain),

13 percent *coyote,* 11 percent *mulato,* 2 percent *castizo,* and 2 percent *lobo* (similar to *coyote*).[20]

Indians provided the major population infusions into the Spanish colonial villages. Navajo, Apache, Comanche, and Ute women and children taken captive by other nomadic bands might later be purchased by Spaniards or sometimes taken directly by them during retaliatory campaigns. Referred to as *genízaros,* these detribalized Indians typically worked as household servants and were brought up as Spanish-speaking Catholics. Between 1700 and 1849, 3,294 nomadic Indians were baptized in New Mexico. Once they reached marriageable age, they were to be freed, although many Spaniards maintained *genízaros* in debt peonage from generation to generation. One authority on this history, Fray Angelico Chávez, estimates that *genízaros* made up about a third of New Mexico's settled population in 1800.[21]

Pueblo Indians also entered Spanish villages by two routes. As a cultural self-preservation mechanism, Pueblo villages ostracized residents who became too acculturated to Spanish ways. Those ostracized then had little choice but to enter Spanish society at its bottom rung. In addition the rotating labor draft after the reconquest, known as *repartimiento,* also placed Pueblo women in Spanish households, where some became pregnant. If a woman gave birth to a light-skinned child after returning to

9. HOUSE WITH CARVED POST, ZAPATA CAPITAL AND BEAM, ARROYO TENORIO, SANTA FE, ABOUT 1912. AMONG THE FINEST EXAMPLES OF SPANISH COLONIAL WOOD DETAILING. (JESSE L. NUSBAUM)

her pueblo, she too might be ostracized, although more often she would give the child up for adoption at the local mission. These *hijos de la iglesia* (children of the church) were placed in Spanish homes and typically categorized as *coyotes*. Rámon Gutiérrez estimates that they made up approximately 10 percent of the settler population during the 1700s.[22]

The neutral term for a person of mixed parentage, *mestizo,* was applied to those who had begun to be absorbed into Spanish society, while denigrating animal names were often applied to those less acculturated or with darker skin. *Mulato,* for instance, originally meant a young mule (the sterile hybrid of a male donkey and a female horse). *Coyotl,* from Nahuatl, the language of the Aztecs, was adopted in Spanish as a new word for wolf and also as a term to describe people of mixed Indian-Spanish parentage, with perhaps a trace of Black ancestry. The original Spanish word for wolf, *lobo,* became a roughly synonymous racial term. Both words continue to have negative connotations in Spanish: *lobo* is slang for a drunk or a womanizer, and a *lobero* is a swindler or confidence man, while *coyote* has been applied to stockbrokers and smugglers.[23]

A small Spanish aristocracy dominated the *casta* hierarchy of eighteenth-century New Mexico. This wealthy, *rico* aristocracy consisted of fifteen or twenty extended families who congregated in the *villas* of Santa Fe, Albuquerque, and Santa Cruz. Below them were the largest group, landed *mestizo* and *genízaro* peasants, who increasingly considered themselves *español* or *mestizo,* and next were the landless *genízaros* and *coyotes* who lived as servants and laborers. To the side, Pueblo *indios* struggled to maintain their villages as distinct cultural islands.[24]

EIGHTEENTH-CENTURY SANTA FE

New Mexico had been settled in the 1600s to preempt British colonization and to allow the Franciscans to convert Indians to Catholicism. After the reconquest, the decimation of the Pueblo population opened lands for settlement by the increasing Spanish population. By 1776 natural increase and the infusion of Pueblo children

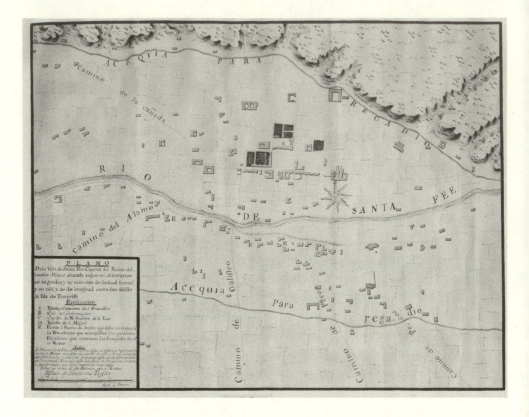

and detribalized nomadic Indians into Spanish communities brought the Spanish population to over ten thousand, compared to eight thousand Pueblo Indians. While the colonization of Texas in the late 1600s blocked the French advance from Louisiana and the California missions begun in 1769 stemmed the Russian spread south along the Pacific coast, New Mexico emerged as the most populous colonial buffer protecting the silver mines of northern Mexico. Government support of the missionaries, provincial officials, and the military garrison at Santa Fe made New Mexico a net drain on the royal treasury. The only source of wealth for the governor and the local elite was the export of sheep, wool, *piñon* (pine nuts), and Indian slaves to the silver mines. Spanish slave raids brought retaliation from the Apaches, who had gotten the horse from the Spanish by 1650, and from the Comanches, who also had procured guns from the French. These hostilities restricted Spanish settlement to the upper Rio Grande, from Albuquerque north to Taos.[25]

Our first clear picture of Santa Fe's town plan comes during this turbulent period, with its population at about fifteen hundred. Drawn by Lieutenant Joseph de Urrutia on a military inspection tour in 1766, this detailed plan reveals the extent to which Santa Fe followed the Laws of the Indies (figs. 10, 11).

10. *PLANO DE LA VILLA DE SANTA FEE DEL REINO DEL NUEBO MEXICO*, 1766.
(JOSEPH URRUTIA)

"The main plaza is to be the starting point for the town," instructed the Laws, and so it was in Santa Fe, with a large rectangular plaza north of the river surrounded by public buildings. Such was the importance of religion to the crown that the church received first choice of the plaza lots. In Santa Fe the main church of San Francisco was placed on the elevated, upriver end of the plaza. The Laws also conceived secondary plazas as places where "the parish churches and the monasteries can be built," envisioning the parish-church-plaza as the unit of urban social organization. San Miguel Church faced onto a modest plaza south of the river in the Barrio Analco, a neighborhood of Hispanicized Indians. The main plaza was also a civic space where the mounted militia drilled and fiestas and markets were held, so the government took second choice; in Santa Fe it selected the north side of the plaza .[26]

Plaza lots not taken by the church or government were to go next to merchants. But in the absence of full-time merchants in Santa Fe, they went to the leading citizens. Property owners, nevertheless, were obligated to build *portales* (porches) facing the plaza and principal streets, "for these are of considerable convenience to the merchants who generally gather there." Although Urrutia did not record *portales* on his map, early documents mention them around town, and a 1791 plan of the Palace of

11. ARTIST'S RECREATION OF SANTA FE IN 1766 BASED ON URRUTIA MAP.
(WILSON HURLEY)

the Governors shows one facing the plaza. In Santa Fe *portales* were constructed of rough-hewn log posts, sometimes topped by carved ornamental brackets called *zapatas*, spanned by horizontal beams, and roofed like normal rooms.[27]

While Santa Fe achieved the basic element of Spanish urbanity—a religious, civil, and commercial center in its plaza—it utterly lacked the regular grid of streets envisioned by the Laws of the Indies. Rather than stay in compact settlements, as prescribed by law and urged by the governor, Spanish settlers across northern New Mexico instead moved their houses close to their fields, once the threat of Indian attack waned in their locale. This put them nearer their work, allowed them to protect their crops, lessened official scrutiny, and permitted some on the frontiers to carry on contraband trade and friendly relations with nomadic Indians. In Santa Fe by 1766, houses built beside their owner's fields stretched for three miles up and down the valley.[28]

COURTYARD HOUSES AND CHURCHES

The flat-roofed adobe houses of Spanish New Mexico ideally employed the courtyard plan, with a single file of rooms wrapped around and opening into a small courtyard (figs. 12, 13). Because many regions and peoples shared these features, the origins of this house type in New Mexico are complex. The courtyard house had been common around the Mediterranean since before the time of Christ and was popularized on the Iberian peninsula during the Roman and Moorish occupations. After the expulsion of the Moors in 1492, it continued as the most common dwelling type in the southern provinces of Extremadura and Andalusia. Elsewhere in southern and central Spain, people built courtyard houses with pitched tile roofs; in the northern and eastern provinces, they preferred compact pitched-roof houses.[29]

Although Spain was politically united under Ferdinand and Isabella in 1492, strong regional cultures persisted in Aragon, Catalonia, Valencia, new and old Castile, Leon, Extremadura, Galicia, and Andalusia. Out of this variety emerged a modern Spanish

12. COURTYARD HOUSE WITH INTERIOR PORTAL, AND ADOBE-WALLED CORRAL,
ABOUT 1902.

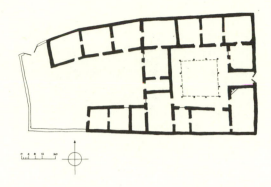

culture, with a conscious beginning when the regional dialect of Castile was codified and elevated to the official state language by Nebrija's Castilian grammar of
1492 and dictionary of 1493. In other cultural realms, unification proceeded less
systematically. Historical anthropologist George Foster has argued that in sixteenth-
century Mexico, a process of cultural crystallization produced a selective, simplified, and idealized version of Spanish culture—a unified "conquest culture" that
had not previously existed in Spain itself. This hybrid culture helped unite the Spanish
colonists from various regions and facilitated the adoption of Spanish ways by native
populations. Town planning practices, as already noted, emerged ad hoc during
the first decades of settlement but were codified by the Laws of the Indies in 1573.[30]

Of all the Spanish regional house types, why did the flat-roofed courtyard house
prevail in Mexico? Foster has argued that Spanish conquest culture drew primarily
from the regions most heavily represented in the first wave of settlers. Once established, this culture resisted infusions from later settlers. Some 30 percent of the early
settlers came from Andalusia (the most from any one province) and another 18 percent from Extremadura and southern Leon. This favored the adoption of that
region's type, the courtyard house.[31]

Like the countries surrounding the Mediterranean, central Mexico had a hot, dry
climate and limited supplies of building timber, which also favored the adoption of
the courtyard house. Moreover in the Valley of Mexico, upper-class Aztecs and
Tlaxcalans (who became Spanish military auxiliaries) also built flat-roofed houses of
stone or adobe with rooms opening onto central courtyards. The Mediterranean-
Andalusian precedent, climatic conditions, and the Aztec-Tlaxcalan building tradition converged to make the courtyard house the primary dwelling of the crystallized
Spanish-Mexican culture. This house type was diffused by the Spanish and their Indian
and Mestizo allies throughout much of Mexico. Particularly in areas that lacked substantial indigenous dwellings, the courtyard house emerged quickly as the new norm.
This was true for much of the present-day American Southwest and for north-central

35

13. GARCIA HOUSE FLOOR PLAN, CLOSSON AND ALTO STREETS, HYPOTHETICAL
APPEARANCE ABOUT 1810. (PATRICIA POLLOCK BASED ON HABS DRAWING)

Mexico, where it remains the prevalent dwelling type in rural areas into the twentieth century.[32]

The similarities between Spanish and Pueblo architecture have led some to attribute aspects of Spanish architecture in New Mexico, such as flat roofs, to Pueblo influence; on the contrary, Spanish domestic forms were well established before they reached New Mexico. The Spanish built comparable courtyard houses in New Mexico and Chihuahua, the next state to the south, where there was no Pueblo population. In addition the Spanish in New Mexico never adopted the terraced, multistory forms of the Pueblos.[33]

The Spanish, meanwhile, affected Pueblo architecture through their introduction of such elements as ground-level doors, standardized adobe bricks, corner fireplaces, beehive ovens (*hornos*), and metal tools that could cut larger roofing timber for wider rooms. This in no way diminishes the importance of the fact that the Pueblos and Spanish shared a building technology of earthen walls and flat roofs, which facilitated the employment of Pueblo builders for the missions and public buildings of Santa Fe.

While Pueblo Indians had a similar tradition of earth and stone construction, including the occasional use of hand-formed "loafs" of dried earth (and rare hand-formed "bricks"), regular adobe bricks were a Spanish introduction. The Spanish would first fill a wooden form with mud and a little straw, added to facilitate even drying. The bricks were next pushed out of the mold, stacked, and cured in the sun. Workmen laid the bricks with earthen mortar, starting directly on the ground or on a stone-rubble footing. Women finished the walls with earthen plaster. Roofs resembled those of the Aztecs and Pueblos: log beams topped by successively smaller poles, branches, brush, and finally a thick layer of earth.[34]

The ideal courtyard house, toward which houses grew, was known in New Mexico as a *placita* (little plaza). Typically built a room or two at a time, a family first constructed a single file of rooms, later an L-shaped, then a U-shaped house, and sometimes, if their resources allowed, a fully developed *placita* (figs. 14-15). While the 1766

Urrutia map shows only five full courtyard houses, by 1846 another map recorded fifty-five. The south-facing, U-shaped buildings along San Francisco Street in 1766, for instance, had all grown into full courtyard houses. The 1846 map, nevertheless, records approximately one hundred single-file, L- and U-shaped houses—the dwellings of the less wealthy. Of the Santa Fe houses described in eighteenth- and early-nine-teenth-century Spanish documents, 17 percent had one or two rooms, 48 percent three or four rooms, 22 percent five or six, 11 percent seven or eight, and only 5 percent over eight rooms. Owners of smaller houses often built free-standing adobe walls to complete their courtyards.[35]

For defensive reasons, doors and windows faced into the placita, with only a single covered passage opening to the outside. Known as a *zaguán*, this passage was closed by heavy, double wooden doors. Because they had no exterior openings, courtyard houses could be built side by side. Away from the plaza and commercial streets, which were lined with *portales*, houses stood at the street's edge, forming walled corridors relieved only by the heavy zaguán doors. Within, the courtyard ringed by *portales* reproduced the civic plaza in microcosm.

Inside the house, one or two rooms often served as the focus of daily life, even in the largest houses. Of the twenty-eight New Mexican houses described in Spanish documents, twenty-four had a *sala,* nineteen a *cocina* (kitchen), sixteen one or more *dispensas* (storerooms), and fifteen an *aposento* (a lodging room, meaning either a bedroom or a room for guests or rent). The most important of these, the sala, is often translated as "living room," although a better translation would be "hall" in the old English sense of a large multipurpose room. While most rooms were about 15 feet square, *salas* measured 15 by 25 or 30 feet. Here guests were entertained, meals were prepared and eaten, and everyone in the household slept.[36]

Matt Field, traveling reporter for the *New Orleans Times Picayune*, described a typical Santa Fe *sala* for his readers in 1840: "In some of the better houses you will find an apartment set aside as a parlor, this invariably being also the sleeping room;

14. ONE ROOM HOUSE OF JACAL (VERTICAL LOG) CONSTRUCTION, 1915. TWO-THIRDS OF SPANISH COLONIAL FAMILIES LIVED IN HOUSES OF ONE TO FOUR ROOMS. (KENNETH CHAPMAN)

15. MANUELITA CHAVEZ DE ROMERO RESIDENCE, 430 CAMINO DEL MONTE SOL, 1912. (JESSE L. NUSBAUM)

16. San Miguel Church, built about 1645, rebuilt 1710-11, upper tower
constructed perhaps 1830, photo 1873. Church towers rose as symbols of
religious devotion above the city of one-story houses. (Timothy O'Sullivan)

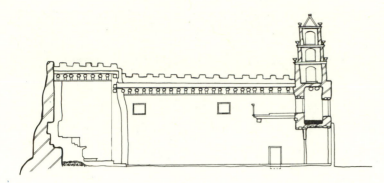

during the day beds are folded close up to the walls and covered with handsome (sometimes really beautiful) Spanish blankets, forming a succession of sofas all around the room." W. W. H. Davis, U.S. attorney in the 1850s, felt this was "an eastern custom, and was undoubtedly borrowed from the Moors."[37]

The *sala* had the largest, sometimes the only, fireplace in the house, as well as most of the furnishings. Wooden furniture of any kind was limited, however. Of the forty-four property inventories from the Spanish period (which primarily cover wealthy families), all list one or more wooden chests, but only seventeen list chairs, fifteen a bench, fourteen a table, only ten a bedstead, and nine a cupboard. The all-important chests ranged from the size of a large shoe box to a deep coffin. These elaborately carved and painted chests, which often had built-in locks, served, in the absence of closets, as the storage place for valuables. Tomasa Benavídez's chest at the time of her death in 1762, for example, contained a used woolen underskirt, a new serge petticoat, one jug and one flask of brandy, one pair of fine pearl ear-rings, and one linen skirt.[38]

Not only did churches receive the choicest locations, but they also towered as landmarks over the one-story residences (figs. 16, 17, 24). "There are two churches," observed Zebulon Pike in 1806, "the magnificence of whose steeples form a striking contrast to the miserable appearance of the houses." Church interiors, too, were the largest in town. *Salas* seldom exceeded 30 feet in length, 15 feet in width and 10 feet in height. The nave of San Francisco Church, by comparison, stretched 162 feet from entrance to altar, was 28 feet wide and 30 feet high, augmented by side chapels off its transept. At the focus of these otherwise dark church spaces were richly decorated altars, bathed with light from the transverse clerestory window (fig. 17). This provincial Baroque combination of gilded altars with hidden light sources was easily the most elaborate form of local Spanish art. The three main churches (San Francisco, San Miguel, and Our Lady of Guadalupe) also boasted three-tiered towers in imitation of the elaborate Baroque churches farther south.[39]

Religious devotion radiated outward from the churches into every corner of the community through a series of *oratorios* (private chapels), shrines, temporary processional

39

17. CROSS SECTION OF SAN MIGUEL CHURCH. THE CLERESTORY WINDOW FLOODED LIGHT ONTO THE ALTARS OF OTHERWISE DIM NEW MEXICO CHURCHES WITH LIGHT. (PATRICIA POLLOCK BASED ON O'SULLIVAN PHOTO AND HABS DRAWING)

altars, and place-names, along with family altars and wall niches for carved saints in many homes. The very name *la Villa de Santa Fe* means "the city of holy faith." Looming to the east are the Sangre de Cristo ("blood of Christ") Mountains, which turn reddish brown in the reflected glow of the sunset. Neighborhoods took their names from the parish churches: *barrio de San Miguel, barrio de San Francisco,* and so forth. Religious processions moving through the streets paused to kneel before temporary altars erected under the *portales* of leading citizens. Bonfires in the streets and on flat, earthen roofs, made Christmas Eve mass an uncommon nighttime celebration.[40]

THE BOURBON REFORMS

Changes in Spanish policies after 1759, known as the Bourbon Reforms, sought to increase tax revenues to the crown by improving defenses and establishing peace on the northern frontier; by fostering new settlements, economic development and trade; and by streamlining and centralizing colonial government. The military inspection tour of 1765–66 (which produced the Urrutia map) led to the consolidation and reconstruction of the frontier garrison forts, known as *presidios*. The curtailment of Spanish slave trading, a program of gifts to nomadic Indians to foster goodwill and dependency, and the pitting of one tribe against another led to a peace treaty with the Comanches in 1786, in addition to selective agreements with Apache bands. This peace, combined with a continued prohibition of trade with the British, Russians, and Americans and the introduction of hard currency on the frontier, initiated a mercantile cash economy and increased trade with central Mexico. In exchange for firearms, metal tools, textiles, and luxuries such as liquor, tobacco, chocolate, and sugar, New Mexico exported corn, beans, wheat, and piñon nuts; animal hides and blankets taken in trade with Indians; and an average of twenty-five thousand head of sheep a year. The local elite prospered, while a growing landless peasantry became enmeshed in debt peonage and a system of livestock sharecropping known as *partido*. With peace, prosperity, and a growing population, a major expansion of settlement out of the upper Rio Grande core began about 1790.[41]

Of the three settlement forms on the Spanish frontier (the mission, the colonial town, and the *presidio*), the presidio came last to New Mexico. It was typically a fortified military garrison in an isolated location, around which a squatter settlement often grew up. For decades after Santa Fe was designated a presidio in 1693, it lacked formal defensive structures, and the soldiers lived in houses scattered throughout the valley. The Urrutia map shows only the governor's house and west of it a building that may have been used by the garrison for storage. This lack of proper defenses so worried the soldiers that in 1780 they pledged part of their retirement funds for the construction of barracks.[42]

In 1791, as part of the Bourbon reforms, a full-blown presidio was finally built under the direction of Governor de la Concha and Lieutenant Manuel Delgado, formerly building superintendent at the San Buenaventura and Carrizal presidios in Chihuahua. Although Delgado knew the regulations promulgated for presidio construction in 1772, he modified the standard plan to accommodate the already existing government buildings and limited resources at hand. The walls were made of adobe instead of the required stone masonry, and they lacked foundations. The new *presidio* was an open rectangle as directed, although to accommodate the oversized garrison of 120 soldiers, it was larger than usual, stretching 1,400 feet north of the plaza and 1,050 feet east to west. The governor's residence and the old building to the west defined the presidio's one entrance. The inclusion of this residence, with its portal, gave it a public face that other presidios lacked. Conversely the immense presidio extending behind the Palace of the Governors added to that building's military character. This combination reflected the governor's dual roles as civil and military leader.[43]

In the prosperity engendered by the Bourbon Reforms, Santa Fe grew from about 1,300 residents in 1760 to 2,542 in 1790 and to perhaps 3,500 in 1810. None of the province's secondary administrative and trade centers (Taos, Abiquiu, Santa Cruz and Albuquerque) reached a population much above 1,000 during the colonial period. As the territory's civil, religious, and social center, Santa Fe attracted many of the region's economic elite. Some *ricos,* as the wealthy with land and livestock holdings were known, like their counterparts in the Valley of Mexico, maintained both a town house and a country house near their holdings. Half of the households in the 1790 census, nevertheless, continued to make their living by farming the valley. In addition to the military garrison of some 100 soldiers, Santa Fe boasted a concentration of barrel makers, weavers, carpenters, cobblers, blacksmiths, tailors, and mule drivers.[44]

Ethnic-racial lines began to blur as marriages of people from different *castas* peaked at over 20 percent in the 1760s and 1770s. Meanwhile the Bourbon Reforms promoted hard work and economic initiative as the route to social mobility. This social-class instability stimulated a growing preoccupation among the rico elite with maintaining their pure Spanish blood (*limpieza de sangre*). Their status rested on landownership and the inherited noble title of *hidalgo,* conferred by the crown on their conquistador ancestors. In order to maintain their "honor, social status, blood purity, and familial wealth," they increasingly petitioned for dispensations to marry their relatives, unions the Church deemed incestuous. A few of the 215 consanguinity dispensations granted between 1760 and 1819 went to first cousins, although most were for couples one or two more steps removed in their relationship.[45]

Table 1: 1790 Census of Santa Fe and Albuquerque[46]

	Santa Fe		Albuquerque	
	Persons	Percentage	Persons	Percentage
español	1,695	67.7	399	34.6
mestizo	221	8.7	549	47.6
color quebrado	380	14.9	0	0
coyote	3	0.1	127	11.0
indio	121	4.8	28	2.5
genízaro	36	1.4	43	3.7
mulato	85	3.3	6	0.5
Totals	**2,542**		**1,152**	

The 1790 census gives a sense of the flexibility of colonial ethnic-racial terminology. While Santa Fe, as the provincial capital, had a higher concentration of Spanish descendants, the differences between it and Albuquerque owe as much to the differing interpretations of local census takers. The high proportion identified as *español* reflects the fact that *mestizos* with a degree of social and economic attainment, as well as their descendants, were often identified as *español*. "The use of this term was a mark of social differentiation, more than the determining factor for biological ethnicity."[47] *Color quebrado* ("broken color," perhaps akin to "half-breed") apparently was used by the census-taker in Santa Fe as a euphemism for *coyote*. Most of those identified as *indio* in the territory, of course, lived in the Pueblo villages, while *genízaros* were concentrated in the frontier defensive settlements.[48]

The cultural inflection of ostensibly racial terminology in historic Spanish Colonial documents makes the assessment of the racial heritage of the Hispanic population of New Mexico difficult. Santa Fe Trail merchant Josiah Gregg cited this estimate from a Mexican territorial official in 1841: "white creoles [Spanish born in the New World], say 1,000; *mestizos,* or mixed creoles, 59,000; and Pueblos, 10,000." Recent historians have variously estimated that "by the close of the nineteenth century genizaros made up a full third of New Mexico's population," and hijos de la iglesia constituted another 10 percent; that people of mixed ancestry in New Mexico accounted for "perhaps more than eighty percent and possibly as high as ninety percent" of the population; and that by 1800 two-thirds of the New Mexico's population were "Hispanic mestizos."[49]

SANTA FE, MEXICO

With Mexican independence in 1821, *casta* terminology, with its residual racial-social hierarchy, was officially abandoned, as everybody became simply "*mexicano.*" The decade-long revolution leading to independence had so weakened the central government and loosened its economic ties with the frontier provinces that the focus of New Mexico's trade quickly shifted from central Mexico toward the United States, with the opening of the Santa Fe Trail in 1821. New Mexico exported mules and hard currency, which stimulated the frontier economy of Missouri. In return New Mexico received manufactured goods, primarily cotton textiles and metal tools. With the withdrawal of royal subsidies, the missions fell into disrepair, while the territorial government relied on tariffs from Santa Fe Trail trade. The old *rico* families and a few others who entered the middle class under the Bourbon Reforms controlled as much as half of the trade. The economic integration of New Mexico into the United States economy laid the groundwork for its political incorporation during the 1846 U.S.–Mexican War.[50]

Santa Fe prospered and grew during the Mexican era as a result of the Santa Fe Trail trade (fig. 18). The eastern half of the plaza was filled by government buildings facing the east side of the new square plaza, while the houses of the wealthy Ortiz and Pino families lined the new street leading from the plaza to San Francisco Church. Although much of the old presidio lay in ruins, one visitor in 1837 "found the place full of soldiers, citizens, and a miscellaneous gathering of humanity of all stations of life, the plaza being crowded with all kinds of vehicles, beginning with the cart that was made entirely of wood . . . to the well constructed wagon that had brought a consignment of merchandise over the Santa Fe Trail; together with teamsters, camp cooks, roustabouts, horses, mules, burros, pigs, and goats."[51]

"The butchers who killed sheep," remembered Demetrio Pérez, who visited Santa Fe in the 1830s, "placed the meat on perches which they placed under the shade of the cottonwoods planted in front of the Old Palace; on the west side, under the spacious porch of the Palace, the bakers were installed together with the fruit vendors and others who sold their diverse kinds of food for the people were dependent on the market for their supply, for at that time there was no public building for the sale of such articles." "Besides that," continued Pérez, "there were several women who cooked dinners which were served to those who wished to take them there, and under the shadow of the cottonwoods the tables were placed for the boarders." The U.S. attorney in the early 1850s, William Davis, found the market still supplied with "mutton, an occasional porker, red peppers, beans, onions, milk, bread, cheese, and during the proper season, grapes, wild plums, and wild berries. In the winter, Indians and others bring in, almost daily, fine venison and wild turkeys, and now and then the carcass of a large bear is exposed for sale."[52]

The multiple uses of the portales mirrored the lack of specialization in building types—a frequent characteristic of vernacular building traditions. The church and presidio were the only specialized architectural forms. Otherwise the *portal*, the standard square room, and the somewhat larger *sala* were adapted for every purpose. Some tables and chairs under a *portal* made a restaurant; a length of rope, some mats, and a portal served as a marketplace; a room on short-term lease became a hotel. The same room could later be occupied by a saloon and, still later, by a trader trying to dispose of his wagonload of dry goods before returning to Missouri or pressing on to Chihuahua. A *sala* used as a ballroom one evening became a courtroom the next day; and later a gambling hall, public meeting room, lecture hall, or school. The plaza itself served as anything from a parade ground or bullring to a campground, storage yard, and social center.[53]

A robust city of forty-five hundred people on the eve of the U.S.-Mexican War, Santa Fe was the largest settlement on Mexico's northern frontier. Although its old presidio lay in decay, the towers of its three churches and two chapels stood as landmarks of continuing devotion. The 250-year tradition of flat-roofed adobe construction persisted, as more and more houses grew to the full courtyard shape. At the hub of trade between the United States and northern Mexico, Santa Fe's plaza had finally blossomed into something resembling the mercantile center envisioned by the Laws of the Indies. The village had emerged gradually as a partially realized outpost of the Spanish colonial empire. With its annexation to the United States in 1848, Santa Fe would become a provincial outpost of a youthful, national empire.

2

INTO THE AMERICAN
MELTING POT, 1846 TO 1912

On a clear, warm September day in 1846, a squad of army volunteers from Missouri and Kentucky returned from the Sangre de Cristo Mountains carrying a 60-foot lodge-pole pine—the tallest they could find. The Army of the West under General Stephen Watts Kearny had occupied Santa Fe only two weeks before, and already the embankments of Fort Marcy were taking shape on the hill above town, from which "every house in the city can be torn by the artillery to atoms." When the volunteers reached the plaza, they planted that pole at its center. A few days later, their general assembled the leading Mexican citizens of Santa Fe, and as an honor guard fired a rifle salute, a 15-by-30-foot Stars and Stripes was run up this makeshift flagpole. Governor General Diego de Vargas, who forced Pueblo leaders to kneel before a cross erected in the plaza in 1692, would have understood.[1]

The occupation of Santa Fe during the U.S.-Mexican War of 1846, and the annexation of New Mexico and California to the United States two years later, resulted from international political and economic developments manifest locally in twenty-five years of Santa Fe Trail trade. By the 1830s, an industrializing United States began to compete with Britain for Latin American and Far Eastern markets. New Mexico offered only a modest market in itself, but it was the main trade route to the interior of Mexico. It also offered a southern, fair-weather route to California ports and hence to the Far East.[2]

Existing economic and marriage ties between rico families and American traders facilitated the bloodless occupation of New Mexico in 1846. The following year, however, an uprising in the north, known as the Taos Revolt, was brutally suppressed. Army artillery bombarded the village of Mora and the Taos Pueblo church, where Mexican patriots had taken refuge. Six revolt leaders were subsequently executed at Taos. The pacification of Navajo, Apache, and Comanche raiders proceeded fitfully for another thirty years.

During the 1850s and 1860s, the U.S. Army maintained a military garrison in Santa Fe, the American Catholic Church dispatched a new bishop, and German-born Jewish

18. PLAN OF SANTA FE, NEW MEXICO, 1846. STRUCTURES CONCENTRATED
AROUND PLAZA, BUT LINEAR SETTLEMENT STRETCHED ALONG RADIATING ROADS.
(J.F. GILMER, U.S. ARMY CORPS OF ENGINEERS)

merchants gradually came to dominate the territory's commerce. An infusion of Anglo-American lawyers and appointed territorial officials united with the old rico families to form a new ruling elite. A series of loose alliances of these lawyers, officials and investors, sometimes called the Santa Fe Ring, worked to control the territory's primary resource—land. By 1912, when statehood was belatedly granted, 80 per cent of the former common lands of the Mexican farmers and ranchers had been alienated through judicial and legislative chicanery.[3]

MANIFEST DESTINY AND RACIALISM

The arrival of Anglo-Americans after the opening of the Santa Fe Trail in 1821 and the occupation of 1846 initiated a new era of racial-ethnic consciousness, colored by a recent shift in the nature-nurture debate. As participants in the Enlightenment, the leaders of the American Revolution believed that all people belong to a single human race and that environment, not race, accounts for differences between peoples. To their way of thinking, the rise of the English and American people resulted from their development of democratic government and public education, paired with economic and personal liberty. The extension of these institutions to the rest of the world would naturally improve other peoples.[4]

However, this idealism ran head-on into the realities of slavery and frontier Indian wars. Washington, Jefferson, and other revolutionaries, we recall, owned slaves. Grassroots prejudices against Blacks and Indians during the first decades of the nineteenth century gained legitimacy with the formulation of pseudoscientific theories of racial superiority in Europe and the United States. By the 1830s, the economic and military ascendance of the United States was explained not by the superiority of its institutions but by the innate superiority of the Anglo-Saxon race. By condemning Blacks and Indians as racially inferior, Anglo-Americans could reconcile the suffering caused by slavery and the removal of Indians from their lands with the constitutional rhetoric of freedom and equal protection before the law.[5]

The U.S.-Mexican War helped crystallize pseudoscientific theories of race in America. A few leaders argued in the old Enlightenment vein that the development of Mexico had been inhibited by a lack of public education and a middle class, as well as by religious and military domination. They held that regeneration through republican government was still possible. About 1835, however, attacks escalated against Mexicans as an inferior race that lacked an innate propensity for democracy, and, like the Indians, had not developed the land to its full potential. After all, the racialists argued, most Mexicans are either Indian or a "mongrel" mixture of Spanish, Indian, and Black. The racialists thereby extended existing prejudices against Indians and Blacks to Mexicans. In 1845 a journalist coined the term *Manifest Destiny* to describe the belief that the superior Anglo-Saxon race had been chosen by Providence to march with the sun in an arc of conquest west across the continent and on to Asia. Following a recurrent pattern of racism, it became common to speak of "dirty" Mexicans and to call them a "degenerate," "bastard," "impure," "barbaric," half-civilized" race. The most common epithet, *mongrel,* echoed the canine and half-breed associations of the Spanish *coyote, lobo,* and *mulato.*[6]

49

William Gilpin, a volunteer in the Army of the West who would later become the first territorial governor of Colorado, wrote in a Senate report on the eve of the U.S.-Mexican War: "The *untransacted* destiny of the American people is to subdue the continent—to rush over this vast field to the Pacific Ocean . . . to set the principle of self government to work—to regenerate superannuated nations . . . to turn darkness into light—to stir up the sleep of a hundred centuries—to teach old nations a new civilization—to confirm the destiny of the human race—to carry the career of mankind to its culminating point—to cause stagnant people to be reborn . . . !"[7]

American politicians and journalists performed elaborate mental gymnastics to rationalize the degree of racial mixing among Americans and to define what they meant by the "Anglo-Saxon" or "American" race. The English, Germans, Scotch-Irish, Dutch, French, and Swedes had formed distinct ethnic groups during the colonial era. But with the development of a hybrid American culture, the wide-spread adoption of English, and increasing intermarriage, these ethnic boundaries blurred. So when the racialists spoke of Anglo-Saxons, they did not mean the descendants of the fifth- and sixth-century Germanic settlers of Britain, who after all, did not exist as a pure racial strain thirteen centuries later in America. They meant instead all whites of northern and western European ancestry who spoke English and shared American culture.

This conflation of race, language, culture, and nationality allowed politicians of Scotch-Irish descent, for example, to speak of the "Celtic-Anglo-Saxon" race, which accounted for the Welsh, Scotch, Irish, and French admixture. Others lauded the Norse contribution of Scandinavians and the Norman ancestors of England and France. Still others discovered the shared Germanic roots of Anglo-Saxons and modern Germans. Many came to believe that they belonged to a particularly progressive branch of the Anglo-Saxons—a separate, unique, and superior American race. Few acknowledged the contradiction of denigrating Mexicans for "mongrelization" while lauding the increased vitality of Americans caused by racial "mixing."[8]

Two additional themes surfaced in racialist thinking in the 1840s that affect social beliefs in New Mexico to this day. Pueblo Indians were first praised during this period as a more pure and, therefore, industrious and moral people than the "mongrel" Mexicans. This attitude underlies the subsequent Pueblophile and Hispanophobic prejudices of some Anglo romantics. Likewise the recognition that the Mexican elite claimed Castilian ancestry was a harbinger of the reassertion of Spanish identification. John C. Calhoun, for instance, argued on the floor of the Senate in 1848 that some Mexicans had "Castilian blood in their veins—the old Gothic, quite equal to the Anglo-Saxon in many respects—in some respects superior."[9]

After the war, the Anglo-American lawyers and officials who allied themselves with the old rico families adopted many of their prejudices toward working-class Mexican *peones*. Vastly outnumbered locally, Anglo officials tempered their racialist rhetoric, although racist attitudes in the rest of the United States delayed statehood for over

sixty years and facilitated the alienation of Spanish-Mexican lands and the local stratification of occupations and economic classes along ethnic lines. Although the
United States Census classed both groups as white, in the popular press and everyday
language, everyone distinguished between "Mexicans" and "Americans."[10]

Intermarriage, nevertheless, became a significant social phenomenon in Santa Fe.
By the 1870 census, over 10 percent of all married Mexican women had American
husbands. Because of their lower total numbers, this represented 62 percent of married American men. The women were primarily from the working class, while their
husbands were predominantly craftsmen, government officials, merchants, and professionals; 60 percent had been born in the states, and the rest were from northern
Europe.[11]

Reconstructing the economic, social, and psychological dynamics of these marriages is difficult. The women offered their husbands a chance to have a home and
children and to draw upon extended family social and economic networks—in short,
an opportunity to become a permanent member of the community. The men
offered their wives the prospect of upward social mobility because of their occupa-
tional skills, financial resources, literacy, and greater experience with the new economic and political order.[12]

Because few single women traveled west over the Santa Fe Trail, only a handful of
Mexican men married American women. Many, perhaps most, who did were ricos
educated in the Midwest, where they met their wives. These included J. Francisco Chávez,
president of the Territorial Senate, Miguel A. Otero, congressional delegate from New
Mexico, and his son, Miguel A. Otero II, the territorial governor. In the late nineteenth century, children of mixed Hispano-Anglo ancestry began to be called *coyotes,*
the term formerly applied to a person of mixed Indian-Spanish ancestry. *Lobo* came
to mean someone of three-quarters Hispanic or Anglo ancestry.[13]

Coyote children learned to move between the home, neighborhood, and religious
world of their Mexican mothers and the commercial, civic, and secular world of their

51

American fathers. Census enumerator sheets for 1870 indicate that a third of the mixed families lived with only Mexican neighbors, another third with a few mixed or American families nearby, and a third were found in the cluster of American men and families in the government-commercial center around the plaza. The names they gave their children hint at the identities they anticipated for them. Half of the couples chose only Spanish first names, one-sixth only English ones, and the remaining third who chose mixed names, generally gave the girls Spanish names and the boys English ones. Even then a coyote might introduce her- or himself as María or Carlos in one context and as Mary or Charles in another.[14]

THE ARCHITECTURE OF PROGRESS

Many American newcomers on approaching their first Mexican village had difficulty even distinguishing it from the surrounding landscape, so different were flat-roofed adobe buildings from what they knew east of the Missouri River (fig. 19). They groped for metaphors to describe Santa Fe. One traveler likened it to "a dilapidated brick kiln or a prairie-dog town"; another recalled that it "struck my mind with the same effect as a fleet of the flat-bottomed boats which are seen in the spring and fall seasons, descending the Ohio river." Americans equated adobe buildings, which to their

19. MONTOYA HILL, NORTHEAST OF PLAZA, 1912. (JESSE L. NUSBAUM) HOUSES AND ROOMS STEPPED WITH THE ROLL OF THE LAND.

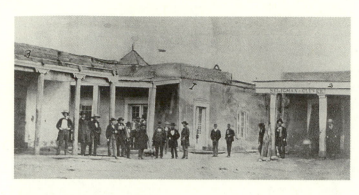

eyes seemed to be in a perpetual state of decay, with loose women, gambling, cowardice, a lack of proper hygiene, and immoral clergy—all symptoms, in their minds, of the decline of Christian civilization in New Mexico. "Great indeed was the contrast between the beautiful and magnificent city which my imagination had pictured," Daniel Hastings, a private who marched behind General Kearny, wrote in his diary, "and the low dirty and inferior place which I then beheld."[15]

Only two weeks after the American occupation, another soldier observed in his journal, "lumber is high, from three to four dollars per hundred, and has to be obtained by whip saw. The general has ordered the machinery of a mill, which is expected out this fall, and they are preparing to have everything ready for it when it comes." By the spring of 1848, a new American newspaper, the *Santa Fe Republican* could boast:

> The Merchants have filled up large and convenient rooms in place
> of the small and crowded ones, and the doors, windows and other
> marks of improvement that strike the eye everywhere indicates
> a most rapid improvement. The ruins of old houses which were
> scattered all over town, have given place to new and better built
> ones, and as fast as workmen and materials can be procured, new
> buildings are going up. Not a street in the place presents the
> appearance it did this time two years ago, and if things continue,
> in one year more, the whole appearance of the city will be changed.

Decorative elements applied to old adobe buildings were physically superficial, but at the same time symbolically significant as the tangible signs of a new regime.[16]

Around the plaza, Americans replaced the tree trunk columns and rough beams of Mexican *portales* with whitewashed, milled posts and trim. By the early 1860s, only two of the old porches remained (figs. 20, 21). Americans began to ship window glass in greater quantity over the Santa Fe Trail and to cut windows and larger doors into

20. SOUTHEAST CORNER OF THE PLAZA, ABOUT 1855. SPANISH-MEXICAN STYLE PORTAL (LEFT), AMERICAN TERRITORIAL STYLE PORCHES (CENTER AND RIGHT).

21. HEADQUARTERS BUILDING, FORT MARCY, NORTHWEST CORNER OF PLAZA, BUILT 1870, PHOTO APRIL, 1881. (BEN WITTICK)

existing adobe buildings. But because of the high expense of freighting fired bricks over the trail, they were reserved for fireplaces and cornices protecting the tops of adobe walls.

These renovations about town employed a simple version of the Greek Revival style, referred to locally today as the Territorial style. American masons laid brick cornices in patterns resembling Greek dentil courses (fig. 22). Using only molding planes and miter box saws, carpenters fashioned raw lumber into door and window frames simulating columns, entablatures, and pediments. They wrapped molding around the tops and sometimes the bottoms of columns to evoke the capitals and bases of classical columns. In the rest of the country, where the Greek Revival flourished as a virtual national style from the 1820s to the Civil War, wooden approximations of Greek architectural details such as these constituted a widespread carpenter's vocabulary, and this was easily adapted to Santa Fe. While the evocation of Greek democracy matched the spirit of the early American republic, in the West, with the rise of Manifest Destiny, it also became a sign of the new American imperialism.[17]

The long popularity of the Greek Revival in Santa Fe is striking. In the East by the 1840s, the style began to be challenged by other, more picturesque styles, primarily the Gothic, Italianate, and Romanesque Revivals. These expanded on the idea, already present in the Greek Revival, that architecture could evoke romantic associations with historic periods and exotic lands. By 1850 the Italianate palazzo, which evoked Renaissance merchant princes, became the preferred facade treatment for town houses and commercial buildings in many eastern cities. Yet in Santa Fe, as in many conservative rural areas of the nation, the Greek Revival persisted, with only a dash of carpenter Gothic and Italianate detailing. Santa Fe's distance from the eastern style centers partly explains this lag. But the Greek Revival also blended easily with those formal patterns of Spanish architecture, such as the portal, that continued to be strong in Santa Fe. As early as 1849, Americans erected two business blocks of two-story buildings fronted by crisp white porches on the plaza (fig. 23).

22. BORREGO HOUSE, CANYON ROAD, BUILT ABOUT 1865. FIRED BRICK CORNICE
IN THE FORM OF A CLASSICAL DENTIL COURSE PROTECTS THE ADOBE WALLS BELOW.

If local residents resented the Americanization of Santa Fe, their feelings seldom made their way into the historic record. When the army repaired the dilapidated Castrense chapel on the south side of the plaza for use as a warehouse, no objections were reported. But when a federal judge remodeled it in 1851 for use as a courtroom, Hispanic jurors refused to serve, and public demonstrations followed. The new bishop, Jean Baptiste Lamy, intervened with a petition for the return of the building to the Catholic Church. This gave the authorities a face-saving way out of the dispute. But in 1859, feeling that the area had become too noisy and congested for religious contemplation, Lamy sold the chapel to Simon Delgado.[18]

Delgado was the oldest son of a family of upwardly mobile Mexican merchants. His grandfather, Manuel Francisco Delgado, was a military officer dispatched from Mexico to the Santa Fe presidio in 1778, during the Bourbon Reforms. He stayed to become active in real estate and livestock, and his son, Manuel, prospered as a merchant in the Chihuahua and Santa Fe Trail trade. Simon chose to raze the chapel and erected a two-story building containing a store, warehouse, and residence, fronted by a whitewashed Territorial style portico. With the completion of the Delgado Building, stores lined three sides of the plaza and the Governor's Palace the fourth, marking a shift of the plaza from a social and religious center to a commercial district.

23. JOHNSON BUILDING, NORTHWEST CORNER OF THE PLAZA, BUILT 1847, WOODEN ARCHES AND SUNBURST BALUSTRADE ADDED ABOUT 1871, PHOTO 1872.

Significantly, however, the chapel property went to the Delgados, the only Mexican Catholic family that would continue to compete with the leading German Jewish and American merchants.[19]

Bishop Lamy was born in south-central France in 1814. As the brilliant son of a devout family of limited means, he entered the clergy. After ordination in 1838, he volunteered to serve as a missionary in frontier Ohio and Kentucky, where his religious zeal, physical endurance, and administrative skill attracted the attention of the American church hierarchy. So when New Mexico was transferred to their jurisdiction, they nominated Lamy to head the church there. Lamy reached Santa Fe in 1851 as apostolic vicar, was subsequently named bishop and later elevated to archbishop. He shared the Americans' distaste for the local culture and adobe architecture. Lamy launched a vigorous campaign to modernize the churches and suppress certain aspects of folk Catholicism, such as the *penetentes,* a lay religious fraternity. They saw to many community social needs and also performed such Holy Week penitential observances as self-flagellation and simulated crucifixion.[20]

The sale of the Castrense Chapel funded the remodeling of the main parish church, the *parroquia,* at the head of San Francisco Street (fig. 26). Lamy hired workmen to add adobe crenelations atop the walls, cut large rectangular windows into the nave and side chapels, and insert a small rose window above the main entrance. Most strikingly he replaced the three-tiered, Mexican-era towers with shorter brick towers, pierced by pointed arches and capped by more battlements—all in the image of the Gothic cathedrals that inspired him as a young priest in Europe and which he continued to see on his frequent fund-raising and recruitment trips home.[21]

Lamy recruited thirty-one French priests by 1866, out of a total of fifty-one in the dioceses. Together they began to remake churches throughout the territory. Typically they first added new belfries and windows. If these had pointed openings, the church took on a faintly Gothic air; if round-headed, a Romanesque feel. After the railroad arrived, the clergy added hard stucco, often scored and painted to look like stone,

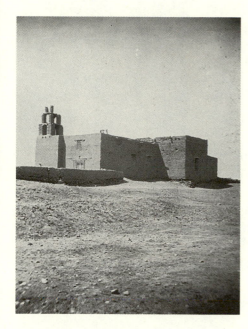 

and pitched roofs, which better protected the building from rain, but destroyed the Spanish Baroque clerestory lighting effect.[22]

The late Spanish colonial church of Our Lady of Guadalupe near the new Santa Fe depot was in disrepair when Lamy turned it over to the Reverend James Defouri in 1881, for use by the growing congregation of English-speaking Catholics (fig. 24). The renovation carried out that fall, "in the modern style," typifies the transformations worked by Lamy's priests (fig. 25). Contractor Florence Donoghue demolished the deteriorated, three-tiered tower to make way for a steep roof, topped by a pointed spire. He added tall doors and windows, which further accentuated the church's new vertical proportions. Even the old adobe forecourt wall was replaced by a white picket fence to provide a cleaner, crisper setting.[23]

Lamy dreamed above all of building a great cathedral for Santa Fe. For such an important project, he recruited the architects Antoine and Projectus Mouly from France and stone masons from France and Italy. Being from the south of France as was Lamy, the Moulys knew both the medieval Romanesque cathedrals of that region and the preeminent French Byzantine-Romanesque Revival building of the day—Leon Vaudoyer's Marseilles Cathedral, under construction from 1845 to 1893 (the design was set by 1853). Not surprisingly their design for Saint Francis Cathedral in Santa

24. NUESTRA SEÑORA DE GUADALUPE CHURCH, BUILT ABOUT 1810, PHOTO 1880. (BEN WITTICK)

25. OUR LADY OF GUADALUPE CHURCH, REMODELED 1880-81, FLORENCE DONOGHUE. (F.A. NIMS)

Fe, with its Romanesque arches, its polychromatic stonework, and its transept dome and domed towers (which were never built) is a provincial cousin of the Marseilles Cathedral emigrated to the New World (fig. 27). In 1869 the masons laid the foundations around the old parroquia, which remained in use (fig. 26). When they finished the new facade and nave in 1886, they tied them to the side chapels of the venerable adobe church. The old nave was then dismantled beam by beam, adobe by adobe, and carried out the new doors. Crews filled low spots in the streets with the debris, while many of the ancient wooden beams and corbels, carried away by parishioners, survive to this day in the houses of Santa Fe.[24]

CIVIC IMPROVEMENTS

The lack of a strong local government meant that civic improvements were pursued ad hoc by the booster community. These businessmen, lawyers, real estate agents, newspaper men, and the occasional territorial official or army officer who stayed to put down roots published promotional booklets, organized improvement campaigns, and boosted the development prospects of Santa Fe at national conventions and world's fairs. Every western city had similar boosters who projected personal energy, enthusiasm, and optimism and made the physical appearance of their community the tangible sign of a progressive spirit.

Captain John Ayers of the California volunteers, for instance, instigated the construction of a plaza park in 1862. The army had just turned back a Confederate expedition at the Battle of Glorieta Pass, and something had to be found to occupy a garrison sitting out the rest of the war. Ayers, who had known landscaped village commons in his native New England, set his men to work transplanting trees from the mountains to the plaza and "got up a subscription from the citizens to fence it in." Walkways converged on a central focal point, which was filled in 1866 with a picturesque bandstand where the Fort Marcy band played evening concerts. But a year later, this "Pagoda" was pushed to the side to make room for a monument to the American (and Mexican

26. ST. FRANCIS CATHEDRAL UNDER CONSTRUCTION AROUND LA PARROQUIA, ABOUT 1881. BISHOP LAMY'S EUROPEAN-INSPIRED ASPIRATIONS ENVELOPE THE OLD, ADOBE PARISH CHURCH. (GEORGE C. BENNETT)

27. ST. FRANCIS CATHEDRAL (TOWERS AND TRANSEPT NEVER COMPLETED), 1885. DESIGN BY PROJECTUS AND ANTOINE MOULY, 1870. PLAN REVISIONS BY FRANCOIS MALLET, 1878.

58

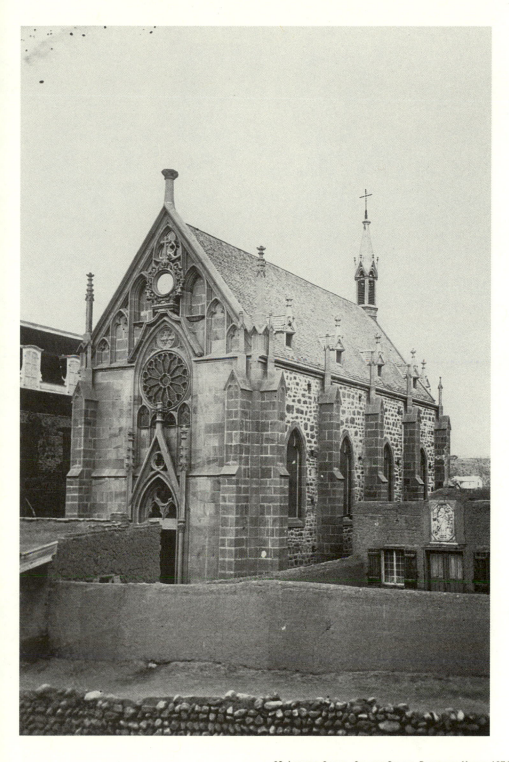

28. Loretto Chapel, College Street, Projectus Mouly, 1874-77. In a city still overwhelmingly built of adobe, this chapel modeled on Saint Chapel in Paris was a marvel. (Ben Wittick)

and Pueblo) dead of the Civil and Indian Wars. Two Irish-born architect brothers named M'Gee designed this stone obelisk (fig. 29). Similar stone monuments were also erected along the new border with Mexico in the 1850s and at key intersections in the survey grid that was then being pushed west across America. The plaza monument, too, quickly became a standard reference for local property surveys. The rational geometry of a monument centered in a symmetrical park combined with the Egyptian associations of an obelisk and the white-washed Greek Revival porches of the surrounding buildings to create a unified environment—a distinct frontier echo of Enlightenment neoclassicism.[25]

Facing the plaza park on the north, the Governor's Palace had received a simple Territorial style porch during the first wave of improvements in the mid-1850s (fig. 30). The building housed the governor's offices and residence as well as the United States Depository, various other government offices, and the territorial legislative chambers, which doubled as courtrooms. When U.S. Attorney Thomas Catron added new doors, windows, and hard stucco to the facade of his office in 1872, the newspaper felt that "by the tasty front he has put beneath the somber palace portal, he has relieved the monotony of a terrible stretch of primitive rudeness, and set a jewel in a mud wall."[26]

29. LOOKING EAST OVER THE PLAZA WITH THE TOWERS OF THE PARROQUIA IN BACKGROUND, ABOUT 1867. FRONTIER NEO-CLASSICISM: AN OBELISK, RADIAL PATHS AND WHITE-WASHED COLONNADES. (NICHOLAS BROWN)

U.S. Marshall John Sherman triggered a complete remodeling of the Palace's facade in 1877, when he added a plank sidewalk, wrapped his porch posts with elaborate moldings, and capped them with a heavy cornice. People felt this made the rest of the palace look "sad," "unsightly," and "mournful," so Territorial Secretary William Ritch took charge of raising funds from the Treasury Department and civic-minded citizens and persuaded contractors to work at reduced rates (fig. 31).[27]

Born in New York in 1830, Ritch migrated across the upper Midwest as a young man seeking his fortune. After serving as a lieutenant in the Forty-sixth Wisconsin Infantry during the Civil War, he returned to become a state senator, and the owner and editor of a small-town newspaper. When failing health caused him to seek a sunny, dry climate, his political connections landed an appointment from President Ulysses S. Grant as New Mexico territorial secretary, second in command to the governor. Ritch would hold the post for twelve years and continue until his death in 1904 as one of Santa Fe and New Mexico's most energetic boosters.[28]

"The heaviest and most artistic portion of the work designed and let out by Mr. Ritch," the *New Mexican* reported, "was the cornice and balustrade, extending from the heavy brick cornice at the east along the front to the U.S. Marshall's office on the west . . . reflecting credit on the taste displayed by Mr. Ritch, and the workmen employed." In truth this showpiece of Santa Fe builders' best style was quite provincial compared to the rich Second Empire-style government buildings of Grant's administration, with their mansard roofs and boldly projecting columns and cornices.[29]

The voice of boosterism was ever present in Santa Fe's newspapers, speaking of this or that sign of progress, and of this merchant or that young attorney as being thoroughly wide-awake—that is, wide-awake to opportunities for turning a profit, while at the same time improving the appearance of the city. Speaking of the large "bazaar" windows that were being installed around town in 1872, the *New Mexican* observed,

61

30. PALACE OF THE GOVERNORS, PORCH REMODELED ABOUT 1855. THE EARLIEST IMAGE OF THE PALACE, AFTER IT HAD ALREADY RECEIVED THIS MODEST TERRITORIAL STYLE PORCH. (U.S. ARMY SIGNAL CORP)

31. PALACE OF THE GOVERNORS, PORCH REMODELED 1877 TO 1878, WILLIAM RITCH AND OTHERS. (BEN WITTICK)

The days for crawling through dark holes in a mud wall have passed, and show and advertising have taken place. Look for instance at the superb show windows crowning the front entrance to Staab & Co.'s, Johnson & Kock's, E. Andrews, Spiegelberg Bros., Sol Spiegelberg and others. . . . Our Mexican friends are too careless in this respect, and we would suggest that they take more pains in rendering the fronts of their stores more attractive to customers and passersby.[30]

The newspapers were always campaigning for building improvements, ranging from boardwalks, plank roofs, and display windows to flagstone walks, stuccoed walls, and metal roofs. One merchant put a boardwalk under his portal in 1872, and during the next two summers they spread around the plaza and along San Francisco Street, with the newspapers urging on the owner next in line. Then five years later, flagstone side-walks became a new sign of progress. Likewise the newspaper extolled the new metal roofs added to many business blocks in the mid-1870s as cleaner than the old dirt roofs with their short spouts, which poured dirty water into the streets.[31]

Often these building improvements were practical. A roof that does not leak and a sidewalk that does not get muddy, after all, have obvious advantages. But the speed with which plank sidewalks gave way to flagstone and board roofs to metal ones reveals that symbolic as well as practical considerations were at work. Progressive values are clearest in the practice of scoring and painting the stucco over adobe walls to resemble stone or brick. Hard-plastering an adobe wall protected it from the elements, but "tattooing" or "stenciling" it, as the practice was called, to resemble stone, also emphasized its new permanence symbolically and asserted eastern styles and building materials over local adobe (figs. 31, 55).

The Greek Revival buildings surrounding the plaza and the newspapers' rhetoric of boosterism gave the impression that Anglo-Americans controlled Santa Fe. But when the old newspapers mention fifteen hundred or two thousand people taking part in a Corpus Cristi procession, with a like number lining the streets to watch, all in a city of fifty-five hundred people, one is forced to reconsider that first impression. Behind the new whitewashed porches were old-style adobe buildings, and a block or two away from the plaza, the Mexican building tradition was even more in evidence. Americans owned most plaza property and controlled many aspects of the economy and government, but their relatively small numbers and limited architectural resources restrained their desire for change. What they did accomplish depended in large part on the cooperation of Hispanic community leaders and an ability to blend eastern styles with the local adobe tradition. This changed with the coming of the railroad.

63

THE RAILROAD BOOM

As the railroad was built west across Kansas in the 1870s, Santa Fe faced its approach with ambivalence. The voice of boosterism spoke through the *New Mexican* with pride of Santa Fe's position as the capital of the territory, regional military headquarters, and seat of the bishop of Santa Fe, of its commercial supremacy and the prestige of its antiquity. Santa Fe could only prosper with the arrival of the railroad, the boosters constantly reassured themselves. But another, less-often-heard voice darkly warned:

> That Santa Fe can never amount to anything more than what it is;
> that it has already reached its greatest importance as a town; that
> its location and mountainous approaches are virtually a bar to the
> approach of railroads. . . . The old Dons will neither improve their
> property or sell to others on terms that will admit of their improv-
> ing; that there are no mines or extended agricultural resources or
> sufficient other natural advantages to build up a town; in short,
> that a town never should have been located here . . . there shall
> never be anything above the present adobe piles.

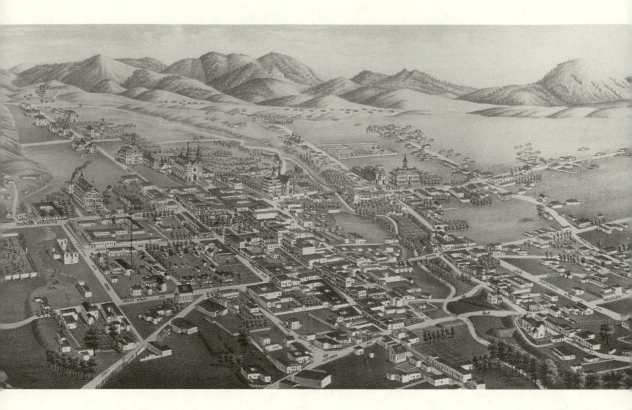

To which the *New Mexican* replied: "The citizens of Santa Fe must themselves show some measure of confidence in the city if they expect railroads and manufacturers and commercial men to show confidence in the town and come here and invest their capital."[32]

Railroad companies typically expected established communities to subsidize their construction as they extended westward after the Civil War, such was the importance of a rail connection to a community's continued economic health. But when the agents of the Denver and Rio Grande Railroad arrived in town in June of 1878, seeking a subsidy to bring their line to Santa Fe, the leading citizens were surprised, even insulted, that New Mexico's leading city should have to pay for a rail hookup. They resisted, and the D.&R.G. withdrew. After nine months contemplating the prospect of being completely bypassed, Santa Fe's leaders initiated contact with the other railroad building toward New Mexico, the Atchison, Topeka and Santa Fe. Negotiations revealed that in order to follow the most hospitable terrain across the territory, the A.T.& S.F. in fact planned to bypass Santa Fe. In the end a substantial county bond issue was voted to pay for an eighteen mile spur line to Santa Fe from Lamy (a new whistle stop on the main line, named for the archbishop).[33]

This spur line arrived in February, 1880, south of the river, nearly a mile from the

32. "Bird's Eye View of the City of Santa Fe, N.M., 1882." After the railroad arrived, multi-story institutional buildings rose quickly over the existing flat-roofed courtyard houses. (J.J. Stover)

plaza. William Berger, a newly arrived real estate promoter, sought to establish a rival city center there beside the depot (fig. 32, lower right). He platted a speculative subdivision south and east of the depot and promoted two auctions of lots by offering free lunches and carriage rides from the plaza. The *New Mexican* was prepared even before the railroad's arrival to champion such initiative: "There is nothing on the plaza that is of value, or but what could be thrown up without a regret. A good hotel and a half dozen good brick building[s], anywhere within two miles of the plaza would be quite sufficient to change the center of business. . . ." However, only warehouses, coal and wood yards, and a scattering of houses appeared near the depot.[34]

It soon became apparent that Santa Fe's business community had no intention of relocating. All five business blocks erected in 1880 and 1881 stood on or near the plaza. When local businessmen organized to build a new hotel to accommodate the influx of tourists and investors from the East, they never seriously considered locating it near the depot. Instead, the Spiegelberg brothers, the city's leading merchants, donated land one block northwest of the plaza, in the opposite direction from the depot. The carriage ride from the depot to the new Palace Hotel would pass directly through the plaza (fig. 33, p. 17).[35]

But high property values and rents caused by crowding the temporary boomtown into the old business district deterred prospective investors. When enterprising young men who had followed the railroad to Santa Fe became discouraged by the lack of opportunities and moved on to Albuquerque or Las Vegas, New Mexico, the business community reacted. In typical ad hoc booster fashion, a public meeting was called early in 1881 to consider widening Water Street, parallel to and a block south of San Francisco Street, which runs along the south side of the plaza. The *New Mexican* proposed that a few blocks west of the plaza, it be curved south to join with San Francisco and form one broad avenue leading to the depot. "It is very certain that Santa Fe must have a business street somewhere, and that pretty soon," argued Territorial Secretary Ritch, "San Francisco street is not at all suited to business purposes, and is wholly

33. PALACE HOTEL, WASHINGTON AVENUE, CHARLES WHEELOCK, 1881.
A FASHIONABLE HOTEL WAS ESSENTIAL FOR ANY WESTERN CITY HOPING TO IMPRESS
PROSPECTIVE INVESTORS. (J.R. RIDDLE)

inadequate to the requirements of business. Besides this there is absolutely no way of reaching the Plaza from the depot side of the town except through unpaved narrow, burro alleys, which make an unfavorable impression upon every stranger who comes to the town." Midway through the meeting, a Spanish speaker rose to ask that the proceedings be translated. This brought the American boosters up short. While they of course provided the translation, it also occurred to them to add Mexicans to the committee already formed to solicit the cooperation of Water Street property owners.[36]

The Water Street committee at first reported receiving the approval of all of the property owners. Coincidentally, however, the newspaper began threatening higher taxes for property owners who, the paper claimed, were setting exorbitant prices for their participation in the widening project. When the list of those giving final approval was published, the paper pointedly noted that everyone on the north side of the street had agreed. As Americans held most of the north side property and Mexicans still owned much of the land on the south side of Water Street, the clear implication was that Mexicans had thwarted the project.

The development of a water system caused even more trouble. The *New Mexican* placed the waterworks high on its list of important improvements along with the Palace Hotel, a gasworks, and new business blocks. As they saw it, houses would at last receive inside plumbing and the system's dam would store irrigation water, which would otherwise be lost in the heavy spring run off. But to native farmers, this meant the loss of control over irrigation water; the ditch association, an important community organization, would surrender its jurisdiction to a private company.

Early in 1881, the county commission granted a water system franchise to a St. Louis engineer and capitalist, J. P. Kennedy. Later it was openly admitted that the commission lacked the legal authority to do this (not until 1884 did the territorial legislature empower water companies to condemn property for laying pipe lines). In 1881, however, legal objections were brushed aside. Some farmers and those whose flour mills were powered by ditch water opposed the project, until the water company offered to reimburse their losses and guarantee normal irrigation waters. Yet shortly thereafter, a dozen small farmers armed themselves and went up the canyon to stop the laying of pipe. The following spring, when irrigation began again, a water company workman was arrested and fined in the locally elected, Hispanic-controlled probate court for taking water without the permission of the ditch association. The next spring, water pipes were broken and the water diverted back into the riverbed. When the company's superintendent rode up the canyon to check on the problem, he was fired upon.[37]

From the American occupation of 1846 until the coming of the railroad in 1880, Americans had gradually changed Santa Fe, but always with the support of the larger Mexican population. The railroad boom disrupted this cooperation. Faced with the loss of control of a basic resource (in this case water, though elsewhere in New Mexico it was land), the native population turned to long-established legal remedies in the probate court and the quasi-governmental ditch association. However, they lacked the funds or understanding of the American courts to pursue drawn-out litigation in the appeals courts. Violent resistance was sporadic, uncoordinated, and ultimately ineffectual, and obstruction exercised through the refusal to sell property to Americans for development or new roads proved to be only a delaying tactic. Property long held by a Mexican family would often pass into American hands in the liquidation of an estate. By 1886 Spanish-surnamed property ownership in Santa Fe was down to 48 percent, and most of this was agricultural land away from the plaza. A pronounced ethnic division of occupations had also emerged, with most Hispanos continuing as farmers and laborers and the recent American and German Jewish immigrants, joined by a few rico intermediaries, taking most positions in business, government, the professions, and skilled trades.[38]

MAIN STREET ON THE PLAZA

Many of the city's prominent German Jewish merchants had deferred their desire for modern business blocks while they awaited the arrival of the railroad. The Spiegelberg

brothers, for instance, operated one of the city's foremost mercantile stores on the south side of the plaza in an old, one-story adobe building. The eldest, Solomon Jacob Spiegelberg, had arrived in Santa Fe from the northern German state of Prussia in 1844 and was joined over the next decade by four brothers. In addition to Santa Fe Trail trade, they became major landowners and in 1872 established the Second National Bank of Santa Fe.[39]

The month the railroad arrived, the Spiegelbergs started construction on a new two-story building, designed to be built in three stages to minimize the disruption of their business (fig. 34). The first portion had adobe walls on the rear and sides, as well as on the front of the second story. These were stuccoed, and the front was painted to look like granite blocks. Materials imported from the Midwest were concentrated on the facade: cast-iron columns and 7-by-15-foot windows on the first floor, pressed-metal window hoods and a bracketed cornice on the second. Although they used adobe, the Spiegelbergs had the first Italianate business front in town. This facade type, which had been popular in the East since the 1850s, would radically alter the appearance of the plaza, since it both did away with the portal and dwarfed earlier adobe buildings.[40]

In 1882 the Spiegelbergs decided to complete the remaining two-thirds as a separate building, designed to house their Second National Bank and Lucas's jeweler on

34. SOUTH SIDE OF PLAZA, ABOUT 1889. MAIN STREET U.S.A. BEGINS TO UNFOLD AROUND THE OLD SPANISH PLAZA.

the first floor, with rental offices on the second. The cast-iron columns and proportions of the first section were repeated, but the window hoods and pressed-metal cornice were more elaborate. Most importantly the Spiegelbergs dispensed completely with adobe and instead built a basement and first floor of stone, with a second floor of brick.[41]

As long as fired bricks had to be shipped in, even if by rail, they were used sparingly. A temporary brickworks supplied the Sisters of Charity Hospital construction in the late 1870s. Several contractors and hardware men tried their hands at brickmaking, but none was successful until builder Florence Donoghue set up a brickworks in the summer of 1882. His only competition came from a brick and terra cotta operation established later at the state penitentiary.[42]

With the importation of heavy machinery, more lumber and stone also began to be produced locally. Before the railroad, lumber was reserved for windows, doors, and porches. After its arrival, larger mills were established, and entire houses and the floors and internal walls of business blocks were made of wood. Stone quarried near the Bishop's Lodge, north of town, supplied Saint Francis Cathedral and the Loretto Chapel in the 1870s. During the 1880s, additional stone quarries opened at Cerrillos (white sandstone), 2 miles up Santa Fe Canyon (brown sandstone), 300 feet behind Fisher's brewery at the head of Palace Avenue (type not specified), and in Arroyo Hondo (gray sandstone).[43]

The Clair Hotel, built on the southwest corner of the plaza in 1891, drew from a national network of suppliers and builders (fig. 36). Locally produced bricks and pine were used for hidden portions. Cast-iron columns and large windows came from the Midwest, red pressed Golden Brick from Colorado, and red Flagstaff Sandstone trim from Arizona. Local laborers demolished the existing 1849 adobe building, dug the basement, and worked as helpers for the outside craftsmen. Carpenters and stone-cutters, developer, architect, and building superintendent all were from Denver, while a "pressed brick gang" from Cincinnati laid the walls.[44]

Most houses and smaller business buildings, however, were designed and constructed

69

35. STAAB BUILDINGS, LOWER SAN FRANCISCO AVENUE, BUILT 1884, PHOTO ABOUT 1935. (T. HARMON PARKHURST)

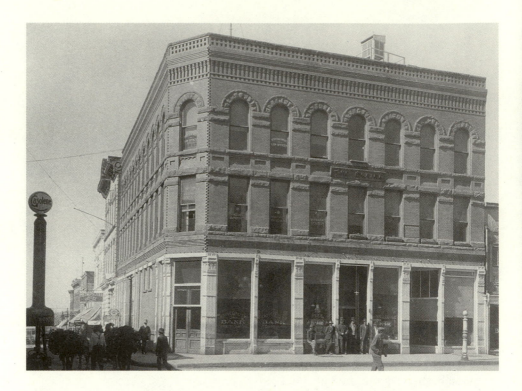

by local building contractors. Many of them were French and Italian stonemasons who had been recruited by Archbishop Lamy. Their knowledge of masonry complemented the local adobe building tradition. The city's leading builder, Florence Donoghue, was born in Dublin in 1832, emigrated first to Missouri, and then, in 1865, to the mining camp of Elizabethtown, New Mexico, where he amassed a fortune. With these resources he set himself up as a Santa Fe building contractor in 1875 and established his brickworks seven years later. In 1881 he was entrusted with the renovation of Our Lady of Guadalupe. Three years later, he formed a partnership with French mason and builder Quintus Monier, and together they built the new territorial capitol building (figs. 37 background right, 39). These French, Italian, and Irish builders were all Catholic, and many married local women, which gave them strong social ties to the Mexican working class from which workmen were drawn.[45]

Architectural styles, too, arrived in abundance with the railroad. The Greek, Romanesque, and Gothic Revivals, which had filtered into Santa Fe earlier, were augmented by the Italianate, Queen Anne, and Second Empire styles. Particular historical and cultural associations made each appropriate for specific uses. The Romanesque and Gothic Revivals, for instance, were popular for churches, because they evoked

36. CLAIR HOTEL, SOUTHWEST CORNER OF THE PLAZA, BUILT 1891, PHOTO ABOUT 1911. (JESSE L. NUSBAUM)

medieval European cathedrals. The style based on the architecture of the French Second Empire (1852-70) was associated in the popular imagination with Paris, the center of nineteenth-century fashion and culture. The urban origins of the Second Empire style, its resulting large scale, and its decorative richness made it especially popular for mansions and public buildings. The booster community chose the Second Empire style for the Palace Hotel (fig. 33),while the French-born Lamy and his clergy also favored the style for church schools and hospitals.[46]

The sole commercial style around the plaza during the 1880s was the Italianate. Mail-order catalogues offered relatively inexpensive cast-iron columns and pressed-metal cornices and window hoods, loosely patterned after Renaissance palazzi. For Santa Fe's cultured few, Italianate business blocks recalled the mercantile prosperity of Renaissance Florence; for the majority, however, they must have evoked the commerce of Main Street America. The style offered a richness of eye-catching detail and associations with prosperity and taste. The Queen Anne style, loosely derived from eighteenth-century English houses, reached Santa Fe with the construction of the Polhemus House about 1890 (fig. 38).

As the Richardsonian Romanesque and the various classical revivals arrived from the East, they too were incorporated into the local repertory. The railroad brought Santa Fe into the industrial age and punctuated the shift from the local vernacular tradition of modest adobe buildings to an era of specialized builders and building types and of imported materials and styles. That the adobe vernacular was Spanish and Mexican in origin and the forces of modernization in New Mexico allied with the incoming Americans is a coincidence of history. Any cultural conflict in architectural matters is overshadowed by the more important shift from a preindustrial to an industrial way of building. Vernacular architectural traditions around the world met the same fate, as farming villages were incorporated into the international industrial economy. Only the timing of their eclipses varied, depending on proximity to industrial and trade centers and to the lines of transportation.[47]

37. PANORAMA OF SANTA FE, ABOUT 1890. LEFT TO RIGHT: ST. VINCENT'S SANATORIUM, CATHEDRAL AND COURTHOUSE; BACKGROUND RIGHT: CAPITOL. (DANA B. CHASE)

38. POLHEMUS HOUSE, FAITHWAY STREET, BUILT ABOUT 1890. (TOM NOBLE)

TRICULTURALISM AND THE STATEHOOD CAMPAIGN

Eastern politicians shied away from annexing more of Mexico in 1848, because the establishment of colonial holdings contradicted residual republican ideals. Many were also unwilling to admit large numbers of what they considered "inferior" Mexicans into the American democracy. New Mexico was in fact the only substantial concentration of Mexicans that the United States did annex, and then mainly to secure a land bridge to the strategic but much less populated territory of California. New Mexico functioned as an internal colony, administered as a territory by key officials appointed by the president. The greatest obstacle to statehood was its Mexican population. The boosters of statehood sought to Americanize this population through education in the English language, through conversion to Protestantism, and through the modernization of agricultural and commercial practices. At the same time, far beyond the power and oftentimes even without the knowledge of the average Mexican, Congress and the courts stripped the traditional villages of most of their land. Simultaneously the image and, ultimately, the name of this population was rehabilitated from the foreign and derogatory *Mexican* to the romantic and ennobling *Spanish*.[48]

The emergence of the identifying term *Spanish-American* in English-language publications proceeded gradually from about 1870 to 1920 as part of the campaign for statehood and coincided with the rise of a rhetoric of triculturalism. In broad terms, this was the effort to fit New Mexico legally and conceptually into the American nation. Santa Fe's Fourth of July parade in 1874 included individuals personifying the Goddess of Liberty but also Don Quixote and Sancho Panza—an early recognition of the local Spanish heritage. Then in the wake of the United States centennial celebration of 1876, the boosters of statehood increasingly emphasized parallels between the American and Mexican wars of independence from European domination.[49]

The theories of racial superiority that gained currency in America during the 1840s rose again on a new wave of xenophobia at the end of the century. In 1882, for instance, the *New York Times* published an anonymous racist diatribe from Trinidad, Colorado, under the heading "Greasers as Citizens." The writer challenged New Mexico's bid for statehood by claiming that the Mexican population harbored anti-American passions. Recently arrived chief justice of the New Mexico Supreme Court, L. Bradford Prince, who would emerge as the leading champion of statehood, flatly denied this in a letter to the *Times*, adding that "the better classes of people . . . are fit representatives of the land of Cid and successors of the heroic discoverers and conquerors of the soil"—an echo of Senator Calhoun's earlier invocation of Castilian blood. The Trinidad letter also charged that "about two-thirds of the population of the Territory is of the mongrel breed known as Mexicans—a mixture of the blood of Apache, negro, Navajo, white horse thief, Pueblo Indian, and old-time frontiersman with the original Mexican stock." While factually correct, this assertion was infused with racism. Prince challenged it by citing the U.S. census, which classed Americans and Mexicans together as "Whites" and showed only 172 people of African descent in the territory in 1870. "While some Pueblo villages are quite near Spanish towns," he continued, "yet no marriage or similar connection take place between races. . . . How any Navajos or Apache blood can mix with the Mexican in these days, when the tribes are on reservations far from the centers of population, I am at a loss to imagine. The fact is that there is not now and has not been for a long time any such mixture, with very rare exceptions; fully as rare as in other sections of the country where the Caucasian race meets the Indian." So pervasive was racialist thinking in American society that when Prince challenged racist sentiments, he resorted to racialist terms by claiming Spanish ancestry for the better class of people and denying the existence of racial mixing.[50]

The suppression of the history of racial intermixing and the rise of the rhetoric of racial separation following the arrival of the railroad corresponded to growing residential segregation across the Southwest. Families newly arrived from the East settled in predominantly Anglo-American new towns, which developed at a distance from the old Spanish-Mexican towns where the native population remained concentrated.

Residential segregation was less pronounced in Santa Fe than in most other southwestern cities, because of the small scale of Anglo-American immigration and new construction between 1880 and 1912 and later because of the desire of artists and other romantic newcomers to live in old adobe houses. But gradually the area they favored on the east side of town, especially around Canyon Road and Camino del Monte Sol, became predominantly Anglo, while the Guadalupe-Westside area emerged as a *mexicano* working-class barrio. Nevertheless in Santa Fe the rhetoric of racial and cultural separation and the arrival of more Anglo women and families with the railroad combined to cause a decline in the proportion of mixed marriages.

In the dedication of his 1882 book *Historical Sketches of New Mexico,* Prince rhapsodized about the "worthy sons of the Conquistadores, who . . . carried the cross of Christianity and the flag of Spain to the ends of the earth." That this celebration appears under "TO THE MEXICANS," suggests that Prince saw the ancestors as Spanish but had not yet extended this term to the contemporary population. His dedication, which extols "THE PUEBLOS" and "THE AMERICANS," is apparently the first written expression of New Mexican triculturalism—the notion that New Mexico is made up of three separate cultures living in harmony. In today's rhetoric, Prince's Mexicans, Pueblos, and Americans have become Hispanics, Native Americans, and Anglos.[51]

The Spanish-language press, which flourished in New Mexico from the 1880s until the 1920s, was not entirely willing to cede the term *American* to English-speaking newcomers. Noting that the Spanish-speaking population had been American citizens since 1848, self-styled "nuevomexican" journalists did employ the *mexicano/americano* dichotomy, but they also increasingly substituted other formations, such as *hispano-americano/anglo-americano.* While working for the full rights of citizenship and the preservation of their distinct ethnic enclave, they increasingly spoke of themselves as *nuevomexicano, hispano,* and *nativo.*[52]

Santa Fe natives, nevertheless, continued to refer to themselves primarily as "mexicano" in Spanish and occasionally wielded the term *Mexican* with conscious pride.

In 1897, for instance, Miguel Otero II, proclaimed at his inauguration, "It is not the least of my joys on this occasion that I stand before you the first native-born governor of this fair territory. I am proud of the fact that I am a Mexican." While this statement received a sustained ovation from the thousands who thronged the Santa Fe plaza, Otero's background was more complex than he suggested. Born in St. Louis in 1859, his mother was Mary Blackwell and his father a congressional delegate from New Mexico, who later established a prominent mercantile wholesale business. Although Otero was raised in New Mexico, he graduated from Notre Dame and, like his father, married an American women. Otero cast his identity forceful as a native Mexican that day, for he and his audience both understood that his appointment meant that an unjustified racist onus was beginning to lift from their shoulders.[53]

BOOSTERISM IN THE FACE OF DECLINE

The first railroad boom of 1880 and 1881 had been disappointing; a few public and commercial buildings went up, but Santa Fe's economy stagnated. The arrival of the Denver and Rio Grande Railroad from the north in 1887 stimulated a second boom in booster rhetoric and paper transactions, but when the census showed a decline in population from 6,635 in 1880 to 6,185 in 1890, the boosters grasped for something to stem the ebbing tide.[54]

Incorporation became the new panacea. Albuquerque and Las Vegas are surpassing Santa Fe because they are incorporated, people began to say; "manufacturing capital is shy of engaging in enterprises where they can have no adequate protection from municipal governments." Boosters paid delinquent poll taxes for those who would vote yes on incorporation. The *New Mexican* daily predicted doom for the city if incorporation failed. Investors would quit Santa Fe, the paper warned, and the territorial capital would be removed to a more prosperous city. E. T. Webber, the Denver capitalist then building the Clair Hotel on the plaza, made his threats tangible a few days before the election, when he sent his workmen home, left six carloads of materials unloaded on a depot siding, and threatened to abandon the project altogether if incorporation failed.[55]

Only the degree of the victory was a surprise: incorporation passed 709 to 102. The *New Mexican,* which had ridiculed a certain backward element of the "Mexican" population before the vote, now congratulated young "Spanish Americans" for coming down on the side of progress. The promised investment never materialized, however, as Santa Fe's unfavorable position on the railway continued to hamper its development, while the national depression known as the Panic of 1893 made matters even worse.

Santa Fe's economy became increasingly dependent on the territorial and federal governments, and on the Catholic Church. These institutions erected all the major new buildings in the five years following incorporation: a reconstructed state capitol, a terra cotta works at the penitentiary, a hospital at the Indian school, the Sisters of Charity convent, and a stone apse for the cathedral. Residential construction, too, stagnated as the population continued to decline.

Most institutional projects after the turn of the century went to the architectural firm of Rapp and Rapp, headed by Isaac H. Rapp. Isaac and his younger brother William Morris Rapp were sons of a Carbondale, Illinois, building contractor, Isaac Rapp, Sr. The senior Rapp, a successful and practical man similar to Florence Donoghue of Santa Fe, had also founded the Carbondale Planing Mill, which produced doors, windows, and wooden molding. Although Isaac, Jr., and William would style themselves architects, architecture schools had not yet been founded in the Midwest, and they apprenticed under their father. (Their younger brothers, Cornelius and George, would later attend the new school of architecture at University of Illinois, and in 1906, establish the Chicago-based firm of Rapp and Rapp, leading national specialists in theater design.) Carbondale had been a booming Illinois Central Railroad town in Isaac's youth, and when he struck out on his own in 1888, he settled in the new railroad town of Trinidad, Colorado. After William joined him in 1892, they opened a second office in the next major town down the line—Las Vegas, New Mexico. Isaac, the chief designer

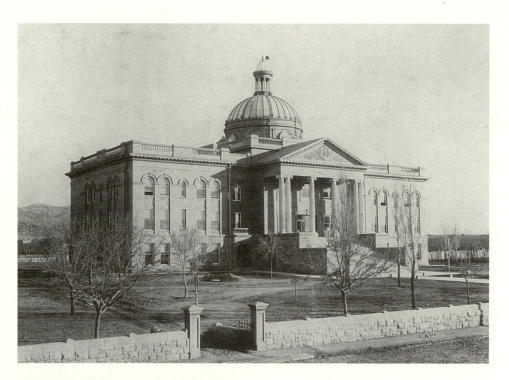

39. STATE CAPITOL, RAPP AND RAPP, 1900. (CHRISTIAN G. KAADT)

40. FIRST NATIONAL BANK, RAPP AND RAPP, EAST SIDE OF PLAZA, 1911. THE LAST
OVERTLY AMERICAN BUILDING ERECTED ON THE PLAZA. (T. HARMON PARKHURST)

and more outgoing of the two, would finally move to Santa Fe in 1909. The success of his 1900 design for a new territorial capitol (fig. 39) brought increasing work in Santa Fe: the Laughlin business block, Catron High School (1905), the First Ward Grade School (1906), the city jail (1906), the Territorial Executive's Mansion (1908), St. Vincent's Sanatorium, the Elks' Theater, and a reconstruction of the county courthouse (1910) (fig. 37, right). While his early work in Trinidad and Las Vegas ranged from the Gothic and Moorish Revivals to the Richardsonian Romanesque, Rapp now adopted the academic classicism popularized by the 1893 Columbian Exposition in Chicago. His 1911 First National Bank, on the east side of the plaza, with its white classical details, symmetry, and restraint would have been at home on any American main street (fig. 40).[56]

Throughout the railroad boom-and-bust years, the *New Mexican* criticized Mexican merchants who were slow to modernize their buildings. Shortly after the arrival of the railroad, it had editorialized that portales "are homely, they make the streets look narrow and have not a business like appearance." They should come down, the paper argued, and most did. Shortly after incorporation in 1891, the paper renewed its campaign: "The unsightly, unhealthy and dangerous portals on the principal street must go, get a move on yourself and remember that you are living in the 19th century and not the 16th." When Juan B. Lamy (the archbishop's nephew) ordered his portal torn down, the paper congratulated him for being "sensible" and "patriotic." Those who followed his example would give their buildings more air and sunlight—a growing concern in a city beginning to tout itself as a tuberculosis health resort.[57]

In time only the 1859 Delgado building on the south side of the plaza retained its portal (fig. 34). The *New Mexican* called weekly for its removal; if necessary, the city should condemn it as a public nuisance and pull it down. But when the city council went Democratic in the fall of 1892, the paper lamented that no action could be expected and relaxed its attack. A year later merchant Felipe B. Delgado quietly removed the portal.[58]

As the city continued to decline, even its position as territorial capital, so vital to the its identity and remaining economic base, came into jeopardy. During each legislative session, Santa Feans staved off efforts to relocate it to Albuquerque. Finally in 1897, the U.S. Congress permanently designated Santa Fe the capital, through the efforts of the new territorial governor, Miguel A. Otero, II.[59]

One line of booster rhetoric even turned economic stagnation into an advantage. Compared to those boisterous adolescents Albuquerque and Las Vegas, this argument went, Santa Fe offered quiet, repose, and refinement, complemented by its beautiful location and climate. In the early 1890s, a campaign to attract consumptives featured promotional brochures and newspaper testimonials to the curative powers of Santa Fe's quiet, sunshine, and mountain air. The *New Mexican* also prophesied that men with economic interests elsewhere in the state would establish their families in Santa Fe because of its good schools, mild climate, and central location, while the wealthy from the Plains states would also summer there. All that was needed to make the city into a leading health resort and upper-class enclave were a few more shade trees, clean streets kept wetted down in the dusty season and lighted at night, an improved plaza park, and a few historical markers.[60]

While the leading citizens of Santa Fe embraced these many projects, they felt ambivalent about the prospect that would ultimately reverse the city's decline—tourism. They struggled to reconcile their progressive booster spirit with the promotion of Santa Fe's antiquity. Even as tourism began to contribute to its economy, the Americanization of the plaza area neared completion. Santa Feans sensed that they were destroying their city's attractiveness for tourists, although often this had to be pointed out to them by outsiders. "Tourists who wish to visit the town should not delay," wrote one visitor from Indiana in 1892, "for the ruthless hand of progress will soon destroy the haloed glow of romance that broods with its benign wings over the antique walls of this ancient city."[61]

3   THE RELUCTANT TOURIST TOWN

As Santa Fe sank deeper into economic stagnation at the close of the nineteenth century, it also became ensnared in a double bind of conflicting expectations. Local boosters struggled to prove that the territory was progressive and Americanized enough to be admitted as a state. Simultaneously tourism rose as a potential solution to the city's economic woes but demanded a contrasting romantic identity. As a result Santa Fe's public identity, and that of the territory in general, split into two contradictory images.

The official image of Santa Fe offered up by businessmen and territorial officials portrayed a venerable city fast becoming Anytown, U.S.A. The contrasting tourist image developed by curio dealers, photographers, and writers for such national magazines as *Harper's Weekly* and *American Architect* reveled in the romance of ancient adobe villages. Promotional books and pamphlets distributed by the Territorial Bureau of Immigration presented the official image, while stereographs, postcards, and magazine illustrations formed the tourist image. Architecture was essential to both as new, eastern-style civic buildings represented the city's progressive spirit, while aging adobe houses and Spanish missions emerged as symbols of its picturesque allure.

After its annexation to the United States in 1848, New Mexico's residents watched with growing impatience over the next sixty-four years as newer, more sparsely settled western territories became states. A half dozen times New Mexico reached the threshold of statehood, only to be turned away. Sometimes its cause became enmeshed with national issues, such as slavery or the gold standard. Other times internal New Mexico political bickering or the Catholic Church's insistence on public funding for parochial schools scuttled the effort. Although similar problems faced the other western territories, Colorado, Montana, Wyoming, Idaho, Nevada, and Oklahoma each gained admittance in turn. Even Utah, suspect because of Mormon polygamy, preceded New Mexico by sixteen years.[1]

The crucial difference, of course, was New Mexico's Spanish-speaking, Roman Catholic population, which congressmen and the eastern press alike considered essen-

tially foreign. A large part of "the people is ignorant and utterly destitute of enterprise and public spirit" wrote the *New York Times* in 1875, reflecting this general prejudice.[2]

PROGRESSIVE AND TOURIST IMAGES

To project a more positive image to the nation, the territorial legislature established the Bureau of Immigration in 1880. Territorial secretary and leading Santa Fe booster William Ritch was elected the first president of the bureau's board of directors and edited its early publications. Like promotional agencies in the other western states and territories, the bureau sought to attract investors and new settlers. An increase in the number of Anglo-American settlers held particular significance for New Mexico's campaign for statehood. The image of an Americanizing territory conjured up by the bureau's book-length *Illustrated New Mexico,* which went through six editions in the early 1880s, sent a similar message to Congress.[3]

Images of new courthouses, schools, churches, business blocks, and residences in bureau publications projected this progressive spirit. The up-to-date Second Empire style of the Palace Hotel and the Staab House demonstrated that Santa Fe was a modern, perhaps even refined city. The halftone reproduction of photographs was not perfected until the 1890s, so wood engravings were used. Although engravers usually worked from photographs, they adjusted secondary details to enhance the primary message. The people and carriages in bureau illustrations, for instance, are often too small for the buildings (fig. 42). Conscious or not, this distortion of scale gives the buildings an inflated scale, equal to the territory's dream of progress. Engravings of the grandiose plans of the territorial capitol and Lamy's cathedral, neither of which was ever fully realized, also appeared year after year. Meanwhile the proliferation of power lines in many woodcuts emphasized the development of modern utilities.

Progress and antiquity, nevertheless, stood side by side in one bureau illustration (fig. 43). On the left, an Indian women with a water jar on her head poses beside an

41. GOLD'S OLD CURIO SHOP, LOWER SAN FRANCISCO STREET, ABOUT 1895. (CHRISTIAN G. KAADT) "THE CURIO DEALER THINKS IT WOULD BE VANDALISM TO MODERNIZE THE HOUSE CONSIDERING HE INTENDS TO DUB IT THE 'OLD CURIO SHOP.'"

ox-drawn cart in front of old San Miguel Church, while on the right, a modern carriage glides past the mansard-roofed Saint Michael's College. The bureau typically deflected tourists' interest in local color away from Santa Fe by providing images of nearby Tesuque Pueblo. But a national magazine such as *Harper's Weekly* or *Century,* with no stake in the campaign for statehood, focused its coverage on the older, Mexican portions of Santa Fe and more broadly on the "Cliff Dwellers," as the Anasazi who left behind the Mesa Verde and Chaco Canyon ruins were then known. In 1881 the *American Architect,* too, began to champion the picturesque qualities of Pueblo villages and prehistoric ruins.[4]

In Santa Fe professional photographers such as Brown and Bennett catered to the romantic interests of early tourists. The head of the firm, William H. Brown, learned the new trade of photography in his father's St. Louis studio during the early 1860s. The Browns freighted their large, delicate cameras and processing chemicals with them over the Santa Fe Trail and established the city's first studio in 1866. After exhausting the immediate local demand for portraits, they pressed on to Chihuahua, stopping at communities along the way to set up their temporary studio. The younger Brown reestablished himself back in Santa Fe from 1880 to 1884. Suffering from tuberculosis, he stayed close to his studio on the west side of the plaza, while his new

42. PROPOSED TERRITORIAL CAPITOL, E.S. JENNISON, REPRODUCED FROM *ILLUSTRATED NEW MEXICO*, BUREAU OF IMMIGRATION PUBLICATION, 1885, ONLY ONE WING CONSTRUCTED (SEE FIGURE 37). THE GRANDIOSITY OF BOOSTER ASPIRATIONS.

partner, George Bennett, roamed the countryside, at times in the company of pioneer archaeologist Adolph Bandelier, taking picturesque views of ruins, villages, and countryside. Itinerant craftsmen plying a new communication media, Brown and Bennett sought to increase their income in 1880 by issuing a catalogue of New Mexico stereographs, including fifty-five views of Santa Fe. They offered these views by mail, wholesale to other photographers, and in 1883 sold five hundred twelve-image sets to the Palace Hotel (fig. 44).[5]

Brown and Bennett included a few modern institutional structures such as the Second Empire style college building in their catalogue. But if the Bureau of Immigration was happy to leave the misapprehension that the painted stucco of the college was stone, the photographers captioned their view "San Miguel College, an Adobe Building," as if to say: "Santa Fe may appear modern on the surface, but underneath it is still exotic." They focused their cameras primarily on the old unimproved quarters of town in stereos entitled "Burro Alley," "El Horno," "Mexican Residence," and "The Dirt Roofs."

Brown and Bennett's most popular subject, with six separate views, was San Miguel Church, which had emerged as the city's first landmark, much as the Old North Church was Boston's first. Another ten views record details of local adobe architecture—things

43. SAN MIGUEL CHURCH AND SAINT MICHAEL'S COLLEGE,
FROM *ILLUSTRATED NEW MEXICO*, BUREAU OF IMMIGRATION PUBLICATION, 1885.
THE PICTURESQUE AND PROGRESS STANDING SIDE-BY-SIDE.

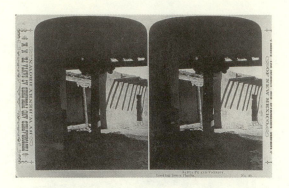

quite exotic to the rest of the country. The view "Looking into a Plazita," taken from under a portal to enhance the three-dimensional effect, epitomized the use of architecture as romantic setting. Brown and Bennett's 1880 catalogue assured its customers that "Santa Fe has hardly been altered during the last century, there is scarcely a frame building in the place." By contrast when an Albuquerque newspaper referred to Santa Fe in 1889 as that "dusty adobe town," the *Daily New Mexican* replied indignantly that six and a half million fired bricks were to be used in new buildings that year alone.[6]

The conflict between progress and antiquity came into sharp focus in 1886, when the county commission proposed the construction of a two and one-half story brick courthouse in the middle of the plaza. The use of this public ground would conserve the county's limited resources, the commissioners felt, while providing Santa Fe with its own courthouse square like other American towns. A flood of letters to the *New Mexican* deplored what one called the irreparable loss of "the pleasantest park in any town of the territory." One man writing from Las Vegas, New Mexico, predicted that this would initiate the destruction of Santa Fe's distinct character: "The quaint old city would soon lose its envied name of being curiously picturesque and the things which now attract thousands of strangers within your gates, would only be said of: Here is where the beautiful old plaza was, here is where the old church stood, and so on until every vestige of antiquity would be blotted out." Santa Fe residents fought to protect their plaza park, but perhaps only an outsider could frame the issue in terms of historic preservation, such was the ambivalence Santa Feans felt about living in a quaint old city. An embarrassed county commission quickly shifted the courthouse to a site on upper Palace Avenue, opposite the cathedral (fig. 37, lower right).[7]

CLASSICISM VERSUS PUEBLO STYLE

The first suggestion that a new building could or should evoke New Mexico's indigenous architecture came, somewhat surprisingly, from a New York architect—Stanford White of the era's preeminent architectural firm, McKim, Mead and White. In 1887

44. STEREOTYPIC VIEW, "LOOKING INTO A PLAZITA," FROM THE BROWN AND
BENNETT SERIES, 1880.

White designed a building for the Ramona Industrial School for Indian Girls at Santa Fe (fig. 45). The school was endowed by publication royalties from Helen Hunt Jackson, the picturesque travel writer turned Indian-rights advocate. In her most popular work, the 1884 romantic novel *Ramona,* Jackson sought to dramatize the plight of Indians in southern California, just as abolitionist Harriet Beecher Stowe's *Uncle Tom's Cabin* had personified the injustices of slavery before the Civil War.[8]

Stanford White moved in the same elite East Coast circles as Jackson. When he visited his brother, a New Mexico mining engineer, in 1883, he described the country around Socorro where his brother worked as looking "like the entrance to Hell." Although White had traveled through New England sketching American colonial buildings to inspire his Colonial Revival designs, he paid no special attention to local Pueblo and Spanish colonial architecture. The Ramona School paper, nevertheless, reported that his design "embodied his conception of the typical style of architecture suited to the history, climate and surroundings of New Mexico. It reveals in some of its most prominent features, the ancient cliff dwellings of New Mexico and Arizona, with low tile roofs, projecting vigas, its porticos, and quadrangular structure around a spacious court." The *New Mexican,* too, was dutifully impressed with the building's exotic "Zuni Pueblo style."[9]

These allusions to ancient cliff dwellings and Zuni Pueblo seem fanciful in retrospect, but for a generation of Santa Fe residents accustomed to Romanesque and Classical public buildings, a few imported details such as iron grilles and red tile roofs went a long way toward creating an exotic appearance. That none of these details were found in historic New Mexican architecture escaped notice. Instead White found elements from Mediterranean and Italian sources most appropriate for Santa Fe. The building's vaguely Renaissance style, along with the symmetry of mass and detail and motifs such as the Syrian arch and hipped roofs make it a typical product of the McKim, Mead, and White office, and similar, in fact, to their pivotal Boston Public Library (1888-92). The school soon constructed a smaller, more conventional brick and wood-frame Shingle Style building.

45. PROPOSAL FOR ROMONA INDIAN GIRLS SCHOOL, STANFORD WHITE, 1887.
ALTHOUGH NEVER BUILT, THIS IS THE FIRST ATTEMPT TO DEFINE A STYLE
APPROPRIATE TO NEW MEXICO.

Throughout the 1880s, while lavishly illustrated articles in *Harper's Weekly* and *Century Magazine* fostered popular interest in the ancient "Cliff-dwellers" and the contemporary Pueblo Indians, scholarly research also gained momentum. The federal Bureau of Ethnology, established in 1879, dispatched Frank Cushing to Zuni Pueblo, where he lived for four and a half years, learned to speak Zuni, was adopted by a family, and underwent initiation into a religious society. His subsequent publications on Zuni social organization, myth, and ritual presented the first detailed picture of the complexity and richness of a Pueblo culture. The bureau also sponsored the field research and publication in 1891 of Victor Mindeleff's *A Study of Pueblo Architecture*, a detailed illustrated report, which emerged as a source book for Pueblo Revival architecture in the following decade. The pioneer archaeologist Adolph Bandelier, too, began his exhaustive archaeological reconnaissance of New Mexico in 1880 and five years later made Santa Fe his home base. Bandelier sought to make his scientific findings more accessible to the public with *The Delight Makers,* an 1890 novel recreating life in the twelfth-century Anasazi world. It met with limited popularity at first, one commentator speculates, because Bandelier "had written about the enemy, the Indians, as if they were real (that is, white) people struggling in a muddled social world rather than mythical creatures grazing in a long-extinct forest."[10]

No New Mexican architect was prepared by inclination or training to enlarge on White's suggestive gesture or to capitalize on the growing popular fascination with the Southwest. Easterners might yearn for romantic images of Indian and Spanish life in New Mexico and for complementary architectural settings, but New Mexicans (both Anglo-Americans and Hispanos of means) continued to build in a variety of Eastern styles, as the Queen Anne and Richardsonian Romanesque gave way during the 1890s to the Colonial Revival and Neoclassicism.

The 1893 Chicago Columbian Exposition punctuated this shift in architectural taste with a great white classical city (fig. 2). McKim, Mead and White and other architects of the exposition promised an American Renaissance of classicism worthy of a country then emerging on the world stage. New Mexico embraced the exposition's dominant classicism in a building it shared with the territories of Arizona and Oklahoma (fig. 46). (The selection of neoclassical for a new territorial capitol in 1900 demonstrated that even if New Mexico had possessed the resources for a separate building at Chicago, its boosters would likely have wrapped their aspirations in classicism.) The territories' building, like Bureau of Immigration pamphlets distributed to fairgoers, advanced the cause of statehood through a rhetoric of Americanization.[11]

Intent on elevating "Culture" with their Great White Way, fair organizers consigned amusement rides, sideshow curiosities, and commercial exhibitions of exotic cultures to a separate pleasure zone—the Midway Plaisance. There, after walking down the crowded Streets of Cairo, marveling at the Tower of Babel and a Moorish Palace, and pausing to eat in the Moroccan Cafe, fairgoers came upon a great brown lath-and-plaster mountain near the end of the midway—the Cliff Dwellers (fig. 47). Climbing through cliffs filled with crumbling ruins, they encountered cliff dwellers in the flesh, portrayed by Laguna Pueblo Indians. One guidebook, nevertheless, claimed that the exhibit represented "the last castles of an extinct race." Meanwhile California, Texas, Colorado, and Florida each explored a romanticized Spanish-Mediterranean image in their state building. While these buildings laid the conceptual groundwork for the subsequent rise of the Pueblo style, such a regional style was simply not yet compatible with New Mexico's official image.[12]

THE LAND OF SUNSHINE

Southern California advanced most rapidly in the promotion of its Spanish Mission culture, spurred on above all by the son of a New England preacher, Charles F. Lummis. As a student of the romantic art historian Charles Eliot Norton at Harvard in the early 1880s, Lummis learned to value local history and traditions, and adopted the belief that art could "shape and sustain emerging social currents and institutions through moral uplift." Stricken with malaria in 1884, Lummis resolved to recuperate by

walking across the country to California, where the *Los Angeles Times* agreed to publish his travel dispatches. His exposure to the immense desert Southwest landscape and the Pueblo and Spanish-speaking peoples left him feeling like "a man who got outside the fences of civilization and was glad of it." "Though my conscience was Puritan," he exulted, "my whole imagination and sympathy and feeling were Latin."[13]

Three years on the city desk at the *Times* led to a stroke, followed by another three years recuperating with a *rico* family in New Mexico. A stint in the field with the archaeologist Adolph Bandelier left Lummis with a trove of observations, notes, and photographs, as well as a desire to make the rest of the country proud of this region "which Americans know as little as they do of inner Africa." Between 1892 and 1894, Lummis unleashed five books, including *A Tramp across the Continent, The Land of Poco Tiempo,* and *Spanish Pioneers,* in which he countered the Black Legend with tales of valiant conquistadors. One result was an invitation from the Los Angeles Chamber of Commerce to edit its magazine. Lummis insisted on complete editorial control, which allowed him to campaign for reform in Indian policy and the restoration of the California missions, and against American imperialism, ethnocentrism, and racism.

As editor of *The Land of Sunshine* from 1894 to 1909 (renamed *Out West* in 1902), Lummis cultivated western writers and painters to help wrap boosterism in a mantel

46. NEW MEXICO, ARIZONA AND OKLAHOMA BUILDING, WORLD'S COLUMBIAN
EXPOSITION, CHICAGO, 1893.

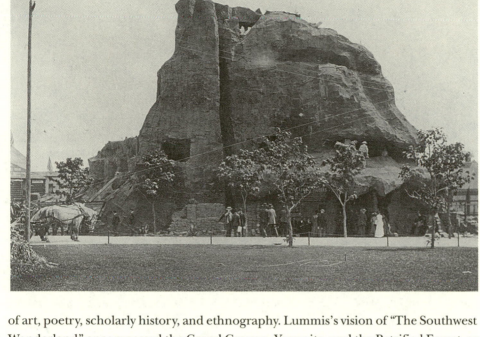

of art, poetry, scholarly history, and ethnography. Lummis's vision of "The Southwest Wonderland" encompassed the Grand Canyon, Yosemite, and the Petrified Forest, as well as the cliff dwellings, Pueblo villages, and the California missions. In the Southwest, argued Lummis, the Anglo-Saxon race was encountering both a temperate Mediterranean climate, and a Latin Catholic culture for the first time. Saxons could thrive as never before, if they learned to temper the excesses of modern materialism and the Protestant work ethic with an outdoor life-style and the Spanish generosity of spirit, personal restraint, social purpose, and joy in life. As the circulation of *Out West* climbed to 12,500, it became apparent that Lummis's romantic sentiments were shared by a small but growing minority.[14]

Allied with Lummis was the Santa Fe Railway advertising department, established in its Chicago offices in 1895 and headed from 1900 to 1933 by William H. Simpson. With newspaper and magazine advertisements, brochures, time tables, and colored lantern slide shows (for school classes, civic groups, train passengers, and hotel guests), it promoted the same natural and cultural attractions as Lummis did. Simpson purchased and traded rail passes with painters and photographers to obtain images of these attractions for use in the railway's publications and for distribution to national magazines, state promotional agencies, and local chambers of commerce.

47. THE CLIFF DWELLERS EXHIBIT, WORLD'S COLUMBIAN EXPOSITION, CHICAGO, 1893.

Beginning in 1906, Simpson assembled a collection of over six hundred paintings, the majority from the Taos and Santa Fe art colonies. In addition to displaying these works in their railroad stations and hotels, Simpson initiated an annual calendar in 1907, each reproducing one of his paintings of Pueblo or, less often, Navajo Indians (fig. 48). These bright-colored calendars reached as many as three hundred thousand homes, offices, and schools a year. Situated in an ahistorical world devoid of modern manufactured objects, dressed in traditional costumes and often posed before a multistory pueblo, these calendar Indians are dignified but aloof—their eyes almost never meet the viewer. Instead they stare vacantly into the distance (seeing, as historical pageants and later Hollywood movies would have it, a vision of the coming white man), or they gaze intently at a piece of pottery, a feather head dress, their weaving, or jewelry work—conveniently the very crafts sold in the railway curio shops. The image of an Indian with a sharply sculpted nose and jutting jaw, shown in full or partial profile, became an increasingly stylized logo for the Santa Fe Railway, as it christened its luxury trains "The Chief," "The Navajo," and "The Super Chief." So complete was the railway's appropriation, that they spoke of "the Santa Fe Indian" and "the Santa Fe Southwest." Curiously, though, the city of Santa Fe and Hispano New Mexico remained marginal to the railway's promotional image until about 1915. If Lummis believed that Anglo culture could be tempered and morally elevated by drawing inspiration from traditional Spanish and Indian cultures, the Santa Fe Railway employed the Grand Canyon and Pueblo Indians primarily as fodder for corporate advertising.[15]

The architectural manifestation of southern California's image-making campaign—the California Mission style—was sparked by the California Building at the 1893 Chicago fair. The following year, the Atchison, Topeka and Santa Fe Railroad began building Mission style depots to greet travelers along their lines stretching west from Kansas to California. The Southern Pacific and Union Pacific quickly followed suit.[16]

The Santa Fe Railway brought the California Mission style to New Mexico in 1897, with a Harvey House hotel in Las Vegas, the Castañeda. The construction of the largest

Harvey House, the Alvarado, at Albuquerque between 1901 and 1904, solidified the style's position in New Mexico. White stucco or buff brick walls, red tile roofs, veranda-lined patios, curved and stepping gable parapets, and towers adapted from the California missions became the hallmarks of the style.[17]

New Mexico's boosters finally crossed over the threshold into regional image making with the territorial building at the 1904 Louisiana Purchase Exposition in St. Louis (fig. 49). Although Neoclassicism again predominated, the territory turned to California for inspiration, asserting that "the Mission style of architecture, characteristic of the country, was adopted." As the leading architects of northern New Mexico, Rapp and Rapp received the Saint Louis commission. In a sense the California Mission style was simply another mode for them, perhaps somewhat more appropriate for New Mexico than Eastern styles, but still a borrowed image. The underlying formality of their design, too, derives from the prevailing classical taste.[18]

By comparison, the Cliff Dwellers, another midway attraction, had a wonderful naive enthusiasm (fig. 50). In place of the fake cliffs of Chicago was a Pueblo village of wood frame and plaster, again staffed by Pueblo Indians. The contrived parapet profiles and the shallowness of the Saint Louis Cliff Dwellers give it a stage-set quality. Vertical

48. "THE END OF THE SANTA FE TRAIL," GERALD CASSIDY, PURCHASED BY SANTA FE RAILWAY AND REPRODUCED ON 1940 COMPANY CALENDAR. THE RAILWAY AND THE CITY WORKED CLOSELY TOGETHER AFTER 1912 TO PROMOTE THE SOUTHWEST.

wooden bars in the windows incongruously evoke prisons. While the lectures and exhibits featuring the territory's educational facilities made a good impression at the New Mexico building, the *New Mexican* had to concede that the Cliff Dwellers "is doing more to advertise New Mexico than any individual show at the fair."[19]

For the first decade of the century, however, the Mission style continued to seem entirely appropriate for New Mexico because of its general Spanish colonial associations. Although classical revival designs predominated in Santa Fe's public buildings, the Mission style was increasingly adopted by those desiring a picturesque Southwestern image. The Women's Board of Trade Library, Senator Bronson Cutting's house, and the remodelings of Rosario Chapel and Guadalupe Church all employed the Mission style. In 1909 the territorial superintendent of public education issued a series of standard school plans in the Mission style. In 1911 Rapp and Rapp recycled their 1904 world's fair design in a new Elks Club Building (fig. 51), and in 1912 the Santa Fe Railway erected one of their trademark Mission depots in the city.[20]

Throughout this first decade, the *New Mexican* noted a growing flow of tourists through the city. In 1904, the owners of the Sunmount Tent City (for consumptives and tourists) contemplated building some adobe cottages, "in regular Mexican style, Mexican fireplaces and roofs, with the exception that they will have modern matched

49. NEW MEXICO BUILDING, LOUISIANA PURCHASE CENTENNIAL EXPOSITION, ST. LOUIS, RAPP AND RAPP, 1904. THE CALIFORNIA MISSION STYLE SEEMED AN APPROPRIATE SYMBOL FOR NEW MEXICO DURING THE 1910S.

wood floors and bath rooms. It is found that a good many eastern people would like to come here and live during their sojourn in adobe houses." [21]

STATEHOOD AND THE MUSEUM OF NEW MEXICO

As the campaign for statehood dragged into the new century, it remained convoluted and frustrating. When Captain Maximilian Luna and Sergeant George Washington Armijo distinguished themselves as members of Teddy Roosevelt's Rough Riders during the Spanish-American War of 1898, doubts about the loyalty of Hispanos to the United States lessened. Political in-fighting and an occasional filibuster continued to thwart action in Congress, however. In 1906 Congress offered the voters of New Mexico and Arizona admission as a single state under the name *Montezuma,* which the populace of each territory resoundingly declined at the polls. In 1910 Congress finally authorized separate statehood, and after a constitutional convention New Mexico became a state on January 6, 1912.[22]

Despite a growing local inclination to cater to tourism in the decade before statehood, Santa Fe lacked the promotional skills to revitalize its civic identity or to define its own architectural style. As late as February 1912, the Santa Fe Railway refused to extend lowered summer tourists rates on travel to the city; its namesake city did not

50. CLIFF DWELLINGS AND DWELLERS EXHIBIT, LOUISIANA PURCHASE CENTENNIAL EXPOSITION, ST. LOUIS, 1904. A MIDWAY AMUSEMENT THAT DID MORE THAN THE STATE BUILDING TO ADVERTISE NEW MEXICO AT THE FAIR.

yet figure into its promotional plans. In 1909 with the founding of the Museum of New Mexico, a new breed of cultural worker arrived in Santa Fe: a former college president skilled in administration and lobbying for government funding, archaeologists trained to analyze cultural artifacts, artists schooled in the romantic tradition, and a photographer with a passion for Pueblo ruins (chapter 4).[23]

When the Bureau of Immigration was allowed to die through lack of an appropriation following statehood in 1912, the museum staff immediately assumed responsibility for publicizing Santa Fe and New Mexico. As newcomers with little stake in the old dream of progress or the statehood campaign, they were free to embrace the tourist image of Santa Fe and elaborate it as the city's new official image. The museum's efforts to excavate Anasazi ruins and protect contemporary Pueblo villages quickly became interwoven with the promotion of Santa Fe as the staging point for tours of these attractions.

Museum photographer Jesse Nusbaum produced images of Santa Fe, nearby ruins, and pueblos beginning in 1909, which repeated most of the subjects in Brown and Bennett's 1880 stereograph catalogue. Nusbaum had learned the building trade from his father, a contractor and brickyard operator, and took up photography as a high school student in Greeley, Colorado. He graduated from Colorado Teachers College in 1907, with a specialization in manual arts instruction. While Brown and Bennett were struggling businessmen augmenting their portrait business with the sale of stereos, Nusbaum was employed by a fledgling cultural institution because of his combination of formal education and practical skills.[24]

As Nusbaum's photographs began to appear in magazine articles, postcards, world's fair publications, railroad travel brochures, and the museum's own new journal, *El Palacio,* Santa Fe's tourist image became its official image. Nusbaum's photograph of noted San Ildefonso Pueblo artist Julian Martinez descending into a reconstructed kiva, for instance, appeared in both *El Palacio* and a series of postcards he issued (fig. 52). When the museum's assistant director, Kenneth Chapman, sent a packet of Nusbaum photographs to William Simpson at the Santa Fe Railway in 1913, he

51. ELKS' CLUB, LINCOLN AVENUE, RAPP AND RAPP, 1912. (JESSE L. NUSBAUM)

noted that "it seems to be the general opinion among the Chamber of Commerce that we can well dispense with views of ordinary business blocks and residences which might be found anywhere in order to emphasize the quaintness of old doorways, interiors, etc." To which the newly interested Simpson replied, "Like your idea of playing up more strongly the picturesqueness of old Santa Fe. . . . Would like, for example, to have a good photograph of the de Vargas procession." When this new historical pageant was next enacted, Nusbaum was busy as official photographer of the event, and a mutually beneficial partnership between the railway and museum commenced.[25]

The residue of Santa Fe's old split identity lingered in the state's 1916 San Diego exposition booklet, in which photographs of weathered adobes and San Miguel Church mixed with fashionable brick civic buildings. The museum staff was already hard at work, though, giving the newly unified image a more tangible architectural form, through the definition of the Santa Fe style. As new revival style buildings took shape in the teens and early twenties, they displaced earlier public buildings completely from promotional publications. For thirty years following the arrival of the railroad, local ambivalence hindered the development of tourism. Once statehood was achieved and Santa Fe resolved its contending identities, the romantic image of the city became the central vehicle for economic resurgence and the blueprint for its physical transformation.[26]

52. RECONSTRUCTED KIVA IN CEREMONIAL CAVE, FRIJOLES CANYON (NOW BANDELIER NATIONAL MONUMENT), RECONSTRUCTION AND PHOTO BY JESSE NUSBAUM, 1910.

INTERLUDE:
ADOBE CAMOUFLAGE

"The honest use of materials," a central tenet of architectural modernism, holds that materials should be used in a forthright way that reveals their character and structure. As a result of this taboo against disguising materials, modernist architects have always felt uneasy about contemporary Santa Fe, which from this point of view excels at "the dishonest use of materials." Few developments, however, are more revealing about a

53. AMELIA HOLLENBACK HOUSE, JOHN GAW MEEM, 1932. (JACK PARSONS)

helped protect them from wind and rain erosion. Vulnerable points around roof drains, at the bases and tops of walls, and walls facing the prevailing winds were inspected and patched annually, and the whole building replastered every few years. The circular hand strokes of the women plasterers stayed on the surface for a time. Often extra clay was added to the plaster to increase its resilience. Some clay deposits were especially prized for their distinctive hues: not only all manner of browns, but also pinks, yellows, dark purples, and *jaspe,* a clay with flecks of mica that glints in sun light. The Spanish, more than the Pueblos, liked to whitewash inside their homes and under open portales with a form of gypsum known as *tierra blanca.* Perhaps this is why Spanish descendants more quickly adopted white and pastel commercial paints, than did their Pueblo neighbors, who have continued to prefer earth tones.[1]

culture or a period of history than the desire for things to appear differently than they really are.

Before the industrial revolution, folk builders worked with the materials at hand. Out of expediency, these were left close to their natural color and texture. In the arid regions of Asia, Africa, and the New World, this has meant that houses were, and are, built from the earth. In New Mexico, whole Pueblo and Spanish villages took on the color of the local landscape. The hue of the earth and earthen buildings varied not only from place to place but also from moment to moment as the light changed with the weather, the time of the day, and the season.

The smooth layer of earthen plaster typically applied to New Mexican buildings

Some Americans seeing adobe architecture for the first time were unsure if they were looking at unfinished buildings or ruins, or even a part of the landscape. They felt that adobe was untidy, even unclean, so when cement plaster became available in

54. CASA SAN YSIDRO (WARD ALLEN MINGE HOUSE), CORRALES, N.M., RESTORED BEDROOM. (ROBERT RECK)

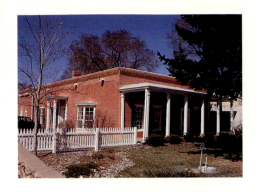

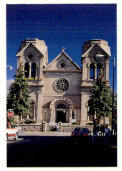

the 1870s, merchants and the wealthy quickly stuccoed their adobe buildings. But rather than leave the plaster in its natural grey color or paint it an adobe color, as people would a generation later, they scored and painted their walls to simulate brick or stone work, a practice known as "tattooing" or "stenciling." The Tully House, built in 1851 of adobe with a protective red brick cornice, for instance, was stuccoed and painted in a brick pattern. After it was decided in 1912 to return Santa Fe to its historic appearance (that is, its pre-1846 appearance), most tattooed buildings were painted an adobe brown. Only in 1974 did the last remnants of 1870s tattooing begin to receive attention, when the Historic Santa Fe Foundation restored the painted brick of the Tully House.

French-born Bishop Jean Baptiste Lamy's desire to modernize Santa Fe matched that of the American officials and businessmen. He recruited Italian stone masons and French architects to build a fitting new cathedral. Begun in 1869, it employed a Byzantine-Romanesque Revival styling reminiscent of the Marseilles cathedral, then fourteen years in construction. The general

mid-nineteenth-century taste for rich effects of ornament, material, and contrasting color (what in the English-speaking world is often termed Victorian) looks garish in times of more restrained taste. Fortunately for Santa Fe's later restorationists, the sandstone available near the city ran into a fairly limited range of browns. The cathedral and other period buildings, such as Loretto Chapel and the old federal building, may conflict stylistically with the later adobe revival image, but they serendipitously adhere to Santa Fe's earth-toned pallet.

Most Santa Fe traditionalists would say that the single most out-of-place building, the one that most violates its spirit, is the bright pink Masonic Scottish Rite Temple. Ironically this building began in 1910 as a first attempt to design something appropriate for Santa Fe (chapter 4). The architects Hunt and Burns, from Los Angeles, specialized in the California Mission style, which usually employed white or buff stucco. To distinguish the temple from their work in California, they incorporated Moorish motifs and stuccoed the building pink. Striking out in a new direction, as the Temple does, is an accomplishment in itself; adjusting

55. Pinckney and Maria Tully House, 1851; stenciled 1870s.
(Author)

56. St. Francis Cathedral, Mouly and Mouly, and Mallet, 1869-1886.
(Author)

nuances comes later. Once the adobe pallet of the Pueblo-Spanish Revival emerged, the Masons could have camouflaged their building with adobe-colored stucco, as other owners of non-Santa Fe style historic buildings have. Instead they have maintained the bright pink, out of their own sense of tradition and distinctiveness.[2]

The ironic change from adobe buildings disguised as stone or brick to stone, brick, and concrete buildings simulating adobe epitomizes the reversal of Santa Fe's identity between 1875 and 1915. The building contractors of Santa Fe had spent the generation after the arrival of the railroad in 1880 learning wood, brick, and stone construction techniques, the nuances of eastern styles, and how to make corners square and

walls plumb. By the time the city's image became more picturesque, in the teens, reinforced concrete had joined the builders' repertory. It would take another generation to replace habits of precision with the ability to simulate undulating adobe buttresses with modern materials. Left to their own devices, builders often employed "an atrocious color; it is very dark and funereal in aspect, caused by putting lamp-black in the stucco." Apparently adobe had become so associated with what was low and unclean that even though the plastering contractors were being asked by the new romantic generation to evoke adobe, their own minds continued to make base associations.[3]

By 1920 an unwritten consensus formed that all new buildings should employ the

57. Scottish Rite Temple, Hunt and Burns, 1911. (Robert Reck)

Pueblo-Spanish style, to which was added the Territorial Revival style in the 1930s. A 1930 competition sought a design to remake the buildings around the plaza in this new, historical spirit. John Gaw Meem, a young local architect, won with a proposal to reinstate portales on three of its sides. Although funds were not forthcoming to execute this proposal, the plaza area was gradually transformed, as new construction adhered to the historic styles, and conspicuous railroad era buildings were stripped of details, stuccoed, and painted an adobe color. Finally in 1966, the plaza portales were rebuilt, based on fresh designs by Kenneth Clark and Meem.

Although the two primarily employed the Pueblo-Spanish style, they chose the classically derived Territorial Revival for the por-

tal fronting the 1891 Catron block, to complement its formal Italianate design. The true character of the building's ornamental window hoods and cornice now lies veiled under adobe camouflage. This profoundly antihistorical desire suppresses the railroad era Americanization of the city in favor of a sanitized, selective version of pre-1860 Santa Fe (chapter 7).

In the Guadalupe-Westside neighborhood, the Spanish-Mexican vernacular has continued to evolve down to the present, quite apart from the Pueblo-Spanish Revival. Builders there continue the tradition of masonry construction and room-by-room accretion. An infusion this century of Anglo-American suburban ideals led Mexican-American builders in Santa Fe and across

58. La Fonda Hotel, John Gaw Meem, design 1927, under construction, 1929. Reinforced concrete structure with hollow clay tile curtain wall and fired brick, undulating buttresses. (T. Harmon Parkhurst)

59. La Fonda Addition, 1995. (author)

60. Catron Block, 1891; portal, John Gaw Meem and Kenneth Clark, 1967. (author)

the Southwest to employ a 10 to 20-foot front yard setback. They continue, nevertheless, to define the sidewalk's edge with low masonry walls or masonry piers linked by picket fences, wrought, chain link, or decorative concrete block. These owner-built enclosures and the houses themselves reveal a taste for vivid colors (turquoise blues and greens, as well as lighter pastels and white) and a taste also for textured stucco, polychromatic brickwork, wrought iron, shrines, and ornamental stone veneers. This vibrant Baroque aesthetic contradicts the muted Arts and Crafts palette of earth tones that predominate on the wealthy Anglo east side.

61. Montoya House, Westside neighborhood, 1950s. (Author)

62. Jose N. Trujillo House, Westside neighborhood, 1947-1992. (Author)

A conscious challenge to the Myth of Santa Fe emerged from the Westside barrio about 1970, in the form of Chicano activism (chapter 5). Chicanos emphasize their dual Indian and Spanish ancestry. Central to their ideology is the legend of Aztlán, the Aztec homeland north of Mexico City, which Chicanos locate in the Southwest. Spanish and Mexican migrations into the Southwest and the contemporary struggle to reclaim alienated lands are both viewed as a return to the mythic Aztlán. Murals across the Southwest proclaimed the Chicano challenge to accepted versions of history. Fifteen or so murals were painted in Santa Fe between 1970 and 1972 by Los Artesanos Guadalupanos de Aztlán, begun under the auspices of a methadone maintenance center as a constructive response to problems of unemployment and drugs in the barrio. Of the two most prominent murals, one faced a four-lane highway built through the barrio in 1967, while the other stands to this day on Canyon Road, in the heart of the fashionable art gallery district. Aztec warriors, symbols, and pyramids combine with armor-clad conquistadors to express a dual Indian-Spanish heritage. The clenched fists and

muscled arms of contemporary Chicanos represent the power of united political struggle. Wrapped around corners and radically foreshortened, these arms, along with the underlying perspective grids, work to obliterate the physical presence of the buildings. Given the importance of adobe-colored buildings for Santa Fe style, many romantic Anglos and members of the Spanish-American elite found both the form and the content of these murals disturbing.[4]

Historical revival architecture remained popular in Santa Fe through the 1950s and 1960s, when modernism reigned throughout much of the world. The Pueblo-Spanish Revival continued to evolve during these years (chapter 8); even adobe colors passed through generations of fashion. In the 1950s, a light egg-shell brown predominated; by the seventies it was superseded by a dark brown, popularized by Antoine Predock's 1969 design for the La Luz condominiums in Albuquerque. A national resurgence of ornament and historical evocation began in the late 1960s, crystallizing by the late 1970s as postmodernism. Working with fewer monetary and craft resources than nineteenth-

103

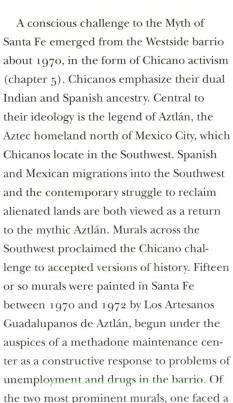

63. Canyon Road Mural, Los Artesanos Guadalupaños, about 1972. (Eva Cockcroft)

64. St. Francis Road Mural, Los Artesanos Guadalupaños de Aztlán (Gilberto Guzman, Geronimo Garduno and Samuel Leyba), 1972. (Eva Cockcroft)

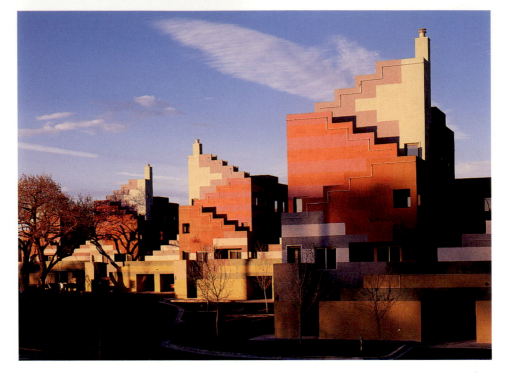

century historicists, postmodernists developed a variety of inexpensive devices to enliven their designs. Abstracted and inflated historical details were rendered with superficial appliques or as cut-out profiles on porches. Finishes became richer, including polychromatic brick, stucco, and tile work, as well as chrome, brass, granite, and marble. This movement infused New Mexican regionalism with a fresh vitality that has brought forth blue- and burgundy-colored standing-seam metal roofs and polychromatic stuccowork. Mainstream Santa Fe style designs regularly use two or three earth tones, while Predock often makes a more daring use of color.

65. TEASTOR-GREY HOUSE, TESUQUE, N.M., ANTOINE PREDOCK, 1984. (AUTHOR)

66. BEACH APARTMENTS, ALBUQUERQUE, ANTOINE PREDOCK, 1984.
(ROBERT RECK)

PART TWO

MODERN SANTA FE

4 ROMANTIC REGIONAL ARCHITECTURE, 1905 TO 1930

Following statehood in 1912, Santa Fe reconciled itself to the role urged on it by eager tourists, and the Museum of New Mexico began vigorously to cultivate its image as a picturesque ancient city. The museum staff adopted organizing principals from the City Beautiful movement, along with the formality but not the overt classicism of Beaux Arts design. At heart, though, museum staff members were disciples of the romantic movement. Widely recognized as an artistic phenomenon, this two-centuries-long tradition has political and economic components as well, which provided the foundation for the museum's cultural crusade. The cultivation of local traditions in opposition to industrial modernization was the romantic thrust most important to Santa Fe.[1]

THE ROMANTIC TRADITION

In the fifteenth century, the rediscovery of classical Rome and Greece and the European discovery of the New World initiated a break from the Middle Ages. Over the next three centuries, the notion that ideal beauty could be derived from classical art and architecture gradually took hold in Europe and was carried to its colonies. Gentlemen of taste derided anything medieval or local in flavor as uncultured, even barbarous.[2]

Beginning in the mid-1700s, however, artists, writers, and architects of what is now know as the romantic movement, men as various as Johann Goethe, Horace Walpole, Sir Walter Scott, and the brothers Grimm, became interested in traditional folklore and vernacular buildings. Rather than rely on classical precedents for the immutable standards of art, the romantics turned to personal experience and found inspiration in nature, exotic lands, and the past—especially the Middle Ages.[3]

The influence of this romantic movement on the visual arts came primarily through the notion of the "picturesque." Indeed late-eighteenth-century British aestheticians frequently used *romantic* and *picturesque* interchangeably, as terms for similar qualities in different arts. The term *picturesque* was first applied to landscape paintings, then to landscape gardens composed to look like those pictures, and finally to architecture set in these landscapes. A building designed to complement a romantic English garden could be picturesque in three major senses: first by its association with a bygone epoch or exotic land; second by its informal floor plan and asymmetrical facade composition; and third by its appropriateness to its setting, whether by its use of local materials or its careful siting on the land.[4]

At first the romantic-picturesque aesthetic often amounted to little more than a taste for the exotic, satisfied by pseudo-Greek ruins, Gothic country houses, and oriental garden pavilions. But by the 1830s, it emerged as a more fully articulated philosophy. During the first decades of the century, architectural theory was revolutionized through detailed studies of historic architecture—studies not only of classical and Renaissance precedents, but also of the Gothic and Egyptian traditions. Writers such as Vaudoyer and Viollet-le-Duc, in France, and Pugin and Ruskin, in England, realized that architecture is shaped by climate, available materials, the state of structural engineering, and the nature of society. Classical architecture no longer stood as the repository of eternal, ideal forms, but instead came to be viewed as one approach to architecture among many, each valid and understandable as the result of its own time and place.[5]

The English romantics, who would most influence American architecture, adopted a moralizing tone when they lashed out at the evils of industrialization. Nowhere was the Industrial Revolution more advanced than in England, and nowhere was its assault on traditional cultures more intense. For English architectural critics such as Augustus Pugin, John Ruskin, and William Morris, industrialization was a logical extension of the rationalizing, standardizing impulses of classicism. Repetitive industrial work, they argued, was destroying the spiritual fulfillment represented by the simple but honest work of the medieval craftsmen. A return to the medieval spirit led, on the one hand, to the emergence of the Gothic Revival as the premiere romantic style, and on the other, to the formation of utopian socialist communities, which promised a spiritual rebirth through handcraftsmanship and the end of capitalist exploitation. The romantic tradition in England after 1860 and in the United States after 1890 is known as the Arts and Crafts movement. While emphasizing handcraftsmanship and the honest use of local, rustic materials, Arts and Crafts adherents also began to look beyond Gothic cathedrals to the simpler vernacular buildings of village and countryside in their search for locally appropriate forms.[6]

Ironically when the romantic attitude was combined with the benefits of industrialism, in particular fast travel and the control of infectious disease, the outcome was tourism. Tourism offered, and still offers, a temporary escape from the drudgery of industrial and bureaucratic work. Tourist attractions mirror romantic interests: unspoiled nature, ancient history, distant lands, and exotic peoples. A boundary drawn around a seemingly pristine fragment of nature yields a national park; those picturesque villages least touched by industrialization become attractive tourist destinations. Emerging in the nineteenth century as an integral component of the industrial world, tourism infused mass culture with the romantic spirit.[7]

At the same time, romantic rhetoric and architecture were appropriated for nationalistic purposes. Augustus Pugin argued, for instance, that the decline of English architecture had been the direct result of the introduction of Renaissance classicism; the revival of English Gothic architecture asserted national identity. Likewise Finnish resistance to Russian domination at the turn of the twentieth century engendered interest in Finnish folklore and a national romantic architectural style.[8]

The romantic-picturesque aesthetic began to take hold in the 1840s in the United States, and by the 1870s American architectural journals began to call for a distinctly American architecture, a desire intensified by the nationalistic rhetoric of the 1876 centennial celebrations. Many architects sought inspiration in the study of New England colonial architecture, both vernacular buildings and Georgian mansions. One led to the open plans and picturesque massing of the Shingle style, the other to the more formal Colonial Revival. Academic architects based in the Northeast also began to employ Mediterranean images for projects in Florida and the Southwest, witness Stanford White's 1887 Ramona Indian School.[9]

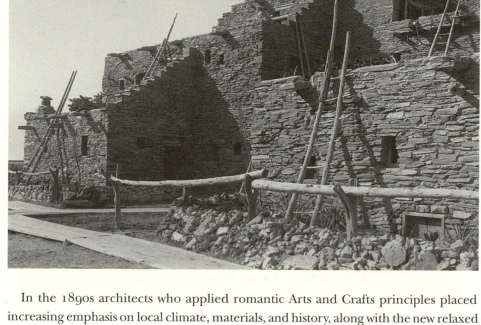

In the 1890s architects who applied romantic Arts and Crafts principles placed increasing emphasis on local climate, materials, and history, along with the new relaxed American life-style. The Mission style of southern California and a revival of mid-Atlantic Colonial forms around Philadelphia emphasized regional history, while Chicago's Prairie style and southern California's wooden craftsmen houses by Green and Green, and their modest bungalow cousins resulted from a more synthetic approach.[10]

PUEBLO-SPANISH STYLE EXPERIMENTATION

For a time in the 1890s and early 1900s, New Mexico belonged in the popular imagination to the larger Hispanic Southwest, then being championed by Charles Lummis from Los Angles and projected architecturally as the Mission style. But gradually a Mission style variant emerged, based on the less formal adobe missions of New Mexico and on Pueblo villages. Pseudopueblos of lath and plaster were popular attractions at the major American world's fairs from 1893 to 1915.[11]

Pseudopueblos also dotted the tourist path through the Southwest, notably at Manitou (Colorado), Albuquerque, and the Grand Canyon. These brought Pueblo Indians to the tourists in the years before the rise of the automobile and good roads. The Santa Fe Railway built the most authentic example—the Hopi House at the Grand Canyon

67. THE HOPI HOUSE, GRAND CANYON, ARIZONA, MARY COLTER, 1905.
ERECTED BY BUILDERS FROM THE HOPI PUEBLOS,
AUTHENTIC IN THE SMALLEST DETAILS. (JESSE L. NUSBAUM)

(fig. 67). Designed in 1904 by Mary Colter and constructed by a crew of Hopis, the building resembled the Hopi village of Old Oraibi and displayed such accurate details as stair-step buttresses, projecting roof beams, stone roof drains, and chimneys made of old pottery. As the railway's interior designer, Colter shaped Harvey House hotel lobbies, lunch rooms, and the occasional building. Her exposure to the Arts and Crafts aesthetic in a San Francisco art school around 1890 is apparent in her emphasis of hand-crafted details and exposed natural materials.[12]

Experimentation with the Pueblo idiom intensified about 1905. Under the direction of University of New Mexico president William Tight, architect E. B. Cristy remodeled the administration building and designed four new structures in the Pueblo style between 1905 and 1909. National magazine articles emphasized the suitability of the Pueblo style to New Mexico's climate and landscape and the "communal life of the University." Curiously no one mentioned the equally important Spanish component of these campus buildings. With Tight's dismissal in 1909, experimentation with the style paused at the university, not to be officially revived until 1927.[13]

Others experimented with the Pueblo image across the Southwest. When Kansas City architect Louis Curtis was asked by the Santa Fe Railway to design El Ortiz Hotel at Lamy, New Mexico, in 1909, for instance, he gave the railroad's trademark Mission style a New Mexican twist (fig. 68). In place of red tile he designed flat roofs and added projecting vigas, exposed adobe on the sides, and hand-carved zapata capitals to provide a more rustic, local feeling. The precisely capped parapets, nevertheless, reveal a debt to the California Mission style.[14]

This early dispersed interest in the Pueblo style was fueled by tourism, institutional and corporate identity, and the romantic inclinations of individuals. It might well have remained a minor strain of Southwestern regionalism such as the Moorish or Mayan Revivals, but at Santa Fe in 1912 the promotion of tourism became linked with the desire for an architectural image to represent the new state of New Mexico. Within a few years a romantically inclined art colony also emerged. This fusion of tourism,

114

68. EL ORTIZ HOTEL, LAMY, NEW MEXICO, LOUIS CURTIS, 1909.
(JESSE L. NUSBAUM)

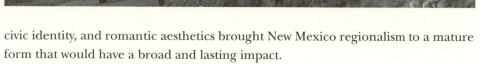

civic identity, and romantic aesthetics brought New Mexico regionalism to a mature form that would have a broad and lasting impact.

Santa Fe's Scottish Rite of Free Masonry lodge initiated the conscious search for an architectural image appropriate for the city. The epitome of the turn-of-the-century fraternity craze, the Scottish Rite practiced the most elaborate mythohistoric rituals, complete with scripted parts, costumes, and stage props (chapter 6). In need of a new building to accommodate their burgeoning New Mexico membership, the Scottish Rite turned first to one of their own, Isaac H. Rapp; however, Rapp's 1909 neoclassical design was rejected as stylistically inappropriate. Another Scottish Rite Mason, museum director Edgar Hewett, next recruited the Los Angeles firm of Hunt and Burns, which had championed the California Mission style since the 1890s.[15]

Hunt and Burns' design for the Santa Fe Scottish Rite Temple (sometimes also called the Cathedral) employs a Moorish variant of the Mission style, with elements adapted from the Alhambra—the Moorish citadel-palace in Granada, Spain (fig. 69). The entrance tower modeled after the Alhambra's Gate of Justice serves as the pivot of Hunt and Burn's picturesque composition, balanced to the left by the auditorium and stage backdrop tower and to the right by a dining hall, which terminates in another hipped-roof pavilion (not visible in fig. 69). Inside, a colonnade drawn from an

69. SCOTTISH RITE MASONIC TEMPLE, HUNT AND BURNS, 1912.
(JESSE L. NUSBAUM)

Alhambra courtyard supports the auditorium balcony. Overhead a vault of painted clouds contains thirty-two star-shaped lights, representing the thirty-two ritual degrees of the Scottish Rite.[16]

The Moorish aura of the design conjured up a Spanish yet non-Californian architectural image for Santa Fe. But even as the Temple was under construction, the staff of the recently formed Museum of New Mexico had begun to define a revival style based directly on local Spanish architecture. The opening of the museum's *New-Old Santa Fe* exhibit, which presented their efforts, was scheduled to coincide with the dedication of the Scottish Rite Temple, on November 17, 1912. (Indeed Sylvanus Morley, who directed the museum exhibit, took a Scottish Rite degree during the dedication celebrations.) The *New Mexican* noted that: "In connection with the question of modeling all buildings in Santa Fe along the line of Mexican and Spanish architecture, several persons have spoken of the new cathedral as being entirely foreign to Santa Fe. But when one thinks of it, this marvelous example of Moorish architecture is really the most fitting type to be erected in Santa Fe, for to a certain extent it is the grand sire of the architecture of New Mexico." In an era when wealthy easterners and their architects tapped into the roots of modern classicism in the Renaissance, it was only logical to follow Santa Fe architecture to its roots in Spain.[17]

The connection of the Alhambra to Santa Fe was made more explicit in 1915, when J. G. Vysekel, a commercial artist for Mandel Brothers of Chicago, was hired to paint a mural above the theater's proscenium arch (fig. 70). The mural depicts Ferdinand and Isabella receiving the keys to the Moorish city of Granada, with the Alhambra on a hill in the background. The scene is reversed in a second mural on the stage curtain, which places the viewer in the Alhambra, looking back across Granada to the siege town established by Ferdinand and Isabella's army—Santa Fe, Spain. New Mexicans of this era would also have been familiar with the local Spanish folk drama "The Christians and the Moors," which kept alive the connection between the Spanish reconquest of the Iberian Peninsula and the conquest of the New World and implicitly equated the

Moors with Native Americans. The Temple's rich multilayered historical allegory trans-ports a person from modern-day Santa Fe to a fantasy courtyard of the Alhambra. Although the Scottish Rite Temple initiated the definition of an architectural style appropriate for Santa Fe, the museum quickly took the city in a dramatically differ-ent direction.[18]

THE MUSEUM OF NEW MEXICO

The catalyst for the development of the Santa Fe style was the joint Museum of New Mexico—School of American Archaeology, founded in 1909, and the catalyst for the museum was Edgar Lee Hewett (figs. 71, 120). Born in 1865 to a prosperous Illinois farm family, Hewett spent the better part of his youth in Chicago. An ambitious young man, he progressed quickly from high school teacher to principal in Missouri and then from superintendent of schools for Florence, Colorado, to director of teacher training at the Normal College in Greeley, Colorado, where he also earned a bache-lor's, then a master's degree. In 1898, at the age of thirty-three, Hewett became the first president of New Mexico Normal College, in Las Vegas. When territorial gover-nor Miguel Otero blocked his contract renewal in 1903, Hewett plunged into archae-ology, an interest cultivated since his arrival in the West. He explored ruins near Santa

70. AUDITORIUM OF SCOTTISH RITE TEMPLE; PROSCENIUM MURAL, "THE SURRENDER OF GRANADA," J.G. VYSEKEL; STAGE SCREEN, VIEW FROM ALHAMBRA TO SANTA FE, SPAIN; 1915. FERDINAND AND ISABELLA RECEIVE KEYS TO THE MOORISH ALHAMBRA IN SANTA FE, SPAIN.

Fe then left to study for a doctorate in archaeology at Geneva, Switzerland. He returned in time to spearhead support for the 1906 Antiquities Act, the first federal preservation legislation.[19]

Like others of the generation following the Civil War, Hewett carried the commercial booster spirit into expanding social realms—first public education, then cultural work. He struggled, on the one hand, against the long-standing prejudice that the only legitimate field for archaeology was the classical Mediterranean world and, on the other hand, against the suspicions of such academic anthropologists as Franz Boas, of Columbia University, that Hewett was more interested in cultivating the popular fascination with the Southwest than in scientific scholarship. Indeed Hewett's strengths were the popular presentation of archaeology and anthropology, fund-raising, self-promotion, and behind-the-scenes political maneuvering. His autocratic management style alienated subordinates, while a contentious streak led him in time to quarrel with nearly all of his allies.[20]

The one man Hewett deferred to was his patron, Frank Springer (fig. 72). Seventeen years older than Hewett, Springer was born to an Iowa pioneer family in 1848. Paleontology captured his imagination at the University of Iowa, but he entered the law. Springer followed the Santa Fe Trail to New Mexico in 1873, where he amassed

71. RITO DE LOS FRIJOLES SUMMER ARCHAEOLOGICAL SCHOOL, 1910. STANDING, L. TO R.: W.W. ROBBINS, ARTIST DONALD BEAUREGARD, ANTHROPOLOGIST JOHN P. HARRINGTON, ARCHAEOLOGIST F.W. HODGE, MUSEUM DIRECTOR EDGAR L. HEWETT, ARCHAEOLOGIST NEIL JUDD, MAUDE WOY, ANTHROPOLOGIST BARBARA FREIRE-MARRECCO. SEATED: ARCHAEOLOGIST SYLVANNUS MORLEY, PUEBLO ARTS EXPERT KENNETH CHAPMAN, CARPENTER PERCY ADAMS, PHOTOGRAPHER-ARCHAEOLOGIST JESSE NUSBAUM, GOLD, JULIUS HENDERSON.

a fortune in the adjudication of land grants (which kindled an interest in local history) and mine and railroad development. In his spare time, Springer produced a steady stream of scientific publications, which distinguished him as the leading American authority on fossils of the marine animals known as crinoids. As the president of the first board of regents of the Normal School, he recognized a kindred spirit in Hewett, through whom he could pursue his historical interest. Until his death in 1927, Springer remained Hewett's most powerful political ally and an indispensable patron for Hewett, Hewett's disciples, and the museum.[21]

Hewett also cultivated institutional backing from the Archaeology Institute of America, headquartered in New York. At the end of the nineteenth century, the so-called robber barons who had become immensely wealthy in commerce and industry (the Whitneys, Rockefellers, Vanderbilts, Pulitzers, and others) adopted the role of aristocratic patrons of the arts to legitimize their new social standing. Concentrated in the Northeast, these urban elite patrons shared a passion for the European Classical tradition with a generation of scholars and artists who sought to create a new American Renaissance. Organizations such as the Society of Beaux Arts Architects, the American Fine Arts Society, the American Academy in Rome, and the Municipal Arts Society of New York proliferated. Founded in 1879, the Archaeology Institute of America flourished through its field schools in Rome, Athens, and Jerusalem. The institute supported Hewett's New Mexico fieldwork in 1904 and 1905 and on his return from Europe, appointed him director of their School of American Archaeology. When they began looking for a suitable home for this field school, Hewett lobbied for Santa Fe over the other aspirants: Colorado Springs, Denver, and Los Angeles. The matter was settled in 1909, when the New Mexico legislature offered the Palace of the Governors as a headquarters building, along with a yearly appropriation of $5,000.[22]

One year earlier, Hewett conducted his first summer school excavations at Frijoles Canyon, northwest of Santa Fe. His campfire chats inspired the twenty young archaeologists drawn from eastern universities and the Normal College with a passion to

72. Rito de los Frijoles, lawyer-entrepreneur-patron Frank Springer,
Santa Clara Pueblo governor Santiago Naranjo,
illustrator Kenneth Chapman, artist Carlos Vierra, 1915.

unearth the secrets of ancient America and bring them to life for the public. The following June, Hewett selected three of these students to be his first professional staff at the museum.

Twenty-one-year-old Jesse Nusbaum (fig. 71) already had two years experience documenting archaeological digs with his camera, while his skills as a builder would be invaluable in the renovation of the dilapidated Governors' Palace and the reconstruction of archaeological sites. Nusbaum would leave to become the first director of the Mesa Verde National Monument in 1920; he returned to Santa Fe in 1929 to head a new rival of the museum—the Laboratory of Anthropology.[23]

Thirty-three-year-old Kenneth Chapman (figs. 71, 72) had known Hewett since he arrived in Las Vegas to convalesce from tuberculosis in 1899. His five years of experience as a commercial artist and engraver in the Midwest landed him a job teaching art at the Normal College. A quiet gentle man, Chapman developed during his years at the museum into an accomplished illustrator of scholarly works on paleontology and archaeology and a leading expert on Indian arts.[24]

The final staff member, Sylvanus Morley (fig. 71), was the son of a mathematics professor at a small Pennsylvania College. He specialized in New World archaeology at Harvard, graduating in 1907. That summer his perseverance and meticulous note taking on an archaeological reconnaissance of the Four Corners region attracted Hewett's attention. Morley's slight build, nearsightedness, and kinetic energy led the Tewa workers at Frijoles in 1908 (among them Julian Martinez of San Ildefonso Pueblo and Santiago Naranjo of Santa Clara Pueblo) to nickname him "hummingbird." Morley left the museum in 1915 to oversee the Mayan excavations of the Carnegie Institute of Washington, D.C. He blossomed as a raconteur, public speaker, and leading authority on Mayan civilization.[25]

Hewett attracted others to the museum's crusade of cultural revival and preservation. Architect Isaac Rapp, who designed the Normal School's main building, Springer Hall, when Hewett was president there, moved to Santa Fe the year the museum opened.

And the last director of the Bureau of Immigration, also editor of the *New Mexican*, Paul A. F. Walter, became the founding editor of the museum's journal, *El Palacio*, in 1913.

Finally there was the painter Carlos Vierra (fig. 72), son of a Portuguese-American family from near Monterey, California. Vierra studied art in San Francisco and worked for two years as a cartoonist and marine illustrator in New York, before coming to Santa Fe for his health in 1904. He became known first as the top marksman in the local National Guard unit, but he also operated a photographic shop on the plaza before formally joining the museum staff in 1912.[26]

THE PLAN OF 1912

As the School of American Archaeology, Hewett and his protégés excavated Anasazi ruins during the summer and Mayan temple cities in the Yucatan during the winter. As the Museum of New Mexico, they began renovating the Palace of the Governors and soon immersed themselves in local concerns. In the spring of 1912, Mayor Arthur Seligman appointed Hewett and Morley to the newly formed Santa Fe City Planning Board and charged them with finding a way to stem the city's thirty-year economic decline. Chair of the planning board was forty-year-old Harry H. Dorman, the son of a New York textile manufacturer who had come to Santa Fe in 1901 for his health. A founding member of the Progressive Republican party and close ally of Senator Bronson Cutting, Dorman served as secretary-treasurer of the *New Mexican* newspaper and operated a successful real estate and insurance business. Dorman sent out dozens of letters requesting advice from large cities and nationally renowned experts, such as pioneer city planner John Nolen and landscape architect Frederick Law Olmsted, Jr. (son of Central Park's designer). Although the board could not afford to hire a professional planner, they received encouragement, planning treatises, and city plans from across the country, all steeped in City Beautiful rhetoric.[27]

Then at its height, the City Beautiful movement was the planning and civic improvement arm of the American Renaissance. Inspired by the example of the 1893 Chicago exposition (fig. 2), City Beautiful proponents sought to reestablish a sense of order and refinement out of the commercial and industrial jumble of rapidly growing cities. Their aesthetic campaign emphasized the construction of parks, boulevards, and grand civic plazas ringed by white marble city halls, libraries, museums, and opera houses. Their preferred style was Beaux Arts classicism, so named because it emanated from Paris's *École des Beaux Arts*. The City Beautiful-Beaux Arts approach imparted a formal dignity to individual buildings and visual unity to civic ensembles. Wealthy patrons commissioned allegorical murals and monumental statues to ennoble public buildings and squares, and to enshrine their version of local history and civic virtue.[28]

Under this influence, the board produced a comprehensive city plan in the fall of 1912 (fig. 147). "The City of Santa Fe is planning extensive improvements," wrote Dorman in true City Beautiful spirit, "that include the laying out of parks and boulevards, the extension of streets, the restriction of manufacturing plants to a suitable district, the elimination of bill-boards and the bringing about of some sort of architectural homogeneity." But while other cities employed Beaux Arts classicism to achieve homogeneity, this style would be too costly for Santa Fe, according to board member Sylvanus Morley, and would destroy "our most priceless possession, an individuality, which raises us above hundreds of other American Cities. . . ." Remarkably Santa Fe was not only the smallest community with a City Beautiful plan, but its Plan of 1912 broke significant new ground by combining the standard emphasis on architectural homogeneity with a local revival style based on a study of the city's old architecture. The board proposed to accomplish this transformation through the encouragement of tax credits and by requiring the local style on specified "ancient streets." Architectural image became central to stimulating tourism and reversing economic decline. Soon the chamber of commerce was promoting Santa Fe not as another "City Beautiful," but as the "City Different."[29]

If nineteenth-century Anglo-Americans had judged Santa Fe's people and architecture to be uncivilized, this generation of newcomers found them picturesque, even

noble. Winding lanes, which the leading citizens would once have widened and straightened if only they could, became quaint, even essential to the city's progress as a tourist center. The *New Mexican,* which insisted in the 1880s and 1890s that the portales be demolished because they made the streets look narrow and unbusinesslike, now called for their return precisely because they made the streets look narrow and unlike other American cities. Two generations of street names also reveal this shift in attitude. In 1881 a committee of boosters had proposed street names heavy on presidents, progressive spirit, and local merchants: Grant and Garfield, Manhattan, Metropolitan and Railroad, Spiegelberg and Johnson Avenues. By comparison Edgar Hewett now culled new street names from the annals of local history for the 1912 plan: Paseo Coronado, Paseo Casteñada, Camino De Vargas, Calle Escalante, and Calle Analco, as well as Calle Azteca and Santa Fe Trail.[30]

123

The task of preparing a supplement to the 1912 plan describing the Santa Fe style fell to the meticulous Sylvanus Morley, then twenty-nine. This was the first systematic attempt to define a local style distinct from the California Mission style. People had not previously studied local vernacular architecture, and when Morley began, all he could see, in his words, were "the hundred variations of the Santa Fe style." Museum photographer Jesse Nusbaum conducted an extensive photographic survey of Santa Fe, concentrating on the unimproved Spanish sections of town (figs. 9, 15, 19, 73, 155, 157). Museums had specialized since the nineteenth century in the sorting and categorization of their holdings, be they butterflies or pot shards. It is easy to imagine Morley and Nusbaum sorting these photographs into piles on a big table, looking for recurrent patterns—for a formal typology. In such a process, idiosyncrasies that do not easily fit (most of the "hundred styles") get pushed to the side and ignored. The forms and patterns that surfaced, were described, and named would shape perceptions for years to come.[31]

Morley and Nusbaum's research provided the basis for the *New-Old Santa Fe* exhibit, which promoted the planning board's proposals. Sponsored by the city, the chamber

73. ROQUE LOBATO HOUSE, BUILT ABOUT 1800, PHOTO, 1912.
(JESSE L. NUSBAUM)

74. LOBATO HOUSE, REMODELED BY SYLVANUS MORLEY, 1912.
(JESSE L. NUSBAUM) THICKENED PARAPET WALL AND STUCCO BETWEEN VIGAS HELP
EMPHASIZE BUILDING'S MASSIVENESS.

of commerce, and the School of American Archaeology, the exhibit opened in the Palace of the Governors in November of 1912 (fig. 76). Morley borrowed photographs and drawings of some of the Pueblo style buildings scattered across the Southwest. Enlargements of Nusbaum's photographs, a map of the proposed streets, drawings of proposed parks by the artist Carlos Vierra, and restoration models of the Palace of the Governors, La Garita (a small fort at the outskirts of town), and the four historic churches helped make the board's vision tangible.[32]

124

Although no copy of Morley's 1912 architectural study has been located, its essence appears in the instructions for a competition to design a "New-Old Santa Fe" style house issued the following July by the Santa Fe Chamber of Commerce. The style requires a "low and long rather than high and narrow" effect and more specifically, flat roofs, natural-colored adobe walls and buttresses, recessed portals, casement windows, projecting vigas, and *canales* (roof drains). "The California Mission style is not regarded for the purposes of this competition as being the same as the New-Old Santa Fe Style," cautioned Morley. "Contestants are warned to keep away from this style, which has been appropriated by Southern California. Nothing can retard the development of Santa Fe style more than to confuse it with the California Mission Style."[33]

As the chief spokesmen for the planning board, Morley took the initiative even before the exhibition opened, when he rehabilitated the old Roque Lobato house as his residence (fig. 73). Rather than modernize the building with a pitched metal roof and milled woodwork, the common practice since the arrival of the railroad, he preserved the building's low, flat-roofed profile (fig. 74). Morley replaced railroad-era sash windows with casements to emphasize the building's horizontality, and he thickened the parapet wall over the portal to give the building a more massive appearance. When Nusbaum rephotographed it after the restoration, he caught the porch in full shadow to emphasize its sculptural massiveness.

Although the photographic survey of Spanish-Mexican architecture had recorded informal designs such as the cluster of houses on Montoya Hill (fig. 19), it was the

75. U.S. FORESTRY SERVICE BUILDING, JESSE NUSBAUM, ABOUT 1912.
(JESSE L. NUSBAUM)

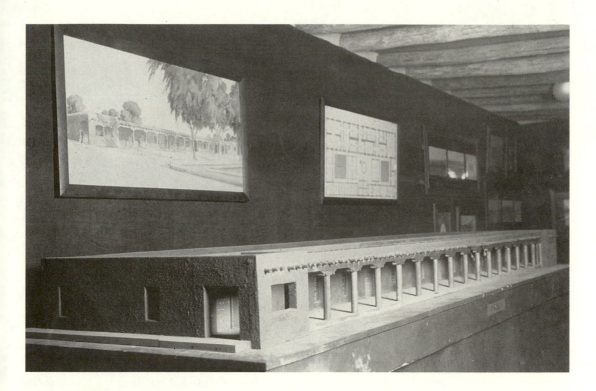

symmetrical, U-shaped type of the Lobato-Morley House that first gained popularity. Morley detected a classical formality in this type, describing it as "the portal or front piazza, flanked at each end by the house." The form soon appeared in new residences and Jesse Nusbaum's design for the local U.S. Forestry Service building. Its most conspicuous expression, however, would be the 1913 portal of the Palace of the Governors.[34]

RESTORING THE PALACE OF THE GOVERNORS

Between 1909 and 1912, Nusbaum oversaw a general rehabilitation of the Palace, and by the fall of 1912 he turned his attention to the plaza facade. No sketches or photographs exist of the eighteenth-century Spanish portal, which had been replaced in the 1850s with a modest Greek Revival style porch (fig. 30) and in 1877 and 1878 with heavier columns and a classical balustrade (fig. 31). The museum's staff and regents agreed that something more appropriate to the building's Spanish history was in order. Nusbaum appears to have taken the lead in formulating the design, with Morley and museum illustrator Kenneth Chapman offering advice. Hewett, who held final authority but was away from Santa Fe at the pivotal time, endorsed their plans. If their renovation had been carried out ten or even five years earlier, the building might well

76. SPECULATIVE RESTORATION MODEL OF PALACE OF THE GOVERNORS MADE BY JESSE NUSBAUM AND PERCY ADAMS FOR THE NEW-OLD SANTA FE EXHIBIT, 1912. PALACE RESTORATION AND EXHIBIT INITIATED THE HISTORICAL RECONSTRUCTION OF SANTA FE.

have received a California Mission style arcade. Instead a portal in the new Santa Fe style was erected (fig. 77).

Although the museum staff had two pieces of evidence on which to base their restoration—the 1766 Urrutia map of Santa Fe (fig. 10) and a wooden corbel found embedded in an internal wall during the renovation—the 1913 portal is best understood as a speculative or interpretive recreation. While rooms project at either end of the building on the Urrutia map, it does not record a portal, so its restoration based on this source alone was conjectural. Jesse Nusbaum had recently completed the photographic survey of Santa Fe and had the example of Morley's house fresh in his mind when he prepared a restoration model of the Palace for the *New-Old Santa Fe* exhibit in November of 1912. "In smaller buildings," he would later write, "residences and the like, such projections of the house enclosing the ends are frequently present. . . . The discovery of the Urrutia map . . . indicated that the Palace was no exception." Nusbaum thereby assumed that the Palace was an oversized version of the U-shaped domestic type.[35]

Two plans that have subsequently reappeared (a 1791 plan of the Santa Fe presidio and the 1846 Gilmer map of the city) shed further light on the building's history (fig. 18). While both record a portal, in neither does it extend the full length of the Palace. In addition both plans show only one projecting room: first on the southeast corner, then on the southwest. This suggests that the vernacular tradition of piecemeal accretions and repairs often left the Palace's facade unbalanced. The museum staff may not have known this, but they certainly knew that in the domestic tradition and in the original Palace, the projections would have been rooms, not open porches. In the 1913 remodeling, however, they opened up these end rooms to accommodate the flow of pedestrians. A long colonnade flanked by open pavilions was a common Beaux Arts facade treatment for museums, theaters, and train stations. The formality of the Palace, therefore, echoes the City Beautiful approach embraced in the city plan of the previous year.[36]

77. PALACE OF THE GOVERNORS, BUILT 1610S, REBUILT 1690S, PORTAL 1913, PHOTO ABOUT 1935. (T. HARMON PARKHURST)

The proportions and details of the new portal were also adjusted to suit Nusbaum, Chapman, and Hewett's desire for a massive appearance. How much room was open for interpretation is apparent in the four images the museum produced of the building: a restoration drawing (which inserts a column and brackets in the openings of the end pavilions) and the restoration model, both shown in the photograph of the 1912 exhibit (fig. 76), along with a mural showing the Palace in 1692 without a high parapet (fig. 78) and the actual building restoration, both done in 1913 (fig. 77). Nusbaum installed tree-trunk posts, far thicker than typical Spanish-era columns, thereby necessitating huge zapata capitals, roughly twice the size of the model corbel bracket found inside the Palace. The high parapet wall atop the portal (the treatment popularized by the Morley House) further heightened the massive appearance. When the Palace was completed, a museum report approvingly quoted a visitor as comparing it to a "Cyclopean monolith."[37]

The facade of the Palace of the Governors stands not as an example of Spanish architecture, but as a key monument in the development and popularization of a regional revival. The Palace, along with the Morley House and the Forest Service Building, represents the new local initiative and City Beautiful formality that shaped the Santa Fe style between 1912 and 1915.

78. ENTRANCE HALLWAY, PALACE OF THE GOVERNORS, ABOUT 1925. MURALS OF VARGAS OCCUPYING THE CITY (LEFT) AND ABORIGINAL SANTA FE (RIGHT) BY CARL LOTAVE, 1913. A THIRD MURAL (NOT SHOWN) OF SANTA FE TRAIL WAGON TRAIN COMPLETED THIS PUBLIC AFFIRMATION OF THE CITY'S TRI-CULTURAL HISTORY.

In true Beaux Arts style, Hewett and his patron Frank Springer commissioned murals to elaborate the historical lessons of the building. The Santa Fe art colony was five years in the future, so Hewett recruited Swedish-born and Paris-trained Carl Lotave, then based in Denver. In recessed panels created by Nusbaum in the Palace, Lotave depicted prehistoric Frijoles Canyon and Puye, thereby connecting the Palace with the School of American Archaeology's field excavations (fig. 146). But rather than recreate these Anasazi villages at their peak, Lotave portrays them abandoned, with only an occasional person gazing forlornly across a twilight landscape. Lotave's panels, like Louis Curtis's well-known photograph, *The Vanishing Race,* which captures a line of horsemen riding toward a forbidding sky, comforted the children of Manifest Destiny with the fiction that the Indians were passing quietly from the scene.[38]

A second set of murals of "the three epochs which this ancient building has seen" adopted the most popular theme for city hall and state capital murals—the progress of civilization (fig. 78). In the first epoch, Lotave again portrayed a solitary Indian, this time crouching by the Santa Fe River, with the sunset red Sangre de Cristo Mountains in the background. The second recreates the "peaceful" reconquest of 1692. And finally Lotave painted a wagon train rolling west over the Santa Fe Trail "that typifies the dawn of the present era, that has brought the rush, the impatience, the progress which have once more revolutionized this mystic land . . ." By wedding the emerging ideology of New Mexican triculturalism with the evolutionary logic of the progress-of-civilization genre, Lotave placed Anglo-Americans at the pinnacle of local history.[39]

SAN DIEGO AND A FINE ARTS MUSEUM

Developments slowed in Santa Fe, as the museum staff turned their energies to San Diego's Panama-California Exposition commemorating the completion of the Panama Canal and celebrating pan-American culture. Between 1911, when Edgar Hewett was named director of exhibits, and January 1, 1915, when the exposition opened, the museum staff created major exhibits for the California, Indian Arts, and Southwest

79. CONSTRUCTION OF INDIAN VILLAGE, PAINTED DESERT EXHIBIT, PANAMA-CALIFORNIA EXPOSITION, SAN DIEGO, DESIGNED BY KENNETH CHAPMAN, 1914. (JESSE L. NUSBAUM) STUCCO OVER WOOD, LATHE AND PLASTER BUILT BY SAN DIEGO CARPENTERS, LOW ADOBE AND OVENS ADDED BY SAN ILDEFANSO PUEBLO BUILDERS.

80. NEW MEXICO BUILDING, PANAMA-CALIFORNIA EXPOSITION, SAN DIEGO, RAPP AND RAPP, 1915. (JESSE L. NUSBAUM) THE FORM OF ACOMA MISSION COMBINED WITH THE TOWERS FROM SAN FELIPE MISSION.

Ethnography Buildings. Portions of the *New-Old Santa Fe* exhibit were redeployed in the New Mexico Building. Carlos Vierra was also commissioned to paint six 4-by-12-foot murals depicting the Mayan temple cities studied by the museum-school.[40]

The museum also designed and supervised the construction of the exposition's leading commercial attraction, the Santa Fe Railway's *Painted Desert* exhibit (fig. 79, pp. 18–19). In its 5-acre compound, the *Painted Desert* featured Navajo hogans, cliff ruins, kivas, and two pseudopueblos. Illustrator Kenneth Chapman designed a scale model of the exhibit, which Jesse Nusbaum elaborated in construction. The railroad freighted in building materials and plants from across the Southwest to add authenticity and issued travel passes to twenty-eight San Ildefonso Pueblo families, including the potters Maria and Julian Martinez. San Diego carpenters erected the wood-and-plaster superstructure, while the San Ildefonsos constructed low adobe walls and beehive ovens. The *Painted Desert* reminded the museum of the roots of the Pueblo-Spanish Revival in pseudopueblos. Moreover as a result of its popularity, the museum staff realized that the tourists they hoped to attract to Santa Fe yearned more for contact with Pueblo Indians than with Hispanos.[41]

The New Mexico Building at San Diego (fig. 80) marked a passage in the development of the Pueblo-Spanish Revival from pseudopueblos and the quasi-archaeological reconstruction of the Palace portal to an eclectic synthesis of elements drawn from various New Mexican prototypes. Rapp, Rapp and Hendrickson (A. C. Hendrickson had become a partner of the firm in 1909) patterned the plan after the Acoma mission (fig. 148), with the church form on the left, a one-story cloister with recessed entryway in the middle, and a two-story open gallery to the right. Onto this they grafted a facade balcony and towers with tiny horns, from the San Felipe Pueblo mission.

Even before the completion of the New Mexico Building, Frank Springer pledged funds to duplicate it in more permanent materials back in Santa Fe. This allowed Rapp, Rapp and Hendrickson to elaborate their San Diego design into a classic demonstration

129

of picturesque eclecticism (fig. 81). The philosophy of eclecticism, defined in 1830s France, recognizes that modern archaeology, scholarship, travel, and communication have made all of history and the world's cultures available to artists and philosophers. It holds that we should select elements (be they ideas or architectural forms) from this storehouse of knowledge according to contemporary needs and taste and synthesize them into a modern philosophy or building design.[42]

As Sylvanus Morley explained in the true eclectic spirit (he was speaking of the New Mexico Building, but his comment applies equally to the museum): "the introduction of the second story balcony between the two towers of the church considerably relieves the monotony of the facade and lightens an otherwise too massive effect [of the Acoma mission]." Rapp, Rapp and Hendrickson further elaborated the museum design with a side entrance patterned on the Laguna mission and terraced forms based on Pueblo villages along two sides. "Six of the ancient Franciscan mission churches, three hundred years old, are reproduced in its facades, without destroying the unity of its appearance;" wrote Santa Fe lawyer and historian Ralph Emerson Twitchell; "they are Acoma, San Felipe, Cochiti, Laguna, Santa Ana and Pecos." Inside, the Saint Francis auditorium recreated a Franciscan mission, complete with elaborate ornamental gouge work, a herringbone ceiling, and a clerestory lighting scheme (fig. 83).[43]

81. FINE ARTS MUSEUM (SOUTHEAST CORNER), RAPP, RAPP AND HENDRICKSON, 1916. THE SAN DIEGO DESIGN FURTHER ENLIVENED WITH PUEBLO TERRACING AND THE LAGUNA MISSION FACADE TO THE RIGHT.

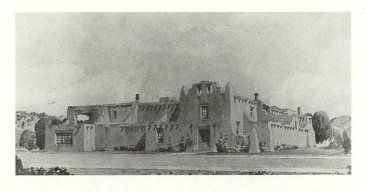

Seen from the plaza, the open loggia at the corner forms the pivot of Rapp's picturesque composition, balanced to either side by church facades. From Lincoln Street (fig. 82), the Laguna mission facade forms the corner pivot, flanked by Pueblo forms, which step out slightly at the distant corners of the building. Vigas, canales, chimneys, windows, and secondary masses further enliven the asymmetrical yet subtly balanced compositions. "The symmetry is that of mass, not exact form," wrote Twitchell soon after the museum's completion. "No matter which way one looks, or from what vantage point, there is a different architectural composition, a new charm, a different pattern and design, in which sunlight and ever-moving shadows have a determining part."[44]

Rapp, Rapp and Hendrickson rose to a new level of creativity, thanks to their interaction with the museum staff. Other than their stiff reworking of the Acoma Mission for a Colorado warehouse in 1908, they had previously contented themselves with Beaux Arts classicism and an occasional Mission style design. Their inexperience with local revival movements led to the embarrassing rejection of their 1910 neoclassical Scottish Rite design. But given this chance to collaborate with the museum, a new spirit entered their work. The picturesque composition and undulating forms of the Fine Arts Museum, its hand-crafted historically accurate details, and the New Mexico Mission style furniture inside betray the strong Arts and Crafts aesthetic favored by Hewett, Morley, Chapman, Vierra, and in particular, Jesse Nusbaum, who designed the furniture and was construction superintendent for the building. Indeed Charles Lummis wrote from Los Angles to congratulate Hewett on the building's dedication: "I had no small fear if with Jess as architect and you as Muddler-in-Chief, the thing would ever be done."[45]

Hewett and Springer decided by the fall of 1912 to commission murals for display in the New Mexico Building and later installation in the Fine Arts Museum. They sought a more ambitious, integrated program than Lotave had just produced for the Palace, so they resolved to cultivate a young artist for the work. Their choice, a twenty-eight-year-old Mormon from Utah named Donald Beauregard (fig. 72), explained that he

82. FINE ARTS MUSEUM (NORTHEAST CORNER), RAPP, RAPP AND HENDRICKSON, 1915. AN ASYMMETRIC, YET BALANCED COMPOSITION FROM ANY VANTAGE POINT. (WATERCOLOR: KENNETH CHAPMAN)

came from "a desert town in the southern part of the state; lived on a ranch and in the saddle until 16—having never seen a railroad until then." He left home to tramp through the mining camps for a year, was recognized as a gifted student at the University of Utah, studied academic painting in Paris from 1906 to 1908, and then served as an artist on Hewett's 1909 and 1910 summer excavations. He returned to Spain and then Paris in 1911 to continue his studies, although he always had "the bread question staring me in the face." So when Hewett arranged for Springer to provide an allowance while Beauregard finished his studies and began work on the murals, he was overjoyed. But within two months, "feeling rather washed out," he consulted the best American doctor in Paris, who prescribed several months in "a higher and sunnier climate in order to prevent any chance of tuberculosis." (The specter of TB cast its dark shadow over the consciousness of that era as AIDS does over ours.)[46]

Although a few months in the Swiss Alps put Beauregard in shape and he returned to his studies in Paris, then Munich, he was dissatisfied with his first sketches for the murals. He began to suffer again, this time with digestive problems, and in September 1913 decided, "to go directly to my old home where of course I can live for practically nothing and get the care only a mother can give." But once in the states, he headed instead to Santa Fe, set up a studio in the Palace of the Governors, and prepared his

83. INTERIOR ST. FRANCIS AUDITORIUM, FINE ARTS MUSEUM, 1918. (WESLEY BRADFIELD) CARVED CORBELS, HERRING-BONE CEILINGS AND AN ELABORATE PROGRAM OF MURALS.

canvases. In a heroic struggle to repay Springer's confidence, to advance "the work in the southwest," and to leave behind some premature fruit of his talent, Beauregard began the murals. From early December until February, unable to eat normal food, sleeping little, and tiring easily, he composed color sketches for all six panels, then chose to begin in oils on the third in the series, a triptych.[47]

The tone of the "Renunciation of Santa Clara" is dreamlike, the setting pastoral (fig. 84). A tableau of figures stand in a field of spring flowers, the leafless branches of poplars silhouetted against a twilight sky. In the left panel, comfortably dressed women and children, a merchant, soldier, and horsemen crowd together. On the right, a middle-aged Saint Francis kneels to tend the bloody hand of a fallen, half-clothed man— a beggar, Christ, all who are sick and suffer. In the center panel, Saint Clair turns away from her mother, who holds a hand up to her temple as she stares down in grief at the sumptuous cloak Clair has just cast off. Clair moves trancelike to accept a white rose from two young women who float gracefully off the ground. As she turns from the crowd on the left toward Francis on the right, Santa Clara renounces the material comforts of her youth for the transcendent life of the spirit.

Beauregard completed the center panel before his fading strength and a fast-growing lump on his neck forced him again to the doctors. Springer, who never hesitated in his support, paid for exploratory surgery in Denver, which revealed stomach cancer. The two-and-a-half-day train and stagecoach journey home to Utah left Beauregard drained but hopeful. His mother wrote Springer in early May: "Your kind letter he opened and read and strong, calm man that he was sobs shook his body and we left him alone for a few minutes since we knew he did not like to have one see the emotion he could not conceal . . . We had him home just two weeks and a day."[48]

Back in Beauregard's Palace studio after word of his death arrived, Hewett arranged the mural series so that it could be seen at a glance. "When one studies the work that he had underway," he confided to Springer, "it is clear that none of us have over

133

ROMANTIC REGIONALISM

estimated it. The subject looms deeper the more one thinks of it, and Beauregard was rising to it with great power." Rather than hurry the murals to completion for San Diego, they suspended work so that Carlos Vierra and Kenneth Chapman could finish them properly, once their own exposition projects were completed.[49]

Beauregard and Hewett had devised an elaborate allegory linking local history, the activities of the museum, and the building itself directly to the city's patron saint, Saint Francis, and to the great tradition of European civilization. Like the lithographic stations of the cross that graced so many New Mexican churches, these panels progress chronologically down the gospel (left) side and back of the epistle side of the (church) auditorium (fig. 83). The "Conversion of Saint Francis" and the "Renunciation of Santa Clara" lead to the "Apotheosis of Saint Francis," above the stage (fig. 128). The figures surrounding Francis personify art, theology, religion, literature, philosophy, and society. Next on the right (but not yet visible in the 1918 photograph), a panel depicts Columbus entrusting his son Diego to a Franciscan monastery, as his vision of Spanish galleons sways in the clouds. On the right wall, the painting of Franciscans "Preaching to the Mayas and the Aztecs" incorporates the temple at Chichén Itzá, which the School of American Archaeology had studied and which Vierra, who completed this panel, had visited in preparation for his San Diego murals (fig.

85. "Preaching to the Mayas and Aztecs," St. Francis Auditorium, Carlos Vierra, 1916-17. Inclusion of Mayan temples studied by museum linking the institution to earlier Franciscan missionaries. (Wesley Bradfield)

85). Three Franciscans study a set of plans in the culminating panel, the "Building of the Missions of New Mexico," the very missions on which the Fine Arts Museum was patterned. This exercise in historical pedigree wrapped the Fine Arts Museum in an aura of religion and European culture and conferred moral and intellectual authority on the institution, including Hewett and Springer.

FORMALIZING THE REVIVAL

If the Fine Arts Museum was one tangible result of the San Diego Exposition, the museum staff and their associates also returned with valuable experience in tourism promotion and a unified sense of purpose. Back in Santa Fe in 1915 they formed an enthusiastic team of artists, designers, architects, builders, and publicists, ready to remake the city and promote the state through a new architectural style. They funneled Nusbaum's photographs to national publications and the Santa Fe Railway publicity department. Their schemes appeared as architectural sketches in their new magazine, *El Palacio*. Kenneth Chapman, for instance, proposed wrapping the Palace portal around the east end of the building to reach a remodeled National Guard armory (fig. 86). At the corner he positioned a tower reminiscent of the Scottish Rite Temple but with a more rounded, North African, adobe feel.[50]

In a series of articles published between 1915 and 1918, they detailed their plans for Santa Fe. A trio of articles by museum director Hewett, painter Carlos Vierra, and San Diego architect William Templeton Johnson analyzed Santa Fe's future. Each summarized the 1912 plan's argument that Santa Fe had once been a tourist attraction in its own right, but an ill-conceived modernization had left it looking like any other American town. Tourists could be attracted again and in greater numbers, they asserted, if the city's Spanish Colonial appearance was restored. They urged the reestablishment of the city's original rectangular plaza and the return of its surrounding portales. All three stressed that new buildings must employ the local style, which they variously termed the New Mexico Mission style, the Santa Fe style, and the Pueblo style.[51]

86. PROPOSAL FOR WAR MEMORIAL HALL, RIGHT, CONNECTED TO END OF PALACE OF THE GOVERNORS, LEFT, KENNETH CHAPMAN, 1919.

A second pair of articles defined the new style in greater detail: one by Mayanist Sylvanus Morley was published in 1915, the other by painter Carlos Vierra appeared in 1918. Morley's article refined his 1912 planning board report, while Vierra's article emphasized developments since the San Diego Exposition of 1915. The 1913 Palace of the Governors remodeling (fig. 77) epitomizes Morley's views, while the 1917 Santa Fe School for Deaf Mutes, by Rapp, Rapp and Hendrickson (fig. 87) represents Vierra's divergent formulation of the style.[52]

"The general effect is low and long," began Morley, "one story is the rule, two stories is the exception, and three, save in church towers, unheard of." The uniform use of flat roofs and the absence of arches, he felt, enhanced the style's horizontality and distinguished it from the California Mission Revival. For detailing he recommended projecting vigas and canales, along with carved corbel brackets and zapatas, which he called the "Santa Fe Capital." Morley emphasized the contribution of the Spanish, who had caused "the breaking up of the great 4 and 5 story communal houses into smaller less cumbersome units." He further credited them with introducing "exterior porches, cloistered courts, balconies, balustrades and towers all tending to lighten the heavy block-like character of native buildings, and to relieve their monotony."[53]

In response Vierra charged that "to accuse [Pueblo architecture] of monotony would

87. SCHOOL FOR THE DEAF, RAPP, RAPP AND HENDRICKSON, 1917. TERRACED
PUEBLO FORMS ENTER THE SANTA FE STYLE.

be to admit superficial knowledge and lack of observation." Vierra felt that the irregularity and variety of Pueblo forms increased their adaptability to modern purposes, citing the School for the Deaf as evidence. Vierra focused almost exclusively on the Pueblo contribution: "In considering the mission structures, too much has been made of its relation to Spanish architecture. . . . What the Franciscans might have done had they been able to obtain Spanish workmanship and materials has little to do with the type as it stands, except to emphasize its Indian character." From today's perspective, New Mexico's missions appear to be the foremost embodiment of the mingling of these two traditions—the interpretation of a Spanish building type by Pueblo builders.[54]

Morley's emphasis on the Spanish contribution resulted from the focus of the 1912 survey on Santa Fe architecture and possibly from the fact that the museum's funding came from the Hispanic-dominated state legislature.[55] Vierra's insistence on the Indian contribution surely reflects his involvement in the enthusiastic post-San Diego promotion of the new state, which made him even more zealous than Morley about distinguishing New Mexico's architecture from California's. Emphasizing the Indian character of New Mexico's buildings in contrast to the Spanish character of California's architecture was one way of doing this. The popularity of the Painted Desert pseudopueblos also had impressed on Vierra the attractiveness of Pueblo architecture to tourists. Moreover multistoried pueblos provided a model for large modern buildings, which the Spanish prototypes did not. And while Spanish style buildings such as the Palace of the Governors were picturesque only in their romantic evocation of the past, buildings patterned on Indian pueblos were picturesque in composition as well. Understandably Morley, the archaeologist, emphasized historical accuracy, while Vierra, a painter schooled in the picturesque aesthetic, championed compositional irregularity.

What is omitted from a historical revival is frequently as revealing as what is included. Isaac Rapp and the museum staff knew, for instance, the historic appearances of Santa Fe's churches from early photographs (figs. 16, 24). Built or remodeled late in the

Spanish era, their multitiered, Baroque towers resemble California missions. Such towers reappeared in the California Mission style during the 1890s. But Rapp and the museum excluded them from the Santa Fe style, in their effort to distance themselves from California.

The round two-story fortified Spanish towers known as *torreones,* to take another example, seem well suited to a picturesque revival because of their romantic associations. But only Charles Lummis, who built his home in Los Angeles (1898-1910), and Ralph Twitchell, who erected his in Santa Fe (about 1920), employed the *torreón.* Perhaps the museum omitted the torreón from their formulation of the style because it first appeared in Los Angeles, or because Hewett's relations with both Lummis and Twitchell were testy, or because the torreón comes from the Spanish and not the Pueblo tradition.

The proponents' rhetoric describing and promoting the style also reveals an over-romanticization of the Pueblos. Magazine articles praised the Pueblo character of University of New Mexico buildings while ignoring their equally important Spanish origins. Although Santa Fe's promoters gave a variety of names to the style ("Santa Fe," "New Mexico Mission," "Pueblo-Hispanic," "Spanish-Pueblo"), by 1930 they had settled on "Pueblo style." To this day corner fireplaces are termed kiva fireplaces in real estate parlance, despite the Spanish origin of that element.

A high priority of the revival boosters was a modern tourist hotel. The notion of modeling one on the terraced Pueblo form surfaced in 1912, when H. H. Dorman sent Isaac Rapp some "Kodaks" of Taos Pueblo, "which show interesting details and which might be used for hotel design." Dorman hoped to elicit an appropriate sketch from Rapp for the *New-Old Santa Fe* exhibit. Although Rapp did not comply, in 1919 *El Palacio* ran the sketch of a proposed Pueblo style hotel by T. Charles Gaastra, an architect who had moved from Chicago to Santa Fe in 1918 (fig. 88).[56]

The following year, a splendid tourist hotel, La Fonda, was built at the southeast corner of the plaza, designed by Rapp, Rapp and Hendrickson (figs. 58, 59, 89-91,

138

88. PROPOSED HOTEL, SANTA FE, T. CHARLES GAASTRA, 1919.
A ROMANTIC TOURIST HOTEL WAS A FIRST NECESSITY FOR THE CITY'S
ECONOMIC REDEVELOPMENT.

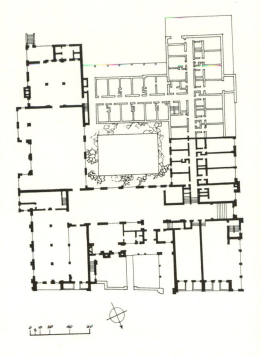

and 151). In an eclectic spirit, they freely adapted Pueblo and Spanish forms for this new building type. The firm deployed Pueblo masses in an even more dramatic composition than Gaastra, with deeply recessed terraces and elaborately contrived undulating parapets. They balanced a three-story bell tower on the left against an entrance on the right, patterned again after Laguna Mission but embellished with a cantilevered balcony. While a typical American hotel of this era had a formal axial entry, with a classically detailed set of doors opening to a half-flight of stairs leading to a grand two- or three-story lobby, La Fonda's guests arrived at an irregular courtyard facing San Francisco Street. Two indirect routes led across the court to the entrance. Rapp positioned this courtyard as part of his picturesque composition and to form an exotic entrance sequence, which doubled as a staging area for bus-tour groups. Inside, low dark-stained wooden ceilings, tile floors, and regional Arts and Crafts furnishings (Navajo blankets, Pueblo pottery, and New Mexico Mission style furniture) satisfied the romantic images conjured up by the hotel's advertising slogan: "Inn at the end of the Santa Fe Trail." In other regards, La Fonda followed the prevailing conventions of hotel design: rental space for shops facing San Francisco Street, the pairing of the dining room with the kitchen and other service functions, and the guest rooms

89. La Fonda Hotel, Rapp, Rapp and Hendrickson, 1921. Pueblo forms with an entrance patterned after the Laguna mission. (Cross Studio)

90. La Fonda, first floor plan; solid black walls, Rapp, Rapp and Hendrickson, 1921; outlined walls, John Gaw Meem, 1927. (Patricia Pollock)

91. La Fonda, lobby, 1921.

on the upper floor, each with a private bathroom and exterior window, arranged on either side of double-loaded corridors.[57]

Two additional public buildings helped solidify the style's position. When Gaastra designed the Cassell Building, on the northwest corner of the plaza in 1920, he adapted the church-auditorium form of the Fine Arts Museum for the centerpiece Oñate movie theater (fig. 92). Around this he wrapped one-story storefronts to create a stepped-back massing (the auto drive-thru was added in the 1920s). The same year, architects for the Treasury Department in Washington designed a new federal building facing the cathedral (fig. 93). Museum director Hewett corresponded with them on the design and evidently provided photographs of early Santa Fe style buildings, for the federal architects also recycled the church form and a mirror-image Palace of the Governors portal into a rigorously formal Beaux Arts plan.[58]

Public rhetoric emphasized the civic symbolism of this new architecture, celebrating the Palace of the Governors as one of the "monuments to the Spanish founders of the civilization of the Southwest." At the dedication of the Fine Arts Museum in 1917, museum patron Frank Springer proclaimed that "we shall find at home the themes for boundless achievement, and our arts shall grow—as this temple has grown . . . —straight from our own soil." A spate of national magazine articles echoed Springer by describing the Santa Fe-Pueblo style as "so directly American," "a true product of America," and "a strictly American style of architecture."[59]

This unexpected emphasis on the Americanness of an exotic, non-Anglo-American architecture reflects the nativist spirit of the post-World War period, an era that produced the Red Scare and yet another wave of xenophobia against immigrants, a time also when Americans with new automobiles increasingly heeded Charles Lummis's oft-repeated slogan, "See America First." New Mexico's architecture was indeed distinctly American, these articles insisted, because it derived from the indigenous Pueblos and from local Spanish architecture—the country's oldest colonial tradition. This heritage had previously raised doubts in the East, which delayed statehood for sixty years,

92. Cassell Building (Oñate Theater), T. Charles Gaastra, 1921, shown after mid-1920s gas station remodeling. (T. Harmon Parkhurst)

93. Federal Building, Supervising Architect, U.S. Treasury Department, 1921. The fine arts museum's church/auditorium form bracketed by mirror image governor's palaces. (T. Harmon Parkhurst)

but the new rhetoric completed the symbolic annexation of the Southwest begun by Lummis in the 1890s and transformed once lowly adobe architecture into a distinctive image for the new state and its fledgling tourist industry.

INTERNAL EXPATRIATES

The museum's promotional campaign geared up just as eastern artists and intellectuals centered in New York were feeling profound disgust at the carnage of World War I, which they saw as a demonstration of the bankruptcy of the modern industrial world. This mood of antimodernism combined with the exotic attraction of New Mexico to bring an infusion of artists, veterans of the progressive-suffrage movement, and a few wealthy patrons to Santa Fe. A small art colony had formed in Taos during the first decade of the century, but by 1915, Santa Fe had attracted only Vierra and two other painters, all suffering with tuberculosis. Artists and writers such as Witter Bynner, John Sloan, Mabel Dodge Luhan, and Marsden Hartley, who arrived in the teens, and others such as Georgia O'Keeffe and Oliver La Farge, who later followed, constituted the romantic wing of the New York intelligentsia. Indeed many of these internal expatriates had lived in Greenwich Village before coming to New Mexico, and they were joined by a steady stream of summer visitors from the East. Just as the nineteenth-century English Romantics John Ruskin and William Morris had once embraced the medieval spirit in their Gothic Revival architecture and Arts and Crafts movement, so these artists in New Mexico drew inspiration from the study of primitive art and began to tout Pueblo ways as a wholesome preindustrial alternative to the insanities of the modern world.[60]

"We feel our people here in the Southwest do have a life in keeping with the soil, the skies, winds, clouds, spaces—," wrote Hewett in 1918, "that they have ordered their lives in honest, simple, harmonious ways." The most tangible and easily adopted manifestation of this spirit was Pueblo architecture. "That which was not essential did not endure," explained Carlos Vierra, "and that which did endure was marvelously enriched with the living, flowing quality of free outline and form. It is in reality a

free-hand architecture, with the living quality of a sculptor's work . . ." As the antithe-sis of precise, industrial-age architecture, hand-shaped adobe came to symbolize the creative spirit and relaxed social mores of the art colonies.[61]

The primary manifestation of this freedom from modern constraints was the artist's own house. Carlos Vierra designed and built the best example of the type between 1918 and 1922 (fig. 94). Vierra's passion for weathered natural materials produced rounded adobe masses and dark wood details. His devotion to Pueblo prototypes inspired terraced forms, although he also drew porch and fireplace details from the Spanish tradition. This exoticism is only skin deep, however. In other regards, this is a typical suburban home of the era, complete with a two-car garage, four baths, a con-crete basement housing modern utilities, and the standard separation of public rooms on the ground floor from the private bedrooms above.[62]

Vierra's house led the move out of the Santa Fe River valley and up onto the dry mesa to the southeast, where land was cheaper. Other artists clustered along Telephone Road, which they rechristened Camino del Monte Sol. They and the thousands who have subsequently followed them to the hills positioned their porches and windows to capture picturesque views of the vast New Mexico landscape. A 1927 prospectus for the Laboratory of Anthropology, for instance, described its site as "on the summit

94. Carlos Vierra House, Carlos Vierra, 1921. A suburban house in the guise of a wind- and water-shaped adobe. (Wesley Bradfield)

of the long slope which rises from Santa Fe toward the foot of the Sangre de Cristo mountains . . . Due to the depth of the institution's property and to the falling away of the terrain to the west and south, no building could ever be erected to cut off the extraordinary views enjoyed from this eminence."[63]

Other artists preferred to start with a one-story, three- or four-room Mexican adobe house; if it stood partially in ruins, so much the better. Sheldon Parsons, who painted presidents, senators, and suffragettes before moving to Santa Fe in 1914 for his health, purchased such a house in the early 1920s. He refurbished it to include modern utilities and conveniences. Adding a large living room and studio wing in the form of a multistory pueblo created an informal, picturesque massing.[64]

Many of the wealthy who arrived in the 1920s on the heels of the first artists were single women, or women couples, college-educated, from the Northeast, with a particular interest in Indian welfare and arts. Miss Amelia Elizabeth White, for instance, was the daughter of Horace White, first biographer of Lincoln and editor of the *New York Evening Post.* For fifty years after settling in Santa Fe in 1922, she was the city's leading philanthropist, supporter of the Indian Arts Fund, Animal Shelter, and Laboratory of Anthropology, as well as patron of the art colony. The painter and builder William P. Henderson designed and constructed a complex of fifteen buildings near the upper end of Camino del Monte Sol for White and her sister Martha and reshaped the arid hillsides with terraces and geometric gardens (fig. 95). Henderson accented stark adobe masses with historic wood details scavenged from nearby mountain villages, while Jesse Nusbaum was engaged to produce the first great collection of New Mexico Mission furniture. In 1926 the Whites enlisted Sylvanus Morley and poet Witter Bynner to christen their swimming pool with a mock Mayan rite, culminating with the sacrificial casting of an Indian princess into the pool—all filmed for later enjoyment.[65]

The mystique of Santa Fe also attracted veterans of the progressive and suffrage movements. Their knowledge of urban housing reforms combined with fantasies of harmonious Pueblo communities to produce clustered housing compounds. Ina Sizer

and Gerald Cassidy, Dorothy Curtis, Sara Woolfolk McComb, Katherine Stinson Otero, Ernest Thompson Seaton, Ann Webster, and the painters' group Los Cinco Pintores each developed compounds, which they christened "plazas," although their site plans bore faint resemblance to Pueblo or Spanish village plazas. Each typically mixed single-family houses and small apartments within a walled compound; the largest totaled twenty-three units. These free-thinking women and men artists acted as social catalyst when they created physical settings that fostered social interaction and mutual support among residents.[66]

Walled compounds, courtyard houses, flagstone patios, and terraced gardens also satisfied the desire for an informal, outdoor life-style (figs. 96, 140). Whenever possible, a stream of water was diverted from the community *acequia* (irrigation ditch) through these outdoor rooms. Fruit trees, a vegetable garden, and above all the artist's home studio symbolized self-sufficiency. Before World War II, many artists sold work out of their studios or home galleries. Customers often sought not only a painting but also a tantalizing glimpse of the bohemian art colony.[67]

Interior furnishings might demonstrate the artist-builder's ingenuity and the owner's connoisseurship of native arts, while a few imported antiques intimated family ties to eastern elites. Navajo blankets, Pueblo pottery, Spanish santos, and tinwork, mixed with Indian genre scenes and landscapes by the art colony. Nusbaum's inflection of the Craftsman furniture style into a New Mexico Mission style became the norm by about 1930. Santa

95. AMELIA WHITE ESTATE, WILLIAM P. HENDERSON, 1922-30. (T. HARMON PARKHURST)

Fe builders also rendered the ultimate Arts and Crafts symbol of the preindustrial house, the inglenook, as the Spanish corner fireplace with built-in adobe benches (fig. 97).[68]

Renowned lyric poet and translator of the *Tao Te Ching*, Witter Bynner, for instance, purchased a three-room adobe in 1922 and expanded it over the next forty years into a rambling thirty-room house. As a friend described it years later: "There are Chinese carvings, painting and jade against the white walls, New England heirloom chests and silver, Navajo rugs on the floor and black and white Mexican serapes on the couches. Your fine library fills the shelves in the study and you watch the changing light on the mountains from its upper portal. Your home is what I feel Santa Fe homes should be—the outer conformity to our native architecture and the inner expression of individual taste."[69] In Bynner's case, an erudite expression of cosmopolitan romanticism.

145

World War I restrained tourism development in Santa Fe, as the number of hotel rooms rose only modestly, from 155 in 1910 to 205 in 1920 (see appendix). But the 1912 plan began to show more substantial economic results in the 1920s, as lodging rooms tripled to 600. That 140 of these were in new motels along the original Route 66 as it dipped into Santa Fe reflected the explosion of automobile ownership and travel. Other tourism-related businesses grew even more rapidly; four curio shops in 1920 became sixteen ten years later, and the single artist listed in the 1921 business directory, photographer T. Harmon Parkhurst, was joined by twenty-eight others in 1930.

The romantic-picturesque tradition, transplanted by the museum and nurtured by the art colony, flourished in Santa Fe. The philosophical and aesthetic underpinnings of the tradition fostered the development of a distinctive regional identity and the promotion of tourism. Picturesque evocation emerged from the start in the Palace of the Governors (combined with Beaux Arts formality). The infusion of Pueblo forms in the mid-teens added compositional irregularity and, for Anglo-Americans, a more fascinating, non-European form of the exotic. After 1920 the response to locale deepened through the use of hand-crafted local materials and the siting of buildings to frame picturesque vistas.

96. INA SIZER AND GERALD CASSIDY HOUSE, COURTYARD ROOM, 1920. OUTDOOR LIVING SYMBOLIZED THE FREE, NEW SPIRIT OF THE ART COLONY AND THE AMERICAN WEST, IN GENERAL.

97. SHELDON PARSONS HOUSE, ABOUT 1927.

5

MEXICANO, SPANISH-AMERICAN: CHICANO, HISPANIC

Santa Fe, like other modern cities, has seen substantial cultural interaction and significant intermarriage between ethnic groups. But while people may grow more alike in their everyday modern lives, perceptions of ethnic difference often paradoxically increase. The Spanish casta system, which had once equated social class with racial heritage and ethnicity, broke down through intermarriage in the late 1700s. After 1846 the immigration of Americans set up a new ethnic hierarchy. While this classic stratification of social class along ethnic lines continued into the twentieth century, the rise of tourism, here as elsewhere, has introduced a second, complicating factor to ethnic dynamics. Select ethnic images and crafts may become the raw materials for tourist advertising and souvenirs, but ethnic leaders challenge these tourist stereotypes and reshape them as rhetorical weapons in intergroup competition for political power, jobs, and resources.[1]

How we mature psychologically as human beings underlies both the us-them dichotomies of ethnic relations and the romantic tourist fascination with exotic groups. Psychologists have observed that during the period of intense socialization around two to three years of age, when children learn rules of behavior and personal hygiene and acquire unspoken cultural systems such as body language, they also solidify their sense of themselves as individuals and begin to identify with their group—principally the family, but by extension the ethnic group, and the nation. As a result a set of dichotomies intertwine in the subconscious: good-bad, clean-dirty, us-them. The desires and impulses that one represses to conform to the expectations of parents and society become a subconscious shadow-half of one's identity, often perceived as feelings of insecurity, guilt, frustration, or anger. We sometimes try to rid ourselves of these feelings by attributing them to, or in psychological terms, projecting them onto others. The process of identifying with one's group ("us") provides shared targets of projection ("them").[2]

This psychology of interwoven dualities helps account for the tendency to glorify one's own group and to denigrate other ethnic groups and nations as aggressive, greedy, promiscuous, cruel, lazy, and above all, unclean—quite apart from their actual character. Comparative cultural anthropologist Mary Douglas has also demonstrated that a concern for cleanliness is often not only a matter of hygiene, but also can serve as a symbolic expression of the desire for social order. That is why religious devotion and chaste behavior, on the one hand, and socializing outside one's group and transgressing social norms, on the other, are often perceived in terms of cleanliness and dirt, purity and pollution: "cleanliness is next to godliness," "pure in thought, word, and deed," "limpieza de sangre" (the Spanish Colonial concern for purity of blood), "ethnic cleansing," "you dirty Nigger lover," "dirty whore," "if you say that filthy word again, I'll wash your mouth out with soap." This is also why people who visit a foreign country and become overwhelmed by unfamiliar odors, patterns of social interaction, and the like often feel dirty, or wake up in the night scratching imaginary bedbug bites.[3]

During the American conquest of New Mexico, as we have seen, brown-skinned people and melting adobe buildings triggered classic ethnic projections. "It is said at St. Fe," wrote one semiliterate American in 1847 before even seeing the city, "Even at meals the men do not think of pulling off their hats and even the Religion is nothing but mockery or they make a mockery of it, on the public square is a slaughter pen which perfumes the town with its nauseous stench and the carcasses of putrefying mammals lie unheeded along the streets, but money is more plentiful than in the States."[4]

A second watershed of personal development occurs during adolescence, as the child becomes an independent adult; the ties to parents and group loosen, and the potential targets of projection become less fixed. For a variety of reasons, some people are attracted to "them," the Other. Some fall in love with a person of another race or ethnic group, others with a person of their own sex. Some are attracted to things classed as deviant by their group—drug use, tattoos, heavy-metal music, fundamentalist Christianity, secular humanism, the life of an artist, and so on. These phenomena are equated here only to the extent that they represent a break from childhood group identification and subsequently require a greater effort by the individual to reconstruct personal identity and the potential targets of projection. An attraction to the exotic (be it a Frenchmen's journey to Tahiti or a Japanese artist's embrace of European modernism, an Anglo's enchantment by things Pueblo or a Pueblo Indian's fascination with the explicit language and thought of Anglos) represents a variation on the psychology of the Other. This often involves a reverse projection of what is repressed or underdeveloped in oneself or one's culture onto the Other, a tendency to see the exotic as self-fulfilled, sexually liberated, and in harmony with nature, for instance, or as self-assured, rational, and authoritative, again without any necessary relation to the character of the Other. Positive and negative projections, fascination and disgust, are intertwined aspects of the complex psychology of group interaction.

SPANISH CULTURAL PURITY

The evolution of ethnic terminology and identities in Santa Fe, particularly those of the Spanish-speaking population, has been shaped in large part through this dynamic of positive and negative stereotypes. The response to malicious stereotypes of "dirty, mongrel" Mexicans during the late 1880s, as we saw earlier, stimulated the development of a rhetoric of tricultural harmony among Indians, Spanish, and Americans. Following the granting of statehood in 1912, the promotion of tourism by the Museum of New Mexico popularized romantic stereotypes of Indians and Spanish. The Spanish-language press also continued its challenge to negative stereotypes and its cultivation of a regional Hispano identity. This growing adoption of the rhetoric of triculturalism, with its shift from the term *Mexican* to *Spanish-American* was helped to fruition by the effects of the Mexican Revolution of 1910 on the U.S. side of the border.

Soon after its founding in 1909, the museum embraced triculturalism and began uniformly to employ *Spanish-American*. Its staff of Anglo-American newcomers realized that tourists were more interested in romantic tales of the Spanish conquistadors than in the still foreign and threatening presence of the Mexican working class. In historical pageants beginning in 1911 and in the 1913 Palace of the Governors murals, the museum elaborated a history of three peoples: Pueblo, Spanish, and American.

The Mexican Revolution led to a concurrent redefinition of Mexican nationalism, which emphasized Indian-mestizo heritage. Pancho Villa personified this foreign nationalism for many Americans, when he raided the border town of Columbus, New Mexico, in 1916. With the retaliatory campaign of General "Black Jack" Pershing into Mexico, and a fresh wave of anti-Mexican xenophobia, it became even more expedient for New Mexico's political leaders to speak of themselves and their constituents as Spanish- rather than Mexican-American.

The increasing use of the term *hispano-americano* in the Spanish-language press after 1890 also aided the adoption of the term *Spanish-American,* while the press's use of *anglo-americano* contributed to another shift in ethnic terminology. When the conviction arose in the late teens that the new Pueblo-Spanish architectural revival was "particularly American" (chapter 4), the meaning of the term *American* came into question. So in the mid-1920s, as the promotion of Pueblo and Spanish culture geared up, Americans took a step down from the pinnacle of public rhetoric and became "Anglos." The adoption of this term made them into one ethnic group among others, with no special claim to superiority. While this did not cause an immediate redistribution of power, it did strengthen the rhetoric of equality and contributed to the lower level of overt racism in northern New Mexico than in other areas of the Southwest.[5]

A revealing pattern in Anglo ethnic attitudes emerges, nevertheless. The tendency to overemphasize the Pueblo contribution to local architecture and thereby deny the equally important Spanish contribution, including on occasion even attributing it to the Pueblos was discussed in chapter 4. John D. Rockefeller, Jr., to cite another example, avidly promoted Indian arts through his Santa Fe Laboratory of Anthropology. But when approached by Nina Otero-Warren, county superintendent of schools, for funding to improve the education of Spanish-Americans, and for inclusion of their arts in the laboratory's programs, Rockefeller rejected her proposal out of hand. Many Anglos projected positive, if highly romantic, attributes onto Pueblos, while showing much less interest in Spanish-American culture and discounting the continuing societal racism they have faced.[6]

Even as the museum was beginning its work after 1910, Aurelio M. Espinosa also commenced his momentous study of the Spanish folklore and language of New Mexico, which would provide a scholarly basis for the use of the term *Spanish-American*. A descendant of Captain Marcelo Espinosa, who rode with Oñate in 1598, Aurelio was born in 1880 at the northern Hispano outpost of Canero, near present-day Del Norte, Colorado. He attended the Universities of Colorado and New Mexico before receiving a Ph.D. from the University of Chicago, in 1909. The following year he embarked on a thirty-seven-year teaching career at Stanford University. Espinosa's steady stream of books and articles led journalist-curmudgeon H. L. Mencken in 1934 to dub him "the greatest living authority on American Spanish."[7]

Espinosa argued that the concentration of archaic Spanish vocabulary and folklore in New Mexico set it apart from Mexico as a particularly pure island of Spanishness. Like any of us, Espinosa saw what he was prepared by his background to see. His heritage as a son of Spanish *hidalgos* and the academic pursuit of pure stocks of folklore combined to send him on a self-fulfilling search for pure Spanish culture. Once, early in his career, however, Espinosa was confronted in his role as associate editor of the *Journal of American Folklore* with an article that contradicted his beliefs.

The young Oxford-educated anthropologist Barbara Freire-Marreco (fig. 71), had collected some Spanish-language folklore at Santa Clara Pueblo. Espinosa introduced her 1916 article with the claim that "The Pueblo Indians of New Mexico have given very little to the great traditional treasure of Spanish folk-lore of New Mexico,—in fact nothing at all. . . ." While Espinosa lauded Freire's two Santa Clara tales as a "demonstration of the vigor and vitality of Spanish tradition," one of the tales concludes when "Jesus Christ held up his hands, and there fell from the roof maize and wheat and beans and chile and onions and all sorts of food"—an event that Espinosa concedes "appears in the Pueblo Indians' own stories." By definition Pueblo Indians could not make a creative contribution to the great tradition of Spanish folklore; they could only preserve pure Spanish tales. When Indian elements appeared, therefore, Espinosa simply discounted them for not being Spanish.[8]

Marreco adds further evidence of cultural interaction between the pueblo and the nearby villages of Guchupange and San Pedro, which she describes as Mexican, but which Espinosa calls Spanish. "Mexicans who are sick sometimes make a vow to dance in the Indian Dances of the pueblo," Marreco reported. She described, for instance, that an old Mexican chastised his son for slandering Pueblo religion by saying to him, "they do these things for the benefit of us and of all the people as well as for themselves." Unable to let this pass unchallenged, Espinosa responded in a footnote that "the Spanish people of New Mexico have mixed very little with the native Indian population, and have taken practically nothing from their language, customs, and beliefs. The Indians, however, have evidently not only learned the language of their ancient masters, but have also taken over many Spanish customs, beliefs, and superstitions."[9]

Espinosa's Spanish folklore mixed comfortably with articles on Appalachian folklore in the *Journal of American Folklore*. Beginning in the 1890s, folklorists sought out evidence of the preservation of Anglo-American culture in the remote hill country. This pure old English stock became one symbolic bulwark against contemporary Central and Southern European immigration, much as the purported Spanishness of northern New Mexico served to distinguish its residents from the new wave of Mexican immigration after 1910. Likewise the myth that the mountain people spoke the English of Shakespeare was echoed in the oft-repeated belief that New Mexicans spoke the Castilian of Cervantes.[10]

Because Espinosa focused on only one aspect of culture, language and oral folklore, his sweeping generalizations about cultural purity lack validity. He showed little interest in the subjects that Spanish colonists would unavoidably have learned from

the Pueblos: transportation routes, sources of building materials, and local environmental wisdom on weather, plants, animals and minerals. If Espinosa had focused on agriculture and food preparation, for instance, the corn, beans and chile, tortillas, tamales, and enchiladas on New Mexican tables would have made it impossible to overlook the Mexican and Pueblo contribution to Spanish-American culture.

In Santa Fe the leading proponents of Spanish cultural preservation were Jose D. Sena, Jr., George W. Armijo, Cleofas M. Jaramillo, Nina Otero-Warren, Aurora Lucero-White Lea, and Fabiola Cabeza de Baca Gilbert (figs. 99, 120, 121). Not only were they all members of the rico elite, but most had strong ties to Anglo-American culture: one of Armijo's grandmothers was Anglo, while three of the women married Anglos. In addition to language and folklore, they emphasized genealogy, costume, and especially Catholicism as key expressions of Spanish identity. In the 1930s New Mexican food and Mexican mariachi music were added to this constellation of conscious ethnic expressions. Beginning in the late teens, this Spanish elite channeled their energies into the Santa Fe Fiesta enactment of the reconquest of 1692 (see chapter 6). In the heightened historicist context of the fiesta, to this day, people think of themselves (and are referred to by Anglo and Pueblo participants) not as "Hispanics," or even as "Spanish-Americans," but as "Spaniards."[11]

98. COURTYARD OF MRS. CLEOFAS JARAMILLO HOUSE, ABOUT 1940.
(T. HARMON PARKHURST)

In 1935 Mrs. Cleofas Jaramillo founded the Sociedad Folklórica (figs. 98, 99). A descendant of landed Spanish families, daughter of a prosperous businessman, educated at Santa Fe's Catholic Loretto Academy, and widow of a Republican politician, Jaramillo's imagination was captured by a magazine article on the Natchez Pilgrimage. Begun in 1932, the pilgrimage toured pre-Civil War mansions, guided by southern belles in ruffled gowns with hoop skirts. The pilgrimage idea swept across the South and into Santa Fe, when Jaramillo persuaded her friends to bring out their heirloom jewelry and gowns for a fashion show and Spanish *merienada* (afternoon tea) during the annual Santa Fe Fiesta. During the balance of the year, the Sociedad, which limited its membership to thirty women of Spanish descent, met to exchange traditional tales and converse in Spanish about customs they feared were vanishing.[12]

153

Jaramillo, Otero, and Cabeza de Baca also began publishing cookbooks, folk tales, and personal reminiscences in the late 1930s. These writings derived their form from a genre of mythologizing Southwestern romance pioneered by Helen Hunt Jackson and Charles Lummis in the 1880s. Mary Austin, a member of Lummis's Los Angeles circle, moved to Santa Fe in the early twenties, where she joined Witter Bynner, Willa Cather, Oliver La Farge, Paul Horgan, Frank Applegate, and others who produced a steady stream of popular folklore and historical romances of Spanish, Pueblo, and Navajo New Mexico.[13]

By publishing their own folkloric reminiscences, the Spanish-American elite sought to preempt what they viewed as the shallow and inaccurate work of Anglos. But by adopting this romantic genre, they unavoidably acquired a set of literary conventions and cultural assumptions. The telltale equation of cultural purity with authenticity and of the modern world with contamination, for instance, permeates Jaramillo's *Romance of a Little Village Girl*: "In this little valley of Arroyo Hondo, situated in the northern part of the state of New Mexico, hemmed in by high mountains and hills, sheltered from the contamination of the outside world, the inhabitants lived peacefully, preserving the customs and traditions of their ancestors." Chicano

99. TENTH ANNIVERSARY BANQUET OF THE *SOCIADAD FOLKLORICO*, LA FONDA HOTEL, 1945. FABÍOLA CABEZA DE BACA GILBERT (SECOND FROM LEFT), MRS. CLEOFAS JARAMILLO (FOURTH).

literary historian Genaro Padilla has noted that this "story of sixteenth-century Spain brought uncontaminated to the verdant little valley where she was born 400 years later . . . spares itself the complexities of sociohistorical process, geographic exigency, profound Native American influences, and cultural evolution consequent to the long migrations into the far northern provinces of Mexico. History is reified out of the need for a simpler story of Spanish adventure, conquest, settlement, isolation (especially isolation) and its adjunct 'purity'. . . ." [14]

While Anglo writers never confronted the historical realities of the American conquest, racism, and land fraud, Spanish-American writers never did more than quietly raise them before quickly moving on. It is difficult to read such a literature, writes Padilla, "without feeling some aversion for the historical amnesia and delusive class pretenses displayed by many of these native writers." Nevertheless he appreciates that by asserting their right to define their own culture and experience, these women "wedged the opening for wider resistance in another time and place."[15]

The absorption with ancestry revitalized the ricos' colonial-era claim to social status by virtue of pure Spanish blood. The leading spokesmen for the Spanish-American elite on genealogy and religion has been Angelico Chavez, who traces his own ancestry through multiple lineages to Oñate's company (fig. 100). His religious devotion and interest in history led Chavez in 1937 to join the Franciscans—the missionaries of colonial New Mexico. A poet, historian, short-story writer, and painter, in addition to being a parish priest, Chavez published the bible of Spanish genealogists, *Origins of New Mexico Families*, in 1953. There he acknowledges that New Mexican women intermarried with Anglos in the nineteenth century "to a degree not generally known or realized" and also that some of the original settlers carried an initial Aztec admixture, which some have used to "cast a false aspersion on a par with immorality or lack of culture." This Aztec element, Chavez assures his readers, "was small enough to be absorbed by the general preponderance of Spanish blood," so that "these New Mexico pioneers . . . were people of whom we can be justly proud." This assumption

that Indian blood is somehow shameful leads Chavez to distinguish the descendants of Spanish colonists from "another element of the population" in 1846: "the genízaros, who were descended from diverse Plains Indians and other nomadic Indian captives. They now had Spanish surnames, many had Spanish blood, and all knew only the Spanish language. Generally, these were the 'poor ignorant Mexicans' described by American writers and travelers of those times."[16]

Spanish genealogy, conquest history, and the preservation of archaic Spanish customs allowed members of Santa Fe's cultural elite to distance themselves from the working-class descendants of mestizos, genízaros, and coyotes. Such preoccupations also helped insulate them from the harsh economic realities faced by other *nuevo mexicanos*. The loss of land and water rights, compounded by the agricultural depression of the early 1920s, forced many New Mexican villagers into the migrant labor force and the working-class barrios of Santa Fe, Albuquerque, and other southwestern cities. The political and economic tumult in Mexico that continued into the 1920s also triggered the first mass emigration north since the colonial period. Dispossessed New Mexican villagers and Mexican immigrants found themselves in head-to-head competition for jobs on the railroads and in mining, timber, and commercial agriculture.[17]

QUESTIONING SPANISH PURITY
New Mexican natives continued to call themselves "mexicanos" in Spanish, but both natives and recent immigrants distinguished between *surumatos* (slang for the Mexican immigrants) and *manitos* (for natives of northern New Mexico, short for *hermanitos*, "little brothers"). In the more formal context of the Spanish-language press, northern New Mexicans often described themselves as "hispanos" or "nativos." In English they universally employed *Spanish-American* to distinguish themselves from more recent Mexican immigrants. (This distinction between recent immigrants and descendants of the colonists continued to be reflected in the 1970 census, when 103,584 people in New Mexico identified themselves as being of Mexican origin and another 119,094

100. Fray Angelico Chávez, about 1945. Parish priest, historian, poet, short story writer, and author of the bible of New Mexico genealogy, *Origins of New Mexico Families*.

155

as being "other Spanish.") This Spanish terminology and the accompanying deemphasis (sometimes outright denial) of cultural connections with Mexico deprived recent immigrants of a symbolic connection to the Spanish-Mexican history of New Mexico, which might have eased their transition into a new country. Ironically Mexican immigration since 1910 has done more than folklore societies to sustain Spanish-speaking culture in the state.[18]

Territorial Governor L. Bradford Prince, folklorist Aurelio Espinosa, and the Spanish elite of Santa Fe transformed the American obsession with racialism into the rhetoric of triculturalism and the cult of Spanish purity. The "citizens of New Mexico—Indian, Spanish and Anglo" had become the formulaic invocation of politicians and regional writers by the 1930s. As Joaquin Ortega, director of the University of New Mexico's School of Inter-American Affairs, put it in 1942, "with its three cultures—Indian, Hispanic and Anglo-Saxon—developing in parallel lines . . ." A knowledgeable scholar such as Ortega would admit elsewhere that "biologically these groups are mixed already in a considerable degree." Likewise the oral traditions of many Santa Fe families also acknowledge mixed ancestry: of an Hispano family with an indio great-great-grandmother and a Yankee soldier great-grandfather; or another with a father recently arrived from Chihuahua and a mother from "Los Jarales down by Belen that some people say was settled by Indians." The public rhetoric of triculturalism suppresses rich family histories such as these.[19]

The clearest challenge to the claim of a special Spanish heritage for northern New Mexico came from Arthur Campa. Born in the northern Mexican state of Sonora in 1905, Campa became an early refugee of the Mexican Revolution when his father, a Diaz loyalist, was killed in 1910. His education at an Albuquerque Methodist school and the University of New Mexico, together with his Mexican birth, gave Campa a special perspective on this debate. A folklorist who would teach at Columbia, the University of New Mexico, and the University of Denver during his career, Campa tilled the same scholarly terrain as Aurelio Espinosa: Hispano folklore and linguistics.[20]

Spanish influences were important in New Mexico, Campa conceded, but they had been filtered through Mexico. "Culturally," wrote Campa, "these two regions are seldom separated by the Rio Grande . . ." New Mexico did develop culturally distinctive customs because of its geographic isolation, Campa was also quick to acknowledge, but regional isolation and cultural variation characterized all of Mexico before the coming of the railroad in the late nineteenth century. New Mexico was in some ways distinctive, but as one regional Mexican culture, not because it was more Spanish than the others. Ironically Campa argued, "The real cultural differences between the region north of the Rio Grande and that below are those which the New Mexican has acquired by close contact with American life. In a sense it is his dehispanization, his falling away from Spanish, that stamps him as a different individual."[21]

In the 1940s and 1950s, Campa asked Spanish-speaking native New Mexicans what they called themselves. Speaking in Spanish, they answered without exception "mexicano." Asked the same question later in English, they replied "Spanish-American." To describe a person from Mexico, they chose "mexicano de México" and "Mexican," respectively. According to Campa, the term *Spanish-American* accomplished three things: "It relieved the interested parties of the imaginary opprobrium of being Mexicans, it transformed them into Spaniards, and it expressed their American citizenship."[22]

Campa had stated his case forcefully by the late 1940s, but it was largely ignored by the proponents of pure Spanish heritage and, at first, had little impact on the popularity of the term *Spanish-American*. The twenty years following World War II were marked by assimilationist trends. Military service in World War II and munitions work on the West Coast changed the courses of many Hispanos' lives. Some returned to their villages, but most stayed on the West Coast or resettled in the larger towns of the Southwest. Hispano veterans, most of whom had seen combat, felt a particular pride in citizenship. The major new Mexican-American political organization was christened the American GI Forum. Many thought of themselves as just plain Americans and chose to raise their children speaking English.

6

June 21 : Santa Fe Cop Kills Chicano

Exactly a month after Felipe Mares was shot to death by Taos police, another young Chicano was gunned down by Santa Fe police. Roy Gallegos, age 19, was killed with a single bullet in the head at about 1:30 A.M. on June 21 by Officer Vance Mabry. Demands from the community for an investigation were ignored by Gov.King and city officials.But this time there are witnesses to what really happened and evidence that officials have deliberately hidden the truth.

Police claimed that Roy had been robbing a drug-store with two other Chicanos, Peter Padilla and Patricio Eloy Gurule, all of Santa Fe. Police claimed that when the 3 were captured, Roy ran away. Police claimed that Officer Mabry called out several orders to stop and then fired a so-called "warning shot" about 100 feet from Roy (they later changed this to 80 feet). Police denied that Padilla was a police informer,as the community believes, and that the whole incident was a set-up. Police also told the press that Mabry was a "veteran officer."

But on July 1 in Santa Fe, a very different version of events was revealed at a press conference sponsored by two barrio organizations: La Juventud del Barrio de Cristo Rey, of which Roy Gallegos was a member, and La Gente. Rev. Miguel Baca, O.F.M., read a statement in which it was pointed out that witnesses to the killing said:
1) Roy Gallegos was handcuffed at the time Mabry killed him. He was also believed to be heavily drugged, making escape very unlikely. He was also running directly toward a large number of state police and National Guardsmen who were across the street.
2) Other police officers shouted at Mabry, "Don't shoot!" but he apparently ignored them. Just before the shooting, when the 3 men were being caught, Mabry said to other officers, "You should have shot those sons of bitches."
3) Mabry is not a veteran; he has been on the police force less than 2 years.
4) Mabry was not 100 or even 80 feet from Gallegos when he fired, but much closer.

Victor Gallegos, Roy's father, also spoke at the July 1 conference. He told how he had gone to see the insurance company about Roy's death and was told to get a report from the police. Chief Felix Lujan told him that he could not

El funeral de Roy Gallegos el día 25 de junio

DECLARACION DE DANIEL GURULE DE LA JUVENTUD DEL BARRIO DEL CRISTO REY A LA OCASION DEL ENTERRAMIENTO DE ROY GALLEGOS
Hemos cumplido con lo que nos pide nuestra fe cristiana por el amor que guardamos a nuestro hermano Roy Gallegos.

Increasingly Hispanos entered the professions and the middle class as residential segregation declined, and Spanish- and Anglo-American intermarriage increased. Although no analysis has been made of Santa Fe County records, marriages between Spanish- and English-surnamed people in Bernalillo County, including Albuquerque, rose from 4.6 percent of all marriages in 1930 to 11 percent in 1964 and 17 percent in 1967.[23]

CHICANO MESTIZAJE

Out of the political repression of McCarthyism and the assimilationist tendencies of the Eisenhower years emerged the Civil Rights movement. The movement accelerated among Mexican-Americans during the mid-1960s, in the campaign to reclaim New Mexico land grants led by Reyes López Tijerina and the California farmworkers' movement led by Cesar Chávez. Tijerina preferred the term *Indo-Hispano,* while Chávez preferred *Mexican-American. Indo-Hispano* was perhaps too explicit or unwieldy to gain broad acceptance, although one still occasionally hears it among grassroots activists in New Mexico. *Mexican-American* still carried the derogatory connotations given it by mainstream America and implied that Mexican-Americans, like any other hyphenated immigrant group, had no special claim to the land. As the Mexican-

101. FROM THE JULY 5, 1971 ISSUE OF *EL GRITO DEL NORTE* WHICH CHRONICLED THE CHICANO MOVEMENT IN NEW MEXICO FROM 1968 TO 1973

American social justice movement gained momentum in the late 1960s, the term *Chicano* crystallized the emerging identity and activist spirit (fig. 101).

Although the origin of the term is not entirely clear, most scholars believe *chicano* is a variation of *mexicano.* As a slang term, *chicano* only rarely appeared in print early in the twentieth century. In Texas and New Mexico, by the 1930s *chicano* was a mildly derogatory term for those with darker skin and family ties to Mexico. As late as 1967, ethnographer Nancie Gonzáles reported that in Albuquerque, *chicano* was a slang term for a gang member, used interchangeably with *pachuco* ("zoot-suiter," somewhat analogous to today's *cholo*).[24]

By elevating a disparaging term to a badge of honor, the Chicano movement called attention to the underprivileged status of the lower class and proudly embraced its Indian origins. Chicano rhetoric and visual imagery also drew heavily from the Mexican nationalist movement of the 1920s. The search for a national identity in Mexico's Indian heritage, known as *indigenismo,* paralleled the academic quest for Anglo-Saxon roots in Appalachia and Spanish roots in northern New Mexico. Orchestral composer Carlos Chávez and muralists Rivera, Orosco, and Siqueiros fused Indian themes with modern European artistic forms. Mexican philosopher José Vasconcelos envisioned the blending (mestizaje) of all the races of the world in Latin America to form *la raza cósmica,* the "cosmic race." Contrary to the European and American desire for racial purity, Vasconcelos's theory was one of inclusiveness and hybrid vigor. And unlike the New Mexican rhetoric of three separate cultures, the Mexican ideology of triculturalism held that Indian and Spanish stocks had mixed to produce the modern Mexican culture and people. So while some Chicanos emphasized a purely Indian heritage, most, like their intellectual counterparts in Mexico, embraced the mestizaje of Indian and Spanish.[25]

The Mexican intelligentsia typically employed the Aztecs and their pyramids, hieroglyphics, history, and agriculture to represent all Mexican Indians. Likewise Chicano rhetoric quickly focused on the mythic Aztec homeland of Aztlán, somewhere to the north of the central valley of Mexico. By locating Aztlán in the American Southwest, Chicanos contended that they were all natives of the region, with a claim to the land.[26]

The first national gathering of activists, the Chicano Youth Liberation Conference, held in Denver in the spring of 1969, issued *El Plan Espiritual de Aztlán.* This declaration of political and economic independence rings with stirring phrases ". . . we, the Chicano inhabitants and civilizers of the northern land of Aztlán from whence came our forefathers, reclaiming the land of their birth. . . . Aztlán belongs to those who plant the seeds, water the fields, and gather the crops and not to the foreign Europeans. . . . With our hearts in our hands and our hands in the soil, we declare the independence of our mestizo nation." In the months that followed, talk of Aztlán swept through the youth, especially college students, who organized as MEChA (*El Movimiento Estudiantil Chicano de Aztlán,* The Chicano Student Movement of Aztlán; *mecha* means "fuse" or "match"). Chicano art entered an intense period of development, as writers, muralists, and community theater groups across the Southwest reinterpreted their history and defined a cultural identity (figs. 63, 64). Their work was overtly political and populist in its desire to reach the entire community.[27]

Aztec rhetoric and symbolism deemphasized local cultural variation. Mexican indigenismo had romanticized the Aztecs as the symbol of all Indians and of a centralized Mexican government; it did not seek an ethnic resurgence of the country's remaining Indian subcultures. In the United States, Chicanos resurrected Aztlán to unite Spanish-speakers across the Southwest in political struggle. Some activists in Santa Fe, nevertheless, found that local history and images resonated better in grassroots organizing; young people connected best with their grandparents not on the basis of the Aztecs, but through local folklore and oral history. Historian and social commentator Gilbert Benito Cordova, for instance, wrote in 1973 of his relatives and neighbors in Abiquiu that, "while the villagers today think of themselves as Hispanos, they are still clearly aware of their *genízaro* origin and take pride in these roots that extend far back into the Southwestern soil."[28]

While the Chicano emphasis of Indian-Spanish mestizaje challenged the myth of Spanish purity, the movement downplayed or ignored the degree of Chicano-Anglo intermarriage and cultural interaction. The term *coyote,* meaning one of mixed Hispano-Anglo ancestry, had carried somewhat derogatory overtones, much like *chicano.* The rising interest in family roots, nevertheless, led some to refer to themselves as Coyotes, with a degree of pride mingled with knowing mischievousness. But because the Chicano movement was an attack on the Anglo power structure, Hispano-Anglo mestiaje posed a conundrum that prevented it from rising to the level of public rhetoric and symbolism. Indeed some Chicano scholars have underestimated the extent of Anglo-Hispano intermarriage and cultural intermixing, just as Espinosa once obscured Spanish-Indian mixing. Visionary *mestiza* poet Gloria Anzaldúa acknowledges this complexity when she writes,

> *To live in the Borderlands means knowing*
> that the *india* in you, betrayed for 500 years,
> is no longer speaking to you,
> that *mexicanas* call you *rajetas,*
> that denying the Anglo inside you
> is as bad as having denied the Indian or Black; . . .
> . . . *rajetas* —literally, 'split,' that is, having betrayed your words.[29]

This political movement and the term *Chicano* received a mixed response in New Mexico and across the Southwest. A 1972 study of preferred ethnic terms among Spanish-speaking and Spanish-surnamed people in Albuquerque found that *Chicano* was already the second most popular term after *Spanish-American.* Among females 54 percent thought of themselves as *Spanish-American* and 23 percent as *Chicano,* but among males both terms were preferred by 38 percent. A generational difference also appeared, with 48 percent of those twenty years of age or younger preferring *Chicano,* but only 15 percent of those forty-one and over. In part this was a regional variation of the generation gap then opening over the issues of the Viet Nam War and the counterculture.[30]

The contemporaneous American Indian Movement (AIM) also developed a rhetoric and mythology to unify Indians from different cultures in political struggle. The shared experience of conquest, repression, reservations, boarding schools, and the classification together as "Indians" laid the foundation for this shared identity. The new term *Native American* asserted an inherent chronological priority to the land, while the concept of Mother Earth paralleled Aztlán.[31]

HISPANICS AND AFFIRMATIVE ACTION

A clash in terminology, such as that between *Spanish-American* and *Chicano,* surfaces political issues and makes academic scholars nervous, because it forces them to abandon their carefully cultivated stance of objectivity. When forced to choose, most opted for a variant of the Spanish terminology—*Hispanic.* Although it began as an adjective, as in *Hispanic culture,* it became a noun, *Hispanics.* While some claim that the term is used solely to describe the shared cultural roots of the varied Spanish-speaking populations in the United States, it often also implies Spanish ancestry.[32]

The term *Hispanic* was also widely adopted by the mass media and governmental agencies during the mid-1970s; by the time of the 1980 U.S. census, it became the primary identifier for the entire Spanish-heritage population. By the early 1980s, its adoption as a self-referent allowed people to put aside the generational and political differences that had characterized the previous terminology. As sociologist Felipe Gonzáles has observed, *Hispanic* served to unite Spanish-speaking and Spanish-surnamed populations throughout the Southwest and the country, in contrast to *Spanish-American,* which had distinguished a long-time population from more recent Mexican immigrants. *Hispanic,* unlike *Spanish-American,* was not employed primarily by political conservatives but by liberal, middle-class advocates of affirmative action. The Hispano

Chamber of Commerce joined with the American GI Forum and the League of Latin American Citizens (LULAC) to form the Hispanic Coalition, while Hispanic caucuses sprang up in the U.S. Congress and a wide range of professional and academic organizations. The local history of the self-identification *hispano* facilitated the adoption of the English term *Hispanic* in New Mexico.[33]

Criticisms of the term *Hispanic* began in earnest about 1987, however, in the scholarly discussion of 1990 census terminology. The major criticisms of *Spanish-American*, of course, carry over: *Hispanic* ignores the important Indian heritage of those in the Southwest, and in this suppression, it is implicitly racist. "It's like a whitewash that the government has come up with to make us more acceptable" said film producer Moctesuma Esparza in a 1990 round-table discussion in Los Angeles. Psychologist Gloria Romero (whose parents are from New Mexico) added, "The further we are from being Indian, the more acceptable we are and the fewer claims we have on this native land."[34]

Argentina-born sociologist Martha E. Giménez also points out that the term *Hispanic* lumps together a heterogeneous population that consists of six different groups: "two minority groups (people of Mexican and Puerto Rican descent), and four immigrant populations (Cubans, Central American refugees, Central American immigrants, and South American immigrants)." Cuban and South American immigrants, in particular, often are well-educated and arrive with capital to start businesses. Recent Mexican and Central American immigrants, by comparison, are economic refugees primarily drawn from the lower class, who often arrive in the United States destitute.[35]

Many Hispanic leaders find political strength in numbers. But if the object of affirmative action is to redress past injustices against Puerto Ricans and Mexican-Americans, Giménez argues, then it is inappropriate to count middle-class Cuban and South Americans in affirmative action totals under the inclusive category "Hispanic": "This situation is politically counterproductive; it sets the basis for political opportunism,

163

it strengthens the perception of people in racial terms, and because it minoritizes for-eign technical workers, scientists, and professionals, it creates a misleading appear-ance of minority advancement." The route to better social science research and better social policy making, she argues, lies in being more precise about the specific sub-groups within the Hispanic population and about the socioeconomic factors, as dis-tinct from ethnic-racial ones, that effect their lives. The specter of affirmative action reverse discrimination has been evoked by Republicans since 1980 to drive a wedge between working-class Whites and the Democratic party, further politicizing the issue and heightening racial-ethnic tensions.[36]

In New Mexico and across the United States, the legal recognition of ethnic iden-tity as the basis for the political allocation of resources has strengthened our perceptions of each other in racial-ethnic terms. Indeed proponents of affirmative action in New Mexico often employ the rhetoric of triculturalism. Because Indians and Hispanics are both considered minorities, affirmative action is not incompatible with the Chicano recognition of a dual Indian and Spanish heritage. The political use of affir-mative action, however, favors the continued suppression of the history of Hispanic-Anglo intermarriage.[37]

Tourism and Ethnic Identity

Eighty years of actively promoting tourism has given Santa Fe a more highly developed set of historical-cultural symbols than most communities. The reconstruction of ethnic identity for tourist consumption, argues anthropologist Dean McCannell, "represents an end to the dialogue, a final freezing of ethnic imagery which is both artificial and deterministic. . . [groups] begin to use their former colorful ways both as commodities to be bought and sold, and as rhetorical weaponry in their dealings with one another . . ." Since 1980s tourism in Santa Fe has not only continued to generate ethnic sym-bols, but the explosion of the tourist economy and the immigration of Anglos to Santa Fe has increased competition for jobs and housing, thereby intensifying ethnic frictions.[38]

The people whose cultures and history provide the attractions for cultural tourism destinations such as Santa Fe typically receive few of the economic benefits. Most tourist dollars are spent on clothing, luggage, plane tickets, car rentals, and rooms in hotels owned by outside investors. Newcomers to Santa Fe established many of the galleries and restaurants that reaped profits from the 1980s tourist boom, while overeducated Anglos flooded the job market. This was countered somewhat by state, county, city, and school personnel systems that favor the hiring of long-time residents. However, the state's per capita income and as a result, government salaries, consistently rank in the bottom five, along with the states of the Deep South.

People with minimum-wage tourism service jobs and modest state salaries could no longer afford to live in chic Santa Fe, and many moved out. Some found affordable property 15 or 20 miles away, while others resigned themselves to the 130-mile round-trip commute from Albuquerque. So despite a birth rate more than double that of non-Hispanic Whites, the Hispanic population of the city remained steady at about 26,500 from 1970 to 1990, while the Anglo population nearly doubled, from under 14,000 to over 27,000, boosted primarily by immigration. This one fact—that the Anglo population surpassed that of Hispanics for the first time in the 1990 census—is now frequently cited as confirmation that Hispanics have been dispossessed.[39]

Resentment over this dislocation is often articulated in ethnic terms. "What we did was 'We painted our downtown brown and moved the brown people out,'" proclaimed city councilor Debbie Jaramillo, in 1991. "Our culture and traditions are facing extinction, our young people are not being given the skills with which to make a good living." "Let's see if the wealthy neighbor or developers will create a trust fund that will cover . . . inflated tax rates," wrote poet and newspaper columnist Orlando Romero. "That's the great American tragedy and for us Hispanics who have loved, lived and stubbornly stayed on this land for hundreds of years, there is no migration, no place to go, no other choice. This is our land and our home." Only four of the thirty-eight irrigation ditches functioning in 1914 remain even partially in operation today, but a mural of the *acequia madre* (the main, or mother ditch) was painted in city hall in 1989, and Jaramillo and neighborhood activists have made the spring cleaning of this ditch into a political event.[40]

Debbie Jaramillo was a secretary in state government when she headed the opposition to a road-widening project through her neighborhood and was elected to the city council in 1988. Her program (and rhetoric) "attempts to stop the rampant development that has transformed the city for the benefit of a few developers and the new rich arrivals." As her proposals for affordable housing, better education, jobs, and small-business loans began to emerge, she increasingly urged their necessity not for Hispanics, but for local residents. While prodevelopment mayor Sam Pick toured the nation promoting Santa Fe cologne, Jaramillo nurtured alliances with Santa Fe's burgeoning neighborhood movement, which included many Anglos. From a lone critical voice in 1988, she was first joined on the city council by a majority favoring socially responsible controlled growth, and in 1994 she won her second campaign for mayor.[41]

In her keynote address to the 1992 Santa Fe Chamber of Commerce annual banquet, then councilor Jaramillo called Santa Fe "a playground of the rich and comfortable," and observed that because of the rising cost of housing, "many residents—a large number of them Hispanics—are crowded into trailer parks on the edge of town"; she warned that "the city's glaring economic disparities could result in the rioting that recently tore Los Angeles apart." But what some saw as an accurate characterization of social conditions coupled with a perhaps overblown evocation of the Los Angeles riots, others saw as an outright "threat of a race riot," made by "a racist who panders to the fears of her constituency," and who is akin to a Black mayor of Detroit "who started out preaching the gospel of hate and fear, of class conflict, of 'Us Against Them', of the Haves versus the Have-nots." One of her supporters responded that "she represents not just an elite few but low-income people of all races," while also acknowledging that "she recognizes that deteriorization in the Hispanic culture." So

Jaramillo and others have increasingly tried to frame the confrontation as an economic class issue, even through ethnic undertones remain strong.[42]

A 1992 video about the annual Santa Fe Fiesta by Diane Reyna, a local news videographer and Pueblo Indian, and Jenette DeBouzek, a folklorist who moved to Santa Fe in 1988, attracted sharp criticism from Spanish-American historians. In my estimation the video is a fitting portrait of the vitality and importance of this annual community-wide celebration, which also raises important social issues in an understated, nonsensational way. One issue is the historical fallacy that the Spanish reconquest, which is being celebrated, was bloodless; another is the hurtful stereotyping of Indians as painted savages during the Fiesta historical reenactment that year. A study guide accompanying the video and small group viewings in living rooms across the city were specifically designed to foster reasoned discussion and reconciliation.[43]

University of New Mexico historians Robert Himmerich y Valencia and Joseph P. Sanchez, among others attacked the video, charged that it perpetuates the Black Legend—the propaganda generated by the Dutch and English beginning in the sixteenth century, which portrayed the Spanish as evil, fanatical, haughty, cruel, and cowardly, stereotypes that continue to underlie many contemporary prejudices against Hispanics. These critics, however, wrongly equate the video's attempt to make people more aware of the functioning of ethnic stereotypes with a desire to perpetuate those stereotypes and engender animosities. The critics' response is understandable, nevertheless, given the controversy surrounding the Columbian Quincentenary celebration, some of which did border on the Black Legend, and given the widespread (often unconscious) Anglo racism toward Hispanics, coupled with the veneration of Pueblo Indians.[44]

Perhaps the person who has most eloquently addressed the damaging effects of historical amnesia and ethnic stereotyping is Joseph Villegas, a community leader from La Cieneguilla, a small village downriver from Santa Fe, currently pressured by real estate development. "Whether you are Spanish or Mexican," he said at a public meeting late in 1991,

167

Puerto Rican, Aztec, Mescalero, Pueblo, Black or White, racism
has no place in our world and is death to our cultures. We have to
teach our children what is morally right instead of what is conve-
nient, easy stereotyping of other people to make us feel better
about ourselves. . . . Much of what we learned in school about our
history is lies. . . . It has taken much soul-searching to be able to
weed out fiction from fact. The truth is that the Spanish people
who came to this continent did injustices to our fellow brother
Indians who lived here. . . . And if we deny it, then we are teaching
our children that it is alright. Is this what we want to teach our
children—that we have the right to impose our ways on another
culture? How do we feel when the dominant culture tries to
impose its ways on us? Por que no dejamos a las otras culturas en
paz? . . . Where there is no truth there is no healing. . . . We want
to think and act and behave in new ways that make us proud of
ourselves for the right reasons. . . . I know who I am. I am Joseph
Lorenzo Villegas, and I am a Mexicano. My son Joseph Jr. will say
the same. Somos Mexicanos. And we will be working with our
Indian brothers, as well as our Anglo brothers, for we have brothers everywhere, all over the world.[45]

How many Anglos have had the courage to say the same to themselves about the
American history of racism toward Indians and Blacks and Mexicans and Asians, and
about the imposition of Anglo-American values from the U.S.–Mexican War to the
English Only movement?

INTERLUDE:
COYOTE CONSCIOUSNESS

Harmony, order, purity—the desire for these qualities has surfaced again and again over the past two centuries, in psychic reaction to rapid social change. We draw park boundaries around fragments of nature, then cultivate the comforting illusion that they contain wildernesses uncontaminated by humankind. Similarly in designated historic districts, we camouflage new buildings as old; we bury utility wires and prohibit garish business signs, all to create harmonious, preindustrial fantasy worlds. In our

102. "COYOTE," WATERCOLOR, LUIS JIMÉNEZ, 1993.

social relations, we often overstate the purity of our ethnic, racial, or national group, while overlooking evidence of cultural interaction and substantial intermarriage. Pushed to the extreme, this desire leads to ethnic cleansing. New Mexico's rhetoric of tricultural harmony, to take our more benign example, overstates the purity and separateness of Indian, Hispano and Anglo.

To balance our need for harmony, order, and purity, we might cultivate an appreciation of complexity, the hybrid, and the creative flux of culture meeting culture. A realistic acknowledgment of cultural interaction and racial mixing can complement the positive aspects of ethnic identity and help hold the negative ones in check. Santa Fe (and other modern societies) might begin by giving equal standing in public symbols, rhetoric, and ideology to the cultural and racial hybrid. Consider, for instance, the potential of the mythic figure representing the marginal, the intermediate, and the mixed with the longest history and deepest resonances in New Mexico—Coyote.

In Navajo, Pueblo, and Apache mythologies, Coyote often appears as a cross between a socially marginal trickster and a Promethean culture hero. Coyote not only shows the limits of acceptable social behavior by transgressing them, but by incessant curiosity he also discovers fire and gives it to humans, puts fish in the rivers, and releases stars into the sky. Coyote's wild enthusiasm gets him into one ridiculous fix after another; it even gets him killed. But he always springs back to life, and new ideals spring immediately into his mind. He is both animal-like and godlike, subhuman and superhuman. He shows what life would be like without social restraint and what it was like before culture (as uncivilized peoples or unsocialized infants). But Coyote also offers a glimpse of alternative ways of living, an opening through which we might pass. Many Native American traditions recognize that a raw, creative vitality permeates the uncharted terrain where Coyote roams.[1]

103. "COYOTE DANCING," WATERCOLOR, HARRY FONSECA, 1982.

The ethnic term *coyote* is itself the product of cultural interaction: a Nahuatl (Aztec) word for a New World animal that was incorporated into Spanish and later, English. In colonial times, *coyote* was a mildly derogatory term for a person of mixed Spanish-Indian ancestry, who might be darker-skinned or less acculturated to Spanish ways than a mestizo. In Spanish slang, a coyote can also be a confidence man or a smuggler. In the late 1800s, the ethnic term was extended to those of mixed Hispano-Anglo ancestry. In New Mexico today, poet John Brandi explains, a coyote is a person who "knows a lot about either side of his heritage, enough to get by securely in each world; & to get away with a hell of a lot in between." Many Native American and Spanish associations clearly derive from the behavior of coyotes —wily scavengers at the edges of livestock herds or human settlements. Naturalists who study coyotes say that in different environments they can seem like different species, so great is their adaptability.[2]

Many people move between cultures, whether because of mixed parentage or the exigencies of the multicultural societies in which they live. Others move to the social fringes out of rebellion against authority or an attraction to the Other. By the nature of human reproduction, we are all mixed-bloods, half-breeds, coyotes. If we are to overcome the us-them dichotomy and resist our human impulse to project negative stereotypes onto other ethnic groups and nations, we must confront and come to terms with our coyote nature. This internal personal reconciliation, along with an honest acknowledgment of the history of inter-mixing, can facilitate tolerance and the development of shared grounds for unified social action. It falls to our poets, artists, and philosophers to give this psychic and social reconciliation a mythic expression.

Native American writers, who have grown ever more numerous and powerful since the 1960s, tap into their oral traditions, frequently revitalizing trickster figures—Raven, Crow, Raccoon, Magpie, and above all, Coyote. He (or she) is a "trickster, transformer, clown, creator," "irrepressibly energetic and apparently unkillable," "given to playful disguises and shape-shifting," "a transformer of reality." "Most typical of the figure is its stamina, curiosity, and malleability," writes Bo Schöler in his introduction to

171

a survey of Native American literature entitled *Coyote Was Here*. "Coyote is continually
changing, growing, moving, returning,
always adding new meaning and making
new things possible. No matter how great
the losses he suffers or how many times he is
defeated, he doggedly keeps returning. Who
can kill a dream?" Native writers, like Coyote,
are dispossessed, driven from their land.
They too seek to create something new,
something sacred and vital, something that
will stand against the materialism of mainstream consumer society. Santa Clara poet
and potter Nora Naranjo-Morse spots Coyote
at New York's Kennedy Airport, "slick/tight
down to his Tony Lamas," "smiling when a
pretty women passed him," "making calculations from behind/the *New York Times*."[3]

Coyote, the wandering rogue, reveled in
the good times of the 1970s and early

1980s. He schemed and profaned his way
through the writings of such Indian and
non-Indian writers as Peter Blue Cloud,
Simon J. Ortiz, Gary Snyder, Peter Coyote,
Pancho Aquila, and John Gardner, and
materialized in the art of T. C. Cannon,
Roberto Marquez, Joseph Beuys, Luis
Jiménez, and Naranjo-Morse. Harry
Fonseca's exuberant Coyote jukes his way
through the modern world, changing from
business suit to a Hollywood sheik's head-
dress to motorcycle leathers.[4]

Howling Coyote first appeared in its classic form about 1982 and emerged as the
cliche-icon of Santa Fe style about 1986,
thanks in large part to the work of Hispanic
wood carvers David Alvarez and Alonzo
Jiménez. Their mentor, Felipe Archuleta,
had long carved whimsical and sometimes
menacing animals—not only rabbits, skunks
and house cats, but also rhinos, giraffes, and
cheetahs. For all the recognition he received
late in life from museums, collectors and art
dealers, noted Christine Mather, "Archuleta
stubbornly refuses to be bought out or in, to
change his lifestyle, be gracious, or even
friendly." Alvarez and Jiménez, by comparison, catered to the tourist market with a

104. "A Well-Traveled Coyote," ceramic, Nora Naranjo-Morse,
Winter 1987.

stylized Howling Coyote, which they produced in large numbers. By the end of the
decade, Howling Coyote statues and T-shirts
filled tourist shops throughout the
Southwest and around the country. Given
Coyote's well-known licentiousness and the
long cross-cultural history of tricksters
depicted with erections (Hermes, Kokopelli), a Freudian would quickly interpret
the form of Howling Coyote as an erect

phallus. But this is a cartoon coyote, with no
danger or lust in his howl, a coyote
rendered harmless by the addition of a
fringed kerchief or a coat of turquoise or
fuchsia—*the* colors of 1980s Santa Fe style.[5]

Preceding Howling Coyote into the pantheon of American kitsch were the cigar
store Indian, the black cast-iron stable boy,
the Mexican dozing under his sombrero, the
Naughty Nellie boot jack, and the armless

105. "White Sports Coat with Pink Carnation," Harry Fonseca,
acrylic on canvas, about 1990.

Venus di Milo. We have learned to censor such overt racist and sexist projections, in this case displacing them onto an animal form. The 1990s advertising campaign for the new Coyote Tequila, apparently aimed at young men, resurfaced much that was repressed in Howling Coyote. In one advertisement, a coyote, silhouetted against the sky, howls over a coy señorita. An Eve of the Desert, she sits in her bright fiesta dress under a lime tree. In the foreground, her framed portrait and a rose (mercifully, not clenched in her teeth) sit to one side, and to the other, a bottle of Coyote Tequila and a breast-shaped Margarita glass. To my ear, the main caption, "Legend has it that the man who created Coyote had a sister named Margarita," echoes the salacious border-town stereotype, "Hey buddy, twenty dollars for a good time with my sister." (The marketing division for Seagram's, which distributes Coyote Tequila, adamantly denies any manipulation of such stereotypes, and understandably also denied permission to reproduce their ad here after seeing this discussion).[6]

Howling Coyote's popularity as a tourist icon peaked in the early 1990s, its place as the reigning curio cliche taken by Kokopelli, the hump-backed flute player. An image that has appeared widely in Southwestern rock art since about A.D. 700, Kokopelli derives his name from a contemporary Hopi kachina with similar attributes. The image came north from Mexico, probably with the traders who also carried sacks of corn, beans, and squash seeds on their backs. In oral traditions, Kokopelli's hump contains seeds, blankets, and babies. After his spring visit, crops begin to grow, and maidens' bellies begin to swell. The beguiling song of his flute complements the potency of his prominent phallus. Again, as with Howling Coyote, the cloying Puritan sensibility intercedes to repress Kokopelli's fertilizing, hybridizing essence, by omitting his erection. In displaced compensation, the insect-like antennae that appear occasionally in rock art Kokopellis blossom as latter-day Plains Indian headdresses.[7]

Can regional cultures survive being turned into sanitized cliches of themselves? In the face of this relentless consumption of cultural images, local cultures (the Other, the outsider, the oppositional) have little choice but to constantly recreate themselves

175

106. CARVED AND PAINTED WOODEN SNAKES BY PAUL LUTONSKY, AND COYOTES BY ALONZO JIMÉNEZ, 1985. (PHOTO: MARK NOHL, COURTESY DAVIS MATHER FOLK ART GALLERY)

107. "HANDCRAFTED FOLKART BROCHURE," SANTA FE COUNTRY FURNITURE STORE, LATE 1980S.

in terms that undermine and challenge the acquisitive, trivializing mechanisms of mainstream, commodity culture. Can we afford to abandon Coyote, Kokopelli, and other localized symbols of creativity and cross-fertilization to mass culture trivialization? How can they be revived and other images developed?

In *Borderlands/La Frontera: The New Mestiza,* Gloria Anzaldúa meditates on the experience of straddling cultural, psychological, sexual, and spiritual boundaries. A visionary Chicana poet and lesbian born on the Texas side of the Rio Grande, Anzaldúa tells us that "being a writer feels very much like being a Chicana or being queer—a lot of squirming, coming up against all sorts of walls. Or its opposite: nothing definite or defined, a boundless, floating state of limbo. . . . Living in a state of psychic unrest, in a Borderland, is what makes poets write and artists create." This personal struggle with contradictions, this juggling of one's identities, like the crossing of genetic streams, yields hybrid vigor. It also fosters tolerance for contradictions and ambiguity and an acceptance of the negative shadow in one's subconscious—those repressed desires and guilty feelings that are so prone to projection onto others.[8]

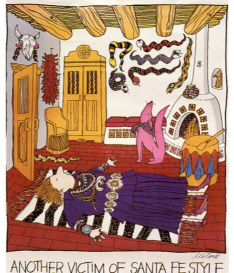

ANOTHER VICTIM OF SANTA FE STYLE

"The work takes place underground—subconsciously," Anzaldúa writes, ". . . where the mestiza stands, is where phenomena tend to collide. It is where the possibility of uniting all that is separate occurs. . . . [The result] is a new consciousness—a mestiza consciousness—and though it is a source of intense pain, its energy comes from continual creative motion that keeps breaking down the unitary aspect of each new paradigm. . . . Because the future depends on breaking down paradigms, it depends on the straddling of two or more cultures. . . ." The work of *mestiza* consciousness is to break down the subject-object duality that keeps her prisoner and to show in the flesh and through the images in her work how duality is transcended. The answer to the problem between the white race and the colored, between males and females, lies in healing the split that originates in the very

177

108. OUTDOOR DISPLAY, FRANK SECKLER STUDIO, 1995. (AUTHOR)

109. "ANOTHER VICTIM OF SANTA FE STYLE," JEROME L. MILORD, 1989.
(COURTESY LEWIS E. THOMPSON PRODUCTIONS)

foundation of our lives, our culture, our languages, our thoughts."

For Anzaldúa the new mestiza epitomizes the modern struggle with opposites because of her mixed race and culture and her feminist confrontation with sexism. But we all confront this inner struggle, "Chicano, indio, American Indian, mojado, mexicano, immigrant Latino, Anglo in power, working class Anglo, Black, Asian." Awareness of our history and of contemporary social conditions precedes inner changes. After all, she writes, "Nothing happens in the 'real' world unless it first happens in the images in our heads."[9]

Anzaldúa equates this psychic reconciliation of contradictions to the fearsome Aztec figure, *la Coatlicue* (quet-lee-quey). Two rattlesnakes form her head, around which hangs a necklace of hands and hearts. This Medusa-like earth goddess, who also wears a skirt of snakes and a belt clasped by a skull with living eyes, unites dualities in a creative, life-renewing tension: creator-destroyer, life-death, womb-tomb, blood spilled on the ground and blood pulsing through our veins. "It is this learning to live with *la Coatlicue* that transforms living in the

Borderlands from a nightmare into a numinous experience."[10]

Among a number of artists exploring mixed identities in the mid-1990s, Anita Rodríguez of Taos possesses a particular verve. Her vibrant pallet, Baroque richness of pattern, and people with their bones and thereby their mortality laid bare in the manner of nineteenth-century newspaper illustrator José Posada declare strong ties with Mexico. When closed, one series of "nichos" displays traditional Hispanic, Christian themes, but when opened reveals a crypto-Jewish heritage that some scholars and northern New Mexicans believe continued surreptitiously after the repression of the Spanish Inquisition. A confirmation opens to a bar mitzvah, a Christmas Las Posadas procession opens on a Hanukkah celebration, or a baptism opens to show the same infant undergoing the ritual circumcision of the *brit milah*. Other of Rodríguez's works contrast contemporary and traditional identities—a low rider swoops past the front of a church resembling the one at Ranchos de Taos. But in each work, the multiple identities are simultaneous, and not ultimately contradictory.[11]

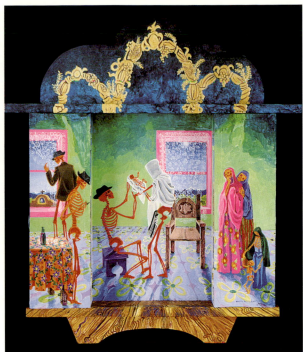

By its very nature, Coyote-Mestiza-hybrid culture is not structured; it is the opposite of a pure cultural heritage or a distinct ethnic identity. There are no rules for Coyote behavior, no Coyote skin color or facial type. Coyote has no pedigree, nor does she want one. As a dweller *en la Frontera,* in a flexible state of opposition and agitated contradiction, Coyote passes under many names and answers to none. Coyotes are regionalists: adaptable and alive to human and natural environments, they read body language and weather in the clouds. Coyotes who see this may laugh at such earnest attempts to flush them into the open. But as the Chicano movement showed, to overcome an epithet (or a trivializing tourist icon) you must put it on as a badge of honor, as a challenge to stereotypes, as a call to organize.

Today Native, Latino, and Anglo America meet and intermingle all along the Mexico-United States border. While Indians, Mexican-Americans, and Mexicans typically learn English out of economic necessity, most of us Anglos in New Mexico have done little to meet our Indian and Hispanic neighbors. Living in an adobe house or wearing Indian jewelry counts for little in this equation. It would help for all children in the border states to learn both Spanish and English, along with healthy doses of Native American, Mexican, Chicano, and American culture and history. Such a study of history, languages, and other cultures may help Anglo-America to overcome the

110. "Secret Rites of Passage," closed, acrylic on board and masonite, Anita Rodríguez, 1995.

111. "Secret Rites of Passage," opened, acrylic on board and masonite, Anita Rodríguez, 1995.

terrible legacy from projecting its profaned, dark, other self onto Indians and Mexicans, or for that matter, onto Asian and African Americans. The best way to exorcise racism from our hearts may be for Americans to become multilingual and multicultural, to let go of the comforting but ethnocentric belief that "we live in the greatest country God ever put on this earth," and learn to live the ambiguous lives of mestizas and coyotes in the borderlands of the modern world.[12]

In Santa Fe those who move between cultures, or stand in opposition to mainstream values, or depart from sexual norms, or marry outside their ethnic group, or are of mixed parentage—in other words, those who are in some sense part Coyote—pre-

dominate. Not everyone who is marginal or mixed has Coyote consciousness, of course, for many people shift effortlessly and unconsciously from one cultural context to another, while others seek the comfort afforded by the emphasis of one side of their identity. But the sometimes painful struggle to bridge cultures, to reconcile conflicting identities, to contain both us *and* them in oneself, can provoke insights into the ambiguities of life and society— insights that can sustain tolerance. This is one way to learn to love thy enemy as thyself. So here's to harmony among the four cultures of Santa Fe: Native American, Hispano, Anglo, and Coyote.

112. "SANTA FE PLAZA, APRIL, 1995," ORIGINAL CHROME, MIGUEL GANDERT.

FROM FIESTA TO
FOURTH OF JULY

Following the approval of statehood by congress, Santa Fe staged a magnificent reenactment of the Spanish reconquest as part of the 1911 Fourth of July celebration. The
wave of enthusiasm released by the ceremonies implementing statehood the following January also triggered the 1912 city plan and the *New-Old Santa Fe* exhibit that
November. The conquest pageant was repeated in 1912, then lapsed. As Santa Fe style
buildings began to provide a convincing backdrop after World War I, the entire population donned regional costumes to reenact historical dramas in a new annual Fiesta.

Santa Fe's rich history of parades and celebrations stretches back centuries. The
key Catholic processions of the Spanish and Mexican periods, Corpus Christi and La
Conquistadora, continue with great vitality to this day. After the American occupation, newcomers acting through their fraternities took the lead in organizing a parallel set of public observances—Fourth of July, Decoration Day (later called Memorial
Day), and the inauguration of governors. This dual system of public ceremonies at
the end of the nineteenth century (Catholic religious processions and the Protestant-
and Jewish-dominated secular celebrations) paralleled the split in the city's promotional image between historic traditions and progressive efforts to Americanize. After
statehood was granted in 1912 and the divided promotional image resolved into a
single romantic identity, the separate religious and civic celebrations too were eclipsed
by the community-wide Fiesta.

181

**Proclamation from the Spanish Archives of
New Mexico, 1712**
In the Villa of Santa Fe, on the sixteenth day
of the month of September of the year seven-
teen hundred and twelve, gathered and met
together in the house of residence of the
General, Juan Paez Hurtado, Lieutenant
Governor and Captain General, . . . the pur-
pose being that, recalling how this Villa had
been conquered on the Fourteenth day of
September of the past year of sixteen hun-
dred and ninety-two by the General Don
Diego de Vargas Zapata Lujan Ponce de Leon,
Marquis of La Nava de Brazinas, and that in
twenty years no fiesta had been observed, as this
Villa should have, in honor of the Salutary

Blood of Our Redemption, and so that in the future the said fourteenth day be celebrated, with Vespers, Mass, sermon, and procession through the Main Plaza, . . . it is our will that it be celebrated for all time, a Fiesta in honor of the Exaltation of the Holy Cross. . . . [Signed by nine community leaders.][1]

"Christmas Passed,"
The Weekly New Mexican (January 2, 1864)
As the natural darkness of night sets in, the whole city and the suburbs around light up with a blaze of light. This is in commemoration of the light which shone around the shepherds, the night of the birth of Jesus of Nazareth. Every catholic prepares, before the night is ushered in, a sufficient supply of the driest and most flammable of wood, to make

piles in front and upon the roof of his house. The churches and their spires, are covered with candles, piles of light wood or other means of making a sudden illumination. . . . the glow and splendor of the light which follows, is at once animating, beautiful and grand.

"Corpus Cristi,"
The Daily New Mexican (June 20, 1870):
In the morning the cathedral was filled with an immense concourse of people, Bishop Lamy in person celebrating high mass. At 12 o'clock M, a procession was formed of the teachers and pupils of the Catholic schools of Santa Fe, followed by a dense crowd of people of both sexes . . . moving north to the house of Maj. Sena, passed thence to and around the plaza and back to the Church

113. CORPUS CHRISTI PROCESSION IN FRONT OF THE PALACE OF THE GOVERNORS, ABOUT 1870.

through San Francisco street. Several of our citizens had erected in front of their residences, tastefully ornamented altars, at each of which the procession halted, and appropriate services were performed by the Bishop, who occupied a position midway of the procession under a magnificent canopy. . . . The ceremonies attracted a very large number of spectators who with the participants filled and crowded the streets and all available standing room along the route of the procession.

From *The Daily New Mexican* (June 27, 1870): On Yesterday (Sunday) the image of the Virgin was taken from the cathedral and carried with great pomp and impressive and imposing ceremonies to the Capilla of the Virgin del Rosario, which is situated about a half mile north west of the city. There was a procession of the pupils of the schools which are under the management of the Catholic Church, attended by a brass band; and a very large number of persons of both sexes and all ages joined in the procession.

CATHOLIC PROCESSIONS

The Corpus Christi celebration in Santa Fe, which is tied in the Catholic liturgical calendar to Trinity Sunday, takes place in May or June with a mass in the cathedral, followed by a procession through the streets (fig. 113). In the late nineteenth century, the procession paused at various temporary altars erected at the Palace of the Governors and under the portales of leading Hispanic residents. Jose D. Sena, who prepared an elaborate altar each year, was a leading cultural intermediary, besides being a devout Catholic. Sena organized a company of New Mexico volunteers during the Civil War, becoming a major, a title he would carry through an active political career. At campaign rallies and public celebrations, Sena was renowned as an orator in both Spanish and English.[2]

The procession of La Conquistadora on the Sunday following Corpus Christi transports the statue of Our Lady of the Conquest from the Cathedral, westward past the plaza out San Francisco Street, and on to Rosario Chapel. There she remains for a series of nine daily masses before being returned by the same route. La Conquistadora, a statue of Our Lady of the Assumption (its designation was later changed to Our Lady of the Rosary and recently to Our Lady of Peace) traveled north from Mexico to New Mexico in 1625, and by 1665, a lay fraternity had been established to foster veneration of her. Refugees of the 1680 Pueblo Revolt carried La Conquistadora south to Guadalupe del Norte (present-day Juárez, Mexico). During the "peaceful" 1692 reconquest of New Mexico, the statue stayed behind, while Diego de Vargas and his men marched behind a banner of Our Lady of Remedies. La Conquistadora finally returned to Santa Fe with Vargas, during the bloody reconquest of 1693.[3]

The Conquistadora processions reputedly trace their origin to 1712, when Santa Fe's leading men (veterans of Vargas's company) issued a proclamation calling for an annual celebration of the 1692 reconquest, "with Vespers, Mass, sermon and procession through the Main Plaza" (although this proclamation makes no mention of La Conquistadora). How long this celebration was observed is unclear, although the fraternity and probably the processions lapsed for a time in the mid-1700s. Both were revived in 1770 and have been active continuously since. The celebration of La Conquistadora was shifted from September to June sometime during the poorly documented 1700s. The processions were also extended beyond the plaza to Vargas's reputed reconquest campsite, northwest of town, where Rosario Chapel was built in 1806.[4]

During the Spanish and Mexican periods, these religious processions expressed community-wide religious devotion. As a celebration particular to Santa Fe, La Conquistadora also expressed civic identity. The religious aspect of the parades ceased to be universal with the arrival of Anglo-Americans, but as a result, they took on new significance as expressions of Spanish-Mexican ethnic identity. What anthropologist Ronald Grime wrote about the Conquistadora processions in the 1970s applies equally to the Corpus Christi processions of the 1870s: "They symbolically take possession of what already 'really belongs to us.' Moving through the civic center of the town, the plaza is a way of declaiming symbolically that the event is of citywide, not merely churchwide, significance."[5]

FRATERNITIES AND PUBLIC PROCESSIONS

Most newcomers to Santa Fe after the American occupation in 1846 were single men. They banded together in fraternities, primarily the Masons, the Odd Fellows, and the Grand Army of the Republic (GAR). Although the Masons and Odd Fellows were open to all men, a papal prohibition prevented Catholics, and thus most Hispanos, from joining. As a result these fraternities fostered political and economic alliances among Jewish merchants and Anglo-Protestant attorneys and territorial officials. The GAR, by comparison, was open to northern veterans of the Civil War, and thus had both Anglo and Hispano members. All five Spiegelberg brothers, along with Zadok Staab, Louis Felsenthal, Bernard Seligman, and other German Jewish merchants were active Masons, as were leading boosters such as Territorial Secretary William Ritch and *New Mexican* editor and Republican party boss Max Frost.[6]

The Masons and Odd Fellows were small bastions of American culture in Santa Fe. They offered the new arrivals companionship and an opportunity to form business contacts. Mutual aid programs, burial plots in the fraternal cemetery, and insurance benefits attracted men who had left their social support networks behind them. Their meetings were dominated by secret initiation rituals that embodied moral and spiritual lessons in the symbolism of gradually revealed mysteries. Fraternities often demonstrated their presence through plaza celebrations and parades. Funeral processions for their members formed in the plaza (fig. 114). Americans (which in local terminology was often extended to include northern European immigrants) also dominated Decoration Day parades, which flourished throughout the country following the Civil War. Their answer to the religious processions of June was the Fourth of July parade, which formed in the plaza, followed various routes through the town, invariably passed in front of the cathedral, and returned to the plaza. Inaugurations, which they also typically organized, began when the population met the newly appointed governor at the edge of town (or at the depot, after the railroad arrived) and continued with a parade to the plaza for the swearing-in and speeches, in front of the Palace of the Governors.[7]

Territorial officials joined with Mexican and American businessmen to organize the Tertio-Millennial Exposition of 1883. This forty-five-day fair was meant to commemorate the 333rd (actually 343rd) anniversary of the founding of Santa Fe (actually the exploration of New Mexico by Coronado, in 1540). Designed to publicize the territory and thereby attract investors and tourist, the exhibitions of minerals and produce were complemented by horse races and Indian dances. Earlier Fourth of July processions had occasionally personified the Goddess of Liberty or Don Quixote, but the exposition reveled in three days of elaborate historical processions and reenactments (fig. 115). The arrival of Coronado's expedition and a mock battle with Pueblo Indians were followed in succeeding days by Vargas's reconquest of Santa Fe in 1692-93 and General Kearny's occupation of the city in 1846. Even as Bradford Prince and other boosters of statehood formulated the rhetoric of triculturalism, they also arranged this first public demonstration of the territory's glorious history. In his oration during the Coronado pageant, Major Jose D. Sena, "attired as a Spanish Chieftain," characterized both the conquistadors and "their descendants here gathered" as "Spaniards."[8]

114. DECORATION DAY AT THE CIVIL WAR MONUMENT ON THE PLAZA, MAY 30, 1880. (BEN WITTICK)

115. THE KNIGHTS OF CORONADO, TERTIO-MILLENNIAL EXPOSITION, 1883.

"Coronado's Cohorts,"
The New Mexican Review (July 19, 1883)
The Royal Splendor and Barbaric
Magnificence of Yesterday's Celebration
The Banner of the Cross Again Planted After
a Lapse of Three Centuries

The first of the three days of historic pageants and tableaux promised by the Tertio-Millennial exposition as representing the three centuries over which this celebration extends, was yesterday signalized by one of the most unique and resplendent parades that was ever witnessed by an American assembly . . .

The procession formed very quietly near the church of Our Lady of the Rosary, just north of the city, and wheeled into lower San Francisco street promptly at 10 o'clock. The thoroughfares, the plaza, every door, window and portal on the route was a perfect mass of expectant faces . . .

Jose D. Sena, chief marshal, attired as a Spanish chieftain in crimson, black and gold, with high boots, helmet and sword, and mounted on a spirited charger, led the pageant. He was accompanied by Hon. W. T. Thornton, president of the Knights of Coronado, who was arrayed in green satin and represented to perfection a gallant Spanish knight. Immediately following came the Thirteenth United States infantry band, playing its most thrilling airs. Then came in unique confusion, the various sections of the pageant, their appropriately inscribed banners floating triumphantly in the morning breeze. Those splendid specimens of physical manhood, the Apache chiefs, warriors and hunters, with their gleaming spears and buckskin robes adorned with beads of many hues; the Oriental and innocent looking Zunis of the sixteenth century, with bows and arrows; the sun dried and good hearted San Juan Indians; the mild mannered Pecuris with their Christ-like wreaths of native willow—made up the first section of this novel pageant, and aroused the admiration to the highest pitch by the characteristic wildness of their makeup. Next came the Spanish occupation. Following the Twenty-third United States Infantry band rode Don Felipe Delgado, representing Coronado, accompanied by Spanish court officers and a guard of twenty richly robed knights under the captaincy of Don Vicente Mares. Frank K. Chaves, as the renowned Espejo, followed with a full quota of court officers and a brilliant guard under command of Don Gabriel Martinez. Following these came Capt. Charles Conklin with a host of handsome lieutenants and a band of fifty Spanish warriors covered with gold and silver tinsel and loaded down with helmets, spears and shields that added much to the general appearance of the pageant.

The rear of the second section was brought up by half a dozen black robed priests, bearing banners in memory of the good fathers of the holy faith; who centuries ago braved the trials of this vast wilderness and first planted here the cross of the christian religion.

Camden, New Jersey, July 20, 1883
To Messrs Griffin, Martinez, Prince and other Gentlemen at Santa Fe:
Your kind invitation to visit you and deliver a poem for the 333rd Anniversary of the founding of Santa Fe has reached me so late, that I have to decline, with sincere regret. But I will say a few words off hand.

We Americans have yet to really learn our own antecedents, and sort them, to unify them. They will be found ampler than has been supposed, and in widely different sources. Thus far, impressed by New England writers and schoolmasters, we tacitly abandon ourselves to the notion that our United States have been fashioned from the British Islands only, and essentially form a second England—which is a very great mistake. . . . Today, something outside of them, and to counterbalance them is seriously needed.

The seething materialistic and business vortices of the United States, in their present devouring relations, controlling and belittling everything else, are, in my opinion, but a vast and indispensable stage in the new world's development. . . . Character, literature, a society worth the name, are yet to be established, through a nationality of noblest spiritual, heroic and democratic attributes. . . .

To that composite American identity of the future, Spanish character will supply some of the most needed parts. No stock shows a grander historic retrospect—grander in religiousness and loyalty, or for patriotism, courage, decorum, gravity and honor. (. . . It is time to realize—for it is certainly true—that there will not be found any more cruelty, tyranny, superstition, etc., in the resume of past Spanish history than in the corresponding resume of Anglo-Norman history. Nay, I think there will not be found so much.) . . . .

As to our aboriginal or Indian population—the Aztec in the South, and the many tribes in the North and West—I know it seems agreed that they must gradually dwindle as time rolls on, and in a few generations more leave only a reminiscence, a blank. But I am not at all clear about that. As America, from its many far-back sources and current supplies, develops, adapts, entwines, faithfully identifies its own—are we to see it cheerfully accepting and using all the contributions of foreign lands from the whole outside globe—and then rejecting the only ones distinctively its own—the autochthonic ones?

. . . If I might assume to do so, I would send you the most cordial heartfelt congratulations of your American fellow-countrymen here. You have more friends here in the Northern and Atlantic regions than you suppose. . . .

> Very respectfully etc.
> Walt Whitman

(Reprinted in the *Philadelphia Press*, August 5, 1883, and *El Palacio*, September 1918)

"De Vargas' Vow,"
The New Daily Mexican (June 10, 1893)
Another event in the history of the city and the Catholic church occurs tomorrow. Centuries ago, when the intrepid De Vargas reconquered the Pueblo Indians that held barbaric sway in this city, he was encamped with his forces on the present site of Rosario chapel. Before the decisive battle on the plaza that drove out the Indians and permitted the erection here of the christian banner, De Vargas made a vow promising that if victorious in his undertaking to recapture the city he would erect on the site of his camp a house of worship, and that every year his followers and their descendants should convey thither the image of the Virgin Mary. This is the significance of the beautiful procession which will form at the cathedral and proceed to the Rosario chapel tomorrow afternoon.

189

"Welcome Governor Otero,"

The New Mexican (June 14, 1897)

Hon. M. A. Otero Inaugurated as Governor of the Territory of New Mexico

The City Was Wild With Enthusiasm.

Thousands of people had gathered about the palace, where a flag-draped stand had been erected for the inaugural ceremonies, and when the procession reached this historic adobe pile, the pent up enthusiasm found relief in cheer upon cheer, until the old walls of the palace fairly shook. . . .

Never before in the history of New Mexico has a governor received so enthusiastic a reception in the capital as did Governor M. A. Otero today. Not only did the entire city turn out to greet him but many of the most prominent men of the territory, irrespective of party and politics, were present.

Upon signing the foregoing oath, in the presence of the assembled multitude, Mr. Otero spoke as follows:

Fellow Citizens: It is indeed a pleasure to me to get back into the territory of New Mexico, my native land, and meet the familiar faces of my friends—people who I believe will believe in me—people who think that I will do my duty as I believe it to be! (Applause). . . .

It is not the least of my joys to remember on this occasion that I stand before you the first native born governor of this fair territory. I am proud of the fact that I am a Mexican! (Loud and prolonged cheering). I am proud that at last it has been recognized that in one of us may be embodied the principles of true American citizenship! (Applause).

116. Inauguration parade for Governor Miguel Otero, south side of the plaza, June 14, 1897. (Phillip E. Harroun)

"Rousing Roosevelt Reception,"
Santa Fe New Mexican (May 5, 1903)
The People of New Mexico at Their Capital City Received the President With Great Fervor and True Gladness
Ringing Address Stirs The Hearts Of The People Deeply

The Presidential train arrived at the Santa Fe depot on time at 9 o'clock this morning, and a presidential salute of 21 guns was fired as the train slowed up at the station. As President Roosevelt alighted from the train, he was welcomed by Governor Otero and Mayor Sparks, who introduced the President to the city reception committee. . . .

As the parade moved on to the Capitol grounds, the 10,000 people who had gathered there cheered vociferously. The steps of the building were thronged with handsome and elegantly attired ladies and a sea of fluttering handkerchiefs greeted Mr. Roosevelt as he ascended the steps to the speaker's stand. His appearance was the signal for loud and long continued applause. He was cordially welcomed by Governor Otero who then presented him to the immense crowd.

President Roosevelt was warmly greeted and responded as follows:

"Governor, Ladies and Gentlemen, and more especially, Mr. Mayor as the chief executive of this ancient and historic city: It is with a peculiar feeling of pleasure that I come here to New Mexico, from which territory one-half and, if my memory serves me correctly, a little more than one-half of the members of my regiment [the Rough Riders] came. The man is but a poor American wherever he may have been born, to whom one part of this country is not exactly as dear as another, and I would count myself wholly unworthy of the office I hold if I did not strive to represent the people of the mountains and the plains exactly as much as those of the Mississippi valley or either coast, the Atlantic or the Pacific. I do know your people, Governor, and I need not say how fond I am of them for you know yourself. How can I help being fond of people with whom I have worked, with whom I labored and marched to battle? And there are no men here excepting the veterans of the Civil War to whom I would doff my hat quicker than to my comrades in the late [Spanish-American] war, and you know what comradeship in war means. It has always seemed to me, Governor, that in this respect my regiment was a typical American regiment.

191

117. PRESIDENT THEODORE ROOSEVELT SPEAKING ON TERRITORIAL CAPITAL STEPS, MAY, 1903.

FRATERNITY RITUAL AND HISTORICAL PAGEANTS

Although members of fraternities took prominent roles in public ceremonies and processions, most fraternal ritual occurred in private (fig. 114). The most important fraternity in Santa Fe, the Masons, began with a series of three rituals, known as degrees, performed in a local Blue Lodge. Many stopped there, but those with the inclination and resources continued in the separate lodges of the York Rite (Knights Templar) and the Scottish Rite, with its additional twenty-nine degrees. In the years following the Civil War, many fraternities were created, and the Scottish Rite greatly elaborated its rituals. The Masons' theatrical costuming, scripted speeches, and historical props portrayed Old Testament prophets and pyramid builders, medieval pilgrims, crusaders, and cathedral builders. Other fraternities ranged into Indian ceremony (such as the Improved Order of Redmen and the Order of Iroquois, developed by leading ethnographer Lewis Henry Morgan) and to Imperial Rome (the Tribe of Ben Hur, set up with the help of novelist Lew Wallace, a former New Mexico territorial governor). Many became fascinated with these rituals and joined more than one fraternity. By day they worked long hours in commerce, government, and industry; in the evening and on weekends they immersed themselves in "degree work."[9]

By the first decade of the twentieth century, Santa Fe had active lodges of the Masons (Blue Lodge), the Knights Templar, the Scottish Rite, the Odd Fellows, and the Knights of Pythias. Locally the Elks, who gave more emphasis to social activities including wives and children, had Hispanic members and served as a cultural meeting ground. By the teens, Santa Fe also had an active group of Shriners—a wing of the Masons given to public service, ritual parody, and boisterous parades (fig. 119).[10]

Members of the most ritually active of these fraternities, the Scottish Rite, dominated early Fiesta organizing committees. The core organizers of the 1911 fiesta were leading merchants Samuel Cartwright and James Seligman, both Scottish Rite Masons, and Mayor Celso López. Museum Director Edgar Hewett, the chief architect of the Fiesta's revival in 1919; Norman King, who directed the early 1920s De Vargas pageants;

118. MOORISH COSTUME FROM *LODGE SUPPLIES FOR KNIGHTS OF PYTHIAS*, PETTIBONE COMPANY, CINCINNATI, ABOUT 1900. FROM COPY IN MUSEUM OF NEW MEXICO, HISTORY LIBRARY.

192

Isaac Rapp, the architect of the new Santa Fe style; and photographer Jesse Nusbaum were all Scottish Rite Masons. With the recent experience of building a Moorish style temple, Scottish Rite members also led the 1912 City Planning Board. Harry Dorman, its chair, Sylvanus Morley, who first defined the architectural revival, former governor Miguel Otero, and merchant James Seligman were active in the Scottish Rite, while only Bronson Cutting and Marcelino Garcia were not. Thirty-third-degree Mason Fredrick Muller, veteran of the Indian Wars, captain in the Rough Riders, and long-time county treasurer as well, could be counted on to play a visible part in public ceremonies from the command of President Roosevelt's mounted escort in 1903 to the role of one of Vargas's captains in the 1920 Fiesta pageant.[11]

So popular were fraternities, especially with the emerging urban middle class, that the Catholic Church responded in 1882 by founding the Knights of Columbus, with four ritual degrees. By the early twentieth century, the Knights were active in Santa Fe, as were other fraternities whose local members were predominantly Hispanos, such as the Brotherhood of American Yeoman and the Fraternal Union of America. Active mutual aid societies included La Union Protectiva, El Auxiliar Femenil, and La Alianza Hispano-Americana, which practiced its own initiation rituals. The Alianza staged the 1911 De Vargas pageant, and all three managed the Spanish participation in the 1931

119. SHRINERS' PARADE, 1912. SHRINERS RIDING BURROS AND WEARING MIDDLE EASTERN COSTUMES, DRESSES AND PRISON STRIPES. (JESSE L. NUSBAUM)

Fiesta, while the Knights of Columbus portrayed the Franciscans in early Fiestas. The historicist spirit of the era, which produced a private absorption in fraternal ritual, burst forth in the Fiesta and Santa Fe style architecture.[12]

José D. Sena, Jr., a prominent Knight of Columbus, and George Washington Armijo, a member of both the Alianza and the Elks, led Hispanic participation in the early Fiestas. Son of the famous Santa Fe orator Major José D. Sena, Sena Junior graduated from Saint Louis University in 1885, at the age of eighteen (fig. 120). A stalwart campaigner for the Republican party, like his father, Sena served from 1897 to 1931 as clerk of the State Supreme Court. Ten years his junior, Armijo was the grandson of the powerful president of the Territorial Senate, Colonel J. Francisco Chávez (fig. 121). Educated at the Christian Brothers College in Saint Louis, Armijo served as a sergeant in the Rough Riders, was wounded in battle, and returned a hero of the Spanish-American War. His friend Theodore Roosevelt acted as godfather to his son, Theodore Roosevelt Armijo. First as a Republican and later as a Democrat, Armijo served as city councilor, school board member, county clerk, state corporation commissioner, senator, and speaker of the house. Sena and Armijo, like the senior Sena, were fluent orators in both English and Spanish, given to taking liberties when translating stump speeches to interject commentary and humor. "He was Chesterfield in English, Cervantes in Spanish," people would say of such a man. As they moved from military service into politics, to their pageant roles as conquistadors and back to their public offices, they blended American patriotism with pride in Spanish heritage.[13]

The women on the 1919 Fiesta committee—Mrs. Isaac H. Rapp, Mrs. Thomas Z. Winter, and Mrs. Napoleon B. Laughlin—often headed humanitarian and cultural organizations. The most prominent of the three, Mrs. Kate Laughlin, was born in Tennessee in 1857 and graduated from Mary Washington College, in Virginia. She met her husband, a promising attorney, in Texas, where they married in 1883 before relocating to Santa Fe for his health. While he established a lucrative practice and served a term on the Territorial Supreme Court, she crusaded for child welfare pro-

120. Mayor Nathan Jaffa, Baritone Oskenonton, Museum Director Edgar L. Hewett, Fiesta Organizer Jose D. Sena, 1925 Fiesta.

grams. As a founding member of the New Mexico Archeological Society, Mrs. Laughlin raised funds for Hewett's first excavations and helped establish the museum. All three women were active members of the Women's Board of Trade, which founded the public library. This precursor to the Santa Fe Woman's Club staged an annual fund-raising "Fiesta" on the plaza, enlivened by touches of exotica: a Japanese tea house and "gipsy . . . Princess Bokakac, the world's most reliable astrologist and palmist."[14]

The leading Indian participant in early fiestas, Santiago Naranjo of Santa Clara Pueblo, like the Senas and Armijo, was a prominent cultural intermediary (fig. 72). He guided Hewett on horseback reconnaissances of the Pajarito Plateau, and as the cook for the Frijoles Canyon and Puye excavations beginning in 1908, became friends with ethnographers Barbara Freire-Marreco and John P. Harrington. As governor of Santa Clara in 1911, 1916, 1924, and 1930, Naranjo mobilized these outside allies against the assimilationist policies of the federal Indian Bureau. He dressed like other villagers while at Santa Clara but cultivated a more picturesque image for the outside. When Naranjo put in his heavy silver earrings and began to tie up his braids with long fancy strips of rawhide, his neighbors knew he was going off to Santa Fe. Given to gambling in the evening with the other Pueblo men, he once lost his buckskin outfit. Many Santa Clarans considered him vain, self-centered, and greedy—a person who had forgotten how he was supposed to be—although few understood his outside work on behalf of the village.[15]

The immediate stimulus for the De Vargas pageant of 1911, in addition to the granting of statehood, was a national craze for historical pageants. In England between 1905 and 1910, a series of historical pageants, inspired by the Arts and Crafts movement, sought to renew a sense of community by recreating preindustrial themes and celebrations. The first American pageant, in Philadelphia in 1908, and others that quickly followed were featured in national magazines. These pageants reconciled tradition with a faith in progress, through a succession of costumed historical vignettes. Beginning with the prehistoric Indian times, a typical pageant next portrayed a city's founding, then subsequent episodes in its history, culminating with an allegorical affirmation of its future prospects. These pageants allowed the local hereditary elite, whose members played the first settlers, to assert their priority atop the local social hierarchy and to project Anglo-Saxon values as the community norms. Progressive social reformers often encouraged participation in pageants by all ethnic groups, as an affirmation of democracy and cultural pluralism.[16]

This national mania for fraternities and historical pageants found fertile soil in ancient multicultural Santa Fe. Somewhere between 15 and 40 per cent of all American men were fraternity members at the turn of the century—a reasonable estimate, too, for Santa Fe. Members of the Knights of Columbus, the Scottish Rite, the Alianza, and the Women's Board of Trade, as well as Indian intermediaries, elaborated ethnic identities and portrayed lessons of individual and civic virtue through costume, public ritual, and historical pageantry. Little wonder then that when public ceremony in Santa Fe took on a local cast, the Knights of Columbus and the Scottish Rite's Knights of the Royal Ax yielded to the Caballeros (Knights) de Vargas, while Santiago Naranjo donned a Plains Indian war bonnet before he ascended the Fiesta podium.[17]

Ruth Seligman, interviewed in 1963[18]

. . . the real idea of a town fiesta came from the Episcopal minister named James Mythen—a very brilliant young man who preached the most marvelous sermons. . . . Mr. Mythen got to talking to us and he said, "You know, I don't see why Santa Fe doesn't have some yearly historical event as they do in New Orleans at Mardi Gras. Santa Fe is so full of history."

So Jim and I were very much interested, and a few days after Mr. Mythen left [to return east], Jim asked a few men to come up to the house. We sat around our dining table, and Jim suggested that one of the best things to start with would be the reconquest by De Vargas.

The men fell for it right away. There was Sam Cartwright. I think he was president of the Chamber of Commerce, but it might have still been called the Men's Board of Trade. I'm very sure Celso López was mayor at the time.

We had the mayor, anyway, and four or five other men Jim thought might be interested.

That's how the De Vargas pageant got started. We didn't call it that; we called it the Reconquest . . . or really, we didn't call it much of anything. I think that was in 1910, though I'm not quite sure. We got Jesse Nusbaum interested. He was always a help with everything. Jesse got all the Indians to come in, and George Armijo was the first De Vargas. Of course they didn't know what sort of costumes they should wear, and his costume was too elaborate, with feathers—a plume—and all that. Soldiers having been on the road for months wouldn't be dressed like that, you know.

That's the way it started, right there in our house. In those days all the little towns had fiestas. They used to have cock fights in Agua Fria and things like that, but in Santa Fe they had only a small religious remembrance each year. For a few years we just had the De Vargas parade. . . .

It was Jimmy Mythen's idea to have some historical event and Jim Seligman's idea to have De Vargas. After a few years it was Mr. Twitchell's idea to have a fiesta—they called it the 300th or whatever year it was, but in all

the years I'd lived here we'd never before had one.

"Ho, For The Fourth Of July,"
Santa Fe New Mexican (May 29, 1911)
Work Is Progressing Favorably Upon the DeVargas Pageant
While the DeVargas pageant celebrating the re-entry of DeVargas into Santa Fe in 1692 will be a unique feature of Santa Fe's Fourth of July celebration this year, sports will not be neglected. Besides the Plaza sports in the afternoon, there will be horse-racing and a fast baseball game at the Baseball park on the Southside. . . .

In order that the DeVargas pageant, the decorated automobiles and other features of the day might not go unrecorded, Jesse Nusbaum, of the staff of the New Mexico Museum and School of American Archaeology, has been designated official photographer. He is a "cracker-jack" and his photographs have the merit of being works of art. The pictures he has taken in Guatemala and also in this city have furnished welcome illustrations in many magazines and newspapers of late years. The more reason to have your automobile decorated, for there will be some satisfaction in seeing it reproduced in more than one publication during the next year for Santa Fe's Fourth of July pageant this year will be widely commented upon for introducing the historic feature of the DeVargas pageant.

"Seventeenth Century Glory Recalled in Brilliant Pageant,"

Santa Fe New Mexican (July 5, 1911)
With glorious sunshine to make their gorgeous costumes the more dazzling and eight thousand people to cheer them, the participants in the De Vargas pageant and the parade which followed it, turned the hand of time back to the seventeenth century yesterday morning and afforded a spectacle which was unique, brilliant and tremendously pleasing. . . .

And then came the central figure in the great pageant—the man who had done more than any one citizen of Santa Fe to make it a success—the man, who, descended from the conquistadores and versed in the history of this country, was pre-eminently fitted to represent a leading character in the victory celebrated—Hon. George W. Armijo, Rough Rider of the Spanish-American war and now

His Grace, the Duke Don Diego De Vargas Zapata Lujan, Ponce de Leon, governor and captain general of the kingdom of New Mexico who was making his triumphant entry into Santa Fe, taking the city in the name of His Gracious Majesty, King Carlos the Second of Spain beyond the seas. . . .

Then rode the two captains of the guard, looking all the world like two of the Three Musketeers immortalized by the Great Dumas. One was County Treasurer Celso López, in a scarlet velvet cape over the customary uniform and on his head was the plumed hat customary some centuries ago. The Duke dismounted and walked to the huge wooden cross which had been erected exactly in front of the spot which was formerly the entrance to the Old Palace, a few feet west of the present main entrance. . . . History says De Vargas stood before such a cross when he delivered his famous proclamation.

Duke Armijo followed out this "ritual" and mounted on a platform read the De Vargas proclamation—in Spanish. His son, Theodore Roosevelt Armijo, clad in the dainty costume of a page, stood at his left.

The speech of Mr. Armijo was that of De

Vargas on that memorable occasion, and was taken from the recent history of Hon. B. M. Read:

"Reverend Fathers, Soldiers, People and Natives: On this the thirtieth day of December, 1693, we see finally crowned by a decisive and lasting victory the great task entrusted to me by his sacred and royal majesty, the Catholic King of Spain, Charles the Second (whom God preserve) of effecting the reconquest of the Kingdom of New Mexico which a most wicked rebellion wrested from the hand of its legitimate ruler and one which only drove away his faithful subjects who during three-quarters of a century had peaceful possession of the country civilizing and christianizing the native people. . . ."

"Harking Back To Days Of New Mexico's Romance,"

Santa Fe New Mexican (June 25, 1912)

The pageant last July 4, was a success. No wonder the world is beginning to pay attention, and inquiries are coming in from magazines and newspapers for feature stories of the event, and moving picture concerns are seeking exclusive concessions to the views of the pageant. Thoughtful men and women see in the pageant, the seed of an annual display that will become as famous as the Ober Ammergau-Passion Plays, for it is an event that lends itself to expansion, to amplification.

In addition to the procession, there may be staged a sham battle between the Spaniards in costume and the Indians in war paint and feathers. Such a riot of colors would be

121. GEORGE WASHINGTON ARMIJO AS DE VARGAS, JULY 4TH, 1911.
(JESSE L. NUSBAUM)

spectacular indeed. The medieval play of the Pastores, too, may be given in the same quaint old way that it was played in the villages of Spain and of Italy five hundred and more years ago. . . .

Rehearsals will take place this week. The costumes are all in hand. One hundred descendants of the Conquistadores have been assigned their places of honor in the procession and are vying with each other to repeat and increase last year's success. . . .

Many an incident for a historic novel and romance, and all the local color the writer man wants, can be secured on July 5, when the history of thrilling days will be brilliantly repeated and exemplified.

"Picture Films Of De Vargas Day,"
Santa Fe New Mexican (June 25, 1912)
John S. Harris, secretary of the chamber of commerce was notified by wire this morning that the Kalem Company, the biggest moving picture concern in the United States would take films of the entire De Vargas day proces-

sion on the Fifth of July, and that in addition he would send George H. Medford, an expert scenic dramatist and six able scenic players to aid in staging the big event and to take such part in the procession as was necessary. . . .

Colonel R. E. Twitchell of the Santa Fe railway, who is here, said last night that the DeVargas day event was being featured from one end of Santa Fe system to the other and that the railway would make unusual effort to bring several thousand people to Santa Fe on that day from all over the United States.

"The Scottish Rite Degrees,"
Valley of Santa Fe, Orient of New Mexico pamphlet
The Scottish Rite of Freemasonry teaches the splendid truths of its twenty-nine Degrees, not abstractly, nor in a dry-as-dust fashion, but with splendor. It brings drama to the service of philosophy, leading the seeker through starlit chambers of imagery, revealing constellations of truth—truth that makes us men and sets us free from fear, fear of life, fear of death.

THE MUSEUM'S FIESTA

Although the Alianza Hispano-Americana staged the De Vargas pageant to great acclaim on the Fourth of July in 1911 and 1912, and the Chamber of Commerce spoke with relish of its continuation, the pageant lapsed in 1913 for reasons that remain unclear. Perhaps some Hispanos disapproved of the commercialization of the pageant through newsreels and tourism promotion. The museum staff was also preoccupied by 1913 with preparations for the San Diego exposition. Then World War I intervened. When the pageant was revived after the war, Hispanic participation declined sharply, as the Fiesta was incorporated into the museum's cultural revival program.

Edgar Hewett and his staff at the School of American Research organized the three-day program of processions, performances, and Indian dances for September 1919 (fig. 125). Each day presented a phase of history—"Before Santa Fe Was," "Santa Fe Antigua," and "Santa Fe Moderna"—thereby manifesting the rhetoric of New Mexico's three cultures: Indian, Spanish, and Anglo-American. The School organized the first day's dancers from Santa Clara, San Ildefonso, and Cochiti Pueblos. The second day, the new De Vargas Association presented the "De Vargas Procession," with the Knights of Columbus playing the Franciscan missionaries, but with Anglo-Americans portraying most of Vargas's men. On the final day, the Daughters of the American Revolution and the Santa Fe Women's Club staged the "Kearny Tableau," while the American Legion organized a special tribute to New Mexico's returning World War I veterans.[19]

"The Fiesta Of Santa Fe," Paul A. F. Walter, *Art and Archaeology* (January 1920) Santiago Naranjo, the Sage of Santa Clara, lifted the ceremonial wand toward the Sky Father, late in the afternoon of Thursday, September 11th, 1919, as a signal that the Fiesta had begun, and that his people should assemble for the ancient Racing Ceremony. . . .

Santiago, crowned with a wreath of green corn leaves, clad in ceremonial costume and carrying a wand with streamers, eagle feathers, and other symbolic insignia, took his position at the western goal of the race course. The four world mountains had been

122. SPANISH-AMERICAN FOLK DANCERS, 1921 FIESTA. (T. HARMON PARKHURST)

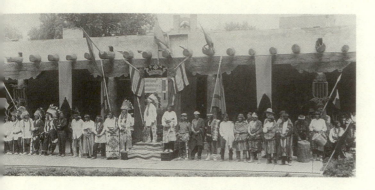

indicated symbolically where Palace and Lincoln Avenues crossed, between and in front of the New Museum and the Old Palace. Tewas and Keres lined the race course. A hush fell over the crowd as the first runners, lithe figures of bronze color, came speeding toward the western goal. The hues of arm bands distinguished the Summer from the Winter people. To and fro they darted like the lightning, scudding like the clouds above them, one set of racers taking the place of another at intervals. First Summer seemed in the ascendancy, but gradually the Winter racers gained and finally triumphed, for was not Autumn at the door and Winter's coming inevitable? It was a thrilling, significant spectacle, dramatizing the procession and the conflict of the seasons.

. . . It was apparent that the performers were very much in earnest, paying no attention to the motion picture camera-men and battery of photographers that were stationed at every vantage point.

"The Santa Fe Fiesta,"
El Palacio (September 30, 1919)
Early in the forenoon [of the second day], Don Diego de Vargas and his Conquerors gathered at the historic Rosario church on

the outskirts of the City. They marched into town over an ancient highway, and in front of the Kit Carson Monument, were joined by the Franciscans led by Col. Jose D. Sena. It was an imposing procession as it came down Lincoln Avenue from the Federal Building and passed the New Museum whose balconies and roofs were as crowded as the streets and Plaza below. Don Diego de Vargas, in the person of Sheriff George W. Armijo, a lineal descendant of one of the Spanish Conquistadores, appareled in glittering Spanish uniform, made a noble figure on his horse. The mounted men who followed in the Spanish uniform of two hundred and more years ago, were quite a jaunty cavalcade. The Franciscans in their simple brown habit with cowl thrown back, marched on foot, representative of the Martyrs, who eighty years before the Pilgrims landed at Plymouth Rock, had brought the story of the Cross to the Indians and had suffered excruciating martyrdom. At the Plaza, the Indian chiefs in their war bonnets and ancient finery, met the intrepid Conqueror and the humble monks. Again it was a spectacle that thrilled and which for color and brilliance it was difficult to excel. The Franciscans erected a huge wooden cross

123. INDIAN PAGEANT, SANTIAGO NARANJO ON PODIUM,1920, FIESTA. (H.C. TIBBITTS)

202

in front of the Palace of the Governors and Don Diego de Vargas dismounted to kneel before it, renewing his pledges of loyalty to the Church and to the King. He then read in Spanish the De Vargas Proclamation which in 1692 announced forgiveness of the Pueblo rebels and assured them of good will and protection on part of the Spaniards. . . .

Where else than in Santa Fe do Pueblo Indians, descendants of the cave and cliff dwellers, descendants of Spaniards and of Moors, the Anglo-Saxon and all the other nationalities that have come to America from foreign shores, mingle so freely and so picturesquely, each true to his type in costume, in appearance, in gesticulation and in language? Add to this the Fiesta spirit, the throngs of cowboys and trappers, the players

and mimers in costumes of centuries ago, and there are created impression after impression, ethnic picture upon picture, a moving, stirring, kaleidoscopic grouping of humanity in stupendous settings bound by the turquoise skies, the snow-tipped Blood of Christ mountains, the yellow foothills and the lush green of the valley orchards. The narrower frame consisted on one side of the venerable, one-story adobe Palace of the Governors, the terraced, towered New Museum with its balconies and buttresses, and on the other of the festively green Indian booths of the Plaza Market. . . .

[On the morning of the third day] salutes from Fort Marcy indicated that General Kearny had entered the City and the Mexican officials took position in the Plaza to greet

124. SOLDIERS ESCORTING THE CABILDO (SPANISH CITY COUNCIL), OPENING OF 1921 FIESTA.

him. General Kearny, Colonel Doniphan and their staff officers and escort wore the stiff, outlandish uniforms of the Mexican war period. The group was joined by the Pueblos in war finery and the entire assemblage then made its way to the Plaza stage. There General Kearny read his proclamation to the people, an interpreter repeating it impressively word for word. The proclamation promised the Mexican people protection and fair treatment together with American citizenship. The Acting Governor replied with great dignity surrendering his authority to the American victors. With solemnity, the American flag was then raised and saluted. There were cheers for the Stars and Stripes led by the Mexican officials. The Santa Fe Band followed with the "Star Spangled Banner" in which the people joined.

"Santa Fe Will Show It's American to Core," *Santa Fe New Mexican* (April 30, 1920) (fig. 127). The mass meeting at the museum promises to be a monster gathering. Governor Larrazolo will address this meeting. The governor is in excellent Spirit and he will no doubt deliver a powerful oration on Americanism. He is regarded as one of the foremost men in the country today in support of its institutions.

It is especially important that all the school children and students should be given the opportunity to take part in the observance of the day. The better they get to understand what American institutions are the better citizens they will be. The idea that law and order are fundamental to the life of a free nation can not be too strongly impressed on the minds of the young. The various fraternal

125. THE KEARNY PAGEANT REENACTING THE 1846 AMERICAN OCCUPATION OF SANTA FE, 1919 FIESTA.

organizations are taking much interest in the observance of the day. The officers of the Elks have sent to every member the following letter:

"On Saturday next (American Day) May 1, 1920, there will be the biggest opportunity within our history to show the citizens of Santa Fe, the Americanism of our organization. . . .

"Every patriotic demonstration promotes the safety and welfare of our state and nation.

Anarchy, Bolshevism, I.W.W. isms, and their isms run riot throughout our fair land. Let the Elks take a forefront in the fight to be waged against the evils bent upon ruining our country and enter into this demonstration with the enthusiasm of which every good Elk is capable."

One feature that should have individual attention is that every boy and girl be provided with a flag.

FIESTA EVOLUTION

Alterations of the Santa Fe Fiesta during the 1920s mirrored national trends in historical pageants. In the wake of World War I, people increasingly felt that an unbridgeable gap had opened between tradition and the modern world. Pageant organizers no longer depicted a chain of local historical events stretching unbroken from Indian times to the present, but instead emphasized detailed depictions of European settlement. Many of the leading prewar pageant directors, grown more overtly antimodern in their outlook, sought to translate folk cultures (in particular that of Appalachia) into elite art forms. They created stylized folk dramas and operas designed primarily as entertainments for urban audiences, rather than the preservation of traditional cultures. Historical pageants that did survive into the 1930s, such as Santa Fe's Fiesta, were transformed into folk plays or annual festivals supported by history museums and tourism.[20]

As local enthusiasm for the Santa Fe Fiesta waned, its staging became a burden on the museum. To make the Fiesta financially self-sustaining, Hewett and company fenced the area in front of the Palace and began to charge admission to the pageants. By 1924 paid performances of Pueblo dances, Hispanic folk plays, and historical romances written by members of the art colony also catered to tourists in the Palace courtyard, Saint Francis auditorium, and Santa Fe's two new movie theaters (figs. 128-

126. MAY DAY DANCERS, SANTA FE FIESTA, 1919 OR 1920.

127. ST. VINCENT'S ORPHANAGE IN AMERICAN DAY PARADE, MAY 1, 1920.
CAPITAL BUILDING AND GOVERNOR'S MANSION IN BACKGROUND.

30). At an open-air amphitheater constructed on the north edge of town in 1926, Hewett interspersed Pueblo dances with classically trained Cherokee, Mohawk, and Choctaw singers. Thomas Wood Stevens, who began his career under William Simpson in the Santa Fe Railway advertising department and who later became a national leader of the pageant movement, purchased a Santa Fe house in 1925. Two years later, Hewett hired Stevens to direct a twelve-episode dramatization entitled "Pageants of Old Santa Fe" at this Fiesta Theater. To attract more tourists, the Fiesta was also moved from the second to the first week of September in 1921 and then to the first week of August in 1925 and 1926. It was returned to Labor Day weekend the following year and finally back to the second week in September in the 1970s.[21]

Pueblo Indians were reluctant participants in Santa Fe pageants that emphasized the Spanish conquest. They fought mock battles with the Spanish in the 1883 and 1912 pageants and even submitted by kneeling before a large cross in 1883. But starting in 1920, Anglos and Hispanos had to be recruited to fill Indian roles. University of New Mexico history professor Lansing Bloom, who organized the Pueblo dances and crafts market in the 1920s, sometimes portrayed the Pueblo governor in the De Vargas pageant. From the 1876 Fourth of July celebration on, however, Pueblo Indians performed excerpts of their own ritual dances as their contribution to public ceremony.

The federal Indian Bureau in the early 1920s sought to limit participation in native religious dances to those over fifty years of age and to not more than one dance a month per village. While Edgar Hewett, along with artist John Sloan, led the opposition to this repression, Hewett was prepared to omit Pueblo dances from the fiesta program pending clarification of Indian Bureau policy. The bureau ruled that Pueblo dances were permissible in the Santa Fe Fiesta, because they were part of "an educational and historical entertainment." In other words, dances were discouraged as a part of the ongoing religious life of the Pueblos but were acceptable as tourist entertainments. In 1922 paid dance performances became part of the new three-day Indian Crafts Market staged concurrently with the fiesta (fig. 130). Anglo judges awarded

cash prizes to Pueblo dance groups based on a scale of 50 points for costuming, 20 points for rhythm, 20 points for "pep," or spirit, and 10 points for audience appeal. The Eagle Dance, for instance, had high audience appeal from the first, because the feathered costumes with great bird wings were so photogenic. The Pueblo dances were moved to the new Fiesta Theater in 1926 but declined somewhat in importance in the 1930s and even more in the early 1960s, when the Indian Market was separated from the Fiesta and moved to August.[22]

Fiesta organizers continued to mine the annals of Spanish and American conquest well into the 1920s. Spanish culture was first represented by Don Quixote and Sancho Panza in the 1874 Fourth of July parade, while the Spanish explorers Coronado and Cabeza de Baca and Santa Fe's reconquerer de Vargas appeared from the 1883 exposition through the late 1920s fiestas. In 1920 a play recounting the trial of the leaders of the abortive Pueblo revolt of 1696 provided an elaborate one-time justification for the Spanish treatment of the Indians. This coincided with the dedication of the Cross of the Martyrs, commemorating the twenty-one Franciscans killed in the 1680 revolt. Mexican independence was reenacted but once, on its centennial in 1921. The Mexican national anthem complemented the U.S. anthem at Fourth of July celebrations and early fiestas but disappeared from the program after 1921, as the local population emphasized its Spanish rather than its Mexican heritage. Anglo-Americans were at first represented by the reenactment of General Kearny's 1846 occupation of Santa Fe and by "Progress of Transportation" processions, which advanced from Spanish carts through Santa Fe Trail wagons and steam locomotive floats to decorated automobiles. The last "Progress of Transportation" was staged in 1920, the final Santa Fe Trail day in 1921, and the last Kearny pageant in 1927.[23]

By the late 1920s, Vargas's "peaceful" reconquest of 1692 had emerged as the sole focus of the annual Fiesta pageant. The selection of this episode rather than the bloody conquest of 1693 (which had been reenacted in 1883, 1912, 1922, and 1924) complemented the emerging public rhetoric of tricultural harmony. Starting in 1920, the

207

Fiesta opened with a reading of the 1712 fiesta proclamation of "Vespers, Mass, sermon, and procession through the Main Plaza" to commemorate de Vargas's 1692 conquest. The most direct descendant of this proclamation—the Conquistadora processions—had occurred in June since the 1700s. The proclamation, nevertheless, gave the modern Fiesta a stamp of historical continuity that few other communities could match. The proclamation also accounts for the preeminence of Vargas rather than Peralta, who founded Santa Fe in 1610. By focusing solely on the Spanish reconquest, the pageant became more an expression of ethnic than community-wide identity.

THE CATHOLIC FIESTA

The linking of the modern fiesta with the 1712 proclamation also stimulated religious participation. The historical pageants of 1883, 1911, 1912, and 1919 had expressed primarily civic and secondarily ethnic identity. The staging of the 1911 and 1912 pageants on the Fourth of July demonstrated a clear patriotic tie. Although the Knights of Columbus portrayed Franciscan missionary friars (*frailes*) in these early Fiesta processions, the Catholic Church did not participate directly.[24]

This infusion of religion into the modern fiesta began in 1920, when an entire day was devoted to the Franciscans and the dedication of the Cross of the Martyrs (fig.

130. JEMEZ PUEBLO DANCERS PERFORMING ON PALACE OF THE GOVERNOR'S COURTYARD STAGE, AUGUST 2-8, 1928 FIESTA.

131). The first fiesta program to include a candlelight procession to the Cross took place in 1925, but unlike later observances, it opened the Fiesta rather than closing it and began from the plaza, not the cathedral. In 1934 the De Vargas pageant day commenced with a high mass at the cathedral and ended with a candlelight procession from the cathedral up the hill to the Cross of the Martyrs. By 1973 the Fiesta was opened by a mass at Rosario Chapel and concluded with another mass at the cathedral, followed by the candlelight procession to the Cross—a sequence now considered traditional. For the clergy and devout Catholics, the bracketing of the Fiesta by masses demonstrates its essential religious character. In later years, this religious sanction has been further emphasized by the knighting of de Vargas and the coronation of a Fiesta Queen by the archbishop in services at the cathedral.[25]

"Official Souvenir Program of the Santa Fe Fiesta," 1920

Tuesday September 14th, 1920. Second Day — De Vargas Day.

8:15 P.M.—Play depicting Court Martial of the Governors of the Pueblos of Nambe and Santo Domingo, and two pueblo warriors charged with treason and conspiracy in the massacre of the Franciscan Friars in the rebellion of 1696.

[Selected] Personnel of Pageant:

General Don Diego de Vargas Zapata Lujan Ponce de Leon, represented by Geo. W. Armijo.

Maestre de Campo Luis Granillo, represented by James Baca.

Don Felipe, Governor of the Pueblo of Pecos, represented by W. M. Danburg.

Five Indians from Tesuque Pueblo.

Luis Cunixú, Jemez Indian, represented by Francisco B. Romero.

Captain Antonio Valverde, represented by Norman L. King.

Ensign Martin de Urioste, represented by William E. Griffin.

Alférez Captain Juan Ruiz, represented by Fritz Muller.

Fray Antonio de Azevedo, represented by Jose D. Sena.

Time: June, 1696.

Place: The Sala de Audiencia in the Palace of the Governors.

A detail of soldiers are on guard . . . . enter:

131. DEDICATION OF THE CROSS OF THE MARTYRS, 1920 FIESTA. (H.C. TIBBITTS)

Don Felipe, Governor of the Pueblo of Pecos, mounted, accompanied by two War Captains and five Indians, mounted, and two Indians, their hands tied behind their backs and lassos around their necks, each lasso in the hands of a War Captain. . . .

Gen. De Vargas: "Arise, sir, what wouldst thou say to me?"

Don Felipe: "The faithful servant of His Majesty and supporter of Your Excellency's most beneficent government most humbly declares that on yesterday this Indian of the Indian Pueblo of Jemez, Luis Cunixú came into the Pueblo of Pecos and was exhibiting an octangular reliquary, made of gilded brass, and in it different relics, a piece of wood of the Cross and an Ecce Homo, which he said he was carrying as proof of the killing of Fray Francisco de Jesus in the Pueblo of Jemez.

Gen. Granillo: "When was the Holy Father Guardian Fray Francisco de Jesus killed and were there any Spaniards with him?"

Luis Cunixú: "The Father was by himself; the interpreter induced him to come out of his cell under the pretext that a woman had to be confessed, and the war captain and the interpreter killed him. When they seized him he called upon our Lord God and the Blessed Virgin for aid and protection; but they killed him with their macanas and dragged his body into the plaza and left it in the door of the church.

Gen. De Vargas: "They are guilty—save one—El Tempano, whose liberty I grant. My sentence I now pronounce. The Tegua Indian, Diego, of the Pueblo of Nambe; the Jemez Indian, Luis Cunixú, and Alonzo Guipui, the governor of Santo Domingo, shall die; they shall be shot at once; Captain Antonio Valverde and the Ensign Urioste and the Adjutant Juan Ruiz shall see that my order is executed. They shall first be confessed by the Rev. Fathers of this Villa. (To Captain Valverde.) Remove the prisoners!" (Captain Valverde gives command to his soldiers; the prisoners, except El Tempano, march between two platoons of ten men each. The snare drum is beaten; the command passes through the eastern gate. Soon shots are heard.)

210

THE COUNTER FIESTA

Men had reenacted the military conquests of Coronado, Vargas, and Kearny in the 1883, 1911, 1912, and 1919 pageants, while the Women's Board of Trade, the woman's Auxiliar of the Alianza Hispano-Americana, and the Daughters of the American Revolution worked behind the scenes, sewing theatrical costumes and operating food booths. This sexual segregation of social life, reflected across the country in the popular fraternities, began to break down by the 1920s. Women won the right to vote in 1920, and were entering the work force as never before. Their emerging economic and political power, along with the availability of contraception, contributed to a relaxing of social mores and a more sexually mixed social life. Young men, for their part, were less attracted by the prospect of evening and weekend secret rituals. Fraternities, allegorical monuments, and historical pageants all began to be publicly parodied, and fraternity recruitment fell sharply after 1920. A gap opened between those who had matured during the great industrial and technological expansion of the 1880s and 1890s and a younger generation shaped by social change and World War I. The artists and writers who began arriving just before 1920 infused Santa Fe with this new spirit of social, political, and artistic change.[26]

Those in the new art colony particularly disliked the museum's commercialization of the Fiesta because they had come to Santa Fe in search of community, and the price of admission to pageants excluded many Santa Fe residents. In response social activist Dolly Sloan and poet Witter Bynner organized a program of free Fiesta events called "Pasatiempo" (pastime, amusement) in 1924. The four-foot-nine daughter of Irish immigrants, Ann "Dolly" Wall married John Sloan in 1901. He was a leader of the New York social realist painters known as "The Ashcan School." Dolly was a manic depressive who medicated herself with alcohol and "almost required a cause to pull herself together." An activist in progressive Greenwich Village circles, she organized rallies and fund-raising campaigns, passed out handbills, and spoke on street corners in favor of birth control, striking unions, and the Socialist presidential candidate Eugene

Debs. Dolly helped organize and John directed the International Workers of the World's great "Pageant of the Paterson Strike" at Madison Square Garden in 1913. The Sloans visited Santa Fe in 1919, bought a house the next year, and returned to spend four months each summer for the next thirty years.[27]

The son of a well-to-do New England family, Witter Bynner graduated *magna cum laude* from Harvard in 1902, then took a job as literary editor of *McClure's,* the progressive New York magazine that was also home to muckraker Lincoln Steffens and novelist Willa Cather. Already a well-known poet, translator, and essayist when he settled in Santa Fe in 1922, Bynner continued to cultivate himself. In travels to Mexico and the Orient, he collected art objects for the rambling adobe house he shared with his companion of thirty-four years, Robert Hunt (son of the Scottish Rite Temple designer, Myron Hunt). An active supporter of women's suffrage as a young man, Bynner became a leading civic figure, even running for the state legislature in 1926, on a platform calling for the removal of Hewett as museum director. The distance between Hewett and Bynner, or for that matter between Hewett and Dolly Sloan, may have been as much a matter of personal temperament as it was a generational difference. The earnest, autocratic, tee-totaling Hewett spearheaded the pious, military pageants that initiated the modern Fiesta, while the tall, gay master of repartee Witter Bynner and the diminutive Socialist dynamo Dolly Sloan instigated the populist and irreverent Pasatiempo.[28]

Pasatiempo included band concerts, community singing and street dancing on the plaza, a children's animal show, and the wildly popular Hysterical Pageant (figs. 132, 133, 137, 138). People from all social strata pulled heirloom clothes from their trunks, made floats and costumes, and decorated their cars, horses, and burros for this parade. Tongue-in-cheek parodies of historic figures, tourists, and tourist stereotypes proliferated. If the De Vargas pageants were historical murals solemnly brought to life, then the ten-foot-tall shirts and pants of one year's Hysterical Pageant were attention-grabbing pop icons—everyday items cut loose from their cultural moorings and inflated to a bizarre size in the manner of modern advertising and the French surrealists. In the

spirit of carnival, for that is what people began calling Pasatiempo, "the grand carnival," artists Will Shuster and Gustave Baumann fabricated Zozobra in 1926 (fig. 134). This effigy of gloom, "otherwise known as King Worry, Dull Care or Old Man Grouch," has been burned ever since to open the Fiesta—a pagan counterpoint to the opening mass.

Mrs. Manuel (Amelia) Sanchez embraced the spirit of the Hysterical Pageant when she organized her friends and relatives in 1927 to dress up in old clothes and hats, add brown makeup and mop wigs, and set out together with a collection of barnyard animals, including a sheep she dyed pink for the occasion. Their parody of popular stereotypes of Mexican hillbillies was a great hit. After the parade, Sanchez took her children home, fed, bathed, and put them to bed, then changed into her mother's wedding gown augmented by a mantilla before rushing back to the plaza in time to be crowned the first queen of Pasatiempo. This role evolved into the Fiesta Queen, who in time would be attended by a full retinue of Spanish and Indian princesses and provide a female counterpart to de Vargas and his caballeros (fig. 142). In the mid-1930s, La Fonda Hotel and La Sociedad Folklórica initiated Fiesta fashion shows of antique gowns. This brought to a close ten years in which tourist promotion was tempered by the addition of community events and the military pageants were augmented by activities for families, women, and children.[29]

132. PASATIEMPO PARADE, FIESTA, ABOUT 1928.

"From the Spanish,"

Santa Fe New Mexican (editorial, August 8, 1925)
What Spain has given to New Mexico is a people, patriotic Americans, with a rich racial endowment from their ancestors, and with a record of seventy-five years of finest fealty to their government. . . .

Through them comes this Spanish heritage of rare courtesy, simplicity, kindliness, of color and music and of graceful movement, of native eloquence, of the patriarchal family, pride, loyalty. . . .

One of the fine things about the Fiesta is its influence toward welding together more in spirit and sympathy the people of these two main branches of our population: "Anglos" re-enacting the roles of heroic Spaniards, native people commemorating the upbuild-ing of an American state, and venerating the Flag of which they have made their full sacrifice. The Fiesta, we believe, is a strong amalgamating force, striking down what barriers the ignorant and those without vision seek to raise. Celebrating the exploits of the Castilians and perpetuating the beauty they have bequeathed us, hand in hand with an honest and vigorous effort to bring to their descendants every advantage that American progress and enlightenment affords—this is the way to fullest amalgamation.

"Zozobra is Fiesta,"

Will Shuster, *New Mexico Magazine*
(August 1950)
In the year 1712 the Marquis de Penuela published a proclamation of Fiesta in commemo-

ration of the re-conquest of New Mexico by Don Diego de Vargas.

Two hundred and some odd years later, E. Dana Johnson, who was then editor of the Santa Fe *New Mexican,* and I got together to hatch out a show for Fiesta.

It was not the Fiesta of the Marquis de Penuela, but actually amounted to a revolutionary protest fiesta, staged by the artists and writers of the community and was called El Pasatiempo. It was protest against the regular Fiesta which was becoming dull and commercialized.

Between us, we worked out the general idea of the show. Dana dug up that wonderful name ZOZOBRA meaning "the gloomy one" from a Spanish dictionary, and I got to work on the details of the show with a budget of fifty dollars.

The first Zozobra was a rather simple affair.

On the night of the show, a circle of bonfires was lighted around the base of the figure. The Kiwanians in black robes circled slowly about Zozobra carrying green torches and chanting a dirge. On cue, Witter Bynner leading a large group of Fiesta merry-makers, all in gay costumes and waving bright colored ribbon whips, dashed out of concealment and drove off the glooms. The effigy was lighted,

roman-candles and red fires were set off, and with much hilarious shouting the merriment was under way.

From that time, Zozobra has become an integral part of Fiesta. It somehow was a fitting symbol for Fiesta. Casting aside all worries and glooms, one entered into the merry spirit of Fiesta with a care-free, light heart. It was an event in which the whole town could participate in spirit.

"Santa Fe Christmas in the '20s,"

Santa Fe News (December 23, 1971)
"I've never lived in a town with so many traditions," one of us remarked, "except perhaps New Orleans. Who starts them anyway?"

Shuster chuckled. "I can answer that partially. Years ago a number of us decided to inaugurate a Santa Fe tradition: a community get-together at the Plaza on Christmas Eve. We built luminarias, prepared farolitos, rounded up musicians and wood-laden burros with their drivers. There was even a Padre who blessed the festivities. It was a big success and we planned to repeat it every year."

"But why didn't it become a tradition?"

"It might have," Shuster said, "but the next Christmas it snowed like hell!"

134. ZOZOBRA, DESIGNED BY WILL SHUSTER, 1947 FIESTA. (ROBERT H. MARTIN)

"Mrs. Terresa Dorman Hostess at Gay Costume Party for Edward Hall,"
[the night before Fiesta opened]
Santa Fe New Mexican (September 3, 1927)
. . . The party was staged at the attractive studio home of Mrs. Dorman on the Camino, with its lovely patio lit by moon beams and its Spanish rooms softly lighted by many candles.

The party was in honor of Edward Hall, vice president of the Ralston Purina Mills, St. Louis who is a visitor here this summer. Among the invited guests were Mrs. Mary Austin, Arthur Field of Montreal, Canada, Dr. Charles Lummis of Los Angles, . . .

Among the interesting costumes were:
Mr. Hall, guest of honor,
"The Nude Descending the Stairs," . . .
Will Shuster, Custodian of a German wine cellar,
Mrs. Ficke, Egyptian dancing girl,
Miss Emerson, Hawaiian beauty,
Mrs. Alice Myers, Indian maiden,
Gerald Cassidy (in stunning costume from Moroco) The Calif Bekr, . . .
Miss Olive Rush, Riding master,
Mrs. Vera Jonson, Tiger,

Mr. Nordfeld, Potentate with triple crown,
Carlos Vierra, Sailor, . . .
Mrs. Ellis, Spanish senorita,
Mr. Andrew Dasburg, French fisherman,
Mrs. Dorthy Harvey, Fiji Islander,
Mr. Witter Bynner, Chinese savant born in Santa Fe,
George Gormley, A Pre-Civil War belle, in old lace gown,
Mamie Meadors, Japanese lady,
John Sloan and Dolly Sloan, New Yorkers.[30]

"215th Annual Santa Fe Fiesta,"
Santa Fe New Mexican (September 3, 1927)
. . . Luminarias
The people of the city are again urged to get candles, place them in paper sacks weighted with sand in the bottom, and set them around their homes or places of business, particularly along the roofs.

"Hysterical Pageant Features Original, Picturesque Stunts,"
Santa Fe New Mexican (September 8, 1927)
The mile-long procession led by the Conquistadores' Band contained every fantastic creation conceivable: . . . the long line of loaded native wood-wagons. . . .

135. WOMAN IN FIESTA COSTUME ABOUT 1935. (T. HARMON PARKHURST)

. . . Mrs. Manuel Sanchez native countrywoman with her red-tinted sheep, children, and rural accoutrements; native wagons with goats and farm products; . . . Lady Godiva (John Windsor) with her taffy tresses, riding a white horse . . . The Indians made a lively section of the parade.

Captains Sedillo and Holmes and their crack polo teams mounted on burros, mallets held stiffly erect, received an ovation. . . . Little Rosina Muniz as "La Rancherita" and Ignacio Vigil as "El Rancherito" led burros loaded with country products; Rosina wore a genuine reboso and Ignacio was a perfect small native farmer; Ben Muniz was an old paisano with a big cabbage on his shoulder . . . . the sisters of Charity entered a group of girls from the orphanage in picturesque fancy dress.

Director A. J. Connell of Los Alamos Ranch school, aided by Masters Hitchcock and Church, contributed a screamingly funny "dude pack train." The tenderfeet had everything possible with them on the half hundred horses, including shower baths, maids and cooks. This was an absolute riot.

"In Character,"
Santa Fe New Mexican
(editorial, September 8, 1927)
For various reasons, the Santa Fe Fiesta, which closed last night, was a little slow about getting into its stride. It gathered momentum with a rush yesterday and the culmination, in the most hilarious and picturesque Pasatiempo ever achieved, brought public enthusiasm up to the highest pitch. . . .

Beautiful Spanish carnivals are held in California and Florida, but the existing links with the Spanish days are so tenuous there must perforce be much that is artificial and in the fashion of movies. In Santa Fe, laden burros, creaking wood wagons are not restored from the past, they merely come in from the country. We not only doll up Anglos in Castillian or Mexican style, the bulk of the crowd celebrants is Spanish-speaking; no costume is needed, they wear their own best cloths; if they don fancy dress, they get it out of the trunks of their grandmothers and grandfathers. No need to dig folk-music out of archives; they play and sing the songs, handed down from their ancestors,

217

which are still extant in the placitas.

Instead of building a more or less accurate replica of old backgrounds, we use buildings which have looked down on Fiestas for nearly four centuries. Instead of striving for some created effect which we think will lure the visitor, we are ourselves; our own present and past make the stirring and thrilling and gorgeous picture.

We never see a Fiesta, moreover, without a feeling of incredulity at the Pueblo Indian ceremonials. They are an impossible anachronism; a dream of the past which will not disappear when we try to wake up; a beautiful and unreal thing, a figment of the imagination, a fairy-story which no imagination can rival.

"Historic Vow of De Vargas is Fulfilled,"
Santa Fe New Mexican (June 14, 1937)
Thanks Have Again Gone Up to Our Lady of Victory for Deliverance
. . . The last novena of high masses vowed by the reconquerer was sung at St. Francis cathedral this morning in the presence of the little statue of Our Lady standing in the sanctuary, having been brought back to the cathedral Sunday afternoon in the second De Vargas procession. It was even bigger than the procession a week ago Sunday when the statue was escorted to Rosario chapel, probably 2,500 people being in line.

The priests at the cathedral have been impressed by the religious zeal marking the annual fulfillment of the vow. In his sermon Father Anthony O.F.M. said: "There is evi-

136. FIESTA GROUP ON ENTRANCE STEPS OF THE FINE ARTS MUSEUM, ABOUT 1935. (T. HARMON PARKHURST)

dence that this last week or so has been a period of grace for this city. More than 1,500 confessions have been heard and devotion of the communicants before and after receiving has been more marked than is usual."

"The Fiesta,"
Santa Fe Examiner (September 9, 1937)
The Fiesta this year was a disappointment to a great many people. For some reason it seemed to have lost a great deal of its punch . . .

For some years there has been criticism of the Fiesta by people who are sincerely interested in Santa Fe and its future, and who have no personal, selfish interest in the affair. The criticism seems mainly to lie in the fact that the Fiesta is gradually being taken out of the hands of those to whom it rightfully belongs, the Spanish-American people of the city, and used by a small group to further their own ends.

When the natives are finally pushed out of the picture, the color, the romance and the atmosphere of the Fiesta will be no more. It will be merely another civic show, of which there are hundreds held annually in this country . . .

The Fiesta should be staged by and for the native people. . . . The native people should be encouraged to have their annual Fiesta with all of its religious and historical significance as it was originally intended . . .

The natives would be the participants, the Anglos from near and far would be in their rightful place as spectators, enjoying a colorful and historically significant glimpses of the days that have faded into antiquity.

Typescript from 1938 Fiesta file,
John Gaw Meem Papers
Is the Santa Fe Fiesta worth the tremendous effort and large sums of money involved? . . .

My personal reaction is a decided "yes"—I'm for it. Of course it's fun, that is if you take part in it and don't just stand on the sidewalk waiting to be shown. Nobody has fun being a wall flower, but it's different if you dance and sing and let people laugh at you in the Hysterical Pageant and let off steam in general after three hundred and sixty-two days of holding in. And you don't get bored if you've just finished helping to decorate the plaza and are proud of it as if you know that some of the glorious sound coming out of the Mariaches is due to your two bucks.

To my mind, nothing contributes more toward the promotion of good feeling,

between Anglos and Spanish Americans than does the Fiesta. Not only that, but it is one of the most important factors in making Santa Fe one of the most tolerant cities in America as far as religious creeds are concerned. You can't work and play together without beginning to like the other fellow. These two facts alone justify the Fiesta.[31]

220

August 26th, 1938

Dear Mr. Meem:

We wish to thank you for your order for the Austro-Mexican Officer Uniform—period 1860.

We are shipping this uniform by express Saturday, August 27th, C.O.D. in the amount of $15.00 plus express charges.

> Very truly yours,
> Western Costume Co., Hollywood,
> California.[32]

"226th Annual Fiesta Is Greatest and Most Successful Yet Held,"

Santa Fe New Mexican (September 6, 1938)

In the hysterical pageant of El Pasatiempo Monday afternoon, all the spirit of true satire, expressed with great artistry for which these events were noted in early Fiestas, was recaptured. . . .

Most spectacular of the entire line were the satirized figures of Hitler, Mussolini and FDR, the "three dictators," goosestepping, saluting, and grinning, respectively. . . .

Leading the floats were the decrepit old parents of El Pasatiempo, Mrs. John Sloan and Witter Bynner, labeled Mama and Papatiempo. They were not marching this year. Instead they were made up as two worn-out viejos, riding in wheelchairs pushed by the two gay niggers, John Sloan and Bob Hunt, who were hardly able to walk inside their enormous rubber feet. Mrs. Otto Nagel was the nurse, Will Shuster the doctor in charge. Poet Bynner should have had a hoarse throat after the parade, for he hacked and coughed completely throughout the hours of the parade.

There was the lovely Maharaja of Vario Abeyta for some more spectacular beauty, Florence Sosaya in her jeweled turban being carried aloft in East India fashion by her attendants swathed in white robes. . . .

Zozobra Burns

The highway leading north to Taos was lined with cars on both sides as far as the eye could see, the highway north to Bishop's

137. HYSTERICAL PAGEANT, 1938 FIESTA. "MAMA AND PAPATIEMPO" DOLLY SLOAN AND WITTER BYNNER PUSHED BY JOHN SLOAN AND BOB HUNT, AND ATTENDED BY WILL SHUSTER.

138. HYSTERICAL PAGEANT, EAST SIDE OF PLAZA, 1938 FIESTA.

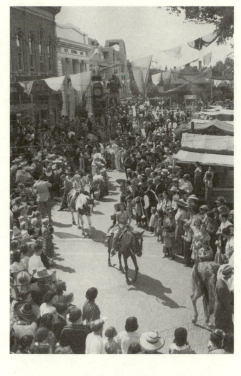

the flames enveloped the papier-mache creation, dispelling the smoke, and Old Man Gloom was destroyed in a final burst of fire.

"350 Persons See Gorgeous Finery of Past Century When Fiesta of Sociedad Folklorica is Held,"

Santa Fe New Mexican (September 9, 1938)
More than 350 persons attended the old-fashioned style show and merienda of the Sociedad Folklorica on Sunday of Fiesta in the Sena Plaza. . . .

A few of the beautiful ensembles included:

Dolman of brown velvet silk, 1850, belonging to Dona Benigna Garcia de Delgado brought from Chihuahua Mexico by Don Felipe Delgado for his bride's trousseau. It is now owned by Josefita Valdez Lucero and was worn by Anita Baca Walton.

Rich deep wine evening gown of heavy grosgrain silk in hooped style from the trousseau of Mrs. Marcelino Garcia, the waist trimmed in beautiful hand-made Mexican drawnwork lace in pinwheel design, 1884. Gold rope necklace that belonged to Dona Ramoncita LaBadie de Baca, grandmother of Ramoncita Baca de Latimer, modelled by Mrs. Latimer. . . .

lodge as well; people sat on rooftops, leaned from upstairs windows—every available spot was taken long before Artist John Sloan touched the torch to the pile of inflammable material at Zozobra's feet.

As the flames from the torch crept through the weeds piled around, a dense cloud of smoke shrouded the gigantic effigy and his contortions, his writhings, from the throngs watching, but the growls of pain from the gaping mouth of the criminal condemned to ghastly death by Judge Lorenzo Gutierrez, Sr., were clearly audible.

Slowly the flames moved toward the feet of the arch-criminal, to the accompaniment of popping firecrackers, shooting skyrockets and a myriad other pyrotechnic displays; finally, as horns blew and people cheered,

139. Fiesta Procession, about 1950. (Santa Fe Railway)

THE 280TH ANNUAL FIESTA

Although begun in September 1919, over the years the Santa Fe Fiesta became, by sleight of words, the "oldest continuous community celebration in the United States" (conveniently forgetting Pueblo ceremonies). From the first, the Fiesta was wrapped in the historical proclamation of 1712. Never mind that La Conquistadora processions had been moved to June in the late 1700s, and that the only previous celebrations resembling the 1919 Fiesta were the 1911 and 1912 Forth of July De Vargas pageants. The 1921 Fiesta program stated that it was "first celebrated in A.D. 1712." The following year the program claimed, contrary to what every native resident knew, that it had been "celebrated annually since A.D. 1712." In 1924 the program more diplomatically called it the "212th Anniversary Fiesta." But by 1938 it was again called the "233rd Annual Santa Fe Fiesta," and so it has been ever since: in 1992, as this is being written, the 280th Annual Fiesta.[33]

From "Ambition Spurred First Spaniards,"
Fray Angelico Chavez, *Santa Fe New Mexican*
(Centennial Fiesta Edition, 1949)
It is true that some individuals mistreated the Indians, but this was contrary to general policy. The truth is that the Pueblo Indians in general were loathe to rebel for many reasons; they did so because of mass hysteria whipped into a mad frenzy by their voodoo witch-doctors who saw the poor aborigines fast slipping away from their own grasp.

From "The Indian Next To You,"
Oliver La Farge, *Santa Fe New Mexican*

(Centennial Fiesta Edition, 1949)
. . . The Indians, who once ran the Spaniards out of here, are in the streets. They are everywhere. The newcomer recognizes the ones who wear their hair the old way, in braids or queue, who stick to the bright headbands, the necklaces, earrings, moccasins, of ancient costume. Finding that our population includes many dark-skinned people anyway, he is much slower to recognize the others, the majority. They come down town every day from school, in school sweaters, in bobby-sox and pedal pushers, and it takes a little time to learn to know for sure that these are Indians.

140. WILL SHUSTER'S FIESTA PARTY, 1948. (SAM ARNOLD)

It takes time to spot the men in ordinary ranch clothes, and the ones in business suits, and the women in ordinary dresses.

By and by you get to recognize them, partly through recognizing friends, until their Indianness is as clear to you as if they retained all the panoply of their ancient forebears. It ceases to disappoint you that they have lost all that costume and mere picturesqueness, because you know that this gum-cracking high school girl is a top-flight buffalo dancer, you have seen this skilled mechanic's footwork in a day-long, man-killing line dance (man-killing, that is, from our point of view), . . .

These people are worth knowing, and up to a point they can be known. Far from being primitive, they are so sophisticated that they are able to throw off the endless irritation of tourist gawking, pointing, loud commenting, and general, inconsiderate rudeness to which they are so steadily subjected in their home villages. Gracefully withdrawn, they conduct their necessary commerce with these loud visitors, they are not even angry, not often that is, because they themselves are too poised and well-bred to let contemptible vulgarity anger them. With the same breeding they politely receive and fend off our own "friends of the Indian" who believe that their friendship to a darker people is a fine gift, and who are so densely obtuse as to feel that they can condescend to them.

More remarkable, although their experience is so often along these lines, they are still prepared to receive those white people who approach them as one would approach anybody else. They will always give you a chance to prove that you are capable of being in fact a friend. After that, your relationship will form, for the same reasons which control your relationships with non-Indians. . . .

"The Santa Fe Fiesta,"

Fray Angelico Chavez, *New Mexico Historical Review* (July 1953)

The present Santa Fe Fiesta, which this year will advertise itself as the 241st, dates from the period around the First World War, when public-minded citizens, "Anglos" who appreciated the unique Spanish historical background of Santa Fe, became aware of the grand possibilities inherent in this decree of 1712. They animated the "hispanos" with pride concerning their forebears, and got them to participate in one big spontaneous folk festival.

223

For the first few years the Santa Fe Fiesta was a genuine Spanish-American folk festival, as it should be, with a touch of Indian participation. Then for a time, certain individuals who took charge emphasized Indian dances and exhibits. For the past decade, "Western" or Hollywood cowboy costumes and hillbilly music have gained the ascendancy. Whatever was left of Spanish-American folklore has been drowned by Mexican music and costuming. This is not to decry the Cowboy-Rodeo-Indian-Mexican influence in the Fiesta, as these elements are all an integral part of the Southwest's historical scene. However, the vacation season has ample room for cowboy, Mexican, and Indian festivities. There are special annual Rodeos already all over the State and in Santa Fe, as well as Indian ceremonies and ceremonials. The Santa Fe Fiesta ought to be a genuine Spanish-American folk festival and nothing else, though not excluding some Pueblo Indian participation, which the Fiesta's original event calls for.

NON-HISPANIC ROLES

After the Kearny pageant was abandoned for good in 1928, Anglo-Americans were limited to viewing the De Vargas pageant, buying native arts, behind the scenes organizing, and the Fiesta Melodrama and Hysterical Parade. While Anglos have figured prominently in the city's history for a century and a half, initiated the 1919 Fiesta, and filled most of the conquistador roles in the early Fiestas, Anglos today have no roles in Santa Fe's mythohistoric Fiesta rituals. Native Americans and Chicanos, who began to challenge the accepted version of history in the aftermath of the civil rights movement, also move at the fringes of the fiesta and occasionally offer up barbed critiques of the proceedings.[34]

Although the Fiesta Queen is thought of by some as a stand-in for La Conquistadora and by others as the younger sister of de Vargas, the role is a modern creation without historical precedent. Queens could presumably be of any ethnic background, but instead are limited to those with Spanish surnames. Even the substantial population

141. EL TORO CREATED BY WILL SHUSTER, SANTA FE RODEO PARADE, ABOUT 1950.
(TYLER DINGEE)

of coyotes, descendants of mixed Hispanic and Anglo ancestry, are excluded from the Fiesta Queen's court (although occasionally a Catanach or Berardinelli portrays one of de Vargas's men). If history stops for Santa Fe revival style architecture about 1870, it begins and ends for public ceremony with the "peaceful" reconquest of 1692.[35]

The energies of Anglos surface elsewhere. Hewett's attempt to fuse the repetitive drumming, singing, and dancing of the Pueblos with European high opera failed in the late 1920s. But in 1955, impresario-conductor John Crosby founded the Santa Fe Opera, which has become one of America's premier summer festivals. In 1973 it was joined by the highly acclaimed Santa Fe Chamber Orchestra and in the 1980s by an explosion of gourmet restaurants and contemporary as well as western and tourist art galleries. These elite cultural activities perfectly complement the burgeoning colony of summer homes for the wealthy. Another predominantly Anglo subculture—the holistic health, feminist, sustainable-growth, environmentalist counterculture—created its own annual festival in 1980—the All Species Day. Its rousing parade, with participants dressed as their favorite plant or animal, shared a sense of grassroots community and irreverent humor with the Hysterical Pageants of the twenties and thirties.[36]

142. FIESTA QUEEN AND HER COURT, ABOUT 1950. (SANTA FE RAILWAY)

"fiesta-siesta," Alianza Federal
mimeographed handbill distributed at the
1969 Fiesta
While the Fiesta de Santa Fe goes full blast—
dancing, singing, plays, eating and drinking,
Reies López Tijerina is imprisoned only a few
blocks away in the Santa Fe jail: A political
prisoner of the same Federal Government
that 123 years ago in the same city bought
out through secret agent the original "ven-
dido" Mexican general Armijo with thousands of gold pieces. For these pieces of gold
Armijo turned over the city—and the entire
southwest—to the Anglos [General Kearney]
without a fight even though he had superior
forces at his command.

Tijerina, who refuses to sell out regardless
of the price—or of the penalty—fights on for
La Raza: for the Spanish history, culture, language and the Treaty of Guadalupe-Hildalgo
and the Mercedes [land grants]: for an end to
discrimination in employment against the

Table 2. Fiesta Organizers and Participants[37]

	De Vargas	Soldiers and Friars' surnames		Chair of Fiesta Committee (later Council)	Committee members' surnames	
		Spanish	Non-Sp.		Spanish	Non-Sp.
1911	George Armijo	43	2	James Seligman	1	2
1919	George Armijo	–	–	Edgar Hewett	0	12
1920	George Armijo	20	23	Ralph E. Twitchell	1	10
1921	Emory Moore	18	22	Ralph E. Twitchell	1	11
1924	Jose D. Sena Jr.	13	11	Edgar Hewett	1	18
1938	Herman G. Baca	–	–	John Meem	3	14
1945	Diego Gonzáles	–	–	Jose D. Sena Jr.	7	13
1957	J.B. Martínez Jr.	–	–	J.B. Martínez Sr.	12	7
1966	Arturo Jaramillo	17	0	Alex Padilla	17	23
1970	Gilbert Martínez	23	2	Edward Gonzáles	35	29
1980	David Rodriguez	23	1	Faustin Chávez	43	17

Indo-Hispano, for an education system that is
something more than Anglo brain-washing
that prepared the Indo-Hispano children for
the prison, the battlefield and the janitor's
broom, and for a system of justice that is not
just an arm of the modern, Washington-nour-
ished Santa Fe Ring that rules New Mexico.

¡Viva Tijerina![38]

From *Symbol and Conquest: Public Ritual and
Drama in Santa Fe, New Mexico,*
Ronald Grime, 1976

Interpreting the Entrada

Though the Caballeros de Vargas have
consulted primary [historical] sources,
they are not attempting to write histories
so much as strengthen values and provide
heroic images with the power to determine

feelings and behavior. The De Vargas figure is a repository, a condensation, of the
virtues which define in part what it means
to be a modern, Hispano Santa Fean. . . .

This De Vargas is a highly idealized
heroic image. In fact, the seriousness of the
image stands in considerable contrast to
similar images in folk dramas like "Los
Moros y Christianos," for example. In this
play the drunkenness of one character provides comic relief in the midst of a serious
battle. In contrast, the Entrada pageant
places all of its emphasis on the dignity,
competence, and piety of the central figure,
so in this respect De Vargas resembles a
modern movie hero more than a figure
from New Mexican folk drama. The
pageant has no humorous elements. . . .

143. Vargas taking possession of Santa Fe, Fiesta, about 1950.
(Santa Fe Railway)

Fiesta Entertainments . . .

Punctuating the intervals between dances were humorously barbed comments, which the largely Anglo audience cheered and enjoyed, even though many of the barbs were aimed at them. The master of ceremonies ridiculed prejudices about Indians while at the same time generating an atmosphere of festivity: "How many of you have seen a real Indian?" he asks. Some hands go up, but the master of ceremonies laughs and ignores them. "We are thinking of not surrendering." He then plays on the wording of a road sign labeled "falling rocks": "The last time we saw Falling Rocks he was chasing Custer's horse." Next he tells an Indian myth in which men were created by being baked in an oven: the black man is overdone; the white man, underdone. The "wonderfully golden, toasty brown Indian" comes out just right. Next: "I once was a cute little Indian!" Then: "Indians, not conquistadores, not Columbus, discovered America." And: "There was a time when Indians really came to the fiesta; I wonder what happened this time." And finally: "You folks have been real nice immigrants today."[39]

"Fiesta Role Seals Bond for Family,"
Camille Flores,
Albuquerque Journal (June 3, 1989)

Javier Martin Alejandro Gonzales remembers the moment he was chosen to represent Don Diego de Vargas in the 1989 Santa Fe Fiesta.

"I look at my father and we both had tears in our eyes," Gonzales said. The bear hug that followed further sealed a bond between the two men, 22-year-old son Javier and father Jorge Gonzales, who at the same age assumed the role of the captain general. . . .

He said he decided as an accounting student at New Mexico State University to "take off the summer following graduation to re-orient myself with my faith and my culture. Sometimes in life they are all you have to carry you through." . . .

"Sometimes I didn't like my coaches very much," said Gonzales with a laugh, referring to his dad, brothers, and to an uncle and cousin who also portrayed DeVargas.

"I thought I at least knew how to say Santa Fe," said Gonzales, who after coaching places the emphasis on the word "feh."

"Holding Up the Sky,"

Pancho Epstein,

Santa Fe New Mexican (April 20, 1990)

This weekend's 10th Annual All Species Day, which dovetails with the 20th Annual Earth Day celebration, is a united effort to raise people's awareness of the problems of the planet. . . . For a two-day period, from 11 A.M. to sundown on Saturday and Sunday, Santa Feans will be treated to, may participate in, and will hopefully learn from annual All Species Day activities that include a parade, sideshows, an ecological fair, displays, magic, theater pieces, poetry, music, singers and speeches. . . .

. . . there will be a multicultural opening ceremony at 11 A.M. on the Plaza Bandstand. "We do everything on time,"

[All Species Day founder and coordinator Chris] Wells said. "I suggest people get to all events early. One thing people can do is car pool or ride a bike. Both will help Mother Earth."

Featured during the opening will be remarks by Mayor Pick, along with speeches from members of the Ecuadorian Rainforest Federation, a federation of Indian tribes from the Amazon. They will be in full-dress regalia. Also speaking will be Santa Clara Pueblo spokesmen Jose Lucero and historian Orlando Romero. . . .

The 10th Annual All Species Day Parade begins at noon Saturday on the Plaza and ends up at Fort Marcy Park. "Its a fun-loving stroll for the whole family," Wells said. "People wear serious as well as humorous

144. ALL SPECIES DAY PARADE, MAY, 1992. (AUTHOR)

costumes. This is a chance for everyone to express his feelings and ideas about the world of nature." . . . The parade includes floats, entries from school environmental clubs, two samba bands and the Santa Fe Schools Elementary Band.

Sunday's festivities conclude at dusk with a walk through a farolito [candles in paper bags filled with sand] labyrinth. This labyrinth is a Hopi design symbolizing Mother Earth and life's transitions. The Hopis say the labyrinth expresses the meaning of spiritual rebirth and the universal plan of the creator. The farolitos will be ignited by the Hiroshima Peace Flame, which has been carried to Santa Fe by a group of global walkers.

"Historic Statue Renamed to Satisfy N.M. Indians,"
Tom Sharpe,
Albuquerque Journal (July 12, 1992)
La Conquistadora, the small statue of the Virgin Mary that has symbolized Hispanic Christianity in northern New Mexico for more than three centuries, has changed her name.

Roman Catholic officials said Archbishop Robert Sanchez renamed the icon "Our Lady of Peace" last week to satisfy American Indians who say the former name denotes cultural domination.

. . . [Isleta Pueblo Indian Joe] Savilla, who with his wife Peggy directs the native Ministries of the Archdiocese of Santa Fe, said the Entrada pageant during September's Fiesta de Santa Fe also distorts the Indian history of New Mexico.

"It's not true history," he said. "They deviate by giving de Vargas a hero's welcome. He was not a hero. They call it a 'bloodless' reconquest. It was not."

. . . Santa Fe Fiesta Council members have been meeting quietly with the archbishop and members of the All Indian Pueblo Council to discuss changes in the Entrada pageant. . . .

"I was so thankful and amazed that it happened now," [Rev. Bill Sanchez] said of Archbishop Sanchez's announcement last week. ". . . with the mixture of blood between us and the culture, we really can't go forward unless there's some reconciliation and unity and healing. The new name is an effort to raise awareness."

"Leaders Call Fiesta Offensive,"
Keith Easthouse,
Santa Fe New Mexican (September 12, 1993)
Prominent American Indians called last
week for an end to Santa Fe's Fiesta, saying
it is essentially a celebration of the conquest of their people by Spain.

Herman Agoyo, executive director of
the eight Northern Pueblos Council, said
reforms enacted last year by the Santa Fe
Fiesta Council to make the celebration less
offensive to Indians have fallen short. . . .

Joseph Suina, associate professor of education at the University of New Mexico,
agreed. . . .

Suina said it would be more appropriate
to celebrate the history of positive interactions between Spanish and Indian peoples
in New Mexico. He suggested a harvest
festival "to celebrate the exchange of food
and tools between Spanish and Indians."

7 RESTORATION IS THE MOST TOTAL DESTRUCTION

Santa Fe has methodically transformed itself into a harmonious Pueblo-Spanish fantasy through speculative restorations, the removal of overt signs of Americanization, and historic design review for new buildings. The initiation of this community-wide historic restoration by the Plan of 1912, at a time when preservationists elsewhere concentrated on individual structures, helped broaden the scope of the American historic preservation movement. Around the country since World War II, the restoration approach has been eclipsed by a preservation ethic emphasizing careful maintenance rather than reconstruction. Although Santa Fe has continued to favor heavy-handed restoration, preservation is now making inroads. Individual buildings in Santa Fe and historic districts elsewhere are often carefully preserved. The net effect of gentrification and historic design review, however, is often the creation of district-wide selective historic fantasies.

As one component of the broader romantic reaction against industrialization and urbanization, the historic preservation movement has been allied with historic revivalism, the pageant movement, the cultivation of ethnic, regional, and national identities, and other forms of tradition making. Before the nineteenth century, builders had employed contemporary materials and methods for new construction and building maintenance. Indeed the great medieval cathedrals, which often took centuries to complete, reveal successive styles and construction techniques. The ancient method, the great nineteenth-century French restorationist Eugene Viollet-le-Duc once wrote, "consisted in adopting the forms in vogue at the time when the edifice had to be renewed or restored—whereas we proceed on a contrary principle—that of restoring every building in its own style." In the restoration of Notre Dame Cathedral in Paris, for instance, this desire for a single unifying style led him to remove a thirteenth-century rose window, which he found incompatible with the rest of the building, and replace it with one of his own design in the style of the twelfth century.[1]

"Restoration," countered preeminent English theorist John Ruskin, "means the most total destruction which a building can suffer: a destruction out of which no remnants

232

can be gathered." His ally, William Morris, characterized restoration as the "Scrape" approach for its inclination to scrape away the accretions of the centuries, and their contrary philosophy as "Anti-Scrape." "Surely," declared Morris in 1884, "it is a curious thing that while we are ready to laugh at the idea of the possibility of the Greek workmen turning out a Gothic building, or a Gothic workmen turning out a Greek one, we see nothing preposterous in the Victorian workmen producing a Gothic one. . . . To my mind it is a strange view of the continuity of history, that should ignore the very changes which are the essence of that continuity." Because the original fabric of a building is essentially irreplaceable, the Anti-Scrape movement advocated diligent maintenance and respect for subsequent alterations—preservation not restoration. If a building is beyond repair, replace it with a new one, they counseled; if an addition is needed, don't disguise it as ancient.[2]

While Europeans had focused on medieval churches, Americans first protected sites linked to political leaders, beginning with George Washington's home at Mount Vernon in the 1850s. Eastern and southern elites established one hundred house museums by 1910 to enshrined Revolutionary and Civil War heros, and thereby hoped to instill patriotism, hard work, and acceptance of Anglo-Saxon leadership among immigrants, the working class, and freed slaves. Because early house museums stood as moral lessons, not as artifacts for historical study, preservation per se was not a high priority, and buildings were freely remodeled to accommodate museum functions. The European debate between restoration and preservation, Scrape versus Anti-Scrape, mattered little. Only with the rise of the Society for the Preservation of New England Antiquities, under William Sumner Appleton after 1910, did the Anti-Scrape, preservation approach begin to spread in the United States.[3]

In southern California, historic preservationists led by the writer Charles Lummis began ad hoc repairs on a few Spanish missions in the 1880s and 1890s, even as these structures inspired the Mission Revival style. But while eastern preservationists were social class descendants and sometimes direct descendants of Revolutionary and

Confederate leaders, those in California were primarily transplants from the East preserving the remnants of another people's history. If eastern elites wore history as a badge of contemporary moral authority, Lummis and company cultivated the missions primarily as a means to promote tourism.[4]

EARLY PRESERVATION IN NEW MEXICO

The ancient practice of building in the contemporary style prevailed in New Mexico into the twentieth century. When Archbishop Lamy commenced a new cathedral in 1869, he chose the then-fashionable Byzantine-Romanesque Revival; and when Territorial Secretary William Ritch led the renovation of the adobe Palace of the Governors in 1877 and 1878, he added a Victorian colonnade and stucco painted to look like stone. But the arrival of the railroad in 1880 brought the first wave of tourists, and with them the awakening nostalgia for America's past.

The first call for preservation was heard in 1883, in response to the Christian Brothers' decision to demolish the dilapidated Spanish Colonial church of San Miguel. The *New Mexican* responded that the city could not afford to lose such a landmark—the "chief monument of the Spanish church militant and flagellant in Santa Fe." A public campaign funded the 1887 repairs by local building contractors Donoghue and Monier. But rather than reconstructing the three-tiered Spanish Colonial tower (fig. 16), which had collapsed in a wind storm during the winter of 1871-72, Donoghue and Monier produced a hipped tower with rounded openings resembling the Richardsonian Romanesque courthouse they were then building across town (fig. 145).[5]

Growing numbers of tourists demanded greater historical authenticity. So when Jake Gold expanded his curio shop in 1893 (fig. 41), for instance, the *New Mexican* noted that "the ancient style of the interior finish will be preserved, as the curio dealer thinks it would be vandalism to modernize the house considering he intends to dub it the 'Old Curio Shop.'"[6]

145. SAN MIGUEL CHURCH, 1887 REMODELING, DONOGHUE AND MONIER.
A VENERABLE MONUMENT REPAIRED USING CONTEMPORARY STYLE AND METHODS.
(T. HARMON PARKHURST)

The Museum of New Mexico initiated the first serious restorations under its director of "Architectural Reconstruction and Photography," Jesse Nusbaum. Nusbaum stabilized Anasazi ruins at Mesa Verde and reconstructed a ceremonial kiva in Frijoles Canyon (now Bandelier National Monument), apparently in the summer of 1910 (fig. 52). He also supervised the restoration of the Palace of the Governors from 1909 to 1913, as well as the construction of the 1914 *Painted Desert* exhibit at San Diego and the 1916 Fine Art Museum in Santa Fe.[7]

The museum characterized its work on the Palace as a "restoration," and although it claimed to have made "every architectural feature historically true," the lack of historical documentation made this project highly speculative (fig. 77). To make the Palace of the Governors serviceable as a public museum, Nusbaum demolished dilapidated walls and reconstructed them with concrete foundations and piers, interspersed with adobe. To make "the whole building uniform," he also applied a contemporary pebble-dash cement stucco, "simulating as nearly as possible the original finish."[8] Formed by throwing a slurry of pebbles and cement stucco onto the walls, pebble-dash provided a rustic surface but in no way resembled earthen plaster applied by hand. Nusbaum also demolished interior walls to form larger exhibit rooms, cut display cases into the adobe walls, and prepared recessed panels for Carl Lotave's Puye and Frijoles Canyon murals (fig. 146).

To create "a noble monument to the memory of the Spanish founders of the civilization of the Southwest," Nusbaum stripped away evidence of "the rush, the impatience, the progress" of the modern world—namely the 1878 portal and recent windows and doors. Their replacements were "designed to conform to the architectural style of the period when the building was constructed." By the fall of 1913, the museum's journal, *El Palacio,* claimed that the work had "progressed sufficiently to give an adequate idea of the unity and massiveness of this historic old structure." This stripping of recent accretions followed by revival style reconstruction to achieve stylistic unity reveal the museum staff as aggressive practitioners of the Scrape approach.[9]

146. FRIJOLES ROOM, PALACE OF THE GOVERNORS, REMODELED 1909-13, MURALS BY CARL LOTAVE. DISPLAY CASES AND MURAL PANELS ADAPT THE ANCIENT PALACE INTO A PUBLIC MUSEUM.

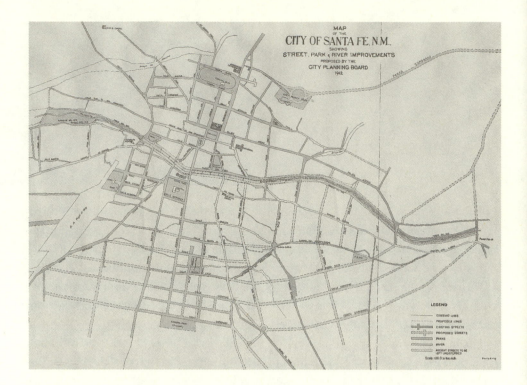

The restoration of the Palace of the Governors and its conversion into a museum paralleled eastern house museums. But Santa Fe's civic leaders also sought the recreation of an entire historic environment—to make the city itself into a tourist attraction. The City Beautiful-inspired Plan of 1912 defined the Santa Fe style with which to create a harmonious historical appearance to attract tourists. Leading proponent Sylvanus Morley also urged "the vital necessity of preserving our historic landmarks and picturesque adobes; and of utilizing them as the dominating note in all plans for civic improvement."[10]

To that end the 1912 plan asserted "that it should be the duty of all city officials to guard the old streets against any change that will affect their appearance. . . . We further recommend that no building permits be issued . . . until proper assurance is given that the architecture will conform exteriorly with the Santa Fe style." The planning board's map of improvements identified "ancient streets to be left undisturbed" (fig. 147). Noted landscape architect Frederick L. Olmsted, Jr., who reviewed the plan, doubted "whether any court would hold it to be within the powers of . . . a City Council, to impose such an obligation upon the owner of private property . . . without provision for the payment of damages." In a time when cities with far greater resources struggled to establish land-use zoning, the political climate was not yet ready for historic design control."

147. "Map of the City of Santa Fe, showing, street, park and river improvements, proposed by the City Planning Board, 1912." (N.L. King)

After lobbying the state legislature unsuccessfully to establish a Capital City Improvement Commission, planning board chair H. H. Dorman began to urge "that everything should be done to create a public sentiment so strong that the Santa Fe style will always predominate." Although the 1912 plan never became legally binding, by the late teens a community-wide consensus did emerge behind the restoration. The city not only began to scrape away evidence of its period of Americanization, but ironically, also demolished a series of historic adobe courtyard houses to make way for the new buildings that solidified the Santa Fe style—the Fine Arts Museum, La Fonda Hotel, the Cassell Building, and a federal building facing the cathedral.[12]

237

THE RESTORATION OF THE ACOMA MISSION

As the romantic Anglo-American community began to reverse the "ill-conceived Americanization" of Santa Fe, they also resolved to preserve the ancient mission churches that had become prototypes for the revival style. During its active years from 1922 to 1932, their Society for the Restoration and Preservation of New Mexico Missions restored churches at Acoma, Laguna, Santa Ana, and Zia Pueblos, as well as the Spanish village church of Las Trampas. The society typically provided tools, modern materials such as concrete and metal flashing, an architect to handle design and structural problems, and an on-site building superintendent to oversee the work. The local Pueblo and Spanish-American villagers, for their part, volunteered labor and supplied adobes or local building stone.[13]

The society's leading backer, Denver timber baron William P. McPhee, for instance, donated $7,000 for the Acoma renovation, equivalent in 1995 to perhaps $250,000. As work at Acoma started in 1924, McPhee's New Mexico Lumber Company was just completing the logging of the common lands of the Tierra Amarilla land grant. The alienation of these lands from the original Mexican settlers is one of the better-documented cases of legislative and judicial chicanery in late-nineteenth-century New Mexico. It is ironic, but not the least unusual, that a leading capitalist, whose

activities undermined traditional communities, also supported the restoration of a tattered remnant of history.[14]

The society's volunteer architect, John Gaw Meem, was a leading preservationist and practitioner of the Santa Fe style from the late 1920s to the 1960s (fig. 183). Born in 1894 to Episcopalian missionaries in Brazil, Meem grew up speaking Portuguese as his second language. His sense of Latino heritage led him on occasion to refer to himself as Juan. A civil engineering graduate of the Virginia Military Institute, Meem served as an officer during World War I, before returning to Brazil as the branch credit manager for a New York bank. Diagnosed with tuberculosis after only a few weeks in this position, he chose to convalesce at the Sunmount Sanatorium in Santa Fe. There sanitorium director Dr. Frank E. Mera and artist Carlos Vierra inspired him with a passion for southwestern architecture. Once Meem recovered his health, he served a brief apprenticeship with a Denver architect, while also attending the evening program of the Beaux-Arts Institute of Design. After opening his Santa Fe office in 1924, Meem continued to be prone to severe headaches and to work himself to the brink of exhaustion. He nevertheless became a nationally known architect and prominent community leader. As chair of the 1938 Fiesta organizing committee, for instance, Meem spearheaded the drive to recapture the spirit of the mid-1920s Fiestas.[15]

148. SAN ESTABAN MISSION, ACOMA, BUILT 1629-44, PHOTO, 1904.
RAVAGES OF THE TIME SINCE THE WITHDRAWAL OF THE FRANCISCAN MISSIONARIES
IN THE 1820S. (EDWARD S. CURTIS)

The restoration of Acoma mission between 1924 and 1930 was the society's longest and most expensive project. Franciscan missionaries directed the construction of the mission of San Esteban in the 1630s beside the then three-hundred-year-old Pueblo village of Acoma (fig. 148). As the best preserved seventeenth-century mission in the United States, it is a National Landmark, an icon of state tourism promotion, and according to architectural historian Vincent Scully, "one of the essential American monuments," "the noblest [church] in the Southwest."[16]

But in the early 1900s, San Esteban stood in disrepair; its roof leaked profusely; its nave walls and towers were badly weathered. The society began in 1924 by replacing the roof. While cultural differences caused some misunderstandings between the Acomas and the society's building superintendent, B. A. Reuter, a major dispute arose in October 1926. "In the reconstruction of the foundation and small terrace at the rear of the Church" (work which used concrete), explained Reuter in a letter to Meem, "I was making it plain that we did not want any cement exposed to view. I noticed the Governor's face get cloudy and serious when I impressed on them that this was an adobe building and that we wanted to keep it an adobe building. That we did not want any rock or cement exposed when we got through. . . . Thereupon the Governor told me that he had all the time been given to understand that we were going to cement the entire outside of the building." Reuter sought to reassure the governor, Baustino Rey, but he soon asserted flatly that he had been lied to and walked away.[17]

Meem had written in the 1924 report of his visit to Acoma that the "Indians are very anxious to plaster all of the outside." Meem envisioned earthen plaster then, and it is apparent from his correspondence with Reuter that the society would never have considered cement plaster. But it is equally understandable that the Acomas assumed cement plaster would be used. After all Anglo-Americans had been hard-plastering adobe buildings throughout the region for fifty years, and the society itself used concrete to reconstruct the roof and foundations. How were the Acomas to know that in the preservation society they had encountered a new breed of Anglo—not the progressive modernizing kind, but the romantic antiquarian variety?[18]

Reuter invited Governor Rey to dinner in hopes of reconciliation, and sent his cook, a twenty-two-year-old Acoma woman, Maria (Aragon?) to tell Rey that she too expected him to come. In a letter written late that same night, Reuter recounted to Meem that when Ray still did not appear:

> I went over to his house got him by the hand put my other arm around him and told him that Maria had supper ready and would be much disappointed if he did not come over. I told him that I had to have a little talk with him, that I had never deceived him and that I loved him. It was too much for his nature and he gaveway washed his hands and came with me.
>
> I had previously posted Maria and got her promise to stay with me until we got this thing all fixed up. . . .
>
> Well I had Maria prepared so after I had introduced the subject and assured the Governor that every drop of blood in your heart was with Acoma and that there must be some misunderstanding and that I really believed adobe would prove better than cement I paused to give Maria a chance to make her speech. She told the governor how she had seen cement fall off of adobe walls in great chunks and how awful it looked and how difficult it would be for the acomas to repair it and how the water then would get behind the other and it would also get loose and fall off and what an artificial spectacle that would be up here on the Rock of Acoma.
>
> Well the Governor fell in just as big chunks as Maria was describing.

With the governor won over, the dispute passed, and the earthen plaster soon went on.[19]

To this day no consensus has emerged about whether earthen or cement plaster is better for adobe buildings. Both are serviceable, given the proper maintenance. The vast majority of adobe houses and most historic churches are now hard plastered. Cement plaster costs more to install but requires less frequent replastering. With a proper foundation and vigilant maintenance, it performs well. But if cracks appear, and are left unattended, the wall can begin to dissolve under the stucco. Earthen plaster, of course, costs less for materials. It more readily shows signs of water damage, and it also allows absorbed water to evaporate more quickly into the air. However, it also requires seasonal maintenance and complete replastering every five to ten years—a significant consideration for the Acomas, not only because of the size of their mission but also because most of them had moved to two newer farming villages, ten miles to the north, and only visited the pueblo on ceremonial occasions. The society justified earthen plaster on technical grounds, although their position was also aesthetic and philosophical.[20]

Their preservation philosophy is more clear-cut in the treatment of the mission's roof drains. These wooden spouts, or canales, were barely long enough to clear the outward batter of the walls, and storm winds blew rain back against the building, eroding what Meem described as "deep arroyos" in the nave's south wall. According to Reuter, "the Indians are well aware of what the spouts do to the south wall against the prevailing winds and they have been insisting that we put some kind of a conducting system there to take care of the water." By a conducting system, Reuter apparently meant pipe downspouts. When Reuter resisted the idea, the Acomas volunteered to pay for the materials themselves. Meem's solution was to construct new wooden canales, lined inside with sheet metal and projecting an additional 5 feet away from the building. Downspouts clearly would have better protected the walls and permitted less frequent replastering, but the society instead insisted on retaining the historical appearance.[21]

The society had a similar aversion to the towers that had been remodeled about 1902 by a local priest, Mexican workmen, and the Acomas (fig. 150). The society found them stiff, unsympathetic, and of too-recent vintage, so they decided to reconstruct their historic appearance. The problem was that the earliest images of the church date to the early 1880s, after wind and rain had already weathered away much of the building. Since the tops of the towers were particularly weathered, their reconstruction would be conjectural.

The ultimate design for the towers is best understood in the context of the evolution of the Pueblo-Spanish Revival style. The 1915 New Mexico Building at San Diego and its descendant, the 1916 Fine Arts Museum, boasted the most prominent early revival style towers (figs. 80, 81). Although the state building and the museum were broadly modeled after the Acoma mission, their towers were patterned after the San Felipe mission to achieve a lighter feeling. This desire for a more vertical proportion continued as late as the society's 1925 fund-raising brochure, which depicted slender towers capped by four small horns reminiscent of San Felipe and the state building (fig. 149). Although Meem began to grapple with the tower design by the fall of 1926, as the south tower was being demolished, work was suspended for the season before he had to make a final decision (fig. 150).

Over the winter, his office landed its first major nonresidential commission, a large addition to La Fonda, the Fred Harvey tourist hotel on the Santa Fe plaza. Meem completed floor plans and elevations for the hotel by May 1927, well before work resumed at Acoma. The visual pivot of Meem's asymmetric yet picturesquely balanced composition for La Fonda is a six-story tower based on the Acoma mission towers, or to be more precise, based on his conception of their historic appearance (fig. 151).[22]

Meem's hotel tower design in turn informed the mission reconstruction. It is true that the hotel tower openings are larger than those ultimately restored at the mission, and that they have balcony railings and corbel brackets. But the batter of the hotel tower, the thickness of the walls surrounding its openings, and its rounded profile all

149. ACOMA MISSION, 1925 FUND-RAISING BROCHURE, SOCIETY FOR THE PRESERVATION AND RESTORATION OF NEW MEXICO MISSIONS. FIRST SUGGESTIONS FOR A POSSIBLE RESTORATION.

150. ACOMA MISSION, FALL 1926. "STIFF AND UNSYMPATHETIC" 1905 TOWERS BEGIN TO COME DOWN.

echoed from the hotel back to the mission (fig. 152). In the process of the restoration, Meem thickened the masonry roofs of the Acoma towers from a few inches to a bit over four feet, while also providing a more massive rounded silhouette. This creative interaction between the design of La Fonda and the restoration of Acoma yielded a new Santa Fe style tower, which Meem subsequently featured in the University of New Mexico Administration Building and Cristo Rey Church (fig. 186). Likewise when San Miguel Church was restored in the mid-1950s (fig. 153), its tower was patterned after Meem's La Fonda/Acoma design rather than on the actual three-tiered Spanish tower known from early photographs (fig. 16).[23]

The society sought to purify the missions of modern accretions. This meant not only the demolition of the 1902 Acoma towers, but also the subsequent removal of pitched metal roofs from the connected residential courtyard. It also meant that any new material used in the restoration (be it cement in the foundation and the roof or sheet metal lining the canales) should be hidden from view once work was completed. While the Acomas shared a desire for the physical preservation of the mission, their principal goal was the reduction of maintenance requirements, not the restoration of a unified historic style. Like the builders of European cathedrals before them, they preferred contemporary materials for repairs and new construction. The preservationists' notion

151. LA FONDA HOTEL, 1927 ADDITION BY JOHN GAW MEEM. ASYMMETRIC COMPOSITION PIVOTS ON A TOWER PATTERNED AFTER MEEM'S BEST GUESS OF ACOMA'S HISTORIC APPEARANCE. (T. HARMON PARKHURST)

that modern materials were acceptable so long as they were hidden from view apparently struck the Acomas as illogical.[24]

Convinced of the correctness of their approach, society officials typically insisted that the work be done their way or they would withdraw from the project. Indeed when the Acomas did not cooperate sufficiently at the beginning of the 1928 building season, the society transferred Reuter to another church, leaving the Acoma mission with the south tower yet to be reconstructed. The following year, when the Acomas made it clear they intended to complete the tower with or without the society's help, Meem wrote to a potential donor that if they undertook the work without expert supervision, "the chances are that the remaining tower would be built in an unsubstantial and inappropriate way and would not match the beauty of the present tower."[25]

FREE STYLE RESTORATION

In Santa Fe too, restoration work continued to be highly speculative. In 1927 artist and builder William P. Henderson restored the Spanish colonial-era Sena House, located just off the plaza (fig. 154). Its provincial Greek Revival porch, added during the American territorial period, had been removed in the 1890s, during the post-railroad Americanization of the city. Henderson first added a two-story wing at the back

152. ACOMA MISSION, TOWERS DESIGNED BY JOHN GAW MEEM,
SUMMER 1927, PHOTO ABOUT 1935. TOWER DESIGN ECHOES BACK FROM
LA FONDA TO THE MISSION. (T. HARMON PARKHURST)

of the rear-facing U-shaped building, to create a large courtyard—hence its current name, Sena Plaza. To unify the old and new portions, he developed a stylized vocabulary of light stucco, heavy posts and lintels, and a Territorial style brick dentil coping. With this restoration, Henderson began to extend Santa Fe's historical fantasy into the American era with the cornice and square rather than tree-trunk posts, but he stopped short when he had the milled beams roughened with a hand-adze and stained dark brown to achieve a rustic effect quite unlike the building's white-washed territorial-era porch.[26]

Santa Fe's supreme fantasy restoration was concocted by Frank Applegate, head of the Department of Sculpture and Ceramics at the Trenton (New Jersey) School of Industrial Arts. An aficionado of Spanish colonial art, Applegate had come for the 1921 Fiesta and never left. He purchased the old four-room de la Peña House near Camino del Monte Sol in 1927, and by the time work ceased with his untimely death, four years later, the house had more than quadrupled in size (figs. 155-58). Applegate shifted the porch lintel and corbel brackets up to a new second-story porch and placed a duplicate lintel below. Like Morley and Meem before him, he thickened the parapet over his porch to achieve a more massive effect. He set old wooden cupboards into existing walls and replaced the crooked log vigas inside with antique corbels and hewn beams.[27]

153. SAN MIGUEL CHURCH, ABOUT 1955. NOT A RESTORATION TO ITS HISTORIC APPEARANCE (SEE FIG. 16), BUT THE ADAPTATION OF THE ACOMA-LA FONDA TOWER. (HARVEY CAPLIN)

154. SENA PLAZA, REMODELED BY WILLIAM PENHALLOW HENDERSON, 1927.

Nusbaum's 1912 view of the interior records bundles of herbs, a mano and metate for grinding corn, utilitarian pots, a large whisk broom, a metal tub, and on the wall, a religious lithograph. Mexican artifacts and modern American utensils disappear from later photographs, replaced by a showy display of Indian arts: Navajo blankets, Apache baskets, a Pueblo drum and kachinas, and a fringed buckskin quiver, hung like a painting on the wall. Bold wall accents that had blocked out architectural elements and changes in wall planes in 1912 were replaced by a "tasteful" unifying dado of the sort used in a variety of period revival styles.

By the late 1920s, John Gaw Meem had several large Santa Fe style houses under construction for wealthy newcomers. One of his clients, heiress Amelia Hollenback, already had houses in Brooklyn and the Pocono Mountains. She often traveled to London, Paris, and Florence, and had visited the Southwest regularly since the late 1890s to attend Pueblo dances. She was approaching fifty years of age when she asked Meem to design a Santa Fe house for her and her companion, Miss Hoffmann. Because Hollenback was nearly deaf, she wrote detailed memos to Meem recapitulating their design conferences, thereby producing an unusually complete record of their collaboration. Near the beginning, she explained:

> I am fond of low ceilings, and like wall niches, and dug-out
> rain spouts. Outdoors I want the roof ladder to be of the
> old type, like the Indians', of round poles with sticks thrust
> through. Some time I intend to put up an outside oven, and—
> if I can find a use for them!—a log dugout watering trough
> and one of those raised pole platforms that are used for dry-
> ing hay or vegetables, storing wood, sheltering wagons, and
> almost everything else. You see, dignity and comfort permit-
> ting, I want something extremely informal that will let us amuse
> ourselves with old ways and old things, but heaven preserve it

155. DE LA PEÑA HOUSE, BUILT ABOUT 1800, PHOTO, 1912. (JESSE L. NUSBAUM)

156. DE LA PEÑA HOUSE, REMODELED BY FRANK APPLEGATE, LATE 1920S,
PHOTO, 1965. (KARL KERNBERGER)

157. DE LA PEÑA HOUSE, 1912. A LEAKING VIGA ROOF, FUNCTIONAL POTTERY AND,
PERHAPS, THE DRYING HERBS OF A *CURANDERA*—FOLK HEALER.
(JESSE L. NUSBAUM)

158. DE LA PEÑA HOUSE, 1965. NEW, ELABORATE CORBELS AND HEWN BEAMS;
ONCE-FUNCTIONAL NATIVE BOWLS, BASKETS, AND THE LIKE DISPLAYED AS ART.
(KARL KERNBERGER)

RESTORATION IS DESTRUCTION

from looking arty! I hope it will look merely natural and sort of inevitable.

And (this request is serious, and should have preceded the above trifles), we are anxious to take sunbaths, but Miss Hoffmann could not climb a ladder.

In this poignant projection onto the exotic Other, Hollenback equates her desire for an informal life of sunbathing and amusement with Pueblo Indians and their architecture. She nevertheless senses the difficulty of achieving this—the possibility of looking arty and unauthentic that hovers over her romantic yearnings.[28]

Hollenback and Hoffmann, as well as their agent, a Mr. Pino, canvased the old Pueblo and Spanish villages for wooden details to use in her house. "The Indians were about to use the old vigas in some new dwelling," Hollenback wrote to Meem during one expedition, "but say they have so many new vigas they would probably just as soon sell the old." When archaeologist Paul Reiter offered her "some prehistoric vigas, discarded from the excavations in Chaco Canyon," she wrote to Meem. "If you think we would have a chance to use them, it would certainly tickle my romantic sense and be of real interest to me. I imagine they would need to project through the walls, as the hacked and burned ends would be part of the exhibit." Although these Chaco vigas were not used (probably because they were structurally unsound), Hollenback assembled a substantial collection of historical wood details, which were fumigated and measured.

Meem next designed each major room around a set of beams: corbels and vigas from the Las Trampas church sacristy in the living room, some beams from the Gran Quivera ruins in the dining room, another set from San Miguel del Vado in Miss Hoffmann's bedroom, some hewn and carved beams from Acoma in Miss Hollenback's bedroom, and a 30-foot-long elaborately carved beam from Bernalillo on the main portal (fig. 53). Also scattered throughout the house were Spanish Colonial and Folk

Territorial doors, a contemporary screen door by folk carver José Dolores López, and Hollenback's collection of Pueblo pottery, Navajo blankets, and Spanish Colonial furniture. When Miss Hoffmann died, soon after the house's completion, Hollenback left it in the hands of caretakers and returned only occasionally over the final two decades of her life.[29]

Meem went to great lengths to create the illusion of a natural setting undisturbed by modern works (fig. 159). Just before construction began, Hollenback complained that someone was taking lichen-covered stones from her property and explained to Meem that "all my days, I have longed for free access to nearby wild land—broken hills and woods and wide views that nobody would ever landscape, nor smooth, nor change at all." To that end Meem quietly saw to it that no more stones were taken. He also had the adobes made off-site, partly to avoid marring the property, and buried the telephone and electrical wires. Rather than turning the house in on itself in the manner of a Spanish courtyard, however, Meem opened it out along the brow of a hill. This allowed him to carefully orient a great deep portal and adjoining terrace toward exhilarating views of the Jemez and Sandia Mountains while also extending the living room to visually screen the garage, a neighboring house, and "quite an expanse of wires and poles."[30]

In addition to interior hallways and a walled patio for sunbathing, Meem incorporated modern conveniences into the Hollenback House, such as a two-car garage, five bathrooms, a fully appointed kitchen, and a buzzer system to summon the servants (fig. 160). The prevailing social structure was also reflected in the selection of George N. Eubank as the building contractor over Mr. Pino, who wished to bid on the house. Meem felt Pino lacked sufficient experience and wrote to Hollenback that Eubank, by comparison, "combined the requisite experience as a builder with a genuine feeling for the native quality of our architecture" and "will be able to give exactly the primitive quality you want in your house by using a certain number of native workmen and directing them expertly while his standing as a contractor will enable you to have him assume responsibility at all times."

Native workmen might be employed to impart a primitive quality, but in Meem's estimation, here as at Acoma, they were not ready to assume overall control.[31]

Although outnumbered by descendants of Spanish colonists and Pueblo Indians, the Santa Fe expatriate community assumed responsibility for defining and protecting the region's cultural heritage. They claimed cultural authority by virtue of connoisseurship: Meem through his detailed knowledge of historic architecture, gained by restoring churches; Edgar Hewett through his Anasazi excavations; Kenneth Chapman by meticulously cataloguing the graphic designs of Pueblo pottery, Frank Applegate through his collection and aesthetic appreciation of Spanish Colonial arts (and in its own right, this book through its scholarly apparatus of footnotes). When Mary Cabot Wheelwright, who would establish a museum of Navajo ceremonial art, prepared a travel itinerary for John D. Rockefeller, Jr., in 1926, she included several "little Mexican towns," but also proposed a call on "Mr. and Mrs. Henderson [who] have a very attractive house built in the old Spanish style." The distinction is subtle, but telling: they live in "little Mexican towns," we build in the "old Spanish style." Unlike their eastern counterparts, Santa Fe's preservationists did not open house museums to commemorate individual Spanish or Pueblo leaders, nor to install their descendants and values atop the contemporary social hierarchy. Instead, like their southern

159. AMELIA HOLLENBACK HOUSE, JOHN GAW MEEM, 1932.
HOLLENBACK TO MEEM; "I HOPE IT WILL LOOK MERELY NATURAL AND SORT OF INEVITABLE." (ANSEL EASTON ADAMS)

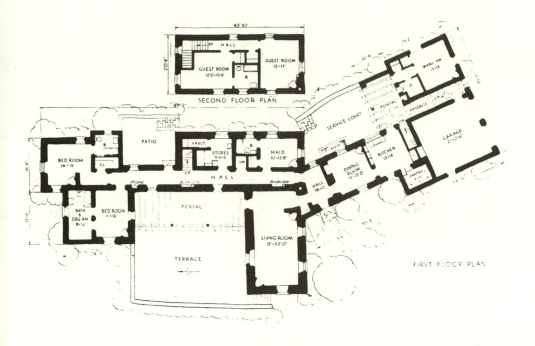

SECOND FLOOR PLAN

FIRST FLOOR PLAN

251

California cohorts, they used architecture to promote tourism and craft romantic retreats for themselves.[32]

As lavish residences began to appear on the hills straddling Camino del Monte Sol in the late 1920s, the remaking of Santa Fe's public face proceeded only fitfully, and several Italianate and neoclassical buildings remained around the plaza. The Old Santa Fe Association was founded in 1926, to encourage the preservation of the city's architectural charter, customs, and public celebrations. Following the depression of 1929, its public profile declined, although association leaders Ina Sizer Cassidy, Sylvia Loomis, and John Gaw Meem consulted informally with those remodeling old buildings or constructing new ones.[33]

In 1930 a competition for the redesign of the plaza was sponsored by Cyrus McCormick, Jr., Chicago heir to the McCormick reaper fortune, who was then building a Meem-designed summer house north of the city. Meem won the competition with a plan to add unifying Spanish style portals on the east and west sides and to remake all of the building facades in either the Pueblo-Spanish or Territorial Revival style. The plan was not immediately executed, for lack of resources and legal authority, but Meem would receive private commissions to remodel the facades of nine plaza buildings between 1937 and 1954.[34]

160. HOLLENBACK HOUSE, PLAN.

Design Control Districts

Elsewhere in America after World War I, the house museum approach broadened to the type of preservation pioneered by Santa Fe—the recreation of large historical environments. Most notable was John D. Rockefeller, Jr.'s, restoration of Williamsburg, the colonial capital of Virginia (fig. 161). Rockefeller had become acquainted with Santa Fe's 1912 restoration plan, when he visited the city in the summers of 1924 and 1926. Beginning at Williamsburg in 1926, Rockefeller funded the restoration of 82 eighteenth-century buildings, the removal of 720 modern buildings (which in this case meant those built after 1800), and the reconstruction of 341 colonial buildings based on often sketchy evidence. The Negro residents of the district, too, were relocated. Rockefeller also had power lines buried and rerouted automobile traffic to a new Colonial Parkway tunnel under the historic precinct to achieve, in the words of his close associate and biographer, Raymond Fosdick, "the harmony of an earlier era." Here was the nineteenth-century Scrape approach on a grand physical and social scale.[35]

Likewise in Santa Fe, when Rockefeller established the Laboratory of Anthropology in a Pueblo-Spanish style building designed by Meem, he sought a similar harmony by offering to pay for the restuccoing of buildings on adjacent properties to match the laboratory. From Colonial Williamsburg and the Laboratory of Anthropology to the Acadia, Grand Tetons, Yosemite, and Mesa Verde National Parks, this son of a business tycoon sought to banish evidence of modern industrialism from select historic and natural enclaves. If the City Beautiful movement failed to impose its dream across entire communities, and the 1912 Santa Fe plan lacked binding legal authority, Rockefeller succeeded at Williamsburg, Rockefeller Center, and elsewhere by simply purchasing all the property involved.[36]

Design control over large environments was also popularized through world's fairs and began to take root in planned communities and legal covenants on residential subdivisions. During the 1920s, planned Spanish-Mediterranean style communities with design control covenants sprang up across the Sunbelt from Florida to California.

Then in 1931, preservationists in Charleston, South Carolina, enacted the first permanent historic design-review ordinance. And by the mid-1950s, approximately ten historic communities from New Orleans to Santa Barbara had also established design-review programs.[37]

Santa Fe's unwritten restoration consensus continued between the world wars, reinforced by the construction of Pueblo-Spanish and Territorial Revival civic buildings under Roosevelt's New Deal (chapter eight). Following World War II, the city's suburban subdivisions also began to carry covenants limiting house builders to "the New-Old Santa Fe, Pueblo or Spanish style of architecture."[38]

Santa Fe's architectural consensus was violated in the mid-1950s, however, by a generation of young modernist-trained architects. Although they suppressed historical ornament in true modernist fashion, their buildings were not the pure glass and metal cubes of the International style, but rather rustic western interpretations of modernism. The 1954 Centerline building design by John Conron and his longtime partner, David Lent, became the favorite target of Santa Fe traditionalists. A native of Boston, Conron served in the Army Air Corps during World War II before studying architecture at Yale with the leading modernists Louis Kahn and Edward Durell Stone. After his apprenticeship in Boston, Conron and Lent chose to settle in Santa Fe in 1952 because, to them, it had the look of a foreign country and was small enough to offer a rich community life. In addition to his architecture, preservation, and interior design practice, Conron has been active in the Fiesta, putting the torch to Zozobra for over thirty years.[39]

For the Centerline building, Conron and Lent remodeled a hipped-roofed red-brick cottage of about 1910 for use as their interior design store featuring American and European modern furniture (fig. 163). The Centerline's articulated wooden structure and cantilevered balcony projecting through a glass curtain wall made it fine Western Modernism, akin to the redwood and plate-glass houses of Californian Harwell Hamilton Harris.

253

161. DUKE OF GLOUSTER STREET, WILLIAMSBURG, VIRGINIA, AFTER RESTORATION BEGUN IN 1928. FOR ALL THEIR OUTWARD DIFFERENCES, AN UNDERLYING RESTORATION DESIRE MAKES WILLIAMSBURG AND SANTA FE FIRST COUSINS.

162. TERRITORIAL GOVERNOR'S MANSION, RAPP AND RAPP, 1908. DEMOLISHED 1950S. (MUGATT)

The effects of the dramatic growth of Santa Fe's population also unsettled the traditionalists. The population rose from 11,176 in 1930 to 27,998 in 1950, and by the mid-1950s, Santa Fe boasted over one thousand hotel and motel rooms (appendix). Traffic became congested on the narrow roads, and parking was scarce around the plaza. The booming strip of motels, service stations, billboards, and neon signs along Cerrillos Road especially offended the traditionalists. The old Santa Fe Trail approach to the city, then called College Street, was threatened with a similar fate, while behind the scenes, the state entertained an expansion of the capitol complex. The Old Santa Fe Association blocked the transformation of College Street, although in time the capitol complex devoured much of the historic Barrio Analco.[40]

In February 1956, the *New Mexican* issued a call for a city ordinance mandating the Santa Fe style: "Our chief danger lies in the fact that we are fast becoming less and less unique, and more and more like any southwestern community of comparable size." City councilor Leo Murphy seized the issue, stating "this situation is going to get out of hand one of these days, if we don't get busy and draw up a code and a systematic plan for orderly growth which also will preserve Santa Fe's distinctiveness." "Relying as we do upon the tourist dollar for a substantial part of our economy," editorialized the *New Mexican* in support of Murphy, "Santa Fe can not afford to allow

163. CENTERLINE BUILDINGS, CONRON AND LENT, 1954. THIS BUILDING, MORE THAN ANY OTHER, SPURRED THE TRADITIONALISTS TO CAMPAIGN FOR HISTORIC DESIGN CONTROLS. (JEAN ROGERS OLIVER)

even occasional architectural misfits to slip by." But in July, a premature design control ordinance was rejected by the planning commission.[41]

The foremost spokesmen for the traditionalists was Oliver La Farge, son of prominent New York architect Christopher La Farge and grandson of leading American artist John La Farge. Born in 1901, he completed a master's of anthropology at Harvard before settling in the French Quarter of New Orleans. There La Farge wrote his first novel, *Laughing Boy*, the story of a young Navajo's confrontation with the modern world, which won the 1930 Pulitzer Prize for fiction. He emerged as an outspoken proponent of Native American rights, and after a decade on the New York literary scene, served in the Air Force during World War II. In 1946 he settled permanently in Santa Fe with his wife, Consuelo Baca, daughter of an Hispano and a French immigrant. La Farge immersed himself in local affairs and was soon the darling of the art colony.[42]

Beginning in 1956, La Farge proselytized in his weekly *New Mexican* column for design control and against the widening of College Street and the expansion of the capitol grounds. These issues propelled Councilor Murphy's mayoral campaign to victory that fall. Meanwhile Ina Sizer Cassidy, a poet who directed the state's WPA Federal Writers Project and for twenty-nine years wrote an arts column for *New Mexico Magazine*, worked with John Meem to mobilize the traditionalists. The *New Mexican*

164. SANTA FE, SINCE WORLD WAR II. (PATRICIA POLLOCK)

contributed one thousand dollars to the Old Santa Fe Association and ran a series of articles and La Farge columns extolling the design control program in Santa Barbara. Membership in the association swelled from some fifty to over four hundred, most of whom turned out for a series of public forums, planning commission, and city council meetings through the end of 1956 and into 1957.[43]

At a time when Santa Fe was still three-quarters Hispano, however, only 3 per cent of association members were Spanish surnamed. Spanish-American leaders had been slow to build Pueblo style houses in the 1920s and 1930s, and now their support for historic preservation was tentative. While conceding that the preservation of some buildings is desirable, Concha Ortiz y Pino de Kleven, a descendant of the two leading colonial families, a former state representative, and for sixty years a cultural leader, remarked in 1990, "I am happy my ancestors built of adobe, so that rather than have them desecrated by ignoramuses, they have, for the most part, gone back to the earth."[44]

La Farge and local architect Irene Von Horvath drafted a second design control ordinance. It required that a "historic Style Committee shall judge any proposed alteration or new structure for harmony with adjacent buildings, preservation of historic and characteristic qualities, and conformity to the Old Santa Fe Style." This encompassed "the so-called 'Pueblo,' or 'Pueblo-Spanish' or 'Spanish-Indian' and 'Territorial' styles." The ordinance described the Pueblo-Spanish Revival as Morley had in the teens, even paraphrasing passages from his writings: flat roofs and adobe-colored walls complementing projecting vigas, canales, buttresses, and portales. The ordinance also allowed a "Recent Santa Fe Style" that adapted historic forms to modern needs but nevertheless employed materials, colors, proportions, and details similar to historic buildings. Cantilevered forms were prohibited, while doors and windows were limited to not more than 40 percent of a building's facades and to no closer than three feet from the corner of a building.[45]

As the council vote on the ordinance approached in the fall of 1957, opposition

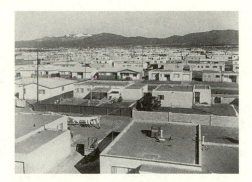

coalesced behind the newly founded Southwest Design Council, consisting of Conron, Alexander Girard, Robert Plettenberg, and other young designers, reenforced by the founding editor of the influential magazine *Landscape,* local resident J. B. Jackson, as well as by a professor of architecture at the University of New Mexico in Albuquerque, Don Schlegel, and by the director of the Roswell, New Mexico Museum, architectural historian David Gebhard. "We are not opposed to—we are in fact heartily in favor of—the preservation of historic buildings and areas," observed council president Conron. "The Ordinance, as proposed, outlines no procedure for the maintenance and preservation of valued historical buildings. Instead the ordinance stresses the importance of limiting future buildings . . . to mimicked copies of historical landmarks." Indeed Conron and other council members proved themselves staunch historic preservationists over the years; they simply doubted that good design could be legislated. "The essence of a free society," wrote David Gebhard with a dash of Cold War rhetoric, "is that it allows the greatest possible expression of ideas. It is presumptuous and entirely totalitarian in spirit for any group of citizens, self-appointed or elected, to set itself up in judgement on such an individual matter as architectural expression." Responded La Farge wryly in his column, "The Southwest Design Council has registered its 'unanimous and firm opposition' to the present ordinance, thus putting us on notice that there is strong sentiment against the measure in both Roswell and Albuquerque."[46]

257

At a final public forum, in which Von Horvath and Meem faced off against Conron and Gebhard, the "amount of frequent applause" indicated strong support for the ordinance. Two nights later, the city council adopted it unanimously.[47]

Landscape editor John B. Jackson, ever the incisive, detached commentator, observed a week later that the city council "has gone on record endorsing architectural uniformity, but much more important, it has also gone on record as endorsing planning." This new resolve, thought Jackson, should first be applied to the city's substandard housing. Likewise the Old Santa Fe Association could perform a public

165. SUBURBAN SUBDIVISION, ABOUT 1965. THE SUPERFICIAL FLAT-ROOFED, ADOBE LOOK, WITHOUT THE SOCIAL SUBSTANCE OF THE NEIGHBORHOOD PLAZA OR THE EXTENDED FAMILY HOUSING COMPOUND.

service by broadening its study from historic buildings "to include the whole subject of local residential streets and alleys and compound layout"; the association should look beyond style to spatial settlement patterns and traditional building types. Conron, who continued for many years as the leading critic of design review, took up the call in 1960 for "a new and more imaginative sub-division ordinance encouraging . . . the development of Santa Fe's most charming aspects—the 'cul-de-sac' and the 'compound.'" Even as Santa Fe reveled in its adobe image, it abandoned these traditional residential patterns for zoning that required front, side, and rear yard setbacks and that yielded a mixture of cookie-cutter subdivisions and custom houses on two-and-a-half-acre lots (fig. 165).[48]

When American's foremost public intellectual and regional planning theorist, Lewis Mumford, visited Santa Fe in 1962, he found nothing aesthetically wrong with these developments: brown stuccoed houses blended well with the landscape. But he saw the abandonment of cul-de-sacs and oasis-like compounds, and of a traditional urban density, as an unmitigated social disaster: "there are values of neighborliness and accessibility, of having choices which you don't have when you are by yourself out in the midst of unoccupied country." Santa Fe has only gradually faced the issues first raised by Jackson, Conron, and Mumford: the need to provide low-income housing and to build upon traditional settlement patterns.[49]

166. SOUTH SIDE OF THE PLAZA, ABOUT 1940. (SEE ALSO FIGS. 34, 116)

The historic styles ordinance addressed only one spatial pattern: the Spanish tradition of portales in commercial areas. Santa Fe's portales had been removed in the 1890s, with the construction of Italianate business blocks set back from the street the width of the sidewalk. The museum staff first called for their return in the teens, as did the 1929 plaza design competition. But architects continued to respect the American set-back pattern as late as the 1950s, when they cut shallow portales into the mass of new buildings such as Woolworth's. "When we go native, as we think," observed La Farge in his column (even as he drafted the ordinance), "we bastardize the portal in its proper sense . . . and produce an inset portal that recedes from the building line." Finally in 1966 Meem drafted an economic revitalization plan that argued that the plaza area "must counteract the parking handicaps by being so attractive in itself that it will draw not only tourists, but high-class business as well." Central to increasing its attractiveness was the return of the "portales, unify all the businesses, faced on the Plaza." Meem and fellow architect Kenneth Clark mixed the Pueblo-Spanish and the Territorial Revival styles in their designs for the ten-and-a-half-feet-tall portales, which offered "the required spaciousness and dignity" (figs. 166, 167).[50]

167. SOUTH SIDE OF PLAZA, 1991. PORTALS, JOHN GAW MEEM AND KENNETH CLARK, 1967. (AUTHOR)

HISTORIC PRESERVATION

The adoption of the design-review ordinance also stimulated interest in Santa Fe's historic architecture and in historic preservation as distinct from restoration. When the planning commission surveyed the city to identify significant buildings in 1956, "to its utter amazement, it found that only some twenty-five buildings comprised the great antiquity of this world-renowned tourist mecca!" So successful had the museum been in its romantic image making that not only had many historic structures been replaced with revival style buildings, but people had come to prefer the revival fantasy to the historic reality. This new attention to Santa Fe's historic architecture responded to Conron's charge that design review without historic preservation would make Santa Fe a revival style sham. It also reflected the rise of Anti-Scrape preservation attitudes across the country, often linked with the modernist denigration of earlier historic revivalism.[51]

The Commission's 1956 report on historic buildings highlighted eighteen pre-1846 structures, another eight early Territorial buildings, and the 1890 Delgado House. Their list included four moderately to heavily restored buildings: the Lobato-Morley House, the Palace of the Governors, Sena Plaza, and the de la Peña-Applegate House. No longer would an atmosphere of historical romance alone confer status, however. "Factual evidence of antiquity" was now required, and the Old Santa Fe Association began combing the archives for such evidence. A spin-off of the Association, the non-profit Historic Santa Fe Foundation, began to publicize real historic buildings with a 1962 brochure; while their *Old Santa Fe Today* has gone through four editions since it first appeared in 1966. [52]

The political arm of the traditionalists, the Old Santa Fe Association, unsuccessfully opposed the construction of the city's first enclosed shopping center, De Vargas Mall, in 1969. They also sought to alert the local Urban Renewal Agency to important historic buildings. The 24-acre renewal area west of the plaza included buildings going back to the 1700s, but it was the run-down home to poor *mexicanos* and their

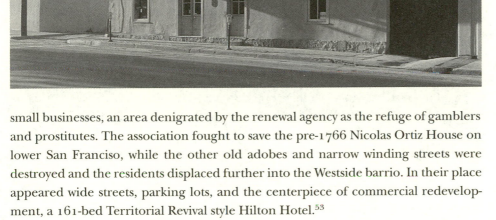

small businesses, an area denigrated by the renewal agency as the refuge of gamblers and prostitutes. The association fought to save the pre-1766 Nicolas Ortiz House on lower San Franciso, while the other old adobes and narrow winding streets were destroyed and the residents displaced further into the Westside barrio. In their place appeared wide streets, parking lots, and the centerpiece of commercial redevelopment, a 161-bed Territorial Revival style Hilton Hotel.[53]

Santa Fe's infatuation with romantic history and the Scrape-restoration approach has only gradually slackened. In 1966 the Padre Gallegos House was relieved of its territorial-era pitched roof and bracketed porch. The subsequent restoration, like most restorations, looks after a few decades like the work of its era—in this case a precise 1950s modernist interpretation of the Territorial Revival. John Gaw Meem's 1969 restoration of the Felipe B. Delgado house, by comparison, was confined to basic maintenance, the replacement of some deteriorated woodwork, and repainting in the original colors (fig. 168).[54]

Meem also headed the 1973 Historic Santa Fe Foundation campaign to save the 1851 Pinckney R. and Maria T. Tully House. While the house's owner, attorney Albert Gonzales, claimed it was not worth saving because it was constructed in the "Gringo era," the planning commission blocked its demolition until funds for purchase and

168. DELGADO HOUSE, RENOVATED BY JOHN GAW MEEM, 1970.
(KARL KERNBERGER)

restoration could be raised. The stucco over its adobes walls had been painted to look like red bricks in the early 1870s, then subsequently restuccoed an adobe color. The restoration of its brick stenciling made the Tully House the city's most emphatic statement of territorial-era Americanism (fig. 55).[55]

RECENT DESIGN REVIEW

Santa Fe architects have continued over the years to complain that design-review regulations prevent them from making a fresh interpretation of the historic styles. Many of the traditionalists, for their part, seem never fully to have grasped that design review protects the early-twentieth-century romantic image of the city, the Santa Fe style formulated by the museum in the teens and codified by city ordnance in the fifties. The ordinance did nothing to protect the city's actual historic architecture, except in the case of the few buildings that conformed to the romantic image. This confusion between revival style and historic architecture came to a head in 1981. A home builder, who had been denied permission to erect a house with a pitched metal roof, pointed out that neighboring historic adobes had corrugated metal roofs. Architects and planners took a fresh look at the city's actual historic buildings and quickly concluded that terneplate and corrugated metal roofs were indeed a part of the historic context. In 1982 the city council approved supplemental guidelines permitting elements such as metal roofs on streets where they are already present.[56]

One metal-roofed design, Ashley Place, a medium-sized commercial building by Santa Fe architect Jack Gaffney, soon came up for review (fig. 169). "It took a long time to figure out what I could do down there in the historic zone," Gaffney recalled. While the stuccoed brick buildings of the twenties had lent themselves to rounded Pueblo style forms, the cost-effective steel- or wood-frame structures of the 1980s produced sharp-edged buildings. Gaffney reasoned that the Territorial Revival, with its formal classically derived forms, was best suited to these contemporary materials. Consciously paralleling the recent neoclassicism of Italian architect Aldo Rossi, Gaffney developed

a spare version of the Territorial Revival. By omitting overt Territorial details, he achieved a pure geometry of square window grids and stacked sharp-edged cubes, topped by a single pyramid—the hipped roof intended for the two-story tower. Gaffney argued that this roof was justified by nearby hip-roofed historical buildings. Although the city staff agreed and recommended approval, the review board voted to approve the project only if the roof were removed. Appeal of this decision would have caused costly delays, so compromise was the only practical course. Gaffney sacrificed the pyramidal roof and compensated with a Territorial Revival brick cornice.[57]

The city's tourist economy exploded in the 1980s, amid the international vogue of Santa Fe style. The number of hotel rooms grew 68 percent during the 1980s, from approximately 2,260 to 3,800. Occupancy rates, nevertheless, climbed from under 60 percent to over 70 percent, and hotel receipts shot from 25 million dollars in 1985 to 86 million dollars in 1992. Art galleries and Indian goods shops nearly tripled, from 107 to 295, during the decade, while gourmet restaurants, chic clothing stores, book-stores, and tour businesses multiplied. Escalating commercial property values encouraged a jump in the scale of new construction surrounding the plaza.[58]

Several large buildings erected in the 1980s precipitated a crisis in the design-review process. The traditionalists' ire fell primarily on the First Interstate Bank building, a

169. Ashley Place, Jack Gaffney, 1983. When the design review board blocked a pyramidal roof for the two-story tower, Gaffney compensated with a more conventional brick cornice. (Author)

mixed office/commercial project occupying most of the block behind the Palace of the Governors (fig. 170). The two-story cube at the building's northeast corner, in particular, attracted derision, graffiti, and raw eggs. "Ugly!" was repeatedly spray-painted here through the course of a year, only to be painted over each time by the bank. In contrast to Rapp's and Meem's use of picturesque composition to suggest incremental growth, the long, repetitious porches of the Interstate building betray the regimentation of large-scale financing and invite associations with faceless bureaucracy.[59]

El Dorado Hotel, which appeared next, captures more of the romance of Santa Fe, especially in its richly detailed interiors (fig. 171). The architects, McHugh, Lloyd and Associates, originally designed landscaping and building ornament at ground level, but as the project began to run over budget, these were scrapped. Private balconies on the fourth and fifth floors remained, however, because they supported higher room rates. Without the street-level detailing, the blank walls and the over-sized cut-out entrances became forbidding. This monumentality is intensified by the obsessive symmetry of the Sandoval Street facade, where each window, each buttress, each balcony is mirrored by another on the opposite side. Before modernism deemphasized such distinctions, this kind of formality was reserved for public buildings and classical designs rather than for a picturesque fantasy such as a tourist hotel. Perhaps through too much reverence, the Pueblo style has taken on a formal grandeur at odds with its humble origins. Traditionalist wags christened this building the *Bastard of Ugly*.[60]

With the construction of these and other massive buildings, the community realized that detailed historic style regulations alone would not protect their image of Santa Fe. In response the city planning department produced a handbook defining fifteen townscape districts. The height and density of new buildings were closely tied to the existing architectural scale in each district. But while they limit size, the townscape guidelines cannot guarantee better design. Several subsequent projects (in the words of local architect Dale Zinn, "designed with a calculator") simply filled the entire developable envelope, leaving the architect little ability to modulate the massing.[61]

170. First Interstate Bank Building, RNL and Dorman Nelson, 1982-83. The corner where "Ugly" was repeatedly spray painted. (Author)

171. El Dorado Hotel, McHugh, Lloyd and Associates, 1984-85. An obsessive formal symmetry at odds with the picturesque tradition of tourist hotel design. (Author)

Nor is it clear that large buildings per se destroy the city's character. John Gaw Meem's locally admired 1929 addition to La Fonda Hotel (fig. 151), for instance, is taller and more densely developed than the 1980s buildings. The focus of Meem's picturesque composition is that six-story tower designed during the restoration of Acoma mission. To the left, a fourth-floor balcony balances against the main tower, while also gesturing to the original 1921 three-story entrance on the left. Secondary masses step down to a cluster of four balconies framed by three-story buttresses, which unify the lower portions of the design. As part of their Beaux Arts training, architects of Meem's generation learned the uses of historical ornament and picturesque composition to evoke preindustrial buildings. Despised by modernists as frivolous concerns, such traditions disappeared from the curriculum of architecture schools after World War II. As a result, a generation of architects was not taught these skills, which had been so essential to the development of Santa Fe's character.

265

THE EMERGING STRUGGLE BETWEEN RESTORATION AND PRESERVATION

Since its creation in 1966, the National Register of Historic Places has helped standardize preservation philosophy across the country, even drawing Santa Fe more toward preservation. The requirement that properties be at least fifty years old to be listed on the National Register of Historic Places reenforces the inclination of preservationists to denigrate recent construction in historic districts—what the register originally labeled "intrusions." Similarly recent additions and alterations to historic buildings represent a "loss of integrity." Both the physical and social means of the work are implied: in a physically complete, original state, uncorrupted, ethically upright. The search for historic integrity, like the insistence on the purity of one's race or ethnic group, becomes a symbolic expression of the desire for social order. Indeed the "loss of integrity" is most often found in neighborhoods that have been passed down the economic scale to the poor or where pragmatic vernacular builders freely employ contemporary materials and replace old windows with new ones, thereby violating the first commandment of historic preservation. The return of "integrity," likewise often takes the form of gentrification by economic and cultural elites who have the "good taste" to remove incongruous accretions—that is, the evidence of the modern world and the intervening lower-class inhabitants.[62]

Federal Preservation Grants in the 1970s and Preservation Tax Credits after 1981 reinforce these attitudes. To qualify for these subsidies, a property must not only be on the National Register but must also adhere to the "Secretary of Interior's Standards for Rehabilitation," which mix the Scrape and Anti-Scrape approaches. In classic Scrape fashion, these standards favor the removal of recent accretions and permit the careful recreation of historic details that may have been lost or become deteriorated. On the Anti-Scrape side, accretions more than fifty years old usually cannot be removed, and new additions may not be disguised as historic.[63]

Santa Fe's Historic Design Review Board began to worry late in the 1980s that Santa Fe style remodelings and new construction had left so few unaltered fifty-year-old buildings that the city was in danger of losing its National Register designation. Property owners stood to lose preservation tax credits, while the perception of a loss of historic authenticity might hurt tourism. "Our city's historic buildings include territorial, even Victorian, styles," editorialized the *New Mexican* in 1991. "Putting pueblo-style trimming on a pitched-roof house or plastering over a red-brick gingerbread home may be as great an affront to historic preservation as aluminum siding on an adobe building." In 1992, eighty years after the museum initiated the Scrape restoration of the community, and thirty-five years after the historic styles ordinance, Santa Fe adopted an ordinance designed to balance the preservation of historic buildings against the community's strong revival style and restoration tendencies.[64]

The Scrape predilection and the reluctance to acknowledge recent history, nevertheless, continues to be widespread, witness recent renovations of the old public library and Our Lady of Guadalupe Church. The 1907 Mission style Women's Board of Trade

Library had been remodeled in 1932 by John Meem in a modest fusion of Spanish Colonial and Territorial Revival styles. Kenneth Clark's 1962 entrance addition was a classic modernist interpretation of the Territorial Revival—apparent not only in the treatment of the entrance as a glass cube but also in the slender proportions of the portal posts (fig. 172).

When the city library moved to new quarters in 1988, the Museum of New Mexico's History Museum, next door in the Palace of the Governors, purchased the building and began to raise funds for its renovation. In the first phase, Clark's glass cube was stuccoed over, to reduce energy losses and avoid potential vandalism to the windows, it was said (fig. 173). His portal was also removed, both because Meem's entrance was being reopened and to make way for a new handicapped-accessible entrance. These issues might well have been addressed in other ways, had the desire existed to preserve the 1962 entrance. Traditionalists instead derided Clark's entrance as a "large fish bowl."[65]

After one generation, buildings inevitably look out-of-date; their proportions seem awkward, their colors not quite right—such is the psychology of fashion. They are freely altered and demolished. But given another generation or two, they begin to be valued as historic; now they are not only preserved, but their harsh treatment by intervening generations is righteously lamented. Santa Fe has yet to adopt the lesson some preservationists have drawn from this phenomenon—namely, that the best work of each generation should be preserved, whether or not it pleases contemporary tastes. That the state's history museum destroyed one of the finest modernist interpretations of Santa Fe style reflects the depth of antihistorical sentiment in the community. To paraphrase John Ruskin: it is a strange view of history that suppresses the continuity of change and accretions that are the essence of real history.

The successive Scrape restorations of Our Lady of Guadalupe have had an added undercurrent of ethnic politics. When the original flat-roofed adobe Spanish Colonial church (fig. 24) was turned over to the English-speaking Catholic congregation in

172. PUBLIC LIBRARY, ENTRANCE ADDITION BY KENNETH CLARK, 1962. ONE OF THE BEST MODERNIST-INFLUENCED INTERPRETATIONS OF THE TERRITORIAL REVIVAL. (ARTHUR TAYLOR)

173. HISTORY MUSEUM ANNEX (OLD LIBRARY), REMODELED BY LABAN WINGERT, AND FRIENDS OF THE PALACE, 1990. REMOVING THE UNFASHIONABLE WORK OF THE PREVIOUS GENERATION. (AUTHOR)

RESTORATION IS DESTRUCTION

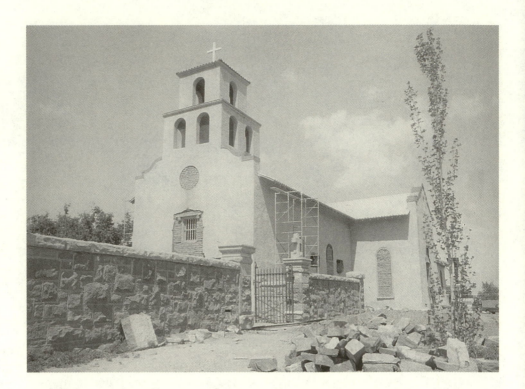

1880, Florence Donoghue added arched windows, a pitched roof, and a steeple (fig. 25). The congregation had become predominantly Hispanic again by 1922, when the church was damaged by fire. The California Mission styling of the new pressed-metal "tile" roof and a new entrance with cast-stone accents (fig. 174) suggests a Spanish identification, contrary to the Pueblo-inflected style then being promoted by the museum. Likewise when a new church was constructed beside the old Guadalupe in 1960, the parish chose the Territorial Revival rather than the other styles allowed by the recently enacted design-review ordinance—the "Pueblo," the "Pueblo-Spanish," and the "Spanish-Indian."[66]

The old church was transferred to the nonprofit Guadalupe Historic Foundation in 1976, to qualify for federal bicentennial grants to convert it into a center for concerts and art exhibits. The group's local architects were Victor Johnson and Robert Nestor, and its chief instigator was Nathaniel Owings of the leading national firm of Skidmore, Owings and Merrill, who had a second home near Santa Fe. They decided to restore the building as nearly as possible to its Spanish Colonial appearance (fig. 175). They squared off the tower openings and replaced 1880s windows and the 1924 entrance with new ones loosely based on pre-1880 photographs. The 1924 hard stucco and crisp brick parapets were also stripped away, in favor of earthen

174. OUR LADY OF GUADALUPE CHURCH, POST-1923 TOWER AND PARAPETS SHOWN, 1976 RESTORATION UNDER WAY. A BUILDING TORTURED BY SUCCESSIVE "SCRAPE" RESTORATIONS. (ARTHUR TAYLOR)

 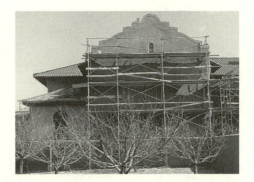

plaster and straight concrete caps. Here funds ran out, with the pitched roof and tower still in place. The result was a hybrid layering of Spanish Colonial adobe body, 1880s modernization, 1920s Mission style reconstruction, and half-completed 1970s Scrape restoration.[67]

As the nearby depot area began to revitalize in the 1980s, the Mission style helped distinguish it from the older plaza tourist district. The Guadalupe Historic Foundation, too, began to change with the addition of more Hispanic parishioners. A 1991 statement of intentions lamented the deteriorated adobe plaster and also explained that "the Foundation now feels that the California Mission Revival exterior is not only what is best remembered by most people," it "is an essential part of the building's history . . ." They resolved to return the arched tower openings, the mixtilinear brick parapets, and cement stucco, but to retain the 1975 Spanish style windows, which they felt were compatible with the Mission style (fig. 176). Before work began, title to the property was returned to the Church, reportedly for insurance purposes. With the brick parapets already restored, the Archbishop's Commission for the Preservation of Historic New Mexico Churches, chaired by Victor Johnson, intervened to prevent the hard plastering. The commission insisted instead on a mixture of earth and lime. Like their traditionalist predecessors at Acoma in the 1920s, the commission's stated reasons for favoring earthen plaster were technical; however, the church's survival from 1923 to 1975 with hard stucco suggests that their motivations were also aesthetic and romantic. After one winter, this lime-adobe plaster weathered so badly that the archdiocese's property manager decided to redo the job with hard plaster.[68]

WESTSIDE GENTRIFICATION

This dispute reflects the broader encroachment of tourist-traditionalist sensibilities on the Westside neighborhood served by Our Lady of Guadalupe. This area expanded in the 1920s, with the migration from surrounding villages caused by the loss of common lands and an agricultural depression, and was encouraged by the growth of tourism,

269

175. SOUTH TRANSEPT OF GUADALUPE CHURCH, 1976 REMODELING. (AUTHOR)

176. SOUTH TRANSEPT 1991 REMODELING RETURNS TO 1920s PROFILE. (AUTHOR)

service, and government jobs in Santa Fe. The Spanish-Mexican vernacular building tradition continued to evolve here, largely unaffected by the revival style remaking of the tourist district.

At the end of the nineteenth century, houses in Spanish-speaking neighborhoods across the Southwest stood side by side at the street's edge and were often oriented toward private courtyards to the rear. In response to the picturesque cottage, the bungalow, and the suburban ranch houses erected by Anglo-Americans, Mexican-Americans built more compact free-standing houses, situated 10 or 15 feet back from the sidewalk. On the west side, owner-builders have continued the Spanish-Mexican traditions of room-by-room accretion, multiple exterior doors, and masonry construction. Many enclose the sides and rear of their lots with tall walls and define the sidewalk's edge with low masonry walls or masonry piers linked by picket fences, wrought iron, chain link, or decorative block (figs. 61, 62, 177, 178). These owner-built enclosures and the Westside houses themselves reveal a taste for textured stucco, polychromatic brickwork, wrought iron, and ornamental stone veneers, as well as for vivid blues and greens, in addition to pastels and whites. This vibrant aesthetic contrasts with the muted Arts and Crafts earth-tone palette that predominates in the wealthy Anglo Eastside neighborhood.[69]

Jose N. Trujillo, the master of the Westside vernacular style, was born and raised in Ledoux, on the east side of the Sangre de Cristo Mountains. Trujillo refers to himself in conversation as "Mexican" more often than as "Hispanic." He joined the Civilian Conservation Corp camp at Santa Fe in 1935, where he learned stonemasonry while building retaining walls along the river. After stints on the railroad in Wyoming and in the army during World War II, he returned to Santa Fe to work as a maintenance foreman for the city housing authority and as a salesman at Big Joe Lumber. Since 1947 he has constructed an extensive compound of two houses, a rental duplex, ornamental walls, and courtyards just west of St. Francis Drive (figs. 62, 178, 179).

Trujillo's tall courtyard walls, lower front yard walls, retaining walls, and low curbs meticulously subdivide the property into car-parking spaces, packed-dirt courtyards,

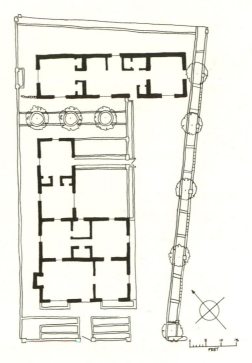

and raised flower and vegetable beds. He combines scavenged stone and wood architectural details, metal tractor wheels and auto wheel hubs, bowling balls, and other jetsam of a modern city with sculptures from friends and invented treatments such as incised pebble-dash stucco. His repetition of ornamental concrete block and a palette of light brown, dark red-brown, and turquoise paint unites the compound. "It's just a bunch of monkey business," Trujillo enjoys telling visitors. "I say to my wife, if you can have all your *monos* in here," gesturing to a living room cabinet filled with figurines and photos of their children and grandchildren, "then I can have my monkey business outside."[70]

Unlike the fading Chicano murals scattered throughout the neighborhood, the Westside vernacular is not perceived as an overt expression of cultural identity. Apart from the study of streetscape characteristics that architect Beverly Spears undertook for the planning department about 1986, Trujillo and this widespread vernacular have remained invisible to most tourists and aficionados of Santa Fe style. Nor has this vernacular been seized by Mayor Jaramillo or neighborhood activists as a symbol of Westside identity.

As the 1980s progressed, the effects of Santa Fe's popularity began to be felt on the west side. The reduction of upper-income tax rates by Ronald Reagan's 1981 tax

177. 900 BLOCK OF MERCER STREET, WESTSIDE NEIGHBORHOOD, 1991. THE DISTINCTIVE MEXICAN-AMERICAN STREETSCAPE OF THE WESTSIDE NEIGHBORHOOD IS LITTLE NOTICED BY AFICIONADOS OF SANTA FE STYLE. (AUTHOR)

178. JOSE N. TRUJILLO HOUSE, WESTSIDE NEIGHBORHOOD, 1947 TO PRESENT. FROM THE MASTER OF THE WESTSIDE VERNACULAR (SEE FIG. 62) (AUTHOR)

179. JOSE N. TRUJILLO HOUSE, PLAN. PART OF A LARGER COMPLEX OF COURTYARDS, GARDENS, HOUSES AND A DUPLEX. (PATRICIA POLLOCK)

plan fueled a construction boom of quarter-million-dollar condominiums and mul-timillion-dollar second homes. The accompanying explosion of real estate values exac-erbated the shortage of affordable low- and middle-income housing. As property values escalated elsewhere in Santa Fe, the Westside attracted young primarily Anglo but also Hispanic professionals, who began to remake the barrio in the Santa Fe style image. Similar social gentrification, often linked to historic preservation, has occurred across the country. In the early 1990s on the west side, it was not uncommon to see a BMW and an Isuzu Trooper parked beside a house recently remodeled in the Santa Fe style, and next door a banged-up black '68 Chevy in front of a Westside vernacu-lar home.[71]

Gentrified properties typically adopt the Eastside pattern (fig. 180) with new six-foot-tall, adobe-colored walls or pole fences at the sidewalk (fig. 181), the better to create a romantic Spanish courtyard and to protect one's property from an "unde-sirable element" that still lingers in the neighborhood. Anglos have not only adopted the pole fence, which Hispanos called *cerca de palo* or *palito* fences, but have completed a symbolic appropriation by rechristening them "coyote" fences in real estate-builder parlance. Some long-time Westside residents told Spears that these changes were destroy-ing the face-to-face interaction and sense of community fostered by the low walls. This ironic inversion finds Anglo newcomers cloistered behind high adobe walls and the Hispanic working class building houses that open emphatically to the street.

In 1983 the city's historic design-review process was extended to the portion of the barrio east of St. Francis Drive, formally mandating the revival style. Santa Fe style, based in part on an earlier stage of the Spanish-Mexican vernacular tradition, is now helping to legitimize the social and spatial transformation of this Hispanic neighborhood. The ordinance establishing the Westside district specified "browns, tans, local earth tones and soft pastels" but prohibited the painting "of buildings with a color that causes arresting or spectacular effects or bold repetitive patterns." While the height of walls and fences is not addressed, the ordinance prescribes "brick, adobe,

 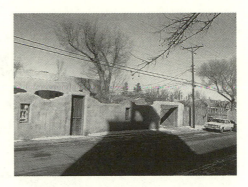

masonry, rock, wood, and coyote fencing," but prohibits unpainted concrete block and chain-link—the predominant vernacular choices. Although some owner-built projects evade the design-review process, the most vibrant examples of the contemporary Hispanic vernacular are now technically illegal in the eastern half of the Westside barrio. (Trujillo lives just outside the review area.) "It is probably no coincidence," wrote Beverly Spears in 1990, "that the creation of the Westside/Guadalupe Historic District and its design controls coincided with a period of sharply escalating property values and real estate speculation in the area." The suppression of the working class Mexicano aesthetic goes hand in hand with their displacement from the neighborhood.[72]

273

The economic forces unleashed by the international vogue of Santa Fe style since 1980 have carried the 1912 plan to realization. This fantasy adobe restoration was envisioned by the museum under Hewett, Morley, and Nusbaum, and later nurtured by the traditionalist enclave led by Meem and La Farge. The recent flood of tourists and second-home builders has reenforced the stereotypic Santa Fe style image. From buried telephone lines to the adobe paint over the Italianate Catron Building, the desire to remove or camouflage evidence of the modern world remains strong. Scrape restorations and equally selective revival style design guidelines have combined to obliterate much of the city's historic architecture, thereby denying the changing tastes and values that constitute any community's real history. The gentrification of the west side through a combination of historic design review and real estate speculation adds a further social dimension to this transformation. The realization of a unified Santa Fe style image obscures Anglo economic control and masks contemporary social inequities. Indeed this absorption with surface and image has proceeded in tandem with the neglect of deeper social and spatial design issues.

180. 500 BLOCK OF CAMINO DEL MONTE SOL, EASTSIDE NEIGHBORHOOD, 1991.
(AUTHOR)

181. DE FOURI STREET, GENTRIFIED PORTION OF WESTSIDE NEIGHBORHOOD.
(AUTHOR)

8 MODERN REGIONAL ARCHITECTURE, 1930 TO 1992

When John Gaw Meem, the architect who would dominate Santa Fe architecture at midcentury, stepped off the train in 1920 chasing a cure for tuberculosis, the city was an outpost of romanticism, its architecture a new and vigorous strain of picturesque eclecticism. Although Meem could have chosen any southwestern city with a sanatorium, from Colorado Springs to San Diego, he was attracted to Santa Fe by railroad promotional photographs of the desert and Pueblo-Spanish style buildings. The leading proponent of the new style, Carlos Vierra, emphasized the evocation of the region's exotic cultures, the asymmetric yet balanced compositions of its buildings, and especially the resemblance of adobe structures to eroded land forms. When Meem recovered his health and opened an architectural office in 1924, his work at first showed the influence of his mentor, Vierra. But by the end of the decade, Meem began to grapple with modernist architectural theory and to formulate a style of his own.

The dilemma for Meem, as for every regional artist in the twentieth century, was how legitimately to continue historical traditions, to respond to local climate, and to foster local community at a time when international economic, technological, and artistic trends drove toward cultural homogenization. How succeeding generations have faced this dilemma is best seen in the writings of the modern regionalist John P. Conron, the sustainable economic theories of Peter van Dresser and other solar designers, the buildings of modern regionalist turned pop impresario, Antoine Predock, and a new residential community known as The Commons. Stylistic regionalism has continued unbroken through the decades, although modulated by a modernist abstraction of forms. A deeper regionalism that responds to local climate and topography and addresses social and economic factors has had a more sporadic history.

At the end of the nineteenth century, European protomodernists such as Voysey, Mackintosh, and Hoffmann simplified and abstracted traditional folk building forms. Such a modernist abstraction of the Pueblo-Spanish style began away from Santa Fe in the late teens. Europeans Rudolph Schindler and Richard Neutra, who transplanted avant-garde modernism to southern California in the teens and twenties, "saw that

the Hispanic/Native American Pueblo tradition of the Southwest was this country's equivalent of the folk traditions of Europe and the Mediterranean." Schindler's 1916 design for a "Country Adobe House" in Taos employed a few stylized historic details but emphasized the rounded sculptural shapes of the building. A more severe abstraction of regional forms—a reduction to blank walls with cut-out voids for doors and windows—appeared in the El Navajo Hotel of 1916 in Gallup, New Mexico, attributed to Mary Colter. Likewise in the 1921 Franciscan Hotel in Albuquerque, Henry Trost rendered projecting canales and stylized vigas in cast concrete (fig. 182). By grouping the windows into recessed panels, Trost gave the tower a vertical emphasis and the appearance of a solid block pierced by slits.[1]

275

Over this stylistic regionalism washed the populist regionalism that swept the country under the New Deal. In its most fully articulated form in the writings of Lewis Mumford, 1930s regionalism responded to the economic collapse of the Great Depression with a vision of decentralized economies organized around regional cities. An indispensable component of city-regional clusters for Mumford was an active cultural life based on the history and special conditions of each area. Regionalist artists, for their part, abandoned the elitism and abstraction of modernism for a social realism accessible to the society at large.[2]

In Santa Fe and elsewhere around the world over the past century, urban elites have often employed romantic regionalism to assert intellectual, aesthetic and moral authority over the working class and the countryside. This contrasting populist impulse, which peaked in the United States under the New Deal, sought to foster political alliances across social class lines. In New Mexico as elsewhere, this populism has proven to be a rearguard action of romanticism, however, because of its tendency to retreat from modern realities into superficial nostalgic stereotypes of traditional cultures. This escapism decreased the regionalist ability to formulate a viable political program and, in architecture, to progress beyond style to the building types and settlement patterns that interact with deeper social structures.[3]

182. FRANCISCAN HOTEL, ALBUQUERQUE, TROST AND TROST, 1923. A MODERNIST ABSTRACTION OF TRADITIONAL FORMS.

The New Deal's coordinated program of economic reform and cultural preservation in New Mexico sought to document traditional Hispanic music, folklore, and customs, and to revive local crafts as a supplement to subsistence agriculture. New Deal officials recognized that the economic plight of Spanish-Americans resulted not only from the depression in wage jobs, but also from overgrazing, soil depletion, and the loss of grant lands. The government sought to improve education, health care, and nutrition, and to modernize farming and stock-raising practices. Federal agencies also began to purchase grant lands from private owners for use by local communities and to shift federal grazing permits from large ranchers to subsistence herders.[4]

These initiatives failed for a variety of reasons. The underlying unresolved paradox in the government's approach was a local version of the dilemma of assimilation versus cultural pluralism. The preservation of traditional values, such as the inclination to put family and village above individual monetary gain, was contradicted by the introduction of technological and economic innovations that undermined these values. Attempts to redress the loss of Spanish-Mexican grant lands created frictions with Pueblo communities and opposition from large ranchers. Most federal programs in New Mexico only began in 1936 or 1937 and were cut short by the outbreak of war in 1941.

This tenuous political program and attraction to nostalgia left the New Deal regionalists vulnerable. As the 1930s progressed, the New York intelligentsia increasingly attacked regionalism as culturally reactionary: Southern writers were tainted by their association with segregation, while midwestern painters such as Thomas Hart Benton and Grant Wood epitomized Anglo-Saxon provincialism. Commercial interests also coopted regionalism, for instance, when Benton was commissioned to paint genre scenes for Lucky Strike cigarette advertisements. As attention shifted to the international stage with the approach of World War II, regionalism was branded as isolationist and, almost overnight, ceased to be a viable nationwide movement.[5]

MEEM'S REGIONALISM

Throughout the 1930s, however, the climate of support for regionalism nurtured New Mexican arts and architecture. This impulse was expressed primarily through major public buildings rather than any experimentation in community design. Pueblo-Spanish Revival buildings predominated in Santa Fe and on the University of New Mexico campus in Albuquerque, were constructed at other sites around the state, and were scattered through California, Arizona, Colorado, and Texas. Across the country New Deal buildings divided evenly between those in a regional historical vein and ones in what was then called the "modernistic" style.[6]

Partisans of architectural modernism believed that a building should not only express its function, its structure, and the nature of its materials, but also the spirit of the modern era. For the strict modernist, ornament and historical evocation contradicted the industrial drive for precision and efficiency. Many American architects of the 1930s nevertheless believed that modernism was compatible with the evocation of an area's traditions. Meem first took up this debate in an address to the 1931 American Institute of Architects national convention in San Antonio: "This is the machine age, and buildings are typified by the use of steel and glass. But our city has no industries, it does not produce machines. . . . Every modern demand can be met within traditional forms,

183. JOHN GAW MEEM WITH 1934 MODEL FOR THE COLORADO SPRINGS
FINE ARTS CENTER, PHOTO ABOUT 1950. MEEM'S MOST MODERN DESIGN,
A BUILDING OF POURED CONCRETE. (TYLER DINGEE)

and still be true to the demands of function and expression of simple materials. We are trying not to imitate the spirit of the times in the great city, but to be true to the spirit of the times in our own section, thus preserving still vital ancient values and adding to the joy and charm of living." Working in a tourist town with little industry, Meem sought to be true to the historicist tradition-making side of modern culture.[7]

At that 1931 AIA meeting, as Meem later acknowledged, he was inspired by a talk given by Eliel Saarinen, a leader of Finnish national romanticism, who had moved to the United States in the 1920s. Meem found encouragement for his beliefs in Saarinen's view that "great epochs in architecture were developed by an intuitive feeling for what he called, 'the fundamental form of the time.' This fundamental form is a composite of everything in a people's culture, in their way of thinking and living."[8]

Fortuitously for Meem, local historical forms mirrored modern forms: terraced Pueblo villages resembled the set-back massing of Art Deco skyscrapers, while rounded flat-roofed adobe buildings echoed Streamlined Moderne shapes. By rejecting the modernist tenet of the honest expression of materials and structure and instead emphasizing an intuitive grasp of the fundamental form of the time, Meem could justify his application of adobe-colored stucco over reinforced concrete and brick. But Meem's regionalism remained primarily aesthetic and stylistic, without engaging in Mumford's economic regionalism or in an examination of building types and settlement patterns that might reinforce traditional culture or foster contemporary community.

Meem saw his buildings as sculpted blocks of adobe, inspired by historic buildings "still a part of the earth as dignified in their simplicity as the land itself." Echoing Vierra, Meem sought "to recreate the past in soft plastic earth shapes to which wind and earth give a final modeling." In Santa Fe's first generation of Pueblo-Spanish style buildings, such as La Fonda and the School for the Deaf, Isaac Rapp had multiplied projecting vigas and canales, corbels, and lintels across taut, sharp-edged forms with thin stepping buttresses. Carlos Vierra began the shift toward sculptural massiveness in his 1921 house.[9]

In his own work after 1927, Meem clustered detailing around porches, entrances, and balconies, thereby freeing large expanses of wall for expressive effects. In both the Laboratory of Anthropology (fig. 184) and the Santa Fe Presbyterian Church, he borrowed the form of the massive rear buttress of Ranchos de Taos Church, broke it in two, and deployed the halves on either side of the entry. To further insure the massiveness of his designs, Meem avoided terminating porches with free-standing wooden posts (as Spanish colonial builders sometimes had) and instead contained them between projecting rooms or thick masonry piers.

In the tower balcony of La Fonda Hotel's addition, designed in 1927 in conjunction with his restoration of Acoma mission, Meem framed the openings with stout masonry piers and a thick parapet (fig. 151). This cubic form with rounded edges became his primary compositional form, adaptable to any scale. His most monumental interpretation of this form was the book tower of the University of New Mexico's Zimmerman Library (fig. 185). As in Trost's design for the Franciscan Hotel (fig. 182), Meem recessed the windows in vertical panels, which he pulled together so that they would read as a group contained in the bulky mass of the tower. Meem terminated the library's lower wings with similar recessed openings surrounded by massive piers and lintels. In Zimmerman Library, La Fonda Hotel, Cristo Rey Church and his other

184. Laboratory of Anthropology, John Gaw Meem, 1929.

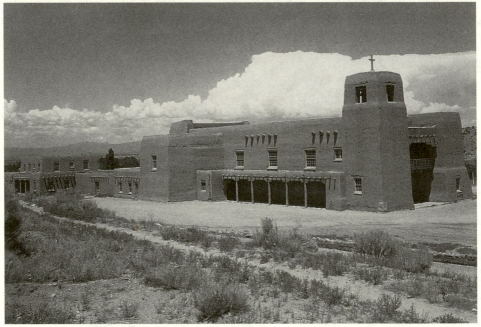

185. Zimmerman Library, University of New Mexico, Albuquerque,
John Meem, 1936. A massive, cubic form repeated at various scales.
(Laura Gilpin)

186. Cristo Rey Catholic Church, John Meem, 1939. The last, great adobe
mission. (T. Harmon Parkhurst)

civic buildings, John Meem shaped reinforced concrete, clay tile, brick, and stucco into dignified monumental forms enhanced with sumptuous buttresses and enlivened with hand-crafted wooden details (fig. 186).[10]

TERRITORIAL REVIVAL

The New Deal helped stimulate a new regional idiom. Based on the provincial Greek Revival buildings of nineteenth-century New Mexico, this Territorial Revival style emerged in the early 1930. Jesse Nusbaum's 1912 photographic survey of historic architecture had included many buildings with faintly classical porches, pedimented lintels, and brick copings—the predominant features of Santa Fe architecture from 1847 to 1880. But Sylvanus Morley's first definition of the Santa Fe style excluded these American-era details in favor of purely Pueblo and Spanish elements. Indeed the Santa Fe style house-design competition sponsored by the chamber of commerce in 1913 forbade "columns or architectural details in the classical orders." Carlos Vierra's second place design, nevertheless, was capped by brick copings, while Meem's 1925 Ashley Pond house and Charles Gaastra's 1925 Gustave Baumann house also employed this one detail of Territorial architecture.[11]

By the late 1920s, Meem had begun to include more Territorial details in his domestic work, such as the pedimented lintels of the otherwise Pueblo- and Spanish-inflected 1928 Vilura Conkey house. This had a certain historical logic: Pueblo and Spanish buildings received their first glass windows in the American era (most with Territorial trim), so that an authentic design would simulate this sequence of accretion. The following year, painter-builder William Henderson employed brick cornices and square wooden porch posts in his renovation of Sena Plaza (fig. 154). Meem's 1929 Robert Tilney House (fig. 187) epitomized the emerging revival, with its pedimented lintels, brick copings, classical porch posts, flat roof, and light-colored stucco. Meem also mixed in an arched transom and grille, as well as wrought-iron brackets under the canales, details derived from the contemporary Spanish Colonial Revival.

187. ROBERT TILNEY HOUSE, JOHN GAW MEEM WITH GORDEN STREET, 1929.
(ANSEL EASTON ADAMS)

281

Meem shares credit for developing the Territorial Revival style with Gordon Street, who joined his office as a designer in 1927. Educated at the University of Kansas and the École des Beaux Arts in Paris, Street opened his own office after five years with Meem and quickly landed a commission to design Harrington Junior High School. There he employed a similar vocabulary of sharp-edged masses, brick copings, occasional white pedimented lintels, and brown Spanish style entry portals.[12]

In 1934 Meem reached the mature formulation of the Territorial Revival in the Federal Emergency Recovery Administration (FERA) Building (now known as the Villagra Building). (The FERA, an umbrella for early New Deal programs, was later superseded by the PWA and WPA). In the FERA Building, Meem employed the same brick copings and white trim he had used in the Tilney House, but omitted the wrought-iron accents (fig. 188). The placement of the FERA Building, facing the entrance to the state capitol, and the use of this new regional classical style symbolically asserted the advent of New Deal bureaucracy. Not surprisingly Meem and Street employed the Territorial Revival for several other New Deal civic buildings in Santa Fe: a municipal building (Meem, 1936), the New Mexico Supreme Court (Street, 1936, fig. 189) and Harvey Junior High School (Street, 1937). While Street continued to add one or two brown wood accents, Meem settled on white classical details and brick copings. The modern tendency to define pure cultural and stylistic categories favored this distillation to all-Anglo detailing in the Territorial Revival.[13]

This formulation of the Territorial Revival quickly became the unofficial style of the state of New Mexico, not under the direction of Meem or Street, but rather in the hands of a new Santa Fe firm, Kruger and Clark. Willard C. Kruger, who emerged as Meem's nemesis in the late 1930s, was a man thirteen years his junior, born in the northeastern New Mexico railroad town of Raton and graduated from Oklahoma A. and M. Kruger and his partner Kenneth Clark served as the staff architect and assistant architect for the New Mexico WPA before opening their own practice in 1938. They adopted the Territorial Revival for most of their government work, including county courthouses in

188. VILLAGRA (FERA) BUILDING, JOHN GAW MEEM, 1934. THE FIRST MATURE
TERRITORIAL REVIVAL BUILDING: CREAM STUCCO, BRICK CORNICES, PEDIMENTED
LINTELS AND A WHITE COLONNADE. (AUTHOR)

Hot Springs (now Truth or Consequences) (1938) and Las Vegas (1942). When Clark returned from the Air Force after the Second World War, Kruger refused to take him back into the firm. Through widely placed campaign contributions and by making his vacation cabins at Tres Lagunas available to leading politicians, W. C. Kruger and Associates emerged as the de facto state architect, a position they held until Kruger's death in 1984.[14]

Although the state toyed with the Pueblo-Spanish style for its capitol complex, it ultimately settled on the Territorial Revival. In the years leading up to statehood, a neoclassical capitol and governor's mansion were erected in Santa Fe (figs. 39, 162), and as late as 1922, a large capitol annex continued this style, ignoring the emergent Santa Fe style. In 1934, however, a state planning study noted the incongruity of neo-classicism for New Mexico state buildings and called for the adoption of the Santa Fe style, which it further characterized as the "Indian-Spanish" type. Meem's 1934 FERA Building and Street's 1937 Supreme Court nevertheless pioneered the Territorial Revival. Kruger and Clark proposed to remodel the old capitol building in the Pueblo-Spanish style in 1938, but this was never executed. Finally in 1950, Kruger and Associates remodeled the capitol in the Territorial Revival style (fig. 190). The removal of the dome and temple-front entry deprived the old capitol of the conventional symbols of government, which Kruger compensated for with a new tower.[15]

189. NEW MEXICO STATE SUPREME COURT, GORDEN STREET, 1936.
(T. HARMON PARKHURST)

Why did the Territorial Revival emerge in the civic buildings of the 1930s to become the unifying style of the capitol complex? The revival's sharp-edged forms were less expensive to execute convincingly with modern materials than the rounded Pueblo-Spanish Revival. The style also synthesized two tendencies of New Deal architecture: the use of classicism to symbolize the power of the modern bureaucratic state and provide assurances of government stability in hard times, and the use of regionalism to express its populist economic and cultural programs. The suggestion of adobe construction provided by cream-colored stucco marked this as a distinctively regional brand of classicism and, one could argue, an architectural synthesis of triculturalism. The Territorial Revival reconciled the capitol with the city's historical identity, while also distancing it somewhat from the tourism economy and local romanticism, which were not shared in all parts of the state.

MODERNISM AND MODERN REGIONALISM

The mood of New Mexico changed during and after World War II. Many who left small towns and villages for the military and West Coast defense work returned to the growing cities with new aspirations and a desire for up-to-date buildings. During the war, the Atomic City, Los Alamos, sprang up 25 miles northeast of Santa Fe on the Pajarito Plateau, where Santiago Naranjo and Edgar Hewett had scouted for Anasazi ruins thirty-five years earlier. Some 60 miles to the southwest, Sandia Laboratory grew up at Albuquerque's Kirtland Air Force Base, giving New Mexico two of the nation's three nuclear weapons research laboratories. From the 1912 plan to World War II, architectural innovation centered in Santa Fe, although the capital remained second to Albuquerque in population. While it grew steadily from 20,325 in 1940 to 34,676 in 1960, Albuquerque leapt from 38,042 to 201,189 in those same decades. Santa Fe would continue to attract young architects with romantic inclinations, but greater opportunities were to be found in Albuquerque.

The number of registered architects in the state doubled in the decade following

190. BATAAN BUILDING (REMODELED CAPITOL, SEE FIG. 39), W.C. KRUGER AND ASSOCIATES, 1950.

284

the war. Santa Fe's four architectural offices in 1940 quadrupled to sixteen by 1960. Most of the young architects who arrived in New Mexico during the 1950s had been educated in eastern and Texan universities recently converted to modernism. In 1960 Don Schlegel, the leading modernist in the new architecture program at the University of New Mexico, explained that the prevailing functional and structural expressionism of the 1950s held "that the utilitarian function of a building in plan, material, and assembly technique should be visually stated. . . . Materials are handled in a manner which best suits their true nature, and they are assembled so that construction techniques are clearly expressed." Likewise George Clayton Pearl, the chief designer for the leading Albuquerque firm of Stevens, Mallory, Pearl, and Campbell, remembers that in 1954, in selecting a set of metal truss supports for the Albuquerque Civic Auditorium, the primary issue was structural honesty—to show clearly that these piers supported a bank of windows and not the roof, which was to rest on a separate structural system. Questions of style, symbolism, and ornamental value were not considered germane. In this 1950s modernist climate, the Pueblo-Spanish Revival became anathema everywhere but in Santa Fe and Taos.[16]

Although Meem was criticized by the young modernists for his use of ornament and history, his insistence on two modernist tenets derived from the romantic tradition helped keep the door open to regionalism: the forthright use of natural materials and a feeling for the elemental simplicity of vernacular forms. While repudiating overt historicism of the sort practiced by Meem, some American modernists also rejected the idealized International Style of steel and glass cubes. By following the romantic threads in modernism, they developed what contemporary journals termed "Modern Regionalism." This approach was most pronounced in the San Francisco Bay area and elsewhere on the West Coast, where Harwell Hamilton Harris, William Wurster, and Pietro Belluschi designed sprawling asymmetric buildings around outdoor patios and employed local natural materials and forms that evoked vernacular wood barns and cottages.[17]

Through the height of modernism in the 1940s and 1950s, Lewis Mumford persisted as the leading champion of regionalism. As with his early criticism of the Beaux Arts–City Beautiful movement, he attacked International Style modernism for its dogmatic application of universal formulas and inadequate response to climate, topography, and local social conditions. Mumford argued that regionalism was a necessary, even if neglected, aspect of true modernism. Conversely a straightforward response to modern economic and technological realities is an inescapable component of any viable regionalism.[18]

The contest between Modern Regionalism and International Style was encapsulated in the 1959 juried show "Contemporary Architecture in New Mexico." Commenting on the show, the director of the Roswell Museum, David Gebhard, allowed that "while it is certainly true that a designer may consciously ignore historical aspects of the area in which he is working, it is open to question whether they should at the same time have ignored the many environmental conditions which brought about old solutions." A chief example of what Gebhard called the "international machine tradition" was Flatow and Moore's 1952 Simms Building—Albuquerque's first steel and glass high-rise—its own version of the United Nations and Lever Buildings. While Gebhard detected the stirrings of a legitimate modern regional architecture in five of the eight buildings exhibited, they included not a single adobe or stuccoed wall, nor anything remotely resembling the Pueblo-Spanish style. Conron and Lent's 1955 Centerline Building in Santa Fe (fig. 163), as Gebhard recognized, was instead reminiscent of San Francisco Bay area regionalism. Descended as it was from the turn-of-the-century Western Stick style with a flavoring of the Japanese wood vernacular tradition, this style looked fresh to postwar eyes because of its thin articulated wooden structure, which bore a formal resemblance to the steel I-beam frames of the International Style. If the aesthetic of the 1930s favored Meem's massive forms, this new aesthetic of attenuated structure clashed with his work and with the state's indigenous adobe buildings.[19]

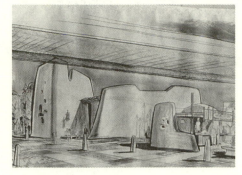

A New State Capitol

Both John Meem, the leading traditionalist architect, and John Conron, the spokesmen for the modern regionalists, came into conflict with Willard Kruger in the mid-
1960s over the design of a new state capitol. Conron's greatest impact came through
his writings in *New Mexico Architecture,* which he edited for over thirty years. His most
ambitious design was an innovative 1963 master plan for the state capitol complex,
prepared by Architects Associated (David Lent, Robert Plettenberg, Philippe Register,
and Conron, the partner in charge), and distributed as a heavily illustrated seventy-
five-page booklet (figs. 191, 192).[20]

The Architects Associated first considered whether the capitol should be relocated
to one of two alternate sites, but it rejected these in favor of the existing site because
of the capitol's importance to the social and commercial life of downtown Santa Fe.
The master plan sought above all to enhance Santa Fe's urban fabric. Low walls would
screen parking from the public plazas and nearby residential areas. To avoid creating superblocks divorced from the city, traffic would continue on existing streets,
although the addition of cobblestone and brick paving would alert motorists that they
were entering a pedestrian zone. The capitol complex would orient to the river, with
landscaped walkways and portals extending north to the plaza and federal oval beyond.
In place of the conventional free-standing monumental capitol building, they envisioned a series of appealing plazas and courtyards—social spaces where people would
meet—made more attractive by art works, restaurants, and small shops. Here was an
attempt to develop the sort of populist regionalism advocated by Mumford, a design
that provided for social interaction as its first consideration.

Conron and the other Architects Associated acknowledged the state's character in
various ways. Their arid landscaping included desert sagebrush planted at the base
of new "mesa wall" buildings and indigenous aspens and pines in courtyards and patios.
Replanting the remnants of orchards that remained about the complex and the use
of plaza and courtyard forms recalled the Spanish heritage. The existing Territorial

287

191. Model for capitol complex plan, Architects Associated,
John Conron partner in charge, 1963. A proposal for a civic architecture
of public plazas and office courtyards.

192. Drawing for capitol complex plan, Architects Associated, John
Conron partner in charge, 1963.

Revival style capitol building acknowledged the Anglo influence in the state's history. The major new architectural components were to be "mesa wall" buildings—a stylized evocation of weathered mesas, earthen pueblos and archeological ruins, and in particular Pueblo Bonito in Chaco Canyon. "But it should be remembered," wrote architectural historian Bainbridge Bunting, "that the Architects Associated is calling for an extension of these traditional architectures—not merely their imitation. The new buildings even though embodying sympathetic echoes of the past must still belong clearly to the present." Although this plan was adopted by the Capitol Building Improvement Commission (CBIC) in September 1962, commission member John Meem found the "concept of these massive walls disturbing—they could become overwhelming."[21]

In May of 1963, to no one's surprise, W. C. Kruger and Associates were awarded the contract to design a new capitol building by the CBIC, headed by new Governor Jack Campbell, whom Kruger had backed in the fall election. Kruger completely ignored the Architects Associated master plan, by designing a free-standing building on a site near the old capitol but not yet owned by the state. The CBIC only amended the master plan to allow this course of action in August, when Kruger presented preliminary sketches. The state was exempt from city zoning and design-review control, but when they got a first glimpse of the rendering of the proposed capitol in December, Santa Fe Mayor Pat Hollis and eight of nine city councilors wrote the governor: "It is urgently requested that the letter and the spirit of the historic ordinance be followed and that the design of the buildings be altered to conform with the architecture of Santa Fe."[22]

What so disturbed the city was that Kruger and Associates' chief designer, Robert Kruger, had crafted a building in the New Formalist style—the abstracted modernist form of classicism popularized in the 1950s by Edward Durell Stone, Minoru Yamasaki, and Philip Johnson (fig. 193). The building's symmetry and self-contained geometric shape, its regularly spaced columns, and broad cornice formed by precast concrete panels resembled new government buildings around the world. Here was the

aloof imported classicism of the 1900 capitol in an updated modernist incarnation. The autocratic antiregionalism of Kruger's design contrasts sharply with the social urbanism of Architects Associated master plan.

Faced with opposition, Kruger stonewalled, refusing to allow newspapers to reproduce the perspective drawings, while pushing ahead with the construction drawings. The week before Christmas, he assured the public that the building had "been erroneously termed modern," when it actually was a "blending of modern construction techniques with the unique architectural heritage of Santa Fe," including "sloping, adobe-colored walls, small window openings, a continuous portal around the building and a flat roof." The round shape, he further assured the public, "is very old in the history of New Mexico, having its origin in the pueblo Kivas."[23]

When Kruger released the finished renderings for reproduction in the *New Mexican* on Sunday, January 12th, Santa Fe erupted in protest. The following Tuesday at ten in the morning, a committee room in the old capitol, previously reserved for Kruger to brief legislators on the project, was packed by over one hundred protestors led by the mayor, city councilors, and Meem. Shock and disbelief quickly turned to outrage, as a flood of letters to the *New Mexican* ridiculed the design as "fantastic and ugly," "Kruger's shocking creation," "that proposed circular monstrosity," "excellent for a college secret society," "dungeon-like," and "based on the concept of an igloo far more than any form native to the southwest." One writer felt "its erection in Santa Fe would constitute an architectural crime," while another added, "the statement of the architect that it was in the 'Monumental Pueblo Style,' was as ridiculous as it was untrue." Reaction from around the state divided between the many who shared Santa Fe's criticisms and the few who echoed late-nineteenth-century boosters when they claimed that adoption of "so boldly conceived a design" would be evidence to "visitors at large that our state is the very epitome of progressive thought and action" and that, by contrast, the new capitol "would show up the surrounding squalor; the pitted streets and filthy hovels."[24]

193. PROPOSED STATE CAPITOL, W.C. KRUGER AND ASSOCIATES, 1965. THE MODERN FORMALIST DESIGN THAT CAUSED A PUBLIC UPROAR.

So great was the public outrage, that Kruger was forced to accept assistance in redesigning the building (fig. 194). Because the construction drawings were nearly complete, the advisory architects, led by Meem, were limited to redesigning the facades in the Territorial Revival style. Meem articulated the four entrances as projecting pavilions and linked them by a monumental Territorial Revival portal. Here in the design of the new capitol, as in the historic design ordinance debate of 1957, the traditionalists, led by John Meem, focused on stylistic image, while the modern regionalists, headed by John Conron, sought to develop a regionalism that progressed beyond facade symbolism to the use of traditional building and planning forms to enhance contemporary social life.[25]

In a postmortem published in *New Mexico Architecture,* architectural historian David Gebhard wrote that the Architects Associated's master plan had asked "How could the site and buildings it contains become a part of the existing community and how could it make a real contribution to the community?" "The substitute plan," continued Gebhard acerbically, "has not even recognized that this is a problem to be faced. What it does propose is a complete separation between the environment of the Capitol complex and the City. The furtherance of this separation is not an evidence of a strong belief which the designer holds on the subject, rather it is evidence of the basic nature of his whole approach—that of working from one expediency to another." When Gebhard also described the unnamed designers as "a local architectural firm, whose work had never really had anything to do with the world of architecture," Willard Kruger threatened to sue *New Mexico Architecture.*[26]

Although none of the mesa wall buildings proposed in the capitol master plan were ever built, McHugh, Kidder and Plettenberg (who had been one of the Architects Associated) employed a similar approach in their design for an expansion of the open-air Santa Fe Opera in 1964 (fig. 195). The roof of the balcony rests on laminated wood posts and beams, a mainstay of modern regionalism, while the seating is wrapped in the boldly curving brown-stuccoed walls. Only the sweeping massiveness

290

194. NEW MEXICO STATE CAPITOL, W.C. KRUGER AND ASSOCIATES WITH JOHN MEEM, 1966. THE UNALTERED FLOOR PLAN WRAPPED IN A MORE HISTORICAL TERRITORIAL REVIVAL STYLE.

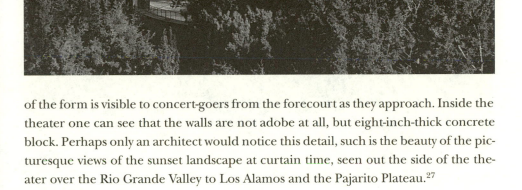

of the form is visible to concert-goers from the forecourt as they approach. Inside the theater one can see that the walls are not adobe at all, but eight-inch-thick concrete block. Perhaps only an architect would notice this detail, such is the beauty of the picturesque views of the sunset landscape at curtain time, seen out the side of the theater over the Rio Grande Valley to Los Alamos and the Pajarito Plateau.[27]

MODERN PUEBLOS, SOLAR ADOBE HOMES, AND THE PITCHED ROOF REVIVAL

Modern regionalism in New Mexico found its fullest expression in the early work of Antoine Predock. A native of Albuquerque, Predock began his studies at the University of New Mexico and completed his bachelor's of architecture at Columbia University in 1962. There he was exposed to Jane Jacobs's social critique of modernist planning and James Marston Fitch's environmental and historical analysis of architecture. Although structural expressionism remained paramount in architectural education, a renewed emphasis on the adaptation of buildings to local environment and materials was afoot. The growing sense that modern public places were not working well sent architecture students such as Predock to Europe to study Renaissance civic plazas and the less formal public squares of Mediterranean hill towns.[28]

195. SANTA FE OPERA REMODELING, MCHUGH, KIDDER, PLETTENBERG, 1965.

(AUTHOR)

In his first major project, a 1969 condominium village in Albuquerque known as La Luz, Predock clustered the individual units together to create shared plazas, through which "a greater sense of community will be evoked than generally exists in suburbia" (fig. 196). Reasserting one of Vierra and Meem's themes, Predock also wrote that "concentrated buildings will recognize particular landscape and view nuances and will generate a strong man-made landscape 'event' analogous to a butte or mountain." "In many ways," he added, "the cluster planning of La Luz and the buildings themselves are very traditional but not by assembling superficial trappings in the name of Pueblo architecture (i.e. fake vigas, elaborately contrived parapet erosion, etc.). In similar ways to the response of the indigenous builder, the buildings at La Luz respond to the climate and landscape of New Mexico." *Architectural Record* added approvingly that "where tradition is called on, it is called on for the way it works and not the way it looks." Despite this modernist aversion to ornament and emphasis on functional determinants, La Luz evokes historic buildings through the use of adobe and functional ornament—cast concrete lintels and roof drains. For a lay public unconcerned with modernist theory, La Luz succeeds in large part because it touches local memory. This degree of modernist abstraction, nevertheless, was too extreme for traditional Santa Fe, where Predock received few commissions.[29]

196. LA LUZ HOUSING DEVELOPMENT, ALBUQUERQUE, ANTOINE PREDOCK, 1967. THIS ULTIMATE MODERNIST ABSTRACTION OF PUEBLO, ADOBE FORMS SET THE TONE FOR MUCH NEW MEXICAN DESIGN IN THE 1970S AND 1980S. (AUTHOR)

Through the heyday of architectural modernism in the 1950s and 1960s, northern New Mexico remained an enclave of regionalism and continued to attract sympathetic artists and architects. The Pueblo-Spanish style in both its romantic and more severe modernist forms remained one of the strongest regional idioms in the country.

Even the emphasis on local economic self-sufficiency of Mumford and New Deal regionalism had a local champion—Peter van Dresser. Born the son of a prominent New York society portraitist in 1908, van Dresser showed early signs of nonconformity. He studied architecture and engineering at Cornell, "but took a leave of absence after three years, unconvinced of the relevancy of academic instruction for the world he hoped to live in." After experimenting with early rockets and editing the journal of the New York-based American Rocket Society, van Dresser moved to Florida in the late 1930s and became active in the Decentralist-Distributist movement, a precursor of the counterculture environmental movement. He set up an organic homestead with "a cypress home on the fringes of the Everglades" and began making solar water heaters.[30]

In 1950, like so many refugees from the American mainstream before and since, van Dresser was drawn by the exotic cultures, the stark landscape, and the hardscrabble economy of northern New Mexico. The following year he built his first experimental solar house, in El Rito, north of Santa Fe. In his comprehensive 1971 statement *Development on a Human Scale,* van Dresser argued for the revitalization of the small-scale decentralized economy of the Pueblo and Hispanic villages. Economic and cultural factors intertwined in his detailed program.[31]

His emphasis on economic self-sufficiency also led van Dresser to campaign for passive solar design. He built a second solar house in Santa Fe in 1958, which combined tilted hot-air collectors with adobe construction and Pueblo-Spanish detailing (fig. 197). The combination of small-scale technology with traditional forms stemmed directly from the regionalist desire that decentralized economic development and local culture be mutually reinforcing. In his writing and designs, van Dresser provided a

197. PETER VAN DRESSER HOUSE, PETER VAN DRESSER, 1958.
AN EARLY SOLAR DESIGN BY THE LEADING THEORIST OF REGIONAL ECONOMIC
SELF-SUFFICIENCY. (AUTHOR)

bridge from thirties regionalism to the counterculture-environmental movement. Although few if any of the twenty-five communes established in New Mexico during the late 1960s survived, many commune members stayed on to become allies of van Dresser and leaders in the passive solar movement.[32]

One commune veteran, solar designer Steve Baer, developed a nonregional architectural vocabulary. Baer's early 1970s house in Corrales, north of Albuquerque, was considered by some the "prototype solar house of the future." The modular building units, which Baer named zomes, are a deflection of Buckminster Fuller's regular geodesic dome into more flexible shapes. Although adobe is used for thermal mass in the building, the house is sheathed in reflective aluminum panels, which imparts a space age image. Solar devices invented by Baer combine with a windmill to evoke an earlier era of rural self-sufficiency. This mixture of old and new low-tech approaches in the Baer house characterizes the pragmatic strain of the counterculture, best known through Fuller's writings and the *Whole Earth Catalogue*.[33]

Given the strength of New Mexico's romantic tradition, however, most communes and solar houses emphasized traditional forms and local materials, especially adobe, which experienced a simultaneous resurgence. Adobe not only provided good insulation and a thermal mass to store the sun's warmth but also was favored by most solar

198. BALCOMB HOUSE, WILLIAM LUMPKINS AND SUN MOUNTAIN DESIGN, 1975.
TAKING THE GREENHOUSE INTO THE HEART OF AN ADOBE HOME. (AUTHOR)

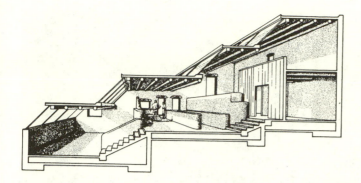

advocates as an easily sculpted organic material. That adobe bricks could be produced on-site and a home erected by the owner combined with the energy conservation of solar design to satisfy the search for appropriate technologies. As in the 1920s and 1930s, the strength of American individualism made the private solar adobe home, rather than the commune, the lasting architectural form of the counterculture.[34]

The 1975 Balcomb House in Santa Fe, designed by William Lumpkins and Sun Mountain Designs, is a quintessential solar adobe home (fig. 198). Born in New Mexico in 1910, Lumpkins apprenticed with Santa Fe architect Irving Parsons. After World War II, he lived for a time in La Jolla, California, before returning to Santa Fe, all the while working to integrate southwestern revivalism, adobe construction, and passive solar design in his architectural practice and a series of house pattern books. The Balcomb House united passive solar technology with the artist's craftsman house of the 1920s. Sculptural adobe walls and rustic wooden details carry over from early revival houses. The addition of a solar greenhouse at the heart of the home provides a more direct connection to nature and a degree of self-reliance through the production of heat and, potentially, vegetables.[35]

New Mexico from Albuquerque north became the leading international center of solar design innovation during the 1970s. In 1979 that research effort was distilled and presented in nontechnical terms by Edward Mazria in *The Passive Solar Energy Book* (fig. 199). In this populist classic, which sold tens of thousands of copies, Mazria translates passive solar techniques, systems, and philosophy into a series of design patterns. This approach, adapted from Christopher Alexander's *A Pattern Language,* facilitates the integration of solar principals into the normal design process. The Solar Energy Group at the Los Alamos National Laboratory, headed by Doug Balcomb, tested and verified the performance of solar technologies in the late 1970s and early 1980s, which gave the movement added creditability. But solar design and construction declined sharply when energy prices began to fall and the Reagan administration terminated energy conservation tax incentives, as well as sharply reducing funding for reusable energy research.[36]

199. KAREN TERRY HOUSE, SECTIONAL ILLUSTRATION BY RUSS BALL FOR EDWARD MAZRIA'S *THE PASSIVE SOLAR ENERGY BOOK*, 1979. FROM THE BIBLE OF THE SOLAR MOVEMENT, A HOUSE THAT RESPONDS TO LOCAL TOPOGRAPHY AND CLIMATE.

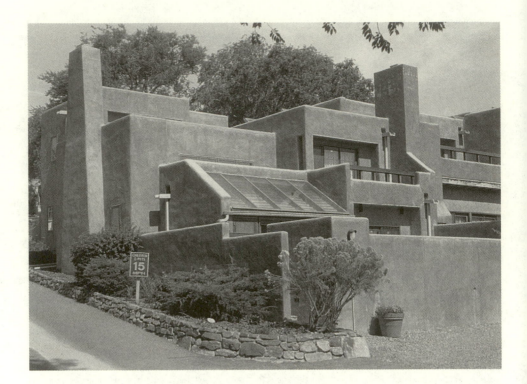

New York native Edward Mazria had become interested in solar design after coming to teach at the University of New Mexico in 1973. He opened an architectural practice in Albuquerque in 1978, which he moved to Santa Fe in 1983. Although passive solar techniques continue to be used in some new houses in New Mexico, Mazria's firm may be the only one that consistently integrates them in commercial and institutional projects such as libraries, stores, schools, and museums. Mazria does not employ the Santa Fe style literally, but instead uses traditional shapes, colors, and textures and adapts traditional building types, as when he based the new Hispanic wing of the Santa Fe's Museum of International Folk Art on a courtyard house. Working with long-time solar builders Wayne and Susan Nichols, Mazria integrated passive solar heating with up-scale condominiums in the La Vereda Compound in Santa Fe during the mid-1980s (fig. 200). Real estate agents learned, however, not to emphasize solar features in their advertising and sales pitches for costly houses and condominiums; most who could afford them do not want to be bothered with solar systems, which they fear will be a burden to operate. Real estate agents instead emphasize the aesthetics of sunlight and landscape views.[37]

The cultural ferment of the 1960s, which produced the solar adobe movement locally, also fueled a broad reaction against modernism. While Jane Jacobs attacked the antiur-

200. LA VEREDA COMPOUND CONDOMINIUMS, EDWARD MAZRIA, AND WAYNE AND SUSAN NICHOLS, ABOUT 1985. (AUTHOR)

ban results of urban renewal, Robert Venturi highlighted the symbolically impoverished language of modern architecture. This reaction led to a resurgence of historic preservation and the emergence of contextualism and later postmodernism. Over the past twenty-five years, architects such as Venturi, Charles Moore, Michael Graves, and Robert A. M. Stern have reintroduced ornament, popular iconography, and historic forms, in an attempt to make architecture more accessible to the general public.[38]

Many New Mexican architects, of course, never abandoned these concerns, and in Santa Fe, both within the design review district and outside it, historicism always reigned supreme. Santa Fe's Inn at Loretto, a tourist hotel designed in 1976 by Harold Stewart, is a traditional and well-received interpretation of the Pueblo Revival (fig. 201). Its battered walls and rounded edges are reminiscent of Vierra's house and much of Meem's work, although its massing is somewhat formal by comparison.

During the early 1980s, a revival of pitched metal roofs added to the Territorial Revival vocabulary. Given that flat roofs often leak and Santa Fe averages 3 feet of snow a winter, pitched roofs have been added to many existing buildings and incorporated into the Hispanic owner-built vernacular since the late nineteenth century. In fact pitched roofs predominate across all of northern New Mexico, except in a handful of pueblos and the romantic precincts of Santa Fe and Taos. In the late 1970s, builder Betty Stewart began incorporating pitched metal roofs in houses in Tesuque, immediately north of Santa Fe. Her romantic eclectic designs typically open up the ceilings inside to reveal heavy dark brown trusses and rafters—an ahistorical evocation of Olde English inns.[39]

Architect Beverly Spears's 1986 study of the rural houses of northern New Mexico, *American Adobes,* emerged as a source book for this revival. Her 1987 design for the Robert Thompson house (fig. 202) combines pitched roofs with adobe construction and simple white trim. Other examples of the type deploy more literal Territorial Revival details. Although the city's 1983 streetscape regulations permitted pitched roofs in some contexts, flat roofs remain the essential element of Santa Fe style for many, and

201. INN AT LORETTO, HAROLD STEWART, 1976. THE NORM FOSTERED
BY DESIGN REVIEW. (ARTHUR TAYLOR)

most pitched roof revival houses have appeared well outside the historic districts. As Blaine Young, another architect working in this idiom, has noted, the pitched roof revival is most popular with established middle-class residents and not with "the second home people" just arrived in Santa Fe with a desire for stereotypical flat roofs.[40]

Only in the early 1980s did overt postmodernism appear in New Mexico in the form of polychromatic stucco, cut-out inflated details, and a double coding of buildings with symbols and forms drawn from the local setting and around the world. Both Jack Gaffney's Ashley Place (fig. 169) and Antoine Predock's Teastor-Grey House (fig. 65) distill local historical elements down to basic geometric forms, as had Aldo Rossi and the Italian rationalists. Gaffney's design is austere, constrained as it was by design review, while in Predock's house, which steps down a hillside north of town, the individual building blocks are playfully set off in brown and pastel stucco.

THE VOGUE OF SANTA FE STYLE

On the whole, Santa Fe in the 1980s opted for image over substance, as it catered to the expectations of visitors and newcomers and neglected the social needs of the community. Just as Mazria's *Passive Solar Energy Book* reflected the counterculture environmentalism of the previous decade, Christine Mather and Sharon Woods's book,

202. ROBERT THOMPSON HOUSE, NEAR ABIQUIU, NEW MEXICO, BEVERLY SPEARS, ABOUT 1987. THE MOST RECENT REGIONAL IDIOM, WHAT IN REAL ESTATE PARLANCE IS KNOWN AS "NORTHERN NEW MEXICO STYLE" OR "MOUNTAIN ADOBE STYLE." (MICHAEL TINCHER)

Santa Fe Style, epitomized the conspicuous consumption of the eighties. Issued in 1986, *Santa Fe Style* rode (and reinforced) the vogue of Santa Fe to sales of 110,000 copies in its first five years, the most of any architecture book of the period (excepting only professional reference books). David Morton, architectural editor for Rizzoli, which published the book, has claimed that it is not an architecture book at all. But the major architectural trends of the decade were precisely the sort of theatrical historicism and packaging of architecture as image/commodity at which *Santa Fe Style* excels.[41]

Mather and Woods employ various rhetorical devices to lift cultural fragments from their original context and place them in a romantic ahistorical past, in preparation for nostalgic reinterpretation. Santa Fe style is at once a leading genre of interior decoration and a life-style for the rich and romantic. Although Mather touches on Pueblo and Spanish traditions in her text, the book's title and the lack of material on contemporary cultures other than upper-class Santa Fe, relegates native groups to the background. The text repeats many of the well-established distortions of local history: "the early colonists lived peacefully with Pueblo Indians," she writes, echoing the Fiesta rhetoric that ignores the bloody reconquest of 1693-96 and the general suppression of Pueblo religion. Likewise statements that "the Spanish colonists developed adobe [from the Anasazi] into bricks in imitation of the stone blocks they had known in Spain," and "portales of pueblo-style homes are supported by carved corbels," obscure the fact that the Spanish introduced adobe bricks, portales, and carved corbels.[42]

The emphasis on photographs of architectural details breaks traditional architecture into design components. Indeed many if not most of the houses that Mather and Woods illustrate, from the 1930s Hollenback House to those of more recent vintage, are themselves collages of antique architectural details. The beautiful photographs facilitate gratification not only by providing design ideas but, more immediately, by supplying rich color images for a generation raised on quick-cut television commercials.

299

No one inhabits these houses (a convention of architectural photography), which encourages the viewer's imagination to move in. Nor do any unsettling hints of the city's cultural and class frictions nor of the ironies of cultural appropriation intrude in the text.

This critique of *Santa Fe Style* applies equally to the six episodes of the PBS show *This Old House* that focused on Santa Fe in 1990. Sharon Woods, who coordinated photographs for *Santa Fe Style,* and other designers and homeowners lead tours through lavish houses, rhapsodizing about the romance of the Pueblo style and kiva fireplaces. The owners of the homes toured and of the house being remodeled, the architect, tour guides, building contractor, and subcontractors—in fact virtually everyone who speaks on camera—is Anglo and, as far as one can tell, most are transplants to Santa Fe. Meanwhile all but one of the foremen, craftsmen, and laborers are Spanish-surnamed. For all the knowing discourse on Pueblo style, not a single Pueblo Indian appears.[43]

When program host Steve Thomas shows up at the remodeling house for a lesson from mason Wayne Leyva, the two shake hands, and Leyva turns his hands, covered with brick dust, palms up for Thomas to inspect. "Look at these hands," says Leyva, "look at how torn up they get building one of these kiva fire places." "Yeah, those are pretty tough lookin' hands there," responds Thomas, looking sheepishly at his own palms. "What are you an artist," jibes Leyva, "you been doing a lot of painting lately." "Aw come on," retorts Thomas. It is one mild, though welcome dissent. But for anyone familiar with the history and social class structure of Santa Fe, the series was a painfully transparent display of romantic self-deception.

THE VISIONARY MYTHMAKER OF SOUTHWEST ARCHITECTURE

In 1990 *New York Times* architecture critic Paul Goldberger observed that Albuquerque-based Antoine Predock appeared to be like "plenty of so-called regionalist architects" before him, slowly building national reputations from provincial turfs by being better than others at designing new buildings that, for all their newness, seem somehow able to enhance rather than diminish the region's architectural traditions. But most of the regionalists live out their careers as admired but minor figures, the very ties to a particular part of the country that first inspired national interest in their work becoming, in the end, a kind of straight jacket, limiting them more than stimulating them. . . . Right now, he shows signs of being the one architect in the country most likely to break out of the regionalist curse and move into what we might call the architectural big leagues.[44]

Goldberger implies that the "regionalist curse" is the tendency to become stagnant because of one's ties to a particular area. In fact regionalists have been condemned to be "admired but minor figures" by definition—the definition of a cosmopolitan intelligentsia for whom "regionalist" has been a marginalizing epithet at least since World War II. In 1976 Pulitzer Prize-winning New Mexican historian and novelist Paul Horgan, who moved to the East himself to escape the regionalist curse, wrote in the *Yale Review*, "I have never seen a statement by a truly gifted artist which admitted to his being a 'regionalist,' no matter how firmly he had been assigned the classification." Predock, who vehemently denies he is a regionalist, sometimes jokes, "Regionalist means not being able to get a job out of state."[45]

For whatever reasons, whether out of frustration from a shortage of major commissions in New Mexico, to transcend the regionalist curse and break into the big leagues, or as a midcareer rejuvenation, Predock struck out in a new direction in the early 1980s. Throughout the 1970s, he had worked primarily in the style perfected at La Luz: brown stucco, geometric abstractions of regional forms, cast-concrete details, and siting for landscape views, with a passive solar admixture in some of his residential

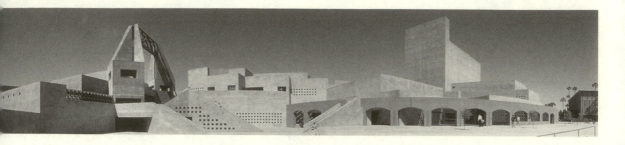

work. He veered away from this pattern in the 1982 Albuquerque United Blood Services Building, with the single bold gesture of blood-red stucco.

By 1984 in projects such as the Teastor-Grey House, near Santa Fe, and the Beach Apartments in Albuquerque (figs. 65, 66), Predock had expanded "the exposition of multi-layered meanings derived from program, place, and culture" to include a much wider range of images and associations, in the manner of postmodern double coding. In the Desert Highlands Housing Community outside Phoenix, Predock evoked, in his words, "the Mayan temple wells; the North African sense of deep passage and transition; . . . Anasazi cliff dwellings; overtly medieval, cool dark, processional sequences; village gate; towers as visual anchors; di Chirico passages; the Taliesin West breezeway; Mark Rothko's dissolving color edges; cowboy movie expectations—cookouts, sunsets, blazing sun, shady ramadas." As Predock also said of the Beach Apartments, "Hollywood is backed up a long way along Route 66," and we might add, in the minds of people the world over.[46]

Predock broke into the architectural big leagues in 1986, by winning four design competitions outside New Mexico, including the American Heritage Center at the University of Wyoming and the Arizona State University Fine Arts Complex. If his imagery and stucco palette had veered exuberantly out of control on occasion in the mid-1980s, in the Fine Arts Complex he reached a more austere synthesis of terraced pueblo and mountain range, hill town and pure geometry (fig. 203). On the formal city side of the complex, two rows of cactus march out of the desert to become colonnades—a southwestern recounting of the primitive origins of architecture. One narrow passageway, pinched in by a wall that look likes Pueblo Bonito redesigned by a latter-day Egyptian rationalist, leads under a monumental metal truss—part triumphal arch, part theater proscenium, part armature for theater lights—to the main courtyard. A monumental flight of bleachers face the theater's fly-tower, which has been extended up to form a brutal, constructivist drive-in movie screen. The imagery is rich and multilayered but not obtrusive; its geometric poetry ennobles this important public place.[47]

203. Fine Arts Center, Arizona State University, Tempe, Antoine Predock, 1986. (Timothy Hursley)

When Disney CEO Michael Eisner began recruiting "the Steven Spielbergs and George Lucases of the architectural world to design new projects," he not only signed up the reigning princes of architecture Michael Graves, Robert A. M. Stern, Arata Isozaki, and Frank Gehry, but also the rising star Antoine Predock. Predock was commissioned to design Hotel Mediterranean, for Disney World in Florida, and Hotel Santa Fe, for the new Euro Disneyland, outside Paris. Particularly in the French project, the local southwestern conditions that have informed Predock's best work were lacking. In place of arid sunny weather he faced gray rainy winters; instead of mountains and panoramic landscape vistas, a flat to rolling countryside; rather than traditional responses to site and deep historical associations, he confronted European stereotypes of the American West, nurtured by romantic Karl May novels and Hollywood westerns. Given these conditions, Hotel Santa Fe was destined to be the very epitome of stage-set scenographic design.[48]

Predock broke Hotel Santa Fe's thousand guest rooms into small clusters, which abstract terraced Pueblo villages and Spanish courtyards (fig. 204). As in the Beach Apartments, horizontal bands of colored stucco restate the landscape strata to produce metaphoric mesas and mountains. A "river" originates atop one terraced pueblo/mountain and meanders down into a series of courtyards; irrigation acequias course through another courtyard, and in yet another, a suburban lawn sprinkler grid becomes a minimalist fountain. Down the middle of the hotel complex runs the yellow center line of Route 66.

This infusion of car culture updates the myth of the American West with the later-day symbols of individuality and boundless opportunity: the endless road stretching to the horizon (and enhanced here by forced perspective). Predock's authenticating relics are not Spanish Colonial doors and ceiling beams, but junked cars shipped over from New Mexico. Drive-in movie and motel forms also help shape the spaces. Cars enter through a movie parking lot and fittingly pass under the giant screen—"a vanishing icon of the West" says Predock.[49]

204. HOTEL SANTA FE, EURO DISNEYLAND, MARNE, FRANCE, ANTOINE PREDOCK, 1990. (CHRISTOPHER MEAD)

For all of its inspired playful invention, when I think of Hotel Santa Fe and of Euro Disneyland, I cannot help but recall the Hameau—that village of picturesque cottages Marie Antoinette had built at Versailles, the royal palace outside Paris. There she and her friends amused themselves by dressing up as peasants and shepherdesses in the years leading up to the French Revolution. Such romantic escapism was then limited to a small ruling elite, while its audience has expanded many fold in the intervening centuries, with the growth of the middle class. Just as the Hameau once diverted attention from the gathering social upheaval, today the shallow gratification of *Santa Fe Style* and Disney theme parks mask growing social injustice, discontent, and the cumulative environmental degradation of unbridled consumerism.

SPECULATIONS ON A CRITICAL REGIONALISM

A critique of the superficiality of much postmodernism has gained momentum in recent years. In 1981 historian-critics Alexander Tzonis and Liane Lefaivre sought to revive and extend Lewis Mumford's brand of regionalism, when they called for a critical regionalism, "a protest against the destruction of community, the splitting of human associations, the dissolution of human contact." Close observation of people interacting in the public places of healthy communities, they argue, "is the condition for reaching the concrete and the real, and for rehumanizing architecture." If romantic regionalism earlier in the twentieth century was intertwined with the rise of the urban bourgeois and consumerism, critical regionalism reacts against the tendency to turn culture and the environment into exploitable commodities.[50]

Architecture critic Kenneth Frampton extended the debate over critical regionalism, when he charged that most of what passes for regionalism today is "cardboard scenographic populism" and "a consumerist iconography masquerading as culture." This tourist-consumer regionalism, like populist regionalism before it, glorifies style and fails to engage architecture at sufficient depth to affect social reality. Local geography and climate, along with political and social traditions and anticentrist sentiments, all help to sustain regional cultures. But argues Frampton, only an ongoing self-con-scious cross-fertilization of the local with contemporary world culture can keep regional cultures vital and relevant.[51]

Close attention to building site and climate is the first level of critical regionalism. "The bulldozing of an irregular topography into a flat site," Frampton argues, "is clearly a technocratic gesture which aspires to a condition of absolute *placelessness,* whereas the terracing of the same site to receive the stepped form of a building is an engage-ment in the act of 'cultivating' the site." Similarly "wherever they occur, the fixed win-dow and the remote-controlled air-conditioning system are mutually indicative of domination by universal technique," which critical regionalism combats with tradi-tional lighting and ventilation solutions, along with modern refinements such as solar heating. From this perspective, Steve Baer's zome solar home, however modern it appears, is more regional than a Pueblo style hotel with air-conditioning and fixed windows. "Through this layering into the site," asserts Frampton, "the idiosyncrasies of place find their expression without falling into sentimentality."[52]

Like Mumford and like Tzonis and Lefaivre, for whom public spaces are "envelopes for concrete events" and "catalysts of social life," Frampton emphasizes the central role of building form and settlement pattern in fostering a deeper regionalism of every-day face-to-face community. Among potentially useful "introverted types," Frampton lists the office atrium, the shopping mall, and the perimeter block (those low-rise urban apartment houses pushed to the edges of a city block to create semipublic courtyards within; Conron's 1963 capitol master plan, in its use of plaza and courtyard, explored local introverted forms). Whatever their potential, the control of shopping malls and hotel and office atriums by private interests has severely limited the range of activi-ties allowed in these public spaces; political speech, for instance, is typically prohib-ited. Indeed privatization characterizes the building forms reshaping America today: the shopping mall, the office park, and the suburban single-family house, found increas-ingly in limited-access communities with perimeter walls, gates, and guardhouses.[53]

306

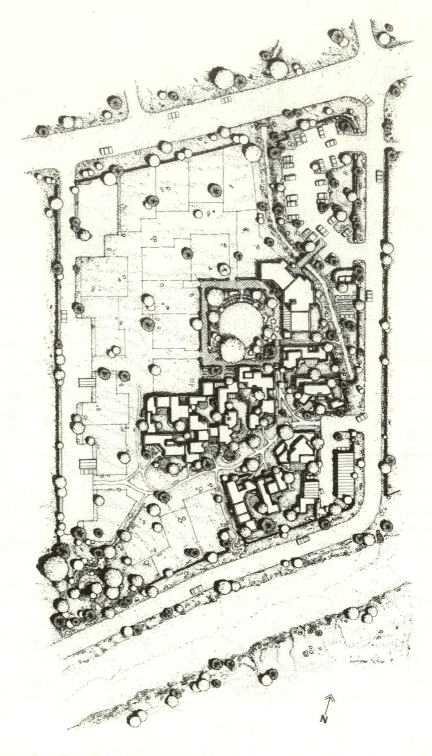

N

205. THE COMMONS, ALTSHULER, BAKER, BROWN, MATHEY AND OTHER
MEMBERS OF THE COMMONS, SITE PLAN, RENDERED BY COURTENEY MATHEY, 1991.
AN ATTEMPT TO CREATE A MODERN VERSION OF THE FACE-TO-FACE COMMUNITY
OF THE TRADITIONAL VILLAGE OR SMALL TOWN NEIGHBORHOOD THROUGH SHARED
SPACES AND FACILITIES.

As we ride in our air-conditioned cars from home to work, school, or the shopping mall, and back again to home and television, we have little contact with other people. Increasingly the choice of which of the products advertised on TV to buy substitutes for real political choice, for face-to-face community, and for our desire to lead productive fulfilling lives. The free-standing house, which provides two-thirds of the dwellings in this country, is the physical manifestation of this isolation—households with two working parents, or a single parent, or a single individual.

THE COMMONS

Many in Santa Fe who make similar critiques are at work developing alternatives. A particularly promising community design initiative is The Commons, a twenty-eight-unit housing project begun in Santa Fe in 1990 (figs. 205, 206). The driving forces behind the project have been developer Donald Altshuler, planner Lynnwood Brown, and architects Paula Baker and Courteney Mathey, all residents of the community. Built on eight acres of rugged sand hills two miles downriver from the plaza, The Commons stands at the developing fringe of the Westside neighborhood. The project self-consciously mixes local precedents such as the plaza, courtyard house, and artists' compound with two of the most imaginative modern design approaches: Christopher Alexander's *A Pattern Language* and the Danish cohousing idea.[54]

The 1977 book *A Pattern Language,* by Christopher Alexander and a team of collaborators, breaks design into 253 patterns that range from construction details and kitchen layout to public places and regional planning. With titles like "Subculture Boundary," "Small Services without Red Tape," "Duct Space," and "Old Age Cottage," each of the patterns raises a design issue such as "Without communal eating, no human group can hold together." Their subsequent discussions weave together traditional wisdom and the research of others with their own observations. Each closes with an underlying design principle such as: "Give every institution and social group

206. THE COMMONS, GATHERING FOR WEEKLY DINNER IN COMMUNITY HOUSE, 1995. (AUTHOR)

a place where people can eat together. Make the common meal a regular event. In particular, start a common lunch in every work place, so that a genuine meal around a common table (not out of boxes, machines, or bags) becomes an important, comfortable, and daily event with room for invited guests." This "pattern language" seeks to create ecologically sound self-sustaining communities that foster human fulfillment and healthy societies. The patterns also make design accessible to the layperson and encourage an incremental participatory building process akin to vernacular architecture.[55]

The other inspiration for The Commons are the Danish *bofællesskaber,* or "living communities," that have developed since about 1970. This type has been christened "cohousing" in English and popularized by architects Kathryn McCamant and Charles Durrett in their book of that title. In Denmark the form consists of clusters of between six and eighty complete private dwellings, arrayed around a common play yard and garden, sharing a community house. The community house combines a kitchen and dining room large enough for shared meals, with laundry facilities, a music and recreation room, workshops, and guest rooms. Those attracted to cohousing seek "the social and practical advantages of a closely knit neighborhood within the context of the 20th century." Participation in the design process and the management and sharing of facilities help create a face-to-face community. Although Americans may resist the decrease of privacy entailed by cohousing, architect Clare Marcus argues that "many of the apparent needs in American society—the yearning for some of the social benefits of small-town life, for a greater sense of community, for safer environments for children, for more intergenerational neighborhoods—can potentially be met in cohousing."[56]

After generations living in free-standing single-family houses, many of us lack the social skills to live closely together with others. This was a major reason most hippie communes failed so quickly. While some of those in The Commons previously belonged to communes but left because they chafed at the social regimentation, they still desired some form of community life. Altschule, Brown, Baker, and Mathey are aggressively realistic about the need to balance community with individuality. They insist they are not a commune: "We are not a single minded ashram here," says Brown. "We thrive on productive loving conflict." Architect Courteney Mathey's favorite word for what they are attempting is *syzygy*—to mix without blending; in biology the conjunction of two organisms without losing individuality.

The Commons was one of the first of the hundred or so cohousing groups in the United States to break ground, perhaps because they successfully readjusted the Danish community-individuality balance. Unlike the Danish approach, which arrives at a single consensus design and builds the entire community at one time, the members of The Commons designed the site plan, public spaces, and community house together, while leaving individuals to design their own houses and build as their finances permit. This tempers the cohousing idea with Alexander's incremental approach, thereby allowing people to learn from their mistakes and make the ongoing adjustments required by a living community.

The site plan of The Commons places parking at the perimeter, with visitor parking concentrated on the northeast corner. A bridge from this lot leads over a small arroyo, through the common house, and to the square-shaped main plaza. One-third of the $30,000 price of a building lot goes toward the construction of the common house, which includes a large kitchen and dining hall with adjoining porch and outdoor seating, a multipurpose room, a laundry, and five guest rooms. The houses of residents with small businesses, artists with studios, professionals with offices, and a masseur with a hot tub spa, all face onto the main plaza. This public square and the common house are designed to host neighborhood events. A footpath leaves the north side of the plaza, loops through four secondary placitas each shared by seven houses, and returns at the southeast corner. The individual houses, which have ranged from $135,000 to $240,000 including the lot, step with the site and incorporate solar heating and private courtyards. Most have a semidetached studio or a cottage for teenagers or grandparents.

The Commons makes a valuable contribution to Santa Fe, by bringing this community-based alternative to life and establishing legal, zoning, and financial precedents for others to follow. The founders of The Commons hoped for a multicultural mix, but all who have joined have been Anglo immigrants. Several felt a need to make a constructive contribution to Santa Fe, where they are sometimes vilified as the source of the community's problems. Most people will continue to cluster by cultural group, although a few coyote compounds, where people of varying backgrounds learn to live together in "productive loving conflict," might help heal some of the wounds in our society.

Since 1912, the Santa Fe style has provided an alluring marketing image for the tourist economy. Monumental New Deal public buildings by Meem and others solidified this strong regional identity, which withstood the ascendance of modernism in the 1950s. The book *Santa Fe Style* epitomized the superficial image commodification of the 1980s; both it and the transplantation of the style to Euro Disneyland betray a frequent lack of engagement in the deeper levels of locale.

A significant undercurrent of climatic and social response, nevertheless, surfaces periodically and is on the ascendance in the mid-1990s. Social networks in Pueblo and Indo-Hispano communities continued to be reflected in plazas and extended family housing compounds. Artists and progressive expatriates also experimented with the compound form in the 1920s, while Conron's 1963 capitol master plan sought to reinforce civic life through the creation of plazas and courtyards. Van Dresser, Mazria, and others have developed a viable solar design technology. Since 1990 a political critique of the negative social effects of tourism has been intertwined with calls for more affordable housing and growing support for neighborhood plazas and housing innovations such as The Commons. These attempts to create a critical regionalism that harnesses the tourist economy for local social needs and develops housing forms that balance individuality with community are gathering momentum. Whether they will be sustained remains for the residents of Santa Fe to answer.

CONCLUSION:
A MYTH WORTH BELIEVING

"There are many reasons why New Mexico and especially Santa Fe does not want Japanese residents and the foremost is the fact that such a colonization would in truth kill the goose that lays the only golden egg this section knows—color and atmosphere." So editorialized the *Santa Fe New Mexican* on March 7, 1942, in opposition to the resettlement of 60,000 Japanese-American citizens from the West Coast to northeastern New Mexico, the last alternative to confining them in what the press termed "concentration camps." *The Socorro Chieftan* cautioned that these Japanese were "just as good Americans as anyone," and "among the things for which we are fighting this war is that of ridding the world of intolerance and bigotry. Let us be careful that, in winning the fight, we are not left at home with the very things we have sworn to eradicate elsewhere." But this noble dissent was overwhelmed by a xenophobic outpouring led by Governor John Miles, State Supreme Court Justice A. L. Zinn, and former governor Clyde Tingley.[1]

Instead the federal government suspended the Bill of Rights to allow the incarceration of 110,000 Japanese-Americans in various western states; all were innocent of any wrongdoing. One internment camp, which held up to 2,100 Japanese men between 1942 and 1946, was placed on the western edge of Santa Fe (fig. 207). The city welcomed this camp because it meant eighty temporary guard jobs and business for local merchants. The camp's remains were obliterated by the Casa Solana subdivision in the early 1950s, and its very existence passed from public acknowledgement. Only in 1991, after the congressional apology and reparations bill, did the Santa Fe camp begin to receive media attention. This black episode in the history of the United States was long suppressed, as unpleasant details that contradict a country's ideals so often are. From the day Japanese relocation was proposed, Santa Fe's leaders understood that their reliance on tourism required special vigilance to suppress any unpleasantness. Tourism intensifies historical amnesia.[2]

The repressed story of the Japanese internment camp conforms to the broader patterns of omission and mystification in the public history of Santa Fe. The first of three

interrelated forms of denial is the omission of the degree to which the waves of Spanish and American conquest have been predicated on the threat and, whenever necessary, the use of force. The object lessons of force—the brutal punishment of the Acomas in 1599 and the execution of resistance leaders at Santa Fe in 1693 and Taos in 1847—are rarely acknowledged publicly. This threat stood behind the Spanish suppression of Pueblo religion and culture, and later the American repression of Spanish and Native American languages and cultures. It also allowed the appropriation of land, water, and other resources by the conquerors. As recently as 1967, the military mobilized against the land-grant repatriation movement. The omission of this history of repression allows past injustices to fester.

312

The degree of cultural and racial intermixing is also systematically downplayed. Anthropologists have tended to focus on traditional Pueblo culture, while deemphasizing Spanish and Anglo influences. The mixture of Pueblo and Spanish elements in historic architecture and revival styles is disguised by a rhetoric of "Pueblo style" and "kiva fireplaces." The terms *Spanish-American* and *Hispanic* further obscure the degree of Indian-Spanish intermixing. Although the Chicano movement brought this history of mestizaje to the surface, the degree of Chicano-Anglo intermixing remains in the background. This pattern is enshrined in the rhetoric of three separate cultures, a rhetoric that tends to heighten ethnic identification, pit one group against another, and obscure the degree of shared experience that forms the basis for common social actions.

A desire for harmony and order also motivates the removal of overt signs of the modern world from historic districts, arts, and celebrations. The Santa Fe Fiesta, although reestablished in 1919 primarily under Anglo leadership, is now perceived as a historic Spanish celebration, with American-era episodes long since purged from its pageants. The architectural revivals freeze time at about 1880, just before the railroad linked the city to the modern industrial world. Similarly historic preservation favors the Scrape approach, which removes recent accretions because of their

207. "LUCKY CLOUD," KANGO TAKAMURA, WATERCOLOR, 1942. PAINTED IN THE JAPANESE-AMERICAN CONCENTRATION CAMP LOOKING EAST OVER SANTA FE TO THE SANGRE DE CRISTO MOUNTAINS.

supposed incongruity, to produce an ahistorical unity of appearance. This pervasive inclination to remove evidence of the modern world betrays a yearning for that mythic bygone era, when cultures were whole and life was simpler and more fulfilling.

These three manifestations of historical amnesia (the omission of violent repression, the denial of racial and cultural mixing, and the suppression of evidence of the modern world) interfere with the public understanding of the origins of contemporary social, economic, and political structures. Members of the *mexicano*-Chicano working class are missing from tourist imagery and political rhetoric, for instance, which long made it easier to ignore their needs. The emphasis instead on a romantic history deprives people of an image of themselves as active agents for contemporary social change. Such a fictionalized reality also inhibits the hybridization of the traditional with the modern, the local with the international, which is necessary for the continued vitality and relevance of any local culture.

A MORE CONSTRUCTIVE SOCIAL MYTHOLOGY

Santa Fe's status as a romantic regional enclave, its tourist economy, and its multiethnic population have made it a particularly active center of mythmaking. But this has been an ambiguous blessing. To the extent that any community shapes its mythic life to please tourists and wealthy newcomers, it will begin to lose sight of its own needs and lack the intellectual, political, and spiritual will to address its pressing social, economic, and environmental problems. It is true that much of Santa Fe's substantial artistic and intellectual creativity is absorbed in romantic escapism. But many artists and social philosophers, from Chicano muralists and Pueblo intellectuals to the founders of the All-Species Day and The Commons cohousing compound, struggle to penetrate the superficial and false images of consumer tourism. They challenge a perverse status quo that permits the displacement of people from their hometown at the same time that they also work to create healthier alternatives.

It is probably no coincidence that as the political debate on how to respond to the negative effects of the tourism boom heated up about 1990, the omissions of history also began to be addressed more openly. Another book could easily, and usefully, be written to detail the social and economic issues facing Santa Fe and to survey the various private and governmental initiatives under way. These range from the grassroots advocates of sustainability through adobe and straw-bale construction and solar and permaculture design, to the city's efforts to stabilize property taxes for long-time residents and provide more low- and moderate-income housing. The formulation of a more constructive social mythology will help mobilize public support for this populist program and sustain it for the long term.[3]

What are some components of a more socially constructive mythmaking? Many issues faced by Santa Fe—cultural and racial hybridization, unredressed injustices, and the atrophy of face-to-face community—are occurring globally. How Santa Fe has begun to reformulate its mythology, therefore, is suggestive for other communities. And if we allow our imaginations free rein while keeping the city's rich history of tradition and mythmaking in mind, other creative possibilities will emerge.

As suggested in the interlude "Coyote Consciousness" above, one modern reality that our myths must help us better cope with is the pervasive interaction among different peoples. But as historian William McNeill observed in 1986, "Iranian Muslims, Russian communists, and American sectarians (religious and otherwise), all exhibit symptoms of acute distress in face of moral uncertainties, generated by exposure to competing truths." The as yet unresolved dilemma is how to acknowledge the validity of diverse cultures without undermining one's own beliefs. One way out, suggested philosopher Paul Ricoeur some thirty years ago, is "a dramatic relation in which I affirm myself in my origins and give myself to another's imagination in accordance with his different civilization. . . . No one can say what will become of our civilization when it has really met different civilizations by means other than the shock of conquest and domination." Myths of cultural purity and national superiority must give way to those that illuminate and ennoble amicable human encounters, authentic communication, and racial mixing, while nevertheless tolerating and even fostering local, regional, ethnic, and religious subcultures.[4]

Mayor Jaramillo has taken the important step of urging her program not as something for Hispanos alone but for all permanent residents. Some fear, however, that ethnic animosities lurk below the surface of her rhetoric. Perhaps some mythic formulation such as the Coyote will give this rhetoric of toleration greater resonance and transform it into a deep sustaining belief.

A MORE INCLUSIVE HISTORY

Santa Fe's public monuments have so far largely conformed to the long-standing patterns of denial, although they also offer an opportunity to express a more inclusive history and social vision. In 1927, for instance, the Daughters of the American Revolution offered Santa Fe a statue entitled *Madonna of the Trail,* as part of its program to commemorate the Anglo pioneer trails west (fig. 208). Local sculptor Frank Applegate and writer Mary Austin attacked this heroic eight-and-a-half-foot statue on artistic grounds, arguing that "the so-called Pioneer Women monument did not represent the real pioneers of this region at all, that the real pioneers were Spanish people and that they had not been consulted and were not represented at all." Rebuffed, the DAR took its statue to Albuquerque. This controversy crystallized the emerging consensus that overt Anglo-American manifestations had no place in Santa Fe's public identity.[5]

Even the Civil War monument erected in 1867 (see figs. 29, 114) now began to seem an incongruous reminder of the American territorial era, made all the more glaring by its location in the middle of the Spanish plaza. Periodic calls for its removal began in the 1950s. The monument is inscribed in English to Union casualties and "to the heroes who have fallen in various battles with savage Indians," that is, nomadic, raiding Indians such as the Apaches, Navajos, and Comanches. As Oliver La Farge

pointed out when removal was first proposed, the heroes of these battles were primarily Spanish-Americans and Pueblo Indians. "Under the Madison Avenue influence," continued La Farge by evoking the symbol of commercial advertising, "we are getting to where we want even our history made bland, sweetened, suited for consumption without any sensation whatsoever. The plaza monument is something else again, an authentic survival of frontier days, of the emotions of those times, of their simplicity and even their crudity. . . . It is altogether too easy to brush such simple things aside, brushing our predecessors aside along with them, in favor of a Madison Avenue version, chocolate-peppermint flavored for tourist consumption." Such a clear plea for a genuine inclusive history has been repeated with each attempt to remove the monument. While it remains in place, the words "savage Indians" were chiseled out one day in 1974. The proposal of sculptor Bob Haozous to relocate the monument to the national cemetery "where it belongs," does have an appealing sardonic logic.[6]

Those who first sought the monument's removal wanted a statue of the leader of the reconquest, Diego de Vargas, to take its place. Removal of the obelisk was again proposed in the late 1980s, but this time to make way for a statue of Santa Fe's founder, Pedro de Peralta. The New Mexico Historic Preservation Division blocked this proposal, and a site beside the post office was chosen instead for the new statue. The jury

208. "MADONNA OF THE TRAIL," AUGUST LEIMBACH, DAUGHTERS OF THE AMERICAN REVOLUTION MEMORIAL, ALBUQUERQUE, 1927. A STATUE REJECTED BY A SANTA FE THAT IN THE MID-1920S WAS EDITING OUT ALL SIGNS OF THE ANGLO CONTRIBUTION TO ITS HISTORY. (AUTHOR)

for the 1990 Peralta statue competition rejected all five finalists: three because they were too abstract and a fourth apparently because its designer had little experience with large commissions.[7]

The fifth rejected entry, a piece by Luis Jiménez, was provocative in both its aesthetics and historical content. Jiménez, an internationally celebrated sculptor who lives in southern New Mexico, depicted Peralta on foot holding a rolled-up document—the royal decree and plans for the city, perhaps, or the Spanish town planning ordinances (fig. 210). This Peralta is framed by an informal triumphal arch formed by a Pueblo Indian and a mestizo carrying a beam engraved "Paseo de Peralta," the name of the avenue passing the site. The historical ambiguity of Jiménez's fiberglass sculptures often makes them controversial, while their play on popular imagery and colorful high-gloss finishes, reminiscent of lowriders, make them highly accessible to the public. By including the common folk who actually built Santa Fe in his Peralta design, Jiménez offered a mild corrective to the romance of the Spanish conquistadors and raised questions of historic social structure and mestizaje. This is precisely the sort of art and history that will lead to healthier myths and deeper social harmony, but this was too much for some Hispanic leaders. His entry was rejected as a "neon Peralta" and led Santa Fe native and former ambassador to Argentina, Frank V. Ortiz, to argue that "the color, design and materials of the sculpture must blend in with the city's historic core."[8]

The controversy engendered by this first competition demonstrated that Santa Fe's Spanish leadership expected a heroic equestrian bronze. A second competition yielded three acceptable entries. Nearby Indian pueblos, however, began to voice their opposition to the whole idea of this "racist statue." Pueblo Governor Patrick Baca wrote, "Our history at Sandia Pueblo is racial and cultural oppression at the hands of the Hispanic conquistadors." Thomas E. Chávez, Ph.D., director of the history museum in the Palace of the Governors, countered that Peralta "was a government official who followed some very enlightened and specific instructions stipulating that he establish

317

209. REMOVAL OF THE BELL OF THE U.S.S. NEW MEXICO FROM THE PLAZA, ABOUT 1973. (DAVID MARGOLIS)

210. "PROPOSAL FOR PASEO DE PERALTA SCULPTURE," LUIS JIMÉNEZ, 1990. PERALTA WITH THE PLAN FOR THE CITY IN HAND PRESIDES OVER THE MESTIZO AND PUEBLO WORKMEN WHO ACTUALLY CONSTRUCTED THE CITY; FROM THE FIRST, ABORTED COMPETITION TO MEMORIALIZE SANTA FE'S FOUNDER.

a new capital in a location that did not displace Indians. . . . Peralta's instructions were in keeping with Spanish policy and Spain was the only European country that consciously considered its moral obligation to the native population of the New World."[9]

Indeed the winning design by Dave McGary, which was installed next to the main post office in 1992, portrays Peralta not as a conquistador in armor with a sword at his side, but instead wearing a cavalier broad-brimmed hat, accompanied by a surveyor (fig. 211). Complementary bronze plaques reproduce the royal decree alluded to by Chávez, along with images of books, tools, livestock, and plants introduced by the Spanish. The commemoration of Peralta rather than Vargas, Peralta's nonmilitary attire, and the accompanying plaques turn the monument into a polemic in the debate over European colonialization that was engendered by the quincentenary of Columbus's arrival in the New World. Like folklorist Aurelio Espinosa, the Peralta monument recognizes only one side of the Spanish-Indian interchange.

The state of New Mexico's primary commemoration of the 1492 quincentenary, by contrast, revels in the conquistador image. This monumental bronze of Governor Juan de Oñate, designed by Reynaldo Rivera and entitled *The Last Conquistador*, embraces modern romantic imagery; it is as though El Cid or a militant Man of La Mancha had just ridden fully armored out of the movies (fig. 212). The monument shows no apparent signs of regret nor any desire for contemporary reconciliation. To place this glorification of the conquistador who so brutally suppressed the Acoma uprising in 1599 in the Española Valley north of Santa Fe, where six thousand Tewa Pueblo Indians live today, displays a monumental insensitivity.[10]

Chiricahua Apache artist Bob Haozous (son of sculptor Alan Houser) responded with a piece entitled *Discover* (fig. 213). His mounted conquistador, with his sword and eyes lifted to the heavens, rests on a base decorated with cut-out figures resembling paper dolls and grade-schoolers' traced hands. But on closer examination, one realizes that the figures are missing hands and feet, and on reflection, that the cut-out hands are the work of the conquistador's blade.

211. "PERALTA, THE FOUNDER OF SANTA FE," DAVE MCGARY, 1992. THE WINNER OF THE SECOND COMPETITION PROVIDED AN EQUESTRIAN BRONZE AND A LITANY OF THE BENEFITS THE SPANISH BROUGHT TO THE INDIANS. (AUTHOR)

212. "THE LAST CONQUISTADOR" OÑATE VISITOR'S CENTER, NEAR SAN JUAN PUEBLO, REYNALDO RIVERA, 1992. NEW MEXICO'S PRIMARY COLUMBIAN QUINCENTENARY MONUMENT COMMEMORATES THE MOST BRUTAL OF CONQUISTADORS. (AUTHOR)

318

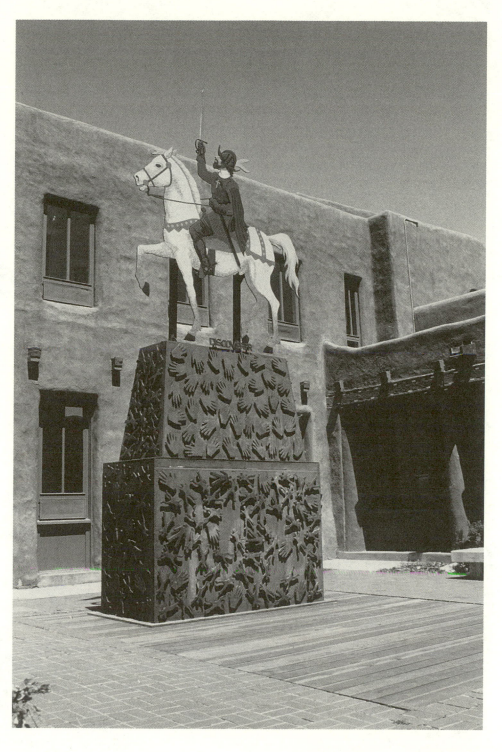

213. "DISCOVER," BOB HAOZOUS, 1992. A NATIVE AMERICAN SCULPTOR CALLS
ATTENTION TO THE WORK OF THE CONQUISTADORS' SWORD. (AUTHOR)

A third artist who has struggled with the subterranean issues of New Mexico history is Patrick Nagatani, a photographer who moved from Los Angeles to Albuquerque to teach at the University of New Mexico. His haunting dreamlike collaged and staged photographs, published in 1991 as *Nuclear Enchantment,* mythologize forty New Mexico sites associated with weapons development, uranium mining, and radioactive contamination (fig. 214). In one image, Japanese tourists (including Nagatani) pose and take pictures of each other in front of the monument at the Trinity bomb test site, as the *Enola Gay* flies overhead; in another a wolf kachina purifies a river strewn with cattle killed by a uranium tailings spill. A woman standing beside Chaco Canyon ruins holds a newspaper with the headline "If Atomic Economy Shrinks, What Next?" while above her a stealth bomber streaks through the sky. In the final image, entitled *"'Generation to Generation,' Strategic Defense Initiative . . .,"* Nagatani stands holding his young son's hand as they look out over Albuquerque from under an umbrella held up against a driving rain and a dark satellite-filled sky.[11]

Santa Fe and the rest of New Mexico, for that matter, could use a set of monuments in the spirit of Jiménez, Haozous, and Nagatani—a public art that challenges romantic history and tourist stereotypes. This might take the form of a statewide three-dimensional update of the 1930s promotional maps that illustrated history, cultures, and attractions with fifty or so vignettes of Indians, conquistadors, and cowboys, campers, skiers, and wild game. Near the fossil beds on the east side of the state, where oil fields give way to the pumping of the Ogalala Aquifer for pivot-arm irrigation, could be deployed a playground-sized set of dinosaurs interspersed with a miniature oil derrick and a windmill. In south-central New Mexico, where the historic Camino Real parallels Interstate 25, might stand a row of statues heading north from Mexico: a conquistador, the Mexican-era entrepreneur Doña Tules Barcelo, a five-year-old Arthur Campa fleeing the 1910 Revolution, and a modern-day maid and construction worker. Or at the Ghost Ranch nature center, north of Abiquiu: a gigantic bleached steer's skull, placed high in the air, in front of the red-brown landscape made famous by Georgia O'Keeffe. And perhaps a cast-concrete three-foot-tall tourist, wearing a camera and holding a howling coyote, could be made available for home landscaping.

In Santa Fe a sculpture of a peach tree cut off at its base, placed next to the 1888 Kit Carson obelisk, might commemorate the scorched-earth tactics he used to subdue the Navajo. On the parade grounds of the old Indian school, a primary site of forced acculturation, I would enjoy seeing statues of Indian children in their turn-of-the-century military uniforms, dancing in a line with kachinas. A bronze Mercedes, executed half-scale so one would have to bend over to see the driver with a car phone at his ear, might make a nice monument to the 1980s boom.

A revival of the more inclusive spirit of early Santa Fe Fiestas would also be welcome. To portray de Vargas or one of his men for the annual Fiesta instills a sense of dignity and civic obligation that participants carry through their lives and that ennobles community life. But other historical events could also be celebrated and taken to heart. In 1980, the three-hundredth anniversary of the Pueblo Revolt was reenacted by runners following the routes of the messengers who coordinated the uprising. Annual commemorative runs along these historic routes, directed by the Pueblos but open to others, would celebrate cultural self-determination and local autonomy.

214. "Koshare/Tewa Ritual Clowns, Missile Park, White Sands Missile Range, New Mexico, 1989," Patrick Nagatani.

Other events that a more complete public history might acknowledge range from the Taos Revolt of 1847, the theft of the common lands, and the arrival of the railroad, to the 1920s immigration of artists and displaced *mexicano* villagers, the Japanese interment camp, and the hippie pioneers of '68.

The Anti-Scrape philosophy of historic preservation, too, epitomizes a healthier inclusivist stance toward history, change, and the modern world. In its broadest sense, it forgoes the search for authentic cultures, untouched wildernesses, and unaltered historic districts and instead finds interest, beauty, and value in all people, places, and periods. Instead of viewing recent buildings as "intrusions," and accretions to historic buildings as a "loss of integrity," we might learn to appreciate them for the rich layering of successive generations of consciousness that they represent. A good declaration of a new Anti-Scrape realism would be to repaint the brown Catron Block, on the plaza, a brick red with white Italianate trim. Next design review might be removed from the west side, or barring that, the guidelines might be rewritten to deemphasize Santa Fe style and encourage the Westside Vernacular. As practitioners of hybrid Coyote culture, modern vernacular builders are not overly concerned with purity of sources or stylistic harmony. So the codification of the current Westside Vernacular runs the risk of taming this creative expression into yet another tasteful revival style genre. A celebration of the raw vitality of the vernacular, in any case, could become a symbol of the neighborhood's resistance to gentrification.

Sustain Modern Local Communities

The aversion to modernity typified by Santa Fe is understandable: our material circumstances advance, but many of us live in increased social isolation, nagged by a feeling of emptiness. And yet no city, culture, or nation can afford to turn its back on modern technology or the capitalist bottom line and expect to remain in control of its own destiny. Rational science progressively improves technology, while its new efficiencies are carried to the corners of the world by the drive for profit. But while technology is cumulative, cultures and their myths are not, precisely because they are embedded in a particular time, place, and community of believers. Although shared technology and ruthless investors increasingly shape our world, the culture they foster glorifies money and material possessions and offers shallow diversions that range from escapist nostalgia to drugs. This international consumer mass-media culture rarely resonates with power and authenticity on fundamental human questions. Indeed those who give their full allegiance to this attitude are prepared to disrupt local social networks and despoil the environment in their pursuit of profit.[12]

Tourism further complicates this predicament by appropriating and manipulating the very cultural life blood of local communities. Managers of national parks, in a parallel situation, ask what is the carrying capacity of natural environments—how many people can visit a park without damaging its plants and animal populations, and what can we do to lessen these negative impacts? But we might also ask, what is the carrying capacity of a cultural environment? How many visitors and new residents invigorate a culture, and how many damage, distort, and overwhelm it? Can a community sustain immigration of 1 percent per year and a steady visitor population of 4 percent? The answer depends on the vitality of the local culture, on the conditions of the interactions of native residents with visitors and newcomers, and on the willingness of everyone to put aside stereotypes and open themselves to real communication. Whatever the threshold, Santa Fe is well past it.

As Santa Fe's political leaders increasingly contend, the city should not add more hotel rooms but should instead concentrate on the development of other sections of its economy. Governmental promotion of tourism could seek to spread the visitor load to other areas of the state and to challenge tourists to overcome stereotypes. Mechanisms are also needed that encourage communications and equitable economic exchanges between visitors and residents. Clearly a conversation over morning coffee between a visitor and the resident-owner of a bed-and-breakfast is culturally healthier and economically better for the community than that between a tourist and a minimum-wage maid passing without eye contact in the hallway of a large hotel owned by outside investors.

The critique of the economic and cultural manipulations of tourism must be a priority of artists, intellectuals, and politicians. The object is not only to challenge tourist stereotypes and harness tourism for community needs, but also to help create a separate space, both psychologically and physically, where local communities can nourish their own myths and social lives. Likewise the trivialization of local cultures into tourist cliches and their denigration as second-rate by cosmopolitan intellectuals must be contested at every turn.

Those who are grounded in a particular place and an unbroken cultural continuity—rural Hispanos and Pueblo Indians, for instance—can seek to revitalize their roots in modern terms. Those raised on invented traditions and consumer iconography—among whom I count myself, most Anglos, and many urban Hispanics and Native Americans—face a tougher dilemma. An important first step is for people to put down local roots. This will allow us to connect more directly with the history that surrounds us and with indigenous knowledge of the environment. Day-to-day, face-to-face interactions among people provide the shared experiences needed to revitalize our myths; so too an intimate experience with plants, animals, soil, and the natural elements can lead to local environmental wisdom. In an era dominated by the quarterly profit statement, we desperately need a deeper understanding of our place in the sweep of history and our role in transmitting the world from our ancestors to future generations.

CONTEMPORARY MYTHMAKING

The writings of architect, historian, and educational consultant Rina Naranjo Swentzell confront mainstream culture with what is most living and creative in her culture. As a child during the 1940s, Swentzell's generation was the last raised when Santa Clara was primarily agricultural and its daily social life still vital around the plaza. Naranjos have been cultural intermediaries for over three centuries, including Rina's uncle

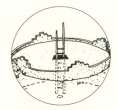

The cardinal landscape.   Anasazi: houses, plaza, and kiva.   Pueblo: houses, plaza, and kiva   Kiva.

Santiago earlier this century and many of her siblings and children, who are potters, sculptors, poets, scholars, and permaculture advocates. She met New Jersey-born Ralph Swentzell at New Mexico Highlands University and married him "because he represented something other than what I grew up as." In the midst of raising her four children, Swentzell became concerned that the BIA was building single-family houses away from the old plaza and decided to study architecture and then the history of Indian education at the University of New Mexico.[13]

Swentzell's writings draw on memories of her youth and talks with village elders and tease out the world view embedded in the Tewa language (fig. 215). As a university-trained scholar, she also studies published Pueblo myths and ethnographies. Her combination of beliefs still central to her life with an analytical consciousness means that she is presenting not pure traditional Pueblo culture, but rather her attempt to make the underlying tenets of Pueblo thought comprehensible and, in a sense, believable in the outside world.

"The Pueblo world," Swentzell writes, "first of all, is an altogether hallowed place where 'the breath,' or life energy, flows through both the animate and inanimate realms in such a manner that even the house, kiva, and community forms breathe of that breath and are essentially alive." This life force, *po-wa-ha* in Tewa, meaning literally "water-wind-breath," flows through the entire world, through clouds, rocks, and pottery as well as plants, animals, and humans. It also flows in and out of the symbolic center of each pueblo, in Tewa the *nan-si-pu,* which means "earth navel," or more literally "belly root." Pueblo ancestors ascended through three previous worlds to this, the fourth level of reality, so the nan-si-pu is both the point of emergence and a point of contact with ancestors and supernatural beings. Although the nan-si-pu is usually inconspicuous—a small pile of stones, a half submerged rock, or a cup-sized depression in a dry plaza—in Pueblo minds it overflows with the life force; "elders of today's Tewa world refer to the *nansipu* as 'the watery place' or as 'the watery place of origin.'"[14]

325

215. ILLUSTRATIONS FROM "PUEBLO SPACE, FORM, AND MYTHOLOGY," BY RINA SWENTZELL, 1990. (RINA SWENTZELL AND JEROME IOWA)

This nan-si-pu is sometimes located in a ceremonial kiva in the village plaza or unprotected in the plaza itself. The surrounding dance plaza forms the primary ceremonial space of the village. Its Tewa name, *bu-ping-geh,* translates as "center of the pueblo/world," or more literally, as "center-heart-place." "As the breath, or *Po-wa-ha,* flows through the voids of our human bodies, so does it flow out of the *nansipu* and into the *bupingeh,* giving life to the physical, social, and religious community." Such a plaza was the very heart of community; "as recently as the 1940s, people slept, cooked and ate outdoors, on the ground level as well as the roof tops, as often as weather permitted." To this day, when it fills with long rows of dancers, their short repetitive steps and compact arm strokes tied to the ceremonial drum beat, the plaza pulses like a heart. By analogy each person carries this life force of the world/community in her or his beating heart.[15]

The buildings surrounding the plaza form the first of four concentric zones that conceptually encircle the nan-si-pu. Outside the village, four boundary shrines traditionally defined the precincts of everyday life. Beyond are the four sacred hills and, visible in the distance, the four sacred mountains, each roughly in the cardinal directions. Like a spider over the middle of its web, a Pueblo metaphor for the mythic location of a village, Pueblo buildings are held between the sacred center and the containing landscape. When a person stands at the heart of the plaza and looks to the sacred mountains on the horizon, 30 to 100 miles away, he or she takes in the bounded order of the world.

Nan-si-pu understood as the center of the world, of course, is ethnocentric, but the Pueblos always recognized that each village has its own belly root. When villages relocated, as they often did before the arrival of the Spanish, the search for a new site was understood as a quest for a new center. *Nan-si-pu* in this sense means not the center of the entire world, but the center of a particular world, a specific human community. This centering of a community in a living, breathing plaza, rooted in the land, is a powerful image of local culture. It contrasts sharply with the physically isolated suburban house, the rational surveyor's grid, and allegiance to a distant cultural center, be it Madrid, Mecca, or Beijing, New York, Hollywood, or the Santa Fe of tourist stereotypes and interior design style.

Imagine if you will, what Santa Fe would be like today if it had adopted the community planning module of the Laws of the Indies in 1957, rather than historic styles design review. These Spanish regulations not only prescribed the plaza as the civic, religious, and social focus for settlements, but also made provision for secondary plazas for each church parish of from two to ten thousand people. Under such a policy, Santa Fe would today have fifteen or so neighborhood plazas to accommodate its 60,000 people. Around each plaza would cluster a post office, library, senior citizens' center, day-care center, and grade school, along with a grocery store, a movie theater, a gym/community hall, and a church or two. While the traditional rectangular or square plaza is a proven prototype, nothing says it cannot continue to be adapted and improved. Because Santa Fe's winters at 7,000 feet discourage outside activities, for instance, some south-facing, Pueblo-like roof terraces sheltered from the wind might be introduced and overlaid with a modern innovation such as the solar atrium.

And what if cluster housing traditions had not been discouraged after World War II by zoning codes, subdivision regulations, and lending practices? The Spanish courtyard house, the residential cul-de-sac, and the artists' and extended family compound might have continued to adapt with socioeconomic changes, leavened along the way by innovations such as cohousing. A diversity of evolving forms would now be able to more subtly accommodate changing household patterns, while fostering healthy social support networks.

Social networks, the production of housing, and myth intertwine at Zuni Pueblo. Each year eight Zuni families build large houses to host the visit of Shalako kachinas (supernatural beings) who are portrayed by dancers wearing masks that make them 10 feet tall. This custom not only mobilizes kinship networks to expand the housing stock, but also invests the village year by year with spirituality. In Santa Fe the construction of housing clusters might be organized as annual community events, with each project christened by a work of public art in the progressive spirit of Chicano murals. What would the political consciousness of a community be if such a mural were painted each year to stimulate an ongoing debate about its history and issues of social change?

There is some talk of retrofitting Santa Fe with neighborhood plazas, and they are to be included in the city's Tierra Contenta subdivision. Each plaza would provide a focus for neighborhood identity, reinforced by mythohistory, an annual cycle of events and celebrations, and its own monuments and murals. On the Westside plaza, a commemoration of Hispano immigration in the 1920s might culminate a school oral history month, during which grandparents would speak of the sorrow of leaving behind their small, intimate villages and the struggles to build a new life in Santa Fe. On the site of the Japanese concentration camp, which backs into a hillside north of the river in the direction of the Tewa pueblos and Los Alamos, might be a small park with an abstract billowing cloudlike sculpture—part po-wa-ha, part *Lucky Cloud,* part A-bomb cloud.

On the new plaza of each ethnically integrated neighborhood, which according to the 1990 census means every Santa Fe neighborhood, could be placed a statue of one of the great coyotes: George Washington Armijo dressed as de Vargas; Santiago Naranjo just finishing putting on his Fiesta buckskins; Witter Bynner as a Chinese Mandarin poet; Oliver and Consuela La Farge as a western dude and a Spanish beauty; and Georgia O'Keeffe in her own austere highly cultivated persona. Here in its neighborhood plazas and housing compounds, Santa Fe's residents could cultivate their own cultural and social life, apart from the distorting influence of tourism.

Of what use are such utopian visions? In Santa Fe and a hundred communities across the Untied States, similar initiatives are beginning under the guise of neotraditional town planning, the new urbanism, or cohousing. It will always be healthy to pause occasionally to imagine a better world in which to live, the people its monuments would honor, the values its ceremonies would celebrate, the face-to-face society its buildings and public spaces would foster. If regional culture is to be a force enriching our lives, it will require a strong local economy to provide jobs and affordable living. Given the economic and political realities of 1990s America, grassroots organizing will certainly be needed to reclaim power for local communities. But such practical actions can best be sustained with a healthy dose of the sort of tradition and mythmaking initiated by the Museum of New Mexico in the second decade of this century. Our job remains to overcome historical amnesia, challenge ethnic and tourist stereotypes, develop a sustainable economy, revitalize community, nurture myths worth believing, and foster a more humane society to pass on to coming generations.

"Very Provincial?" the philosopher John Dewey once asked rhetorically about people not living in New York or some other cosmopolitan center. "No, not at all," he replied. "Just local, just human, just at home, just where they live."[16] In our efforts to lead fulfilling lives that contribute to a better society, may we all be at home where we live.

APPENDIX: TABLES OF POPULATION AND ECONOMICS

Table 1. Population and Ethnic Composition of Santa Fe [1]

	City Population (% increase)	Indio/Genízaro (% of total pop.)	Español	Mulato	Mestizo/Coyote	
1790	2,542	157 (6%)	1695 (68%)	85 (3%)	604 (24%)	
		Indian	White	Freed Slave/ Negro	Spanish Surnamed	Non-Sp. Surnamed
1850	4,846		4,832 (99%)	14 (0.5%)	(93%)	(7%)
1860	4,635 (-4%)	32 (1%)	4,576 (98%)	27 (1%)	(91%)	(9%)
1870	4,756 (+3%)	44 (1%)	4,687 (98%)	34 (1%)	(87%)	(13%)
1880	6,635 (+39%)				(70%)	(30%)
1890	6,185 (-7%)					
1900	5,603 (-9%)					

	City Population (% increase)	Total County Population (% increase outside city)
1910	5,073 (-9%)	14,770
1920	7,236 (+42%)	15,030 (-30%)
1930	11,176 (+54%)	19,567 (+8%)
1940	20,325 (+82%)	30,826 (+24%)
1950	27,998 (+38%)	38,153 (-3%)
1960	34,394 (+23%)	44,970 (+4%)

(% of total pop.)

	City Population	Total County Population	Spanish Lang. or Surname	White (non-Spanish)	Negro
1970	41,167 (+19%)	54,774 (+29%)	26,642 (65%)	13,792 (34%)	153

	City Population	Total County Population	American Indian	Hispanic	White (Non-Hisp.)	Asian-Amer.	Black
1980	48,953 (+20%)	75,360 (+94%)	838 (2%)	26,899 (55%)	20,054 (41%)	172 (.5)	230 (0.5%)
1990	55,541 (+13%)	98,928 (+64%)	1,000 (2%)	26,302 (47%)	27,492 (49%)	312 (.5)	263 (0.5%)

Table 2. Estimated Employment in Basic Economic Sectors for Santa Fe County [2]

	Total Employees (% of Total)	Agriculture	Mining/ Manufactur.	Government	Tourism/ Arts	Other (Secondary Sectors)
1930	7,009	1,316 (19%)	1,257 (18%)	730 (10%)	648 (9%)	3,058 (44%)
1940	7,630	939 (12%)	759 (12%)	1,091 (14%)	782 (10%)	4,059 (53%)
1950	11,632	689 (6%)	615 (5%)	1,807 (16%)	1,214 (10%)	7,307 (63%)
1960	14,351	303 (2%)	674 (5%)	3,034 (21%)	1,758 (12%)	8,582 (60%)
1970	18,509	340 (2%)	760 (5%)	4,057 (22%)	2,564 (14%)	10,788 (58%)
1980	33,062	545 (2%)	1,575 (5%)	7,907 (24%)	4,531 (14%)	18,504 (56%)
1990	49,452	889 (2%)	2,650 (5%)	10,119 (20%)	8,574 (17%)	27,220 (55%)

Table 3. Tourism and Arts Businesses and Occupations listed in Santa Fe City Directories and Telephone Books [3]

	Curio Shops/ Indian Goods	Art Galleries	Artists	Architects	Hotels/ Motels	Lodging Rooms (Increase)[b]
1882	0	0	0	1	3	135
1890	1	0	0	0	3	95 (-24%)
1900	5	0	0	0	4	130 (37%)
1911	3	0	0	0	5	155 (17%)
1920	4	0	1	3	6	205 (29%)
1930	16	1	29	4	16	600 (193%)
1940	17	1	25	4	21	740 (23%)
1951	17	2	26	9	35	795 (6%)
1960	17	8	—[a]	18	31	1,150 (50%)
1970	15	26	—[a]	27	32	1,760 (53%)
1980	8	99	—[a]	43	37	2,260 (28%)
1992	64	231	44	89	61	4,116 (68%)

[a] 1960-1980 telephone books have no heading for artists.

[b] Percentage prorated for ten years, where period covered by data is greater or less than a decade.

NOTES

Because I have dispensed with a comprehensive bibliography in the name of economy, sources are given in full the first time they appear in each chapter. In addition, the following abbreviations have been used throughout:

AJ	*Albuquerque Journal*
BL-CF	Cassidy Family Papers, Bancroft Library, University of California, Berkeley
DNM	*Daily New Mexican,* including title variations, *The New Mexican, The Santa Fe New Mexican,* etc. For a full listing of variations in the newspaper's title, see Pearce S. Grove, Becky J. Barnett and Sandra J. Hansen, eds., *New Mexico Newspapers* (Albuquerque: University of New Mexico Press, 1975).
EP	*El Palacio* (magazine of the Museum of New Mexico)
HNAI	William G. Sturtevant, ser. ed., Alfonso Ortiz, vol. ed., *Handbook of North American Indians, vol. 9, Southwest* (Washington, DC.: Smithsonian Institution, 1979).
JSAH	*Journal of the Society of Architectural Historians*
MNM	History Museum, Museum of New Mexico, Santa Fe
	H Hewett Collection
	PA Photographic Archives
	VF Vertical File
	WL Wiess-Loomis Collection
NMA	*New Mexico Architecture*
NMHR	*New Mexico Historical Review*
NMRC	New Mexico Records Center and Archives, Santa Fe
PSRA	Nicholas C. Markovich, Wolfgang F. E. Preiser, and Fred G. Strum, eds., *Pueblo Style and Regional Architecture* (New York: Van Nostrand Reinhold, 1990).
RAC	Rockefeller Archives Center, Tarrytown, New York
	RF Rockefeller Family Papers
	OMR Office of Messieurs Rockefeller

SANM Spanish Archives of New Mexico. Microfilm edition of 23 reels, cited by reel and frame number. Sources of translations also cited.

SANMII Spanish Archives of New Mexico, Part II. On deposit at the NMRC. Case number and sources of translations cited.

SFG *Santa Fe Gazette*

SFR *Santa Fe Reporter*

UNM University of New Mexico, Albuquerque

    B Bunting Collection, Meem Archives, Zimmerman Library

    M Meem Collection, Meem Archives, Zimmerman Library

    MG Map and Geographic Reference Center, Centennial Library

WNM *Weekly New Mexican*

Introduction

1. John Nichols, *The Milagro Beanfield War* (Holt, Rinehart and Winston, 1974); Robert Redford, dir., Redford and Moctesuma Esparza prod., *The Milagro Beanfield War,* Los Angeles: Universal City Studios, 1988; Anthony DeCurtis, "Robert Redford: The Rolling Stone Interview," *Rolling Stone* (October 6, 1994): 73-77+. "*The Milagro Beanfield War* had to do with the rhythms of a culture that had no information access, that had no television or radio," explained Redford to *Rolling Stone* in 1994. "They just lived as they had for 400 years." The ignorance of the region's history betrayed by this classic romantic construction goes a long way toward explaining the film's reliance on stereotypes.

2. Throughout much of this century, scholars have dismissed tourist crafts, architectural revivals, historical pageants, and the like as unauthentic pseudoculture. A classic statement of this interpretation is Daniel J. Boorstin, *The Image or What Happened to the American Dream* (New York: Atheneum, 1962). In the late 1970s, however, historians and anthropologists began to take modern hybrid cultures seriously and have produced such notable studies as: Eric Hobsbawm and Terence Ranger, eds., *The Invention of Tradition* (Cambridge: Cambridge University Press, 1983), especially Hobsbawm's introduction on "Inventing Traditions" and Hugh Trevor-Roper's chapter, "The Invention of Tradition: The Highland Tradition of Scotland"; T. J. Jackson Lears, *No Place of Grace: Anti-Modernism and the Transformation of American Culture* (New York: Pantheon, 1981); James Clifford, *The Predicament of Culture: Twentieth-Century Ethnography, Literature, and Art* (Cambridge, MA: Harvard University Press, 1988); David E. Whisnant, *All That is Native and Fine: The Politics of Culture in an American Region* (Chapel Hill: University of North Carolina Press, 1983). My understanding owes a considerable debt to these sources.

3. Fredrik Barth, ed., *Ethnic Groups and Boundaries* (Boston: Little, Brown and Co., 1969) is an influential interpretation of this phenomenon. For subsequent research, see chap. 5, n. 1, below.

4. Clifford, *Predicament of Culture,* 235.

5. I paraphrase Clifford here.

6. On subjectivity in the presentation of history, see Paul Ricoeur, *History and Truth* (Evanston, IL: Northwestern University Press, 1965); William H. McNeill, "Mythistory, or Truth, History, and Historians," *American Historical Review* 91 (1) February 1986): 1-10; Hayden White, *The Content of the Form: Narrative Discourse and Historical Representation* (Baltimore: Johns Hopkins University Press, 1987); Greg Dening, *Mr Bligh's Bad Language: Passion, Power and Theatre on the Bounty* (Cambridge: Cambridge University Press, 1992). For the anthropological debate on subjectivity, see Clifford, *Predicament of Culture,* 11-114; George W. Stocking, Jr., ed., *Observers Observed: Essays on Ethnographic Fieldwork* (Madison: University of Wisconsin, 1983); Paul A. Roth, "Ethnography without Tears," with comments and reply, *Current Anthropology* 30(5) (December 1989): 555-69; Michael Carrithers et al., "On Ethnography without Tears," *Current Anthropology* 31(1) (February 1990): 53-58.

Chapter 1

1. Michael L. Elliott, *The Archeology of Santa Fe: A Background Report* (Santa Fe: City of Santa Fe, 1988), 13-18; Linda S. Cordell, "Prehistory: Eastern Anasazi," HNAI 131-51, especially 134-36.

2. Cordell, "Prehistory," 136-44; Elliott, *Archeology of Santa Fe,* 16-18.

3. Elliot, *Archeology of Santa Fe,* 18-21, Cordell, "Prehistory," 144-45; Ramón A. Gutiérrez, *When Jesus Came the Corn Mothers Went Away: Marriage, Sexuality, and Power in New Mexico, 1500-1846,* (Stanford, CA: Stanford University Press, 1991), xxvi; Albert H. Schroeder, "Pueblos Abandoned in Historic Times," HNAI 254.

4. George Hammond and Agapito Rey, *Narratives of the Coronado Expedition 1540-1542* (Albuquerque: University of New Mexico Press, 1940), (quote) 257, 158, 254-57, 308; George Hammond and Agapito Rey, *The Rediscovery of New Mexico 1580-1594,* (Albuquerque: University of New Mexico Press, 1966), 84, 108, 185, 219, 277-78; Victor Mindeleff, *A Study of Pueblo Architecture in Tusayan and Cibola* (1891; reprint, Washington, D.C.: Smithsonian Institution Press, 1989).

5. George Hammond and Agapito Rey, *Don Juan de Oñate, Colonizer of New Mexico* (Albuquerque: University of New Mexico Press, 1953) 2 vols.; Marc Simmons, *The Last Conquistador: Juan de Oñate and the Settling of the Far Southwest* (Norman: University of Oklahoma Press, 1991); Gutiérrez, *When Jesus Came,* 47-49; Thomas D. Hall, *Social Change in the Southwest, 1350-1880* (Lawrence: University Press of Kansas, 1989), 67, 73, 81-82; William deBuys, *Enchantment and Exploitation: The Life and Hard Times of a New Mexico Mountain Range* (Albuquerque: University of New Mexico Press, 1985), 47-81.

6. Hammond and Rey, *Oñate,* I: 354-56, 428-56; Simmons, *Oñate,* 135-46; Gutiérrez, *When Jesus Came,* 52-54.

334

7. Hammond and Rey, *Oñate*, 1:32-34; Gutiérrez, *When Jesus Came*, 54-55.

8. Irene Chávez, trans., "Instructions to Peralta by Viceroy," NMHR 4 (2) (April 1929): 185, 187; John W. Reps, *Cities of the American West* (Princeton, NJ: Princeton University Press, 1979), 35-40. Dora P. Crouch, Daniel J. Garr, and Axel I. Mundigo, *Spanish City Planning in North America*, (Cambridge, MA: MIT Press, 1982), 6-19, contains the best translation of the town planning ordinances of the Laws of the Indies.

9. Crouch, Garr, and Mundigo, *Spanish City Planning*, ordinance 38, p. 9, echoed in ordinances 5 and 110, pp. 7, 12-13.

10. Crouch, Garr, and Mundigo, *Spanish City Planning*, ordinance 111, p. 13. A good discussion of Santa Fe's location is found in Irene Moke, "Santa Fe, New Mexico" (Ph.D. diss., University of Nebraska, 1945), 115-22.

11. George Kubler, *The Religious Architecture of New Mexico* (1940; reprint, Albuquerque: University of New Mexico Press, 1972); Francisco Atanasio Dominguez, E. Adams, and A Chávez, trans., *The Missions of New Mexico, 1776* (Albuquerque: University of New Mexico Press, 1956); John L. Kessell, *The Missions of New Mexico Since 1776* (Albuquerque: University of New Mexico Press, 1980).

12. Kubler, *Religious Architecture*, 67, 133; Alfonso Ortiz, "1000 Years of Pueblo Architecture: 500-1500," paper presented at Pueblo Style and Regional Architecture conference, University of New Mexico, October 1-4, 1988. The seventeenth-century churches of Santa Fe (San Francisco and San Miguel) both face west onto their respective plazas. Those built early in the nineteenth century (Guadalupe Church and Rosario Chapel) face east and south, respectively, reflecting the shift in orientation in the province.

13. Marc Simmons, "History of Pueblo-Spanish Relationships to 1821," HNAI 178-93, especially 181-86, 193; Schroeder, "Pueblos Abandoned," 254.

14. Simmons, "Relationships," 186-87; Joe S. Sando, "The Pueblo Revolt," HNAI 194-97; Charles Hackett, *Revolt of the Pueblo Indians* (Albuquerque: University of New Mexico Press, 1942), 207-8.

15. J. Manuel Espinosa, *Crusaders of the Rio Grande* (Chicago: Institute of Jesuit History, 1942), 151-62. "The Justification of General Don Diego De Vargas," *Old Santa Fe* 2 (5 [should be no. 1]) (1912): 58-65, especially 58, 61; John Kessell, "Vargas and the Spanish Reconquest," *Santa Fe, History of An Ancient City*, ed. David Nobel (Santa Fe: School of American Research, 1988).

16. In addition to the sources in note 15, see also Gutiérrez, *When Jesus Came*, 143-44.

17. Espinosa, *Crusaders*, 151-62; Simmons, "Relationships," 186-87; Gutiérrez, *When Jesus Came*, 143-45.

18. David R. Wilcox, "Multi-Ethnic Division of Labor in the Protohistoric Southwest," (Albuquerque: Papers of the New Mexico Archeological Society, 1983); Elizabeth A. Brandt, "Internal Stratification in Pueblo Communities," paper presented at American Anthropological Association annual meeting, Washington, DC, December 1984.

19. Gutiérrez, *When Jesus Came,* 196, (quote) 198-99; Adrian Bustamante, "'The Matter Was Never Resolved': The *Casta* System in Colonial New Mexico, 1693-1823," NMHR 66(2) (April 1991): especially 143, n. 1 for a survey of the literature on Spanish ethnic categorization; Magnus Morner, *Race Mixture in the History of Latin America,* (Boston: Little, Brown and Co., 1967), 59.

20. On the origins of New Mexico settlers, see George P. Hammond, *Don Juan Oñate and the Founding of New Mexico* (Santa Fe: Historical Society of New Mexico, 1927), 187-210; Angelico Chávez, *Origins of New Mexico Families* (1954; reprint, Albuquerque: University of Albuquerque, 1973), especially ix-xiv; Clevy L. Strout, "The Resettlement of Santa Fe, 1695: The Newly Found Muster Roll," NMHR 53(3) (July 1978): 261-70; Bustamante, "*Casta* System," 143-64; Gutiérrez, *When Jesus Came,* 103, 365 n. 23. Bustamante and I make slightly different tabulations of the castas of the 1,695 settlers listed in Strout, apparently as a result of my assigning a casta to relatives of those with known casta. The small amount of immigration from outside of New Mexico revealed in the 1790 census is discussed by two historians: Oakah L. Jones, Jr., *Los Paisanos: Spanish Settlement on the Northern Frontier of New Spain* (Norman: University of Oklahoma Press, 1979), 130-31; and Gutiérrez, *When Jesus Came,* 149.

21. A. Chávez quoted in David Lavender, *The Southwest* (1980; reprint, Albuquerque: University of New Mexico Press, 1984), 88. See also Gutiérrez, *When Jesus Came,* 153, 180-89; Thomas D. Hall, *Social Change in the Southwest, 1350-1880,* (Lawrence: University of Kansas Press, 1989), 126. The Urrutia map indicates that the Barrio Analco south of the river was originally settled by Tlaxcalans who accompanied the original Spanish settlers. While oral tradition supports this, most other documentation suggests that few Tlaxcalans ever lived here; instead the neighborhood was populated primarily by genízaros; Marc Simmons, "Tlascalans in the Spanish Borderlands," NMHR 39(2) (April 1964): 101-10; Steven M. Horvath, Jr., "The Genízaro of Eighteenth-Century New Mexico: A Reexamination," *Discovery* [School of American Research] (1977): 25-40; Angelico Chávez, "Genízaros," HNAI 198-200.

22. Gutiérrez, *When Jesus Came,* 155-56; Hall, *Social Change,* 102.

23. Gutiérrez, *When Jesus Came,* 197.

24. Gutiérrez, *When Jesus Came,* 148-49.

25. Gutiérrez, *When Jesus Came,* 147-56; Hall 90-95, 105-9.

26. Crouch, Garr, and Mundigo, *Spanish City Planning,* ordinance 112, p. 13, ordinance 118, p. 14. For a brief discussion of Urrutia and his Santa Fe map, see Max L. Moorhead, *The Presidio: Bastion of the Spanish Borderlands* (Norman: University of Oklahoma Press, 1975), 56-57, 170. See also: Reps, *Cities,* 46, pl. 3. Discussion of Santa Fe's pre-1766 town plan is problematic because of incomplete, vague, and sometimes contradictory documentation. The most thorough yet still inconclusive discussion is Linda Tigges, ed., *Santa Fe Historic Plaza Study I* (Santa Fe: City Planning Department, 1990). See also: Christopher M. Wilson, *The Santa Fe New Mexico Plaza* (Ann Arbor: University Microfilms, 1982), 6-10; Ralph E. Twitchell, *Old Santa Fe* (Santa Fe: New Mexican Pub. Co., 1925), 51, note; Ralph E. Twitchell, *Spanish Archives of New Mexico* (Cedar

Rapids, Iowa: Torch Press, 1914) 1:73, archive 181; Angelico Chávez, "Santa Fe Church and Convent Sites in the Seventeenth and Eighteenth Centuries," NMHR 24(2) (April 1949): 92.

27. Crouch, Garr, and Mundigo, *Spanish City Planning*, ordinance 115, p. 14; George Kubler, *Sixteenth Century Mexican Architecture* (New Haven: Yale University Press, 1948), 1:204; SANM I, 364, 756, 787, paraphrased in Boyd C. Pratt and David H. Snow, *The North Central* [New Mexico] *Regional Overview* (Santa Fe: Historic Preservation Division, 1988), 1:243, 250; Marc Simmons, *Spanish Government in New Mexico* (Albuquerque: University of New Mexico Press, 1968), frontispiece; Benjamin F. Taylor, *Short Ravelings from a Long Yarn* (1847; reprint, Santa Anna, CA: Fine Arts Press, 1936), 146.

28. For a fuller discussion, see Marc Simmons, "Settlement Patterns and Village Plans in Colonial New Mexico," *Journal of the West* 8(1) (January 1969), 7-21.

29. Robert C. West, "The Flat-Roofed Folk Dwelling in Rural Mexico," *Geoscience and Man* (Journal of the Geography Department, Louisiana State University) 5 (1974), 111-32, specifically 125-26; Kubler, *Mexican Architecture* 1:188; Philip Bartholomew, "The Hacienda: Its Evolution and Architecture in Colonial New Mexico" (Ph.D. Dissertation, University of Missouri, 1983), 47-48; John Kantner, "A Study of Form and Space in Spanish Colonial Domestic Architecture in New Mexico" (senior thesis, Colorado College, 1989), 252-53, 262, 308.

30. George Foster, *Culture and Conquest: America's Spanish Heritage* (Chicago: Quadrangle Books, 1960), 10-13. Ivan Illich, "Vernacular Values," *CoEvolution Quarterly* 26 (Summer 1980): 33, 34, observes that Nebrija's grammar of 1492 and dictionary of 1493, which were the first to standardize a European vernacular language, Castilian, were presented to the crown as tools "of conquest abroad and a system of scientific control within the entire kingdom."

31. Peter M. Boyd-Bowman, "Regional Origins of the Earliest Spanish Colonists of America," *Publications of the Modern Language Association* (December 1956): 1152-63; Kantner 272-74.

32. West, 126-27. Kantner, "Form and Space," 295-98, notes the similarity of Aztec architecture to the subsequent Mexican courtyard house but discounts it as a significant source, in favor of exclusive Spanish origin.

33. Kantner, "Form and Space," 341; Bartholomew, "The Hacienda," 7, 117.

34. For a discussion of the different types of "adobe" construction practiced by the Pueblo Indians and the Spanish, see Bainbridge Bunting, *Early Architecture of New Mexico* (Albuquerque: University of New Mexico Press, 1976), 9-12. See also Earl Morris, "Adobe Bricks in a Pre-Spanish Wall Near Aztec, New Mexico," *American Antiquities* 9(4) (1944): 434-38; Michael Moguin, "From Bis Sa to Picuris: Early Pueblo Adobe Technology of New Mexico and the Southwest," *Adobe Journal* 9 (Winter 1992): 10-29.

35. Pratt and Snow, *North Central Regional Overview* 1:240-53.

36. Kantner, "Form and Space," 168-77 analyzes SANM documents identified in Pratt and Snow, *North Central Regional Overview* 1:241-52, which name the rooms in houses. For Santa Fe Trail travel accounts and diaries on *salas* and house interiors, see Philip St. George Cooke, *The*

Conquest of New Mexico and California (1878; reprint, Albuquerque: Horn and Wallace, 1964), 15; William W. H. Davis, *El Gringo or New Mexico and Her People* (1857; reprint Santa Fe: Rydal Press, 1938), 51-52; Lewis Garrard, *Wah-to-Yah and the Taos Trail* (1850; reprint Norman: University of Oklahoma Press, 1955), 168-70, 172; Susan Magoffin, *Down the Santa Fe Trial and into Mexico, 1846-7,* (New Haven: Yale University Press, 1962), 103-4, 137, 153-54, 166; J. E. Sunder, ed., *Matt Field on the Santa Fe Trail* (Norman: University of Oklahoma Press, 1960), 204.

37. Sunder, *Matt Field,* 204; Davis, *El Gringo,* 52.

38. Lonn Taylor and Dessa Bokides, *New Mexican Furniture, 1600-1940* (Santa Fe: Museum of New Mexico Press, 1987), 18-22; SANM I, 1, 776; Kantner, "Form and Space," 168-77.

39. Zebulon Pike, *The Expeditions of Zebulon Pike,* ed. Elliott Coves (New York: Francis P. Harper, 1895), 607. The dimensions of 162 and 28 1/2 feet appear in George Kubler, *The Religious Architecture of New Mexico* (1940; reprint Albuquerque: University of New Mexico Press, 1972), 101. Bunting, *Early Architecture,* 56, indicates that New Mexican church naves were generally slightly taller than wide; hence the height estimate of 30 feet.

40. These place-names, along with *barrio de Nuestra Señora de Guadalupe, barrio del Torreón,* and *centro de la ciudad,* were culled by Felipe Mirabal from birth, marriage, and burial registers of 1822-1824 in the Archives of the Archdiocese of Santa Fe: Santa Fe, B-67, M-52, M-53, Bur-52.

41. Gutiérrez, *When Jesus Came,* 298-336; Hall, *Social Change,* 110-15, 134-47.

42. This discussion is based on Max L. Moorhead, "Rebuilding the Presidio at Santa Fe, 1789-1791," NMHR 49(2) (April 1974): 123-42. The best discussion of the history of the Palace of the Governors is Cordelia Snow, "A Brief History of the Palace of the Governors," EP, 80(3) (Fall 1974): 1-22.

43. Janie Louise Aragón, "The People of Santa Fe in the 1790s," *Aztlán* [Chicano Studies Program, UCLA] 7(3) (Fall 1976): 391-417; E. B. Adam, ed., *Bishop Tamaron's Visitation of New Mexico, 1760* (Albuquerque: Historical Society of New Mexico, Publications in History, vol. 15, 1954), 46; SANM I, 1096a; Virginia L. Olmstead, trans., "Spanish Census of 1790 for the Province of New Mexico," and "Mexican Census of 1823 and 1825 for the Province of New Mexico," 2 vols. (typescript, 1973); H. Baily Carroll and J. Villosana Haggerd, trans., *Three New Mexico Chronicles,* (Albuquerque: Quivira Society, 1942), 27, 84, 88-89.

44. Olmstead, "Spanish Census"; Aragón, "People of Santa Fe," 402-12.

45. Gutiérrez, *When Jesus Came,* (quote) 244; see also 199, 215, 244-45, 280, 334-35.

46. Aragon, "People of Santa Fe," 391-417; Antonio Jose Rios-Bustamante, "New Mexico in the Eighteenth Century: Life, Labor and Trade in la Villa de San Felipe de Albuquerque, 1706-1790," *Aztlán* 7(3) (Fall 1970), 357-89, 381.

47. Aragón, "People of Santa Fe," 397.

48. Rios-Bustamante, "New Mexico in the Eighteenth Century," 357-89, 381. I base my equation of *color quebrado* and *coyote* on the similar percentages of these two groups in Santa Fe and Albuquerque and on the use of only one of the terms in each community.

49. Josiah Gregg, *Commerce of the Prairies* (1841; reprint, Philadelphia: J. B. Lippincott Co., 1962), 76. Historians' estimates of racial origins of population of New Mexico cited: Lavender, *The Southwest*, 88; Gutiérrez, *When Jesus Came*, 156, 171, 175; Jones, *Los Paisanos*, 130; D. W. Meinig, *The Shaping of America* (New Haven: Yale University Press, 1993) 2:60.

50. Hall, *Social Change*, 147-64; Gregg, *Commerce*, 76.

51. W. H. H. Allison, "Santa Fe in 1837-38," *Old Santa Fe* 2(2) (October 1914): 176-77.

52. B. M. Read, "In Santa Fe During the Mexican Regime," NMHR, 2(1) (January 1927), 93-94; William H. Davis, *El Gringo* (New York: Harper, 1857), 172.

53. This discussion of the flexible use of the plaza and Mexican architecture is based on the preceding two quotations and Sunder, *Mastt Field*, 213-14; Ralph Bieber, *The Papers of James J. Webb* (Seattle: University of Washington, 1924), 265-73; and announcements of meetings, lectures, dances, etc., in SFG, July 7, 1866, March 23, 1867; DNM, July 27, 1868, August 16, 1869, November 29, 1869, August 10, 1872.

Chapter 2

1. Quote from Stella M. Drumm, ed., *Down the Trail and into Mexico: The Diary of Susan S. Magoffin* (New Haven: Yale University Press, 1926), 140 "attoms" in original. On the flagstaff and ceremonies, Magoffin, *Down the Trail*, 115; John Bloom, "New Mexico Viewed by the Anglo Americans, 1846-49," NMHR 34(3) (July 1959): 170-71; Phillipe Cooke, *The Conquest of New Mexico and California* (1878; reprint, Albuquerque: Horn and Wallace, 1964), 62, 64.

2. Thomas D. Hall, *Social Change in the Southwest, 1350-1880* (Lawrence: University Press of Kansas, 1989), 167-200, synthesizes the scholarly literature on this period.

3. Hall, *Social Change*, 204-48; Howard Lamar, *The Far Southwest, 1846-1912: A Territorial History*, (New Haven: Yale University Press, 1966).

4. My discussion is based on the excellent study by Reginald Horsman, *Race and Manifest Destiny: The Origins of American Racial Anglo-Saxonism* (Cambridge, MA: Harvard University Press, 1981), 9-24, 43, 77, 97-101.

5. Horsman, *Race and Manifest Destiny*, 9-24, 43, 116-38, 189-207.

6. Gutiérrez, *When Jesus Came*, 339, quote; Horsman, 208-48; Doris L. Meyer, "Early Mexican-American Responses to Negative Stereotyping," NMHR 53(1) (1978): 75-92; Susan Reyner Kenneson, *Through the Looking Glass: Anglo-American Attitudes Towards the Spanish-Americans and Indians of New Mexico* (Ann Arbor: University Microfilms, 1978); David J. Weber, "'Scarce More than Apes': Historical Roots of Anglo-American Stereotypes of Mexicans," in Weber, ed., *New Spain's Far Northern Frontier*, (Albuquerque: University of New Mexico Press, 1979).

7. William Gilpin, *The Mission of the North American People* (Philadelphia: Lippencott and Co., 1873), 132.

8. Horsman, 250-71, 302.

9. Horsman, *Race and Manifest Destiny*, 241; see also 211, 260-61.

10. Mario Barrera, *Race and Class in the Southwest: A Theory of Racial Inequity* (Notre Dame, IN: Notre Dame University Press, 1979), 29, 39; Hall, *Social Change,* 210-17.

11. Darlis A. Miller, "Cross Cultural Marriages in the Southwest: The New Mexico Experience, 1846-1900," NMHR 57(4) (October 1982): 335-60; Deena J. González, "The Spanish-Mexican Women of Santa Fe: Patterns of Their Resistance and Accommodation, 1820-1880" (Ph.D. diss., University of California at Berkeley, 1985), 111-53; Deena J. González, "The Widowed Women of Santa Fe: Assessment of the Lives of an Unmarried Population, 1850-1880," in Ellen C. DuBois and Vicki L. Ruiz, eds., *Unequal Sisters: A Multicultural Reader in U.S. Women's History* (New York: Routledge, 1990), 34-50. The low number of Mexican men in 1870 (and of many single-women heads of households with children) may be somewhat misleading, since the census was taken in July, when many men may have been away from Santa Fe working as herders and teamsters, in the mines and railroads of Colorado, or in the last days of the *comanchero* trade and *cibolero* (buffalo hunting) tradition. While I am in general agreement with González's analysis, we disagree on the total number and relative significance of mixed marriages in Santa Fe. My count of mixed marriages in Bureau of the Census, *Ninth Census, 1870, New Mexico, Santa Fe County,* enumerator sheets, reel 4: twenty-six mixed marriages in Precinct 3 (pp. 1-65) and thirty-nine in Precinct 4 (pp. 1-57). González claims in her dissertation (p. 118) that in 1870 "the number of Euro-Americans married to Spanish Mexicans neared three hundred." She appears to have taken Darlis Miller's calculation of 63 percent of Anglo men in mixed marriages (which agrees with my calculations), and assumed, incorrectly, that all five hundred of them were married, in order to arrive at the figure of three hundred. With approximately fifteen hundred Mexican women over fifteen years of age, three hundred in mixed marriages would have been 20 percent. When she subsequently asserts (p. 119) that "not quite two percent of all Spanish-Mexican women were married to Euro-American in 1870," she appears to have misplaced a decimal point. I believe I am correct in my calculation that more than 10 percent of Mexican women (born in New Mexico and having Spanish given names) were married to or in common-law unions with American men (born outside New Mexico and with non-Spanish surnames). (Chris Wilson, letter to Deena González, August 19, 1992.)

12. See sources in note 11, above.

13. I do not know for certain when *coyote* took on this new sense of a person of mixed Mexican-Anglo parentage. Bustamante, "New Mexico," 155, documents the old meaning of "white-Indian mixture" as late as 1860. Bustamante, "New Mexico," 155-56; Arthur Campa, *Hispanic Culture in the Southwest* (Norman: University of Oklahoma Press, 1979), 1; Ruben Cobos, *A Dictionary of New Mexico and Southern Colorado Spanish* (Santa Fe: Museum of New Mexico Press, 1983), 37, 99, all note the new meaning of *coyote* in common usage in the twentieth century.

14. *Ninth Census,* enumerator sheets; D. González, "Spanish-Mexican Women"; Miller, "Cross Cultural Marriages."

340

15. Leroy R. Hafen, ed., *Ruxton of the Rockies* (Norman: University of Oklahoma Press, 1950), 180; Elliott Coves, ed., *The Expeditions of Zebulon Pike* (New York: Francis P. Harper, 1895), 607; Bloom, "New Mexico," 168-69. See also Josiah Gregg, *Commerce of the Prairies* (Norman: University of Oklahoma Press, 1954), 77. For overviews of early American responses to New Mexico, see Bloom,"New Mexico"; Kenneson, *Through the Looking Glass.*

16. Gibson, 230; SFR, May 13, 1848, p. 2. On the first sawmill, see U. S. Department of the Interior, "Public Buildings in New Mexico" (Washington, DC: U.S. Printing Office, 1867), 4.

17. William Pierson, *American Buildings and Their Architects: The Colonial and Neoclassical Styles* (Garden City, NY: Doubleday, 1970), 417-18, 446-52.

18. Stanley Stubbs and Bruce Ellis, "Archeological Investigations," School of American Research Monograph 20 (1955), 6-12; Alvin Sunseri, *New Mexico in the Aftermath of the Anglo-American Conquest* (Ann Arbor: University Microfilms, 1973), 73-74.

19. Stubbs and Ellis, "Archeological Investigations," 9-18, synthesize what is known about the Castrense site. For a biography of Delgado, see Fabiola Cabeza de Baca, "Pioneer Merchant— Don Manual Delgado," *Santa Fe Scene,* undated, NMRC, History File #101; Biographical card index, NMRC; Delgado Family file, MNM-VF.

20. Paul Horgan, *Lamy of Santa Fe: His Life and Times* (New York: Farrar, Straus and Giroux, 1975); Ralph E. Twitchell, *The Leading Facts of New Mexico History* (Cedar Rapids, Iowa: Torch Press, 1912) 2:329, n. 256.

21. George Kubler, in *Religious Architecture of New Mexico* (Albuquerque: University of New Mexico Press, 1940), 101, quotes Salpointe on this remodeling.

22. John Kessell, *The Missions of New Mexico Since 1776* (Albuquerque: University of New Mexico Press, 1980), 17-22.

23. DNM December 21, 1881; Lebaron Bradford Prince, *Spanish Mission Churches of New Mexico* (Cedar Rapids, Iowa: Torch Press), 1915, 121.

24. Kessell, *Missions,* 37-43; Bruce Ellis, *Bishop Lamy's Santa Fe Cathedral* (Albuquerque: University of New Mexico Press for the New Mexico Historical Society, 1985).

25. John Ayers, "A Soldier's Experience in New Mexico," NMHR 24(4) (October 1949), 259-60. On plaza park, see WNM, August 16, 1880; DNM April 17, 1873, September 25, 1874, July 23, 1883, January 18, 1894.

A photograph that shows the bandstand nearing completion has been dated by MNM-PA staff to 1866. On construction of the plaza monument, see SFG February 9, October 26, 1867; March 14, June 13, 1868.

26. DNM July 20, 1872.

27. DNM July 28, 1877, p. 1.

28. For a biography of Ritch, see "Last Resting Place," DNM September 17, 1904, p. 1; and *The History of New Mexico, Its Resources, and People* (Los Angeles: Pacific States Publishing Company, 1907), 505. The latter source is repeated verbatim in Twitchell, *Leading Facts* 4:332, n. 1054.

29. WNM March 9, 1878.

30. DNM September 9, 1872. See also WNM December 19, 1863, p. 1; DNM August 23, 1872, p. 1.

31. Small news items appeared almost every week, especially during the building season, commenting on improvement projects under way and suggesting other necessary ones. To take one year of the DNM as an example, see items for 1872 on page 4: May 11, 13, 22; June 18; July 30, 31; August 1, 13, 24; September 9; October 7, 15, 18, 23; November 9, 15, 20; December 10, 18. See also nn. 57-58, below, on the DNM campaign to have the portales removed from the plaza.

32. DNM December 16, 1874, p. 1.

33. Terry Lehman, *Santa Fe and Albuquerque, 1870-1900* (Ann Arbor: University Microfilms, 1975), 107-97; Carole Rifkin, *Mainstreet: The Face of Urban America* (New York: Harper and Row, 1977), 145-49; John Reps, *The Making of Urban America* (Princeton, NJ: Princeton University Press, 1965), 349-413; William Parish, *The Charles Ilfeld Company* (Cambridge, MA: Harvard University Press, 1961), 95-97.

34. DNM December 16, 1874, p. 1. See also DNM September 24, 26, 1874; and September 25, December 15, 16, 1880.

35. DNM May 3, 10, 1880.

36. For a report of the first public meeting on Water Street, see DNM March 16, 1881. The course of the project is also reported in DNM December 20, 1879; March 10, 16, 17, 18, 20, 22, 29, April 13, May 17, 1881. See also Lehman, *Santa Fe and Albuquerque*, 201-5.

37. *Acts of the Legislative Assembly of the Territory of New Mexico* (Santa Fe: New Mexican Printing Company, 1884), 130. The controversy surrounding the water works is described in the DNM May 17, 20, June 14, 23, July 9, December 22, 1881; March 17, 1882; March 6, May 15, l883; April 10, 1884; December 12, 1888.

38. Hall, *Social Change,* 210-14; Linda Tigges, "Characteristics of Santa Fe Land Ownership of the 1880s" (paper presented at the New Mexico Historical Society conference, 1986), 3, 4, 7.

39. Henry J. Tobias, *A History of the Jews of New Mexico,* (Albuquerque: University of New Mexico Press, 1990), 25-26, 29-30, 42-43, 66-67, 71-72, 113-14.

40. WNM December 17, 1880; DNM February 18, May 24, 1881; 1883 Sanborn Insurance Map.

41. DNM July 4, 1881, February 2, April 21, 22, May 21, November 23, December 8, 1882; February 4, 1883; 1883 Sanborn Insurance Map.

42. The imported materials are mentioned in DNM October 2, 1880; May 3, 1881; February 2, 1882; February 6, 1883. On bricks, see DNM September 28, 1880; May 27, December 31, 1881; April 11, June 7, August 3, 1882; September 3, 1885; May 12, 1886; August 16, 1887;

April 19, 1889; *Biennial Report of . . . the New Mexico Penitentiary. . .* (Santa Fe: New Mexican Printing Company, 1894), 19; Blandina Segale, *At the End of the Santa Fe Trail* (Milwaukee: Bruce Pub., 1948), 158.

43. On local carpenters, see *Census of 1870*, quoted in Virianna Holmes, "Architectural Woodwork" (Ph.D. diss., University of New Mexico, 1979); DNM April 16, 1891.

On local stone, see DNM August 20, 21, 1882; September 30, 1884; February 5, 1885; November 18, 1887; June 7, 1891.

44. DNM August 22, September 10, October 9, 27, November 22, 1890; March 11, April 2, 3, May 18, June 30, December 14, 1891; 1898 Sanborn Insurance Map.

45. "Death of an Old Timer," DNM May 7, 1894, p. 4.

46. This discussion of the characteristics and associations of various styles is largely based on Marcus Whiffen, *American Architecture Since 1780, A Guide to Styles* (Cambridge, MA: MIT Press, 1969). For a general discussion of associationalism in the American architecture of this period, see Walter C. Kidney, *The Architecture of Choice: Eclecticism in America, 1880-1930* (New York: George Braziller, 1974), vii-viii, 1-8. Because associationalism was at first only superficially understood in Santa Fe (c.1880-1910), it receives only cursory treatment here. With the development of the Pueblo Spanish Revival style (c. 1910-20), associationalism was creatively applied to local vernacular architecture. Therefore the place of associationalism in the picturesque aesthetic and in what some authors have called "picturesque eclecticism" is discussed more fully in chapter 6.

47. See Rifkin, *Mainstreet*, 63-64, 72-73.

48. Horsman, *Race and Manifest Destiny*, 239, 243-45.

49. DNM July 3, 1874; L. Bradford Prince, "Claims to Statehood," *North American Review* (March 1893): 346-54, especially 351.

50. L. Bradford Prince, letter to the editor, *New York Times*, February 28, 1882, commenting on a letter of February 6. On late-nineteenth-century xenophobia, see John Higham, *Strangers in the Land: Patterns of American Nativism, 1869-1925* (1963; reprint, New York: Athenaeum, 1975), especially 153-57; Patricia Nelson Limerick, *The Legacy of Conquest: The Unbroken Past of the American West* (New York: W. W. Norton, 1987), chap. 8; Paul Kutche, "The Anglo Side of Acculturation," in June Helm, ed., *Spanish-Speaking People in the United States* [Proceedings of the 1968 Annual Spring Meeting of the American Ethnological Society], (Seattle: University of Washington Press, 1968), 183-85.

51. L. Bradford Prince, *Historical Sketches of New Mexico* (New York: Leggat Brothers, 1883), 3.

52. A. Gabriel Meléndez, *So All Is Not Lost: The Poetics of Print in Nuevomexicano Communities, 1834–1958.* (Albuquerque: University of New Mexico Press, 1997).

53. "Welcome Governor Otero!," DNM June 14, 1897, p. 4. For a biography of Otero, see P. A. F. W.[alter], "Necrology, Miguel Antonio Otero II," NMHR 19(4) (October 1944): 349-53; "Miguel Antonio Otero," NMHR 67(1) (special issue, January 1992).

343

54. See also Christopher M. Wilson, *The Santa Fe New Mexico Plaza* (Ann Arbor: University Microfilms, 1982), 93-96.

55. DNM August 7, 1886. On Santa Fe incorporation, see DNM March 26, 1890; March 16, April 13, May 15, 27, 28, June 2, 3, 1891.

56. Carl D. Sheppard, *Creator of the Santa Fe Style: Isaac Hamilton Rapp, Architect* (Albuquerque: University of New Mexico Press, 1988), 11-16, 43-72, 120, 126.

57. DNM July 22, 1882; October 16, 1891; March 26, 1892.

58. DNM January 19, February 3, April 18, and October 8, 1892; October 26, 1893.

59. For a fuller discussion of the capital location issue, see Lehman, *Santa Fe and Albuquerque,* 245-76.

60. DNM March 4, April 7, July 5, 29, 1890.

61. DNM September 7, 1892, p. 4.

Chapter 3

1. Robert W. Larson, *New Mexico's Quest for Statehood 1846-1912,* (Albuquerque: University of New Mexico Press, 1968), 301-4 (summary).

2. Quoted in Larson, *Quest for Statehood,* 123.

3. Herbert H. Lang, "The New Mexico Bureau of Immigration, 1880-1912," NMHR 51(3) (1976): 193-214. The major publications of the bureau are William G. Ritch, *Illustrated New Mexico,* 5th ed. (Santa Fe: Bureau of Immigration, 1885); Max Frost, *New Mexico: Its Resources, Climate . . ."* (Santa Fe: Bureau of Immigration, 1894); and Max Frost and Paul A. F. Walter, *The Land of Sunshine: A Handbook of the Resources . . ."* (Santa Fe: Bureau of Immigration, 1904). Variant editions of each of these and all other bureau publications are listed in Wilma L. Shelton, *Checklist of New Mexico [Government] Publications, 1850-1953* (Albuquerque: University of New Mexico Press, 1954), 22-29.

4. *Harper's Weekly,* September 13, 1879, April 14, 1883, April 26, 1886, September 7, 1889, July 19, 1890; *Harper's [monthly] Magazine,* April 1854, April 1880. Andrew K. Gregg, *New Mexico in the Nineteenth Century: A Pictorial History* (Albuquerque: University of New Mexico Press, 1968), 82-108, reproduces a sample of wood engravings from *Harper's,* the Bureau of Immigration, and other sources. On professional architectural journals' treatment of historic adobe architecture, see Richard Longstreth, *On the Edge of the World: Four Architects in San Francisco at the Turn of the Century* (Cambridge, MA: MIT Press, 1983), 277-79, 389.

5. W. Henry Brown, *Catalogue of Stereoscopic and Large Views of New Mexico Scenery* (Santa Fe: pub. by author, 1880), copy at MNM-PA. Although Bennett appears to have been responsible primarily for the stereographs and Brown for the studio portrait work, I have chosen to give both of their names to the work because of their business partnership, and their work appears on mounts with their names both separately and together; see Richard Rudisill, *Photographers of the New Mexico Territory, 1846-1912.* (Santa Fe: Museum of New Mexico, 1973),

13-14, 16-17. The Museum of New Mexico Photo Archives have a nearly complete set of these stereographs.

6. Brown, *Views of New Mexico,* sixth paragraph of text (unpaginated); DNM April 19, 1889.

7. DNM April 26, 1886; DNM May 3, 1886.For the commissioners' proposal, see DNM April 24, 1886.

8. White's perspective drawing appeared in DNM April 2, 1888, p. 8, and is reproduced in Leland Roth, *The Architecture of McKim, Mead and White, 1870-1920* (New York: Garland Publishing, 1978). On Helen Hunt Jackson and her novel, see Kevin Starr, *Inventing the Dream: California through the Progressive Era* (New York: Oxford University Press, 1985), 57—63.

9. Charles C. Baldwin, *Stanford White* (New York: Dodd, Mead and Company, 1931), 154; White quoted in Baldwin, *Stanford White,* 154-55; DNM April 5, 1887. Other DNM items on the Ramona School: May 3, August 16, 1887; April 12, 1888; August 15, 1891. The faintly Shingle Style building erected by the Ramona School is represented in MNM-PA, photo #76046.

10. Albert H. Schroeder, "History of Archeological Research," HNAI 5-13; Keith H. Basso, "History of Ethnological Research," HNAI 14-21; Adolf F. Bandelier, *The Delight Makers* (1890; reprint, New York: Harcourt Brace Jovanovich, 1971), (quote) xvii (introduction by Stefan Jovanovich).

11. James W. Shepp and David B. Shepp, *Shepp's World's Fair Photographed* (Chicago: Globe Publishing, 1893); Barbara Rubin, "Aesthetic Ideology and Urban Design," *Annals of the Association of American Geographers* 69 (September 1979): 339-61; Robert A. Trennert, "Fairs, Expositions, and the Changing Image of Southwestern Indians, 1876-1904," NMHR 62(2) (April 1987): 127-50.

12. Shepp and Shepp, *World's Fair,* 318. The California, Colorado, Florida, and Texas buildings are each reproduced in Shepp and Shepp.

13. Starr, *Inventing the Dream,* 81; Turbese Lummis Fiske and Keith Lummis, *Charles F. Lummis: The Man and His West* (Norman: University of Oklahoma Press, 1975), 119-20, 20 (quoting Charles Lummis). For biographies of Lummis, see Starr, *Inventing the Dream,* 75-89; Edwin R. Bingham, *Charles F. Lummis: Editor of the Southwest* (San Marino, CA: Huntington Library, 1955).

14. Fiske and Lummis, *Charles F. Lummis,* 120; Starr *Inventing the Dream*; Bingham, *Charles F. Lummis*; Charles F. Lummis, "The Southwestern Wonderland," *The Land of Sunshine* 4 (1896): 204-13, and *The Land of Sunshine* (1895-1901) and *Out West* (1902-9) in general under his editorship.

15. Edward Hungerford, "A Study of Consistent Railroad Advertising," *Printer's Ink,* reprinted in *The Santa Fe [Railway] Magazine* 17(4) (March 1923): 43-48; Keith L Bryant, Jr., "The AT&SF Railway and the Development of the Taos and Santa Fe Art Colonies," *Western History Quarterly* 9(14) (October 1978): 437-53; T. C. McLuhan, *Dream Tracks: The Railroad*

and the American Indian 1890-1930, (New York: Harry N. Abrahams, 1985); Sandra D'Emelio and Suzan Campbell, *Visions & Visionaries: The Art and Artists of the Santa Fe Railway* (Salt Lake City: Peregrine Smith Books, 1991).

16. David Gebhard, "Architectural Imagery, the Missions and California," *Harvard Architectural Review* 1 (Spring 1980): 136-45; Keith Bryant, Jr., *History of the Atchison, Topeka and Santa Fe Railway* (New York: Macmillan, 1974).

17. On the Castañeda, designed by F. L. Roehrig, see Louise Ivers, "The Architecture of Las Vegas New Mexico" (Ph.D. diss., 1975), 215-20. On the Alvarado, designed by C. F. Whittlesey, see David Gebhard, "Architecture and the Fred Harvey Houses: The Alvarado and La Fonda," NMA 6(1, 2) (January/February 1964): 18-25.

18. Frost and Walter, *Land of Sunshine*, vii.

19. "New Mexico Exhibits," DNM, July 14, 1904, p. 1. For additional fair items, see DNM May 2, December 5, 1904.

20. Carl D. Sheppard, *Creator of the Santa Fe Style: Isaac Hamilton Rapp* (Albuquerque: University of New Mexico Press, 1988), 63-64; the Mission style buildings cited in the text are represented in MNM-PA.

21. DNM April 9, 1904, p. 8.

22. Larson, *Quest for Statehood,* 224-304.

23. President, Board of Regents, School of American Archeology, to W. J. Black, Passenger Traffic Manager, AT&SF, Chicago, February 12, 1912, MNM-H, file 37.

24. Rudisill, *Photographers,* 44-45; Lynn Adkins, "Jesse L. Nusbaum and the Painted Desert in San Diego," *Journal of San Diego History* (Spring 1983): 89; Jesse Nusbaum Collection, acquisition notes and biographical sketch (typescript) MNM-PA. These archives contain the most complete collection of Nusbaum's photographs and postcards.

25. Kenneth Chapman to W. H. Simpson, March 18, 1913, MNM-H, file 37; Simpson to Chapman, March 25, 1913, MNM-H, file 37. I have corrected the misspelling of Vargis in the quotation of the latter.

26. A. F. Koehler, ed., *New Mexico: The Land of Opportunity* (Albuquerque: Albuquerque Morning Journal, 1915).

Interlude: Adobe Camouflage

1. Christine Mather, "Living with Antiques: Casa San Ysidro, Corrales, New Mexico," *Antiques* (April 1978): 820-29.

2. The Scottish Rite Temple was stuccoed pink from its construction; see "Masonic Dedication," DNM November 16, 1912, p. 5.

3. Edgar L. Hewett, "Santa Fe in 1926," *Papers of the School of American Archeology* 39 (1916): 8-12, quote p. 11.

4. Eric Knoll, "Folk Art in the Barrios," *Natural History* 82(5) (May 1973): 56-65; James D.

and Eva S. Crockcroft, "People's Art and Social Change: The Community Mural Movement," *Radical America* 12(2) (March-April 1978): 7-14; Geronimo Garduño, "Artes Guadalupunos de Aztlán," in Eva Crockcroft, John Weber and Jim Cockcroft, eds., *Toward a People's Art* (New York: E.P. Dutton, 1977).

Chapter 4

1. While this chapter focuses on the elite western tradition, resistance to cultural homogenization also has come from other groups with strong traditions, such as the Pueblos and Hispanic-Americans of New Mexico. Although these two forms of resistance often overlap, borrow from each other, and take outwardly similar forms, they should not be confused (as romantics sometimes have). A pueblo's struggle to maintain its language, religion, and way of life is substantially different from the Anglo-American use of Pueblo architectural forms as a symbolic counter to the industrial world, just as a communal dwelling is different from a tourist hotel.

2. Lewis Mumford, "The Theory and Practice of Regionalism," *Sociological Review* 20(1) (January 1928): 18-33, 20(2) (April 1928): 131-41, especially 133-34; Ivan Illich, "Vernacular Values," *CoEvolution Quarterly* 26 (Summer 1980): 22-49; Spiro Kostof, *A History of Architecture: Settings and Rituals* (New York: Oxford University Press, 1985), 403-31; Alan Colquhoun, "Three Kinds of Historicism," *Architectural Design* 53(9/10) (1983): 86-90.

3. Mumford, "Regionalism,"134-36; Kostof, *History of Architecture,* 547-69; Bill Risebero, *Modern Architecture and Design: An Alternative History* (Cambridge, MA: MIT Press,1982), 11-18.

4. Christopher Hussey, *The Picturesque: Studies in a Point of View* (London: Frank Cass and Company, 1927; reprint, 1967); Peter Collins, *Changing Ideals in Modern Architecture* (Montreal: McGill-Queen's University Press, 1965), 42-60.

5. Collins, *Changing Ideals,* 29-41; Colquhoun, "Historicism," 88-89; Phoebe Stanton, *Augustus Pugin:* (New York: Viking Press, 1971); David Van Zanten, *Designing Paris: The Architecture of Duban, Labrouste, Duc, and Vaudoyer* (Cambridge, MA: MIT Press, 1988).

6. Kostof, *History of Architecture,* 571—93; Risebero, *Modern Architecture,* 94-105, 119-23; T. J. Jackson Lears, *No Place of Grace: Anti-Modernism and the Transformation of American Culture, 1880-1920* (New York: Pantheon Books, 1981), chapter on the Arts and Crafts movement; Richard Guy Wilson, "American Arts and Crafts Architecture: Radical though Dedicated to the Cause Conservative," in Wendy Kaplan, ed., *"The Art that is Life": The Arts and Crafts Movement in America, 1875-1920* (Boston: Little, Brown and Company/New York Graphic Society, 1987).

7. Dean McCannell, *The Tourist: A New Theory of the Leisure Class* (New York: Shocken Books, 1976); Eric Hobsbawm and Terrence Ranger, eds., *The Invention of Tradition* (Cambridge: Cambridge University Press, 1983).

8. Collins, *Changing Ideals,* 100-105; Risebero, *Modern Architecture,* 29-32; J. M. Richards,

347

800 Years of Finnish Architecture (London: David and Charles, 1978); David Gebhard, "The Myth and Power of Place: Hispanic Revivalism in the American Southwest," PSRA 143-58, especially 146-48.

9. R. Wilson, "American Arts"; Vincent Scully, *The Shingle Style and the Stick Style: Architectural Theory and Design from Downing to the Origins of Wright* (New Haven: Yale University Press, 1955); Richard Longstreth, "Academic Eclecticism in American Architecture," *Winterthur Portfolio* 17(1) (September 1983): 56-82.

10. Lears, *Anti-Modernism*; R. Wilson, "American Arts"; Scully, *Shingle Style*; Gardnet Teall, "The Modern Colonial House: . . .in the Development of an American Architecture," *The Craftsman* 24(1) (1913): 61-68; David Gebhard, "The Spanish Colonial Revival in Southern California (1895-1930)," JSAH 26(2) (1967): 131-47; Richard Longstreth, *On the Edge of the World: Four Architects in San Francisco at the Turn of the Century* (Cambridge, MA: MIT Press, 1983), especially 27-33.

11. Gebhard, "Myth," 149-50. According to Gebhard ("Myth," 149) and Longstreth (*On the Edge*, 276-77), Pueblo architecture inspired the "Hotel near Montalvo, California, A. C. Schweinfourth, Architect," *California Architect and Building News* 15(4) (April 1894): 39. The predominant features of this design (symmetrical massing, circular piers, a recessed porch, and quatrefoil windows) strike me as an austere interpretation of the Spanish idiom, having little to do with Pueblo architecture.

12. "The Grand Canyon of Arizona at Panama-Pacific Exposition," *Santa Fe [Railway] Magazine* 8(8) (1914): 49-50; Virginia Gratten, *Mary Colter, Builder upon the Red Earth* (Flagstaff, AZ: Northland Press, 1980), 14-19; Christopher Wilson, "The Spanish Pueblo Revival Defined, 1904-1921," *New Mexico Studies in the Fine Arts* 7 (1982): 24-30.

13. E. Dana Johnson, "A University Pueblo," *World's Work* 14 (October 1907): 9468-74; "A Revival of Old Pueblo Architecture," *Architects and Builders Magazine* 10 (1908-9): 282-85; "Pueblo Architecture Adapted to Modern Needs in New Mexico," *The Craftsman* 19(4) (1909): 404-6; Michael Welsh, "Symbol and Reality: The Cultural Challenge of Regional Architecture at the University of New Mexico, 1889-1939," PSRA, 213-22.

14. Gebhard, "Myth," 151-52; David Gebhard, "Architecture and the Fred Harvey Houses," NMA 4(7/8) (July/August 1962): 11-17; Carl Sheppard, *Isaac Hamilton Rapp: Inventor of the Santa Fe Style* (Albuquerque: University of New Mexico Press, 1988), 59-60, 83.

15. Sheppard, *Rapp*, 60-61; *A Century of Freemasonry in New Mexico* (Santa Fe: n.p., 1951), 64; interview with Benjamin William Friedman, secretary, Scottish Rite Temple, Santa Fe, November 28, 1986 (in author's possession); Harold Kirker, *California's Architectural Frontiers: Style and Tradition in the Nineteenth Century* (Santa Barbara: Peregrine-Smith, 1973), 86, 122; David Gebhard and Robert Winter, *A Guide to Architecture in Los Angeles and Southern California* (Santa Barbara: Peregrine-Smith, 1977), 17, 273. Hunt and Burns subsequently adapted elements of their Santa Fe building for Charles Lummis's Southwest Museum; see Richard F.

Bach, "The Southwest Museum, Los Angeles—Sumner Hunt & S. R. Burns, Architects," *Architectural Record* 17(1) (July 1917): 18-26.

16. Oleg Grabar, *The Alhambra* (Cambridge, MA: Harvard University Press, 1978), 29, 39, 44.

17. "Masonic Dedication," DNM November 16, 1912, p. 5; "Noted Masons Confer High Degrees," DNM November 19, 1912, p. 1; Marta Weigle and Peter White, *The Lore of New Mexico* (Albuquerque: University of New Mexico Press, 1988), 409; Ronald Grimes, *Symbol and Conquest: Public Ritual and Drama in Santa Fe, N.M.* (Ithaca: Cornell University Press, 1976), 152-55.

18. "The Scottish Rite Cathedral in Santa Fe," *Scottish Rite Bulletin* (Santa Fe) 56(4) (July-August 1975): 2-8. The artist is identified in the lower right corner of the mural.

19. Beatrice Chauvenet, *Hewett and Friends: A Biography of Santa Fe's Vibrant Era* (Santa Fe: Museum of New Mexico Press, 1983).

20. Hewett feuded with Charles Lummis, Ralph E. Twitchell, L. Bradford Prince, Bronson Cutting, Harry H. Dorman, and Franz Boas. See Chauvenet, *Hewett and Friends*, 109-20; George W. Stocking, Jr., "The Santa Fe Style in American Archeology . . .," *Journal of the History of the Behavioral Sciences* 18 (1982): 3-19; Lummis and Twitchell files, MNM-H1; Prince Collection, SRCA; Archaeology Institute of the Southwest file, Cutting Collection, Library of Congress. The first three museum staff members, Kenneth Chapman, Sylvanus Morley, and Jesse Nusbaum, all chafed under Hewett's abrasive and condescending manner. Chapman soon became concerned over "Dr. Hewett's preoccupation with plans for the 'School', his long absences, and his neglect of the growing needs of the Museum. Before long my disappointment had turned to actual resentment when I observed the erratic and even devious means he was using to make amends for his dilatory ways" (Kenneth Chapman, "My First Quarter-Century in the Southwest, 1899-1926" (typescript), 1954, folder 177, box 18, RAC-OMR, p. 4). After two years Chapman found a full-time position as illustrator for Springer's paleontology books. As this took only about half of Chapman's time, he was free to pursue his study of Indian art and to help out at the museum. Hewett chastised Morley for leaking news of his Mayan discoveries to the press before Hewett could announce the findings himself. Morley left in 1915 to oversee the Mayan excavations of the Carnegie Institute of Washington, D.C. (Morley file, MNM-H). Nusbaum left in 1920 to become the first director of the Mesa Verde National Monument.

In 1924 and 1926, Hewett snubbed John D. Rockefeller, Jr., who was visiting Santa Fe and who had expressed an interest in supporting Indian arts (rather than a restoration of Santa Fe, as local oral tradition has it). Rockefeller chose instead to work with Chapman and Nusbaum in establishing the Laboratory of Anthropology. See Chauvenet, *Hewett and Friends,* 192-93; Herman Bumpus to Executive Committee, American Association of Museums, February 11, 1927 [report on Santa Fe's museums and cultural institutions funded behind the scenes by Rockefeller], folder 172, box 17, RAC-OMR; Kenneth Chapman to

349

John D. Rockefeller, Jr., February 11, 1954, folder 177, box 18, RAC-OMR; Kenneth Chapman, "My Conferences with Dr. Hewett, 1926-1929" (typescript), 1954, folder 18, box 177, RAC-OMR; and additional materials in box 177, RAC-OMR.

21. Chauvenet, *Hewett and Friends,* 37-38, 58; "Necrology, Dr. Frank Springer," NMHR 2(4) (October 1927): 387-93.

22. Chauvenet, *Hewett and Friends*; Richard G. Wilson, "The Great Civilization," in *The American Renaissance, 1876-1917* (New York: Brooklyn Museum, 1979); Michele Bogart, *Public Sculpture and the Civic Ideal in New York City, 1890-1930* (Chicago: University of Chicago Press, 1989); James Gaither, "A Return to the Village: A Study of Santa Fe and Taos, New Mexico, as Cultural Centers, 1900-1934," (Ph.D. diss., University of Minnesota, 1957), 28-36; DNM February 1, August 21, September 18, November 16, 1908.

23. Lynn Adkins, "Jesse L. Nusbaum and the Painted Desert in San Diego," *The Journal of San Diego History* (Spring 1983): 89.

24. "Dr. Kenneth Chapman Succumbs Here at 92," DNM February 25, 1968, p. 1; "Kenneth Milton Chapman, 1875-1968," EP 75(2) (Summer 1968): 35-39.

25. *Morleyana: A Collection of Writings in Memoriam* (Santa Fe: School of American Research and MNM, 1950).

26. Sheppard, *Rapp,* 37-39; Betty Toulouse, "Happy Birthday EL PALACIO!," EP 90(2) (1984): 4-9; Peter D. Harrison, "Carlos Vierra: His Role and Influence on the Maya Image," in *The Maya Image in the Western World* (exhibit catalogue; Albuquerque: University of New Mexico, 1980), 22.

27. The two files of original 1912 planning board materials in MNM-WL give a good sense of the board's extensive contacts around the country, the depth of its exposure to the City Beautiful movement, and its preparations for the *Old New Santa Fe* exhibit. "Dorman Dies; Services Set Here Monday," DNM October 30, 1960, pp. 1, 16.

28. Kostof, *History of Architecture,* 669-73; R. Wilson, "Great Civilization"; Bogart, Public Sculpture; Werner Hagemann and Elbert Peets, *The American Vitruvius: An Architects Handbook of Civic Art* (1922; reprint; New York: Benjamin Blom, 1972); Barbara Rubin, "Aesthetic Ideology and Urban Design," *Annals of the Association of American Geographers* 69(3) (September 1979): 39-61; M. Christine Boyer, *Dreaming the Rational City: The Myth of American City Planning* (Cambridge, MA: MIT Press, 1983); Daniel M. Bluestone, "Detroit's City Beautiful and the Problem of Commerce," *JSAH* 47 (September 1988) pp. 245-62; William H. Wilson, *The City Beautiful Movement* (Baltimore: Johns Hopkins University Press, 1985). "Planning the City," Bulletin no. 4 of the National Conference on City Planning (Boston: Wood, Clark Press, 1913), available in MNM-WL, lists fifty-nine U.S. cities with city plans or organizations to promote planning. Of the five with populations less than 25,000, Santa Fe was smallest in the 1910 census, with 5,072, and Boulder, Colorado, next smallest, with 9,539.

29. H. H. Dorman to Honorable Mayor of Chicago, March 18, 1912, MNM-WL. "Proceedings of the City Council," DNM November 24, 1912, p. 7, reproduces the text of the 1912 city plan; N. L. King, "Map of the City of Santa Fe, New Mexico, Showing Street, Park and River, Improvements Proposed by the City Planning Board" (Santa Fe: Planning Board, 1912), available at UNM-MG. Jesse Nusbaum, "Vay Morley and the Santa Fe Style," in *Morleyana*, 162-73, gives a first-hand account of the activities of the planning board, the *New-Old Santa Fe exhibit*, and the Morley House rehabilitation. For secondary sources on the planning board, see Christopher Wilson, "The Santa Fe, New Mexico Plaza: and Architectural and Cultural History, 1610-1921," (Ann Arbor: University Microfilms, 1982), 107, 133-36; R. Wilson, "Revival Defined," 26-30; Sheppard, *Rapp,* 76-77; Nicholas C. Markovich, "Santa Fe Renaissance: City Planning and Stylistic Preservation, 1912," in PSRA 197-212.

30. DNM April 10, 1881; King, "Map."

31. "Proceedings," column 3; Nusbaum, "Vay Morley." Nusbaum's photographs are housed at the MNM-PA.

32. Nusbaum, "Vay Morley"; Sylvanus Morley to Dear Sir, draft September 13, 1912, final version September 25, 1912, sent to various architects describing Santa Fe style and soliciting their participation in the "New-Old Santa Fe Exhibition"; H. H. Dorman to Board of Regents of the Museum of New Mexico, October 16, 1912; unsigned letter to Brother David (rector of San Miguel), September 11, 1912; Sylvanus Morley to I. H. Rapp, September 20, 1912; unsigned letter to Louis Curtis, October 14, 1912; all MNM-WL.

33. Sylvanus G. Morley, "Keeping a City Old," *Santa Fe Trail* 1(2) (August 1913): 93-95.

34. Morley to Dear Sir, September 13, 1912, MNM-WL; see also n. 32, above.

35. The model corbel is reproduced in Rosemary Nusbaum, *The City Different and the Palace* (Santa Fe: Sunstone Press, 1978), 48. E. Boyd, *Popular Arts of Spanish New Mexico* (Santa Fe: Museum of New Mexico Press, 1974), 38, calls it a "fictional portal."

36. The 1791 plan appears in Marc Simmons, *Spanish Government of New Mexico* (Albuquerque: University of New Mexico Press, 1968), xviii.

37. "Report of the Museum of New Mexico," EP 2(3) (December 1914): 1.

38. Carl G. Lotave file, MNM-VF; "Life and Work of St. Francis," EP 1(2) (December 1913): 1-2, and "Links Historic Past with Living Present," EP 1(2) (December 1913):1-6; Richard N. Murray, "Painting and Sculpture," 153-89, in *The American Renaissance*; Christopher M. Lyman, *The Vanishing Race and Other Illusions* (New York: Smithsonian and Pantheon, 1982).

39. "Links Historic Past," 6.

40. "Museum and School Share in San Diego's Triumph," EP 2(2) (November 1914): 2; Paul Walter, "New Mexico's Contribution to the Panama-Pacific Exposition," EP 3(1) (October 1915): 3-16.

41. "San Diego Triumph"; "New Mexico's Contribution"; Adkins, "Jesse L. Nusbaum,"

351

86-95; "Model of Exhibits at San Diego," EP 1 (4/5) (February and March 1914): 5; Edgar L. Hewett and William Templeton Johnson, "Architecture of the Exposition," EP 3 (3) (April 1916): 41; Acquisition Notes (typescript), Nusbaum Collection, MNM-PA.

42. Collins, *Changing Ideals,* 117-27.

43. Sylvanus Morley, "Santa Fe Architecture," *Old Santa Fe* 2 (3) (January 1915): 298; R. E. Twitchell, ed., *The City Different* (Santa Fe: Chamber of Commerce, n.d. [1919 or 1920]). See also Sheppard, *Rapp,* 79-88; "Architecture of San Diego Exposition," 61.

44. Twitchell, *City Different.*

45. Charles Lummis to Edgar Hewett, September 24, 1917, Lummis file, MNM-H; Lonn Taylor and Dessa Bokides, *New Mexican Furniture, 1600-1940* (Santa Fe: Museum of New Mexico Press, 1987), 216-17. "Modern Development of Pueblo-Spanish Architecture" (typescript), c. 1936, WPA file # 133, NMRC, credits Vierra, Chapman, and Nusbaum as consultants on the design of the Fine Arts Museum.

46. Carl Sheppard, *The Saint Francis Murals of Santa Fe* (Santa Fe: Sunstone Press, 1989), 43, 57, 46. Perhaps a third of Santa Fe's artists and intellectuals during the 1920s had come to recover from TB and other respiratory ailments. The fear of a relapse, often kept alive by lingering health problems, hung over Territorial Secretary William Ritch and *New Mexican* publisher Bronson Cutting, museum staff members Kenneth Chapman and Carlos Vierra, artists Sheldon Parsons and Will Shuster, poet Alice Corbin Henderson, and the foremost architect of the next generation, John Gaw Meem. Many came first to the Sunmount sanitorium to recover their health. Established in 1902 on the basis of Santa Fe's sunshine, clean air, and high altitude, its white frame cottages resembled sanitariums across the Southwest. But when its owner, Dr. Frank E. Mera, commissioned Isaac Rapp to design a revival style building in 1914, the symbolism of a harmonious Pueblo village far from the tensions of urban industrial life was added to Sunmount's image. See Sheppard, *Rapp,* 88-89; Marta Weigle and Kyle Fiore, *Santa Fe and Taos: The Writer's Era, 1916-1941* (Santa Fe: Ancient City Press, 1982), 10. Because TB is communicable through coughing and sneezing, people were as reluctant to publicly admit that they had TB, before a cure was found in 1943, as they are now to admit having AIDS. Euphemisms such as "had lung problems," or "came because of poor health" appeared even in obituaries written years later.

47. Sheppard, *Saint Francis,* 63, 62.

48. Sheppard, *Saint Francis,* 76.

49. Sheppard, *Saint Francis,* 75. I have capitalized *when,* and changed *it* to lowercase to make the quote read more smoothly in this context.

50. Kenneth Chapman, "Proposed New Mexico War Memorial," EP 6 (1) (January 11, 1919): 50.

51. Edgar L. Hewett, "Santa Fe in 1926," Papers of the School of American Archeology,

no. 39 (Santa Fe: School of American Archaeology, 1917), 8-12; Carlos Vierra, "Our Native Architecture in Its Relation to Santa Fe," Papers of the School of American Archeology, no. 39 (Santa Fe: School of American Archaeology, 1917), 1; William Johnson, "The Santa Fe of the Future," EP 3(3) (1915): 11-32.

52. Morley, "Santa Fe Architecture"; Carlos Vierra, "New Mexico Architecture," *Art and Archeology* 7(1/2) (January/February 1918), 37-49.

53. Morley, "Santa Fe Architecture," 283-84.

54. Vierra, "New Mexico Architecture," 47, 40. "To" capitalized in original of first quote.

55. *Acts of the Legislative Assembly of the Territory of New Mexico* (Santa Fe: n.p., 1909), 6-7.

56. H. H. Dorman to I. H. Rapp, October 1, 1912, and unsigned to Wm. Rapp, October 16, 1912, MNM-WL; T. Charles Gaastra, "Proposed New Hotel . . .," EP 7(4) (August 31, 1919): 89; Boyd C. Pratt, "Directory of Historic New Mexico Architects" (manuscript, 1988), UNM-M, 37-38.

57. Sheppard, *Rapp*, 94-98; Gratten, *Mary Colter*, 48-54; *Architectural Forum* 39(5) (November 1923), issue devoted to hotel design. Other Sun Belt resorts, notably the Ponce de Leon Hotel, St. Augustine, Florida (1885-87), and the Glenwood Mission Inn, Riverside, California (1902-11), also employed entry courtyards, but with rigorously symmetrical plans.

58. Chauvenet, *Hewett and Friends*, 132; Pratt, "Directory," 37-38, 93-94; Edgar Hewett to Judge J. W. Hoyle, July 2, 1920, box 44, folder 2, MNM-H.

59. *Acts of the Legislative Assembly*; Frank Springer, "Dedicatory Words," *Art and Archeology* 7(1/2) (1918): 5-7; Rose Henderson, "Santa Fe's Art Museum," *Arts and Decoration* 12(4) (1920): 272, 296-97; Alida F. Sims, "Pueblo—A Native American Architecture," *House and Garden* 41 (April 1922): 50-52+; R. P. Crawford, "Discovering a Real American Art," *Scribners Magazine* 73 (March 1923): 380-84; E. Dana Johnson, "The Architecture of Santa Fe," *House Beautiful* 51(1) (1922): 76-78; Rexford Newcomb, "Santa Fe, the Historic and Modern," *The Western Architect* (January 1924): 4-6, and 16 plates.

60. Carlos Vierra settled at Santa Fe in 1904, Sheldon Parsons in 1913, Gerald Cassidy in 1915, and the poet Alice Corbin arrived with her artist husband William P. Henderson in 1916. With the completion of the art museum, Hewett began to court nationally known artists with promises of studio and gallery space, and life in a community that valued artists as did few others. Hewett persuaded New York painter Robert Henri, a leader of the Ash Can School of social realism, to visit in the summer of 1916, and he helped attract Marsden Hartley, John Sloan, Randell Davey, and Will Shuster from Greenwich Village by 1920. Weigle and Fiore, *Santa Fe and Taos*; Katharine F. Gerould, "New Mexico and the Backwash of Spain," *Harpers Monthly* 151 (July 1925); Mary Austin, "Indian Detour," *Bookman* 68 (February 1929): *653-58, 199-212;* Sally Saunders, "Santa Fe's New Conquistadors," *Outlook and Independent* 155 (August 1930): 607-9; "Artists and Writers" (special section) DNM June

26, 1940; Lois Palken Rudnick, *Mabel Dodge Luhan: New Woman, New Worlds* (Albuquerque: University of New Mexico Press, 1984); Van Deren Coke, *Taos and Santa Fe: The Artist's Environment, 1882-1942* (Albuquerque: University of New Mexico Press, 1963); Arrell Morgan Gibson, *The Santa Fe and Taos Colonies: Age of the Muses, 1900-1942* (Norman: University of Oklahoma Press, 1983); Edna Robertson and Sarah Nestor, *Artists of Canyons and Caminos: Santa Fe, the Early Years* (Salt Lake City: Gibbs M. Smith, 1982); Mary Wachs, ed., *Artists of 20th-Century New Mexico* (Santa Fe: Museum of New Mexico Press, 1985), biographical appendix.

61. Edgar L. Hewett, "On the Opening of the Art Galleries," *Art and Archeology* 7(1/2) (January/February 1918): 50-52; Vierra, "New Mexico Architecture," 42; Henderson, "Art Museum"; Rose Henderson, "A Primitive Basis for Modern Architecture," *Architectural Record* 54(2) (1923): 189-96.

62. Museum patron Frank Springer funded the construction of Vierra's house as a residential demonstration of the new style. Chauvenet, *Hewett and Friends*, 126; Vierra's six volumes of photographs taken c. 1912-20, UNM-M; James H. Purdy, "The Carlos Vierra House," *Bulletin of the Historic Santa Fe Foundation* 51(1) (January 1979).

63. Alfred Kidder to John D. Rockefeller, Jr., December 19, 1927, box 17, folder 172, RAC-OMR.

64. R. Wilson, "Revival Defined," 103; Matthew E. Gallegos, "The Arts and Crafts Movement in New Mexico, 1900-1945" (master's thesis, University of Virginia, 1987), 33-40; "Arizona [actually Santa Fe, New Mexico] Adobe House with the Old Mesa Spirit," *Arts and Decoration* 27(3) (1927): 72; Ruth Laughlin Barker, "The Hearths of Santa Fe," *House and Garden* 51 (February 1927): 86+; Edward Dana Johnson, "Building Old Houses in New Spain," *House Beautiful* 61(1) (1927): 68+; Bainbridge Bunting, "Residence of Mabel Dodge Luhan," NMA 3(9/10) (1961): 11-13; John Lively, "The Nicolai Fechin House," *Fine Housebuilding* 25 (February/March 1985).

65. "Indians Gather at White Residence for Dance Friday," DNM August 7, 1926; Ann D. Clark, "Santa Fe Patroness Dies on 94th Birthday," DNM August 29, 1972, p 1; Sherry C. Smith, "Simple Dignity: The Architecture and Furniture of William Penhallow Henderson," EP 93(2) (Winter 1987): 30-35; J. B. Jackson, paper presented at "Tourism and Growth in Santa Fe" conference, March 9, 1991, video tape, Recuresos de Santa Fe; Lonn Taylor, "Creating an 'Hispanic' Artifact: The Construction and Furnishing of the Martha and Amelia White House in Santa Fe, 1923-1929," paper presented at the Western History Association conference, Albuquerque, October 1994.

66. Gibson, *Santa Fe and Taos Colonies*, 205; Lears, *Anti-Modernism*, 64-65; Gallegos, "Arts and Crafts Movement," 37-40; Michael Belshaw, "The Compounds of Santa Fe," (typescript), 1985, City Planning Department files.

67. Paul M. Sears, "The Business Side of Art in New Mexico," *New Mexico Business* 7(1)

(January 1954): 10-17; Corinne P. Sze, "The Gustave Baumann House," *Bulletin of the Historic Santa Fe Foundation* 19(1) (June 1991): 1-9.

68. Bunting, "Luhan House"; "Rancho Las Acequias in Old Santa Fe," *House and Garden* 100 (September 1951): 120-25; Bainbridge Bunting, *John Gaw Meem: Southwest Architect* (Albuquerque: University of New Mexico Press, 1983), 44-50, 83, 106-10, 128-45; Virginia Fincke, "I Wanted an Adobe House," *Arts and Decoration* 47(2) (1937): 326-28; Theodore Fisher, "American Home Pilgrimages, No. VIII—New Mexico," *American Home* 73(6) (1939): 39-41; Christine Mather and Sharon Woods, *Santa Fe Style* (New York: Rizzoli, 1986), 60-83, 102-3, 122-23, 176-77.

69. Ruth Laughlin Alexander, "On Hal's Birthday," DNM August 12, 1956, p. 5A; Corinne P. Sze, "The Witter Bynner House," *Bulletin of the Historic Santa Fe Foundation* 20(2) (September 1993).

Chapter 5

1. I owe a particular debt of gratitude to Felipe Gonzáles for advice on this chapter, for copying materials from his research files, and for sharing a copy of his article, "'Structural Correspondence': The Political Construction of Spanish American Nomenclature in New Mexico History," March 1990, written for inclusion in Thomas D. Hall and Sylvia Rodríguez, eds., *The Hispano Homeland Debate: Ethnicity and Social Change Among Spanish-Speaking Peoples in the Southwest,* forthcoming. Since I drafted this chapter, Gonzáles's related article, "The Political Construction of Latino Nomenclature in Twentieth Century New Mexico," appeared in the *American Journal of the Southwest* 35(2) (Summer 1993): 158-85. The classic statement on the question of the development of ethnic identities is Fredrik Barth, ed., *Ethnic Groups and Boundaries* (Boston: Little, Brown and Co., 1969), especially 9-38. A Chicano formulation of the relation between social class and ethnicity is Mario Barrera, *Race and Class in the Southwest: A Theory of Racial Inequity* (Notre Dame: Notre Dame University Press, 1979). A valuable survey of historical perspectives is John Higham, "Current Trends in the Study of Ethnicity in the United States," *Journal of American Ethnic History* 2(1) (Fall 1982): 5-15. Susan E. Keefe and Amado M. Padilla, *Chicano Ethnicity* (Albuquerque: University of New Mexico Press, 1987), 13-24, provides a helpful survey of theories of ethnic change. A useful discussion of the tourist phase of ethnicity is Dean McCannell, "Reconstructed Ethnicity: Tourism and Cultural Identity in the Third World," *Annals of Tourism Research* 11(3) (1984).

2. Vamik D. Volkan, "Psychoanalytic Aspects of Ethnic Conflicts," in Joseph V. Montville, ed., *Conflict and Peacemaking in Multiethnic Societies* (Lexington, MA: Lexington Books, 1990), 81-92.

3. Mary Douglas, *Purity and Danger: An Analysis of the Concepts of Pollution and Taboo* (New York: Frederick A. Praeger, 1966), especially 1-6.

4. Volkan, "Ethnic Conflicts," 88-89; J. W. Chatham, unpublished journal, UNM Special Collections, p. 80 of typed transcript.

355

5. In the quotations concerning the Santa Fe Fiesta in the next chapter, for instance, the term *Anglo* does not appear until "From the Spanish," DNM August 8, 1925, p. 4, when it is placed in quotation marks, suggesting that it was a new usage.

6. Raymond B. Fosdick, *John D. Rockefeller, Jr.: A Portrait* (New York: Harper and Brothers, 1956); A. W. P.[ackard], Memorandum of Conversation, Mrs. Otero-Warren, February 28, 1930, and Arthur W. Packard [Office of John D. Rockefeller, Jr.] to Mrs. Adelina Otero-Warren, March 12, 1930, both box 173, folder 17, RAC-OMR. See also Sylvia Rodríguez, "Art, Tourism, and Race Relations in Taos: Toward a Sociology of the Art Colony," *Journal of Anthropological Research* 45(1) (Spring 1989): 77-100. Rockefeller's swift rejection of Warren's request and total lack of interest in Spanish-Mexican culture is particularly telling, since he was publicly vilified as a result of the 1913-14 strike against his family's Colorado Fuel and Iron Company. That strike culminated in the so-called Ludlow Massacre, when company guards set the strikers' tent city afire and shot into it, killing eighteen—half of them "mexicanos."

7. J. Manual Espinosa, "Spanish Folklore in the Southwest: The Pioneer Studies of Aurelio M. Espinosa," *The Americas* 35(2) (October 1978): 219-25; Virginia Simmons, *The San Luis Valley* (Boulder, CO: Pruett Publishing, 1985), 61; Michael Miller, "The Espinosa Family," in Rose Díaz and Jan Dodson Barnhart, eds., *Hispanic Heros* (Albuquerque: Starlight Publishing, 1992).

8. Barbara Freire-Marreco, "New Mexican Spanish Folk-Lore," *Journal of American Folk-Lore* 29 (1916): 536-46; Espinosa introduction, Freire-Marreco, "Folk-Lore," 536; Freire-Marreco, "Folk-Lore," 538.

9. Freire-Marreco, "Folk-Lore," 539, n. 2. "The" capitalized in original Espinosa quote.

10. David E. Whisnant, *All That is Native & Fine: The Politics of Culture in an American Region* (Chapel Hill: University of North Carolina Press, 1983), 8, 57; John R. Chávez, *The Lost Land: The Chicano Image of the Southwest* (Albuquerque, University of New Mexico Press, 1984), 98-99; Aurelio M. Espinosa, *España en Nuevo Mexico: Lecturas elementales sobre la historia de Nuevo Méjico y su tradición española* (Boston: Allyn and Bacon, Norwood Press, 1937).

11. Genaro Padilla, "Imprisoned Narrative? Or Lies, Secrets, and Silences in New Mexico Women's Autobiography," in Hector Calderon and Jose David Saldivar, eds., *Criticism in the Borderlands* (Durham, NC: Duke University Press, 1991),43-60; Carol Jensen, "Cleofas M. Jaramillo on Marriage in Territorial Northern New Mexico," NMHR 58(2) (April 1983): 153-72; Jan D. Barnhart, "Nina Otero Warren," in Díaz and Barnhart, *Hispanic Heros*; "Fabiola Cabeza de Baca Gilbert," in *Women of New Mexico* (exhibit catalogue; Albuquerque: Museum of Albuquerque, 1976), 15-16; Tey Diana Robolledo, ed., *Nuestras Mujeres: Hispanas of New Mexico* . . . (Albuquerque: Norte/Academia, 1993), 42-46. See chapter 6 for biographical sketches and sources on Armijo and Sena.

12. Cleofas M. Jaramillo, *The Genuine New Mexico Tasty Recipes* (1939; reprint, Santa Fe:

Ancient City Press, 1981), 19-20 [historical note by Marta Weigle]; "Sociedad Unit Encourages Old Customs," DNM Centennial-Fiesta edition, September 1949, section 7, p. 5; David Sansing, "Pilgrimage," in Charles R. Wilson and William Ferris, eds., *Encyclopedia of Southern Culture* (Chapel Hill: University of North Carolina Press, 1989), 700.

13. Classic statements of the Spanish-American elite are Nina Otero, *Old Spain in Our Southwest* (New York: Harcourt, Brace, and Co., 1936); Cleofas M. Jaramillo, *Genuine Recipes,* and *Romance of a Little Village Girl* (San Antonio: Naylor, 1955); Fabiola Cabeza de Baca Gilbert, *The Good Life: New Mexico Traditions and Food* (1949; reprint, Santa Fe: Museum of New Mexico Press, 1982), and *We Fed Them Cactus* (Albuquerque: University of New Mexico Press, 1954); Angelico Chávez, *Origins of New Mexico Families* (1954; reprint, Albuquerque: University of Albuquerque, 1973), and *My Penitente Land: Reflections on Spanish New Mexico* (Albuquerque: University of New Mexico Press, 1974).

14. G. Padilla, "Imprisoned Narratives," 48 (includes Jaramillo quote).

15. G. Padilla, "Imprisoned Narratives," 60.

16. A. Chávez, *Origins,* xiv; Kate McGraw, "About to Turn 80, Poet-Priest Still Busy," DNM April 8, 1990, pp. A1, 4.

17. G. Padilla, "Imprisoned Narratives," 44; J. Chávez, *Lost Land,* 84-86, 89-99, 103; David J. Weber, *Foreigners in Their Land: Historic Roots of the Mexican Americans* (Albuquerque: University of New Mexico Press, 1973), 45-50; Mario T. Garcia, *Mexican Americans: Leadership, Ideology and Identity, 1930-1960* (New Haven: Yale University Press, 1989), 14-15, 97-98, 281-84.

18. 1970 census figures cited in Fernando Peñalosa, *Chicano Sociolinguistics: A Brief Introduction* (Rowley, MA: Newbury, 1980), 3. J. Chávez, *Lost Land,* 93; Philip B. Gonzáles, "A Critique of Both Sides in the Hispano Homeland Debate," manuscript, 1991, 4-7. Gonzáles analyzes and translates L. E. Bernal, "Hispano-Americanos, o simplemente Americanos," *El Nuevo Mexicano* May 6, 1920, on the use of *hispano*. Whether or not New Mexico was distinctly Spanish, actual cultural differences existed and were perceived as such between New Mexicans and Mexicans. The use of *manito* in the everyday vernacular, and *hispano* in the Spanish-language press reveals a clear and apparently widespread perception of cultural distinctiveness from Mexico.

19. Joaquin Ortega, *New Mexico's Opportunity* (Albuquerque: University of New Mexico Press for the author, 1942), 2, 8; Joaquin Ortega, "The Intangible Resources of New Mexico," Papers of the School of American Research (Santa Fe: Archeological Institute of America, 1945), 6-7.

20. For Campa's biography, see Garcia, *Mexican Americans* 273-74; Anselmo F. Arellano and Julian J. Vigil, eds., *Arthur L. Campa and the Coronado Cuarto Centennial* (Las Vegas, NM: Editorial Telarana, 1980), 4-5.

21. Arthur L. Campa, "Spanish Religious Folktheatre in the Southwest," *UNM Bulletin*

5(2) (June 15, 1934): 6-7; J. Chávez, *Lost Land,* 99-100; Arthur L. Campa, "Spanish Folk-Poetry in New Mexico," reprinted in *Hispanic Folklore Studies of Arthur Campa* (New York: New York Times/Arno Press, 1976), 14; see also Arthur L. Campa, "The Spanish Folksong in the Southwest, *UNM Bulletin* 4(1) (November 15, 1933): 13.

22. Campa, "Spanish Folk-Poetry," 15; Arthur L. Campa, *Hispanic Culture in the Southwest* (Norman: University of Oklahoma Press, 1979), 5. Campa's chief shortcoming may have been an inadequate appreciation of the extent to which New Mexicans, nevertheless, perceived themselves as culturally different from Mexicans.

23. Nancie L. Gonzáles, *The Spanish-Americans of New Mexico* (Albuquerque: University of New Mexico Press, 1969), 25, 136-78; Edward Murguia, *Chicano Intermarriage: A Theoretical and Empirical Study* (San Antonio: Trinity University Press, 1982), 49, 68; J. Chávez, *Lost Land,* chapter 5; Garcia, *Mexican Americans,* 33-38, 284-89; P. Gonzáles, "Structural Correspondence," 21-24; Donovan Senter, "Acculturation among New Mexican Villagers in Comparison to Adjustment Patterns of Other Spanish-Speaking Americans," *Rural Sociology* 10(1) (March 1945): 31-47; F. Chris Garcia, "Manitos and Chicanos in New Mexico Politics," *Aztlán* 4(2), reprinted in F. Chris Garcia, ed., *La Causa Política: A Chicano Politics Reader* (Notre Dame: University of Notre Dame Press, 1974), 271-80.

24. J. Chávez, *Lost Land,* 130; Campa, *Hispanic Culture,* 7; Norris Hundley, Jr., ed., *The Chicano* (Santa Barbara: Clio Books, 1975), text and nn. 34-37, p. 152; Joseph V. Metzgar, "The Ethnic Sensitivity of Spanish New Mexicans: A Survey and Analysis," NMHR 49(1) (January 1974): 49-74, especially 55; N. Gonzáles, *Spanish-Americans,* 141.

25. Henry C. Schmidt, *The Roots of Lo Mexicano: Self and Society in Mexican Thought, 1900-1930,* (College Station: Texas A & M University Press, 1978); Charles W. Anderson, et al., *Issues of Political Development* (Englewood Cliffs, NJ: Prentice-Hall, 1974), 45, 55-56, 193; Marc Simmons, "Rejoinders," *Annals of the American Association of Geographers* 74(1) (1984: 169-70; Gloria Anzaldúa, *Borderlands/La Frontera: The New Mestiza* (San Francisco: spinsters/aunt lute, 1987), 77.

26. J. Chávez, *Lost Land,* 130; Rudolfo A. Anaya and Francisco Lomeli, eds., *Aztlán: Essays on the Chicano Homeland* (Albuquerque: Academia/El Norte Publications, 1989), especially 1-5, 111-34, 230-41. The best current scholarship suggests that the Aztlán referred to in Aztec oral traditions was in the contemporary Mexican state of Nayarit, 400 miles northwest of Mexico City, although earlier ancestors of the Aztecs likely migrated through the Southwest. More important than the precise location of Aztlán is the fact that it became a powerful symbol for regaining alienated lands and for the social community of the village. Chicano artists and intellectuals have wielded this mythohistoric homeland as a utopian vision for the future—a future of peace, justice, and community, local self-sufficiency, and self-determination.

27. Anaya, *Aztlán,* 1.

28. Gilberto Benito Cordova, *Abiquiu and Don Cacahuate: a Folk History of a New Mexico Village* (Cerrillos, NM: San Marcos Press, 1973), 18, and *The 3 1/2 Cultures of Española* (Albuquerque: El Norte Publications/Academia, 1990); Suzanne Fields, "Santa Fe Chicanos Take Care of Their Own," *Innovations* (Winter 1975): 3-8; Tomás Atencio, "Resolana: A Chicano Pathway to Knowledge" (Ernesto Galarza Commemorative Lecture, Stanford Center for Chicano Research, 1988); Rudolfo A. Anaya, ed., *Voces: An Anthology of Nuevo Mexicano Writers* (Albuquerque: University of New Mexico Press, 1987). The newspaper *El Grito del Norte* chronicled the Chicano movement in New Mexico from 1968 to 1973.

29. Anzaldúa, *Borderlands*, 194.

30. Metzgar, "Ethnic Sensitivity." The self-identification "Chicano" may have been a bit less popular in Santa Fe, as a result of the intensification of Spanish identity by the Fiesta and tourism. Nevertheless *Chicano* clearly was written on the banner behind which significant grass-roots activism marched through the city in the early 1970s.

31. Stan Steiner, *The New Indians* (New York: Delta Books, 1968), 218-19; Sam D. Gill, *Mother Earth: An American Story* (Chicago: University of Chicago Press, 1987).

32. Campa, *Hispanic Culture*, 6-8. A telling discussion of the uses of the terms *Hispano* and *Hispanic* appears in Niles Hansen, "Commentary: The Hispano Homeland in 1900," and Richard L. Nostrand, "Comment in Reply," *Annals of the American Association of Geographers* 71(2) (June 1981): 280-84; J. M. Blaut and Antonio Rios-Bustamante, "Commentary on Nostrand's 'Hispanos' and their 'Homeland,'" Richard L. Nostrand, "Hispano Cultural Distinctiveness: A Reply," and "Rejoinders" by Marc Simmons, Angelico Chávez, D. W. Meinig, and Thomas D. Hall, *Annals of the American Association of Geographers* 74(1) (1984): 157-69. Arthur Campa, who preferred the term *Hispanic,* was quick to challenge Chicano ideology. In the book that culminated his career, *Hispanic Culture in the Southwest* (1979), Campa stated his criticisms: "It is probably true that most Chicanos have considerably more Indian than Spanish blood, but when they ask universities to teach 'Chicano studies' and 'Chicano history,' the meaning of chicano is extended into the Spanish cultural field, because an exclusive 'Chicano culture' simply does not exist" (pp. 7-8). Campa equated *Chicano* with *Indian,* whereas most Chicano theorists used the term to refer to a mixture of Spanish and Indian heritage, even if some overemphasized the Indian component as a corrective to the previous emphasis on Spanishness. The quest for pure cultures led many scholars in the past to the fallacy of viewing origins as an either/or proposition. The Spanish-speaking culture of northern New Mexico and southern Colorado may appear Spanish or Hispanic when compared to that of the Pueblos or Navajos. When compared directly to Spain, however, it becomes apparent that it is a New World hybrid. Acculturation is not simply a one-way process of immigrants or conquered groups adopting the dominant culture, but a complex interaction resulting in cultural changes on both sides. The uncritical use of the term *Spanish-American,* or more recently *Hispanic,* inhibits the scholarly eval-

359

uation of the historical process of cultural interchange between Indians and the Spanish and of the more recent interaction of Hispanic-Chicanos with Anglos.

Keefe and Padilla, *Chicano Ethnicity,* chap. 2, includes a discussion of acculturation and the scholarly literature on the subject, especially as it relates to Mexican-Americans. On the complexity of modern cultural interactions, see: Eric R. Wolf, *Europe and the People Without History* (Berkeley: University of California Press, 1982); and James Clifford, *The Predicament of Culture* (Cambridge, MA: Harvard University Press, 1988). I employed the term *Hispanic* uncritically in Chris Wilson and David Kammer, *La Tierra Amarilla: Its History, Architecture, and Cultural Landscape* (1989; reprint, Santa Fe: Museum of New Mexico Press, 1992).

33. P. Gonzáles, "Structural Correspondence," 31-32.

34. Bob LaBrasca, "A Question of Identity," *L.A. Style* 5(10) (March 1990): 158-63, 176.

35. Martha E. Giménez, "Latino/'Hispanic'—Who Needs a Name? The Case against a Standardized Terminology," *International Journal of Health Services* 19(3) (1989): 557-71; quote, p. 561. See also Marta Tienda and Vilma Ortiz, "'Hispanicity' and the 1980 Census," *Social Science Quarterly* 67(1) (March 1986): 3-20; Alfred Yankauer, "Hispano/Latino—What's in a Name?" *American Journal of Public Health* 77(1) (January 1987): 15-17; David E. Hayes-Bautista and Jorge Chapa, "Latino Terminology: Conceptual Bases for Standardized Terminology," *American Journal of Public Health* 77(1): 61-68; Fernando M. Trecino, "Standardized Terminology for Hispanic Populations," *American Journal of Public Health* 77(1): 69-72. Criticisms of the term *Hispanic* have led some to advance the new term *Latino,* which has gained substantial acceptance in Chicago, New York, Florida, and California, but only limited currency in New Mexico. Like *Hispanic, Latino* is a term of language origin (that is, a culture or language derived from Latin) that has taken on a meaning of national/geographic origin (from Latin American). Because *Latino* was adopted as a virtual synonym for *Hispanic* in the mass media, it immediately assumed the existing ethnic stereotypes. As such, *Latino* is open to the same criticisms as *Hispanic,* and in addition, its acceptance among Hispanics and non-Hispanics may not be as great. Its underlying definition also opens up the possibility of the inclusion of descendants of immigrants from French-, Italian-, and other Romance-language-speaking countries in census and affirmative action totals.

36. Giménez, "Latino/'Hispanic,'" 567.

37. Felix Padilla, "Latino Ethnicity in the City of Chicago," in Susan Olzak and Joane Nagel, eds., *Competitive Ethnic Relations* (Orlando: Academic Press, 1986), 153-72.

38. McCannell, "Reconstructed Ethnicity," 375-92. An excellent analysis of a parallel development to that of Santa Fe is Sylvia Rodríguez, "Ethnic Reconstruction in Taos," *Journal of the Southwest* 32(4) (Winter 1990): 541-55. F. Padilla, "Latino Ethnicity," 1-15.

39. See appendix, table 1 for population figures, and appendix note 1 for sources. Office

of Community Development, *Santa Fe Housing Needs Survey* (Santa Fe: City of Santa Fe, 1987); Kelly Richmond, "Growing Pains," DNM January 21, 1991, pp. A1, 4-5, and editorial; "Santa Fe: A Hot Real Estate Market," AJ July 13, 1992, Business Outlook, pp. 1-2. A seven-part series, "Saving Santa Fe," on local reaction to the negative effects of the tourism boom, appeared the week of October 3, 1993, in DNM.

40. Quotes from Debbie Jaramillo, typescript of speech delivered at Taos, New Mexico, January 10, 1991, author's files; Orlando Romero, "La Villa Real, SFR July 24, 1992. See also "City Council Urges Local Artist Fresco," DNM August 31, 1988; Deborah M. Gonzáles, "Practicing Our Traditions/Reclaiming Our Heritage," *Puntos de Vista,* 4(3) (May 1992): 9; David Baca, "Claiming Your Water Rights in the Santa Fe Basin," *Puntos de Vista* 4(3) (May 1992): 11; David Roybal, "Ex-Lieutenant Governor: King Just Looking to Cash In," DNM July 8, 1992, pp. A1-2 and commentaries, p. A7; Rebecca Roybal, "Debate on La Cienega," DNM July 9, 1992, p. A4; David H. Snow, *The Santa Fe Acequia Study* (Santa Fe: City Planning Department, 1988), 19.

41. Dorsey Griffith, "Debbie Jaramillo," DNM September 4, 1988; "Pick Quips Way through Regis-Lee Talk Show," AJ December 7, 1988, Journal North section; Dorsey Griffith, "Picking His Own Stage," DNM May 7, 1989, pp. A1, 5; Cheryl Wittenauer, "Forum Queries Candidates on Economy, Jobs," DNM February 13, 1990, p. B1; "Pick Wins with 39% of Vote," DNM March 7, 1990, pp. A1,4,5; "Why Debbie Jaramillo?" *Puntos de Vista* 4(1) (February 1992): 3-4; Patricia Frye, letter to the editor, DNM July 10, 1992, p. A10.

42. Bob Quick, "Jaramillo Warns of Unrest," DNM July 1, 1992, p. B1 (Quick's paraphrases of Jaramillo); John Howard and E. J. Alberts, letters to the editor, DNM July 13, 1992, p. A9; Richard Lucero, letter to the editor, DNM July 25, 1992, p. A11.

43. Jeanette DeBouzek and Diana Reyna, *Gathering Up Again: Fiesta in Santa Fe,* 1992, video-cassette.

44. R. Himmerich y Valencia, J. Sanchez, et al., letter To Whom It May Concern, March 12, 1992, author's files; Orlando Romero, "Doing Fiesta a Disservice," SFR July 8, 1992, p. 10. See also Biddle Duke, "Conflicts, What Conflicts?" DNM c. April 1992, p. A1, MNM-VF; Jeanette DeBouzek and Diane Reyna, "Setting the Video Straight," SFR July 22, 1992, p. 7; Joseph P. Sanchez, "The Black Legend: Origins of Anti-Hispanic Stereotypes" (booklet; Washington, DC: National Park Service, c. 1985).

45. Joseph Villegas, "It's Time To Heal Old Wounds," *Puntos de Vista* 4(2) (March/April 1992): 3-5.

Interlude: Coyote Consciousness

1. Frank H. Cushing, *Zuni Folk Tales* (1901; reprint, Tucson: University of Arizona Press, 1992), 203-68; Marta Weigle and Peter White, *The Lore of New Mexico* (Albuquerque: University of New Mexico Press, 1988), 146, 165-67, 185, 314, 389, 469.

2. John Brandi, "How Many Ways Are There to Tell of Coyote?," in James Koller, Gogisgi Carroll Arnett, Steve Nemirow and Peter Blue Cloud, eds., *Coyote's Journal* (Berkeley: Wingbow, 1982), 39. J. Frank Dobie, *The Voice of Coyote* (Boston: Little, Brown and Company, 1949), surveys the history, folklore, and nature writing on coyotes; see also April Kopp, "Coyote: Howl of the Wild," *New Mexico Magazine* (August 1991), 96-101.

3. Bo Schöler, *Coyote Was Here: Essays on Contemporary Native American Literary and Political Mobilization, The Dolphin* 9 (Aarhus, Denmark: SEKLOS, 1984): 9; Nora Naranjo-Morse, *Mud Women: Poems From the Clay* (Tucson: University of Arizona Press, 1992), 74-77.

4. Koller et al., *Coyote's Journal*; Peter Blue Cloud, *Elderberry Flute Song: Contemporary Coyote Tales* (Buffalo: White Wine Press, 1989); *Man on Fire/El Hombre en Llamas: Luis Jiménez* (Albuquerque: Albuquerque Museum, 1994), 134-37; Marta Weigle, "On Coyotes and Crosses": That Which is Wild and Wooden of the Twentieth-Century Southwest" in Richard Francaviglia and David Narrett, eds., *Essays on the Changing Images of the Southwest*, William P. Webb Memorial Lectures (College Station: Texas A & M Press, 1994).

5. For examples of Howling Coyote and other Southwestern tricksters, see Donald Locke, "Jim Pile: New Icons for the Southwest," *Artspace* (Spring 1982): 20-21 [Pile did not include Howling Coyote in his extensive catalogue of kitsch regional icons]; Christine Mather and Sharon Woods, *Santa Fe Style* (New York: Rizzoli, 1986), 118-21; Barbara Babcock, "By Way of Introduction," *Journal of the Southwest* 32(4) (Winter 1990): 383-99; Marta Weigle, "Southwestern Lures: Innocents Detoured, Incensed Determined," *Journal of the Southwest* 32/4 (Winter 1990); advertisements in *Artspace* (Summer 1982): 57; *The Book of Santa Fe* (advertising booklet; Summer/Fall 1986), 17, 86; *The Santa Fe Catalogue* (advertising catalogue, Winter 1991), 45, 72, 88.

6. Coyote Tequila advertising, *Rolling Stone* 614 (October 3, 1991): unpaginated insert following p. 68.

7. Arthur H. Rohn, *Rock Art of Bandelier National Monument* (Albuquerque: University of New Mexico Press, 1989), 82-83; Frank Seckler, "Seckler Studio," advertising brochure for cut-out sheet metal art featuring Kokopelli, 1994.

8. Gloria Anzaldúa, *Borderlands,* 72.

9. Anzaldúa, *Borderlands /La Frontera: The New Mestiza* (San Francisco: spinsters/aunt lute, 1987), 77-91, quotes, 79-80, 87.

10. Anzaldúa, *Borderlands,* 41-51, 72-75. See also Peter T. Markman and Roberta H. Markman, *Masks of the Spirit: Image and Metaphor in Mesoamerica* (Berkeley: University of California Press, 1989), 119, 157-58.

11. Stanley Hordes, "The Inquisition and the Crypto-Jewish Community in Colonial New Spain and New Mexico," in Penny, Mary Elizabeth and Anne Cruz, eds., *Cultural Encounters: The Impact of the Inquisition in Spain and the New World* (Berkeley: University of California Press, 1991).

12. Anzaldúa, *Borderlands*; B. Emily Hicks, *Border Writing: The Multidimensional Text* (Minneapolis: University of Minnesota Press, 1991), 117. Because Pueblo Indians have compartmentalized their culture as a self-preservation strategy, many are hesitant to have outsiders learn their languages and penetrate their basic belief. As a result, I have omitted Pueblo languages from my call for learning second languages.

Chapter 6

1. SANM II, 179, translated in Fray Angelico Chávez, "The First Santa Fe Fiesta, 1712," NMHR 28(3) (July 1953): 183-85.

2. "Death of Major Sena," DNM July 11, 1892, p. 4; *History of New Mexico* (Los Angles: Pacific States Publishing, 1907), 295. The Corpus Christi procession invariably paused first at an altar in front of the Sena family house, just north of the cathedral. One year a long festoon of evergreens looped from their altar to the Cathedral. The procession next turned west on Palace Avenue, passed around the plaza, and returned to the cathedral on San Francisco Street. Santa Fe's leading Hispanic merchant family, the Delgados, usually constructed one or more altars on the plaza. In the 1870s, Fernando's altar stood midway along the west side of the plaza, where the oratorio of Juan Vigil had been in the Mexican era, and Felipe B. Delgado's altar stood on the south side, in front of the building his brother Simon had erected to replace the Castrense Chapel in 1859. These altars, erected amid a clutter of business signs, and the procession, which temporarily displaced Santa Fe Trail wagon trains from the plaza, reasserted older religious associations. For mention and in some cases discussion of the Corpus Christi celebrations, procession route, and location of altars, see SFG June 4, 1864; and DNM June 4, 1864, June 1, 1869, June 20, 27, 1870, June 16, 1873, June 8, 1874, May 20, 1875, June 19, 1876, June 29, 1878, May 24, 1880. See also Ronald Grimes, *Symbol and Conquest: Public Ritual and Drama in Santa Fe, New Mexico* (Ithaca, NY: Cornell University Press, 1976), 57-63, 165.

3. Fray Angelico Chávez, *Our Lady of Conquest* (Santa Fe: Historical Society of New Mexico, 1948), 2-3 n. 3, 7-8, 21-28.

4. Chávez, "Fiesta Council"; Chávez, *Our Lady*. For mention and in some cases a discussion of La Conquistadora celebrations, see DNM June 27, 1870, June 23, 1881, July 4, 1882, July 23, 1884, July 6, 1886; June 11, 1887, July 1, 1889, June 10, 1893, June 2, 1894.

5. Grimes, *Symbol and Conquest*, 68.

6. Mark C. Carnes, *Secret Ritual and Manhood in Victorian America* (New Haven: Yale University Press, 1989), 2-3; *A Century of Freemasonry in New Mexico* (Santa Fe: n.p., 1951); Ralph E. Twitchell, *The Leading Facts of New Mexico History* (Cedar Rapids, Iowa: Torch Press, 1917)5:312-33; Grand Army of the Republic, Knights Templar, and Scottish Rite files, Adella Collier Collection, NMRC; Misc. Programs and Announcements file, L. Bradford Prince Collection, NMRC.

7. "Masonry in New Mexico," WNM January, 2, 1864, p. 2; item on fraternal meeting halls, DNM February 18, 1870; "Grand Celebration," DNM July 3, 1874; "General Orders of Grand Marshall [for 1903 Roosevelt visit]," handbill, Misc. Programs and Announcements file, L. Bradford Prince Collection, NMRC; Twitchell, *Leading Facts* 5:312-33; Henry Tobias, *A History of the Jews in New Mexico* (Albuquerque: University of New Mexico Press, 1990), 48-49. See also annual announcements and descriptions of Decoration/Memorial Day (May 30) and Forth of July celebrations in DNM.

8. "Coronado's Cohorts," DNM July 19, 1883; Wayne Mauzy, "The Tertio-Millennial Exposition," EP 37(24) (December 1934): 185-99.

9. Carnes, *Secret Ritual*, 5, 52, 55, 64, 94-95, 134-35, 138-39. See also Albert G. MacKey, *A Lexicon of Freemasonry* (Philadelphia: Moss and Co., 1869); Lynn Dumenil, *Freemasonry and American Culture, 1880-1930* (Princeton, NJ: Princeton University Press, 1984); Mary Ann Clawson, *Constructing Brotherhood: Class, Gender and Fraternalism* (Princeton, NJ: Princeton University Press, 1989).

10. DNM regularly ran a column entitled "Fraternal Societies" or "Societies," with the meeting times and officers of the fraternities; see, for example, August 24, 1904, p. 6, May 29, 1913, p. 7.

11. Clawson, *Constructing Brotherhood*, 263; EP 5 (September 19, 1918); "Proceedings of the City Council [Planning Committee Report]," DNM December 24, 1912, p. 7; Nicholas C. Markovich, "Santa Fe Renaissance: City Planning and Stylistic Preservation, 1912," PSRA 198; Scottish Rite file, Collier Collection, NMRC; "Noted Masons Confer High Degrees . . ." DNM November 19, 1912, p. 1; Beatrice Chauvenet, *Hewett and Friends* (Santa Fe: Museum of New Mexico Press, 1983), 150; "Historic Pageant for Santa Fe," EP 5 (1918): 62-63; "The Santa Fe Fiesta," EP 7(5/6) (September 30, 1919): 98-106, 128-30, (quote) 99-101; official Fiesta programs, 1920, 1924, MNM-VF; carton 9, BL-CF. For a biography of Muller, see *History of New Mexico*, 154-55.

12. Carnes, *Secret Ritual*, 4; William Whalen, *Handbook of Secret Organizations* (Milwaukee: Brice Publishing, 1966), 76-82; Jose Hernandez, *Mutual Aid and Survival: The Case of the Mexican American*, (Malabar, FL: Kreiger, 1983), 31-37; Olivia Arrieta, "*La Alianza Hispano Americana*, 1894-1965 . . .," Seminar Paper, Southwest Hispanic Research Institute, University of New Mexico, 1994; Sylvanus Morley to George Armijo, September 10, 1912, MNM-WL; John D. DeHuff, "The Santa Fe Fiesta," NMHR 6(3) (July 1931): 324.

13. On José D. Sena, Jr., see *History of New Mexico*, 295-96; "Hearing Set On Retiring Jose Sena, 83," DNM June 27, 1950. On George Armijo, see Twitchell, *Leading Facts* 2:584; "Funeral Mass Wednesday for George W. Armijo, Politician and Orator," DNM February 17, 1947, p. 1; John Grassham, "George W. Armijo," in Rose Díaz and Jan Dodson Barnhart, eds., *Hispanic Heros* (Albuquerque: Starlight Press, 1992).

14. "Fiesta Was a Success," DNM August 24, 1904, p. 1; DNM July 4, 1912, p. 1; DNM

May 27, 1913, p. 5; "Constitution and By-Laws of the Woman's Board of Trade" (Santa Fe: The Eagle Print, 1915); "Mrs. Laughlin, Old Resident, Dead at 86," DNM? May 12, 1944, p. 1 (copy in MNM-VF); P. A. F. W.[alter], "Necrology, Mrs. Napoleon B. Laughlin," NMHR 19(3) (July 1944): 257-58.

15. Chauvenet, *Hewett and Friends*, 93, 95, 191; Santa Clara Pueblo file, MNM-VF; Susan Peterson, *The Living Tradition of Maria Martinez* (Tokyo: Kodansh International, 1977), 90.

16. An excellent study of this phenomenon is David Glassberg's *American Historical Pageantry: The Uses of Tradition in the Early Twentieth Century* (Chapel Hill: University of North Carolina Press, 1990), especially 41-68, 258, and 283-86 on the 1908-16 phase.

17. Carnes, *Secret Ritual*, 1-2; "Historic Pageant," 63.

18. Quoted in Chauvenet, *Hewett and Friends*, 148-51.

19. "Historic Pageant for Santa Fe," 62-63; "The Santa Fe Fiesta" (1919), 98-106, 128-131; Paul A. F. Walter, "The Fiesta of Santa Fe," *Art and Archeology* 9(1) (January 1920): 15-22; Chauvenet, *Hewett and Friends*, 147-61. This and subsequent discussions of the Fiesta also draw context from the fiesta files in UNM-M; the Collier Collection, NMRC; MNM-VF, which contain many fiesta programs; DeHuff, "The Santa Fe Fiesta"; Angelico Chávez, "First Fiesta"; Donna Pierce, ed., *¡Vivan Las Fiestas!* (Santa Fe: Museum of New Mexico Press, 1985); Grimes, *Symbol and Conquest*; and accounts in DNM the week of July 4, 1911 and 1912, second week of September 1919, and c. 1975 to present, first week of September 1920 to c. 1975 (but first week of August 1925 and 1926).

20. Glassberg, *American Historical Pageantry*, 229-78, 286-90.

21. Grimes, *Symbol and Conquest*, 187-88; Chauvenet, *Hewett and Friends*, 156-59, 196; Glassberg, *American Historical Pageantry*, 239, 268; Archeological Institute of America, *The Fiesta Book*, Papers of the School of American Research, New Series no. 13 (Santa Fe: 1925); "Thomas W. Stevens," special "Artists and Writers" section, DNM June 26, 1940 (reprint, Santa Fe: Ancient City Press, 1982); fiesta programs, MNM-VF; DNM for Fiesta weeks.

22. DNM July 3, 1876; Jill Drayson Sweet, "Tewa Ceremonial Performances: The Effects of Tourism on an Ancient Pueblo Indian Dance and Music Tradition"(Ph.D. diss., University of New Mexico, 1980), 84-87, 100-106, 108-9; Will Roscoe, *The Zuni Man-Woman* (Albuquerque: University of New Mexico Press, 1991), 179-93.

23. Chauvenet, *Hewett and Friends*, 151-61; official Fiesta programs, 1920, 1921, 1922, 1924, 1925, 1926, MNM-VF; "Grateful Thanks From Pasatiempo Committee . . .," DNM September 4, 1924, p. 4; "Hysterical Pageant . . .," DNM September 8, 1927, p. 6; John Sherman, "First Fiesta Queen Remembers 1927," DNM September 5, 1984, pp. 3, 5.

24. "Coronado's Cohorts"; Chauvenet, *Hewett and Friends*, 148-51; "Seventeenth Century Glory Recalled in Brilliant Pageant," DNM July 5, 1911; "Harking Back to Days of New Mexico's Romance" DNM, June 25, 1912, p. 7.

365

25. Official Fiesta programs, 1920, 1925; Fiesta program, typescript, August 25, 1934, Santa Fe Fiesta file, Collier Collection, NMRC; Grimes, *Symbol and Conquest,* 268-69.

26. Carnes, *Secret Ritual,* 151-56. On the analysis of generational shifts in attitude, see Mario Garcia, *Mexican Americans: Leadership, Ideology and Identity, 1930-1960* (New Haven: Yale University Press, 1989), 3-7.

27. Glassberg, *American Historical Pageantry,* 128-31; Van Wyck Brooks, *John Sloan: A Painter's Life* (New York: E. P. Dutton and Co., 1955), 34-36, 89-91.

28. Chauvenet, *Hewett and Friends,* 196; for a biographical sketch of Witter Bynner, see James Kraft, The Works of Witter Bynner: Selected Poems (New York: Farrah, Straus, Giroux, 1978), xvii-lxxix; "Witter Bynner Celebrates 75th Birthday . . .," DNM August 12, 1956, p. A5, with appreciations by Paul Horgan, Ruth Laughlin Alexander, John B. Jackson, Oliver La Farge, etc.; Winfield T. Scott, "Witter Bynner Dies . . . ," DNM June 2, 1968, p. 1; John Fludas, "Prankster Poet," *Saturday Review* (February 17, 1979); Lois Palken Rudnick, *Mabel Dodge Luhan: New Women, New Worlds* (Albuquerque: University of New Mexico Press, 1984), 242-50. On a contemporary countercelebration, see Denise L. Lawrence, "Rules of Misrule: Notes on the Doo Dah Parade in Pasadena," in Alessandro Falassi, ed., *Time Out of Time: Essays on the Festival* (Albuquerque: University of New Mexico Press, 1987), 123-36.

29. Sherman, "First Fiesta Queen; "Zozobra, Dull Care, to Burn . . . ," DNM September 7, 1927, 1.

30. For a contrasting perspective on this subculture, from the son of the party's guest of honor, see Edward T. Hall, *An Anthropology of Everyday Life: An Autobiography* (New York: Doubleday, 1992), 39-61.

31. Unsigned typescript, SF Fiesta 1938 file, UNM-M.

32. SF Fiesta 1938 file, UNM-M.

33. "The Santa Fe Fiesta" (1919); Fiesta programs, 1920, 1921, 1922, 1924, 1938, 1945, MNM-VF; "226th Annual Fiesta . . ."; Walter K. López, "Santa Fe: Old, New City," *Vista/Focus on Hispanic Americans* magazine supplement to AJ May 27, 1989, p. 12.

34. Grimes, *Symbol and Conquest,* 139-40, 200-205.

35. Grimes, *Symbol and Conquest,* 116—17, 190, 204, 245—47, 259—64; Camille Flores, "Fiesta Seals Bond for Family," AJ June 31, 1989.

36. On All Species Day, see Pancho Epstein, "Holding up the Sky," DNM April 20, Pasatiempo section, pp. 1, 22; Kelly Richmond, "Global Walk Hasn't Been All Peace and Love," DNM April 21, 1990, p. 1; Cheryl Wittenauer, "Santa Fe Celebrates Species with a Flair," DNM April 22, 1990, pp. A1, A3, B1.

37. "Seventeenth Century Glory Recalled in Brilliant Pageant," DNM July 5, 1911; "September 3/4 and 5 Set as Santa Fe Fiesta Dates," DNM July 25, 1938; "Historic Pageant for Santa Fe," EP 5 (1918): 62-63; Fiesta programs, 1920, 1921, 1924, 1945, 1957, 1966, 1970, 1980, MNM-VF.

38. Quoted in Grimes, *Symbol and Conquest,* 139-40.

39. Grimes, *Symbol and Conquest,* 169-70, 200-202.

Chapter 7

1. E. E. Viollet-le-Duc, *Dictionnaire raisonné de l'architecture française du XIe au XVIe siècle,* trans. Charles Wethered (London: Sampson Low and Searle, 1875), section on restoration reproduced in Cevet Erder, *Our Architectural Heritage* (Bungay, United Kingdom: Richard Clay Ltd. for UNESCO, 1986), 130-35, 193-208, (quote) 201. David Lowenthal, *The Past is a Foreign Country* (Cambridge: Cambridge University Press, 1985), 278, 389-96, 406; E. H. Gombrich, "The Beauty of Old Towns," *Architectural Association Journal* (April 1965): 293-97; Jacques Dupont, "Viollet-le-Duc and Restoration in France," in National Trust for Historic Preservation, *Historic Preservation Today* (Charlottesville: University of Virginia Press, 1966); Nathan G. Weinberg, "Historic Preservation and Tradition in California" (Ph.D. diss., University of California-Davis, c. 1979), 20-23.

2. Ruskin quoted in John Summerson, "Ruskin, Morris, and the 'Anti-Scrape' Philosophy," in National Trust, *Historic Preservation.* William Morris, "Architecture and History," quoted in E. P. Thompson, *William Morris: Romantic to Revolutionary* (1955; revised edition, New York: Pantheon Books, 1977), 239. On the English restorers and the Anti-Scrape movement, see Thompson, *William Morris,* 226-42; Lowenthal, *The Past,* 278-80; Summerson, "Ruskin, Morris"; Nikolaus Pevsner, "Scrape and Anti-Scrape," 35-54, in Jane Fawcett, ed., *The Future of the Past: Attitudes to Conservation, 1147-1974* (New York: Watson-Guptill, 1976); Jane Fawcett, "A Restoration Tragedy: Cathedrals in the Eighteenth and Nineteenth Centuries," 75-116, in Jane Fawcett, ed., *The Future of the Past;* Stephen T. Madsen, *Restoration and Anti-Restoration: A Study in English Restoration Philosophy* (Oslo: Universitetsforlaget, 1978).

3. Charles Hosmer, *Presence of the Past: A History of the Preservation Movement in the United States before Williamsburg* (New York: G.P. Putnam's Sons, 1965), 41-122, 237-59; Michael Wallace, "Visiting the Past: History Museums in the United States," *Radical History Review* 25 (1981): 64-68; John Higham, *Strangers in the Land: Patterns of American Nativism* (1955; reprint New York: Antheneum, 1975), 45-63; James M. Lindgren, "The Gospel of Preservation in Virginia and New England: Historic Preservation and the Regeneration of Traditionalism," (Ph.D. diss., College of William and Mary, 1984), 2-7, 55-342, (quote) 6-7; Jane Holtz Kay, *Preserving New England* (New York: Pantheon, 1986), 46-47. William Sumner Appleton, "Destruction and Preservation of Old Buildings in New England," *Art and Archeology* 8(3) (May-June 1919): 130-83 describes the approach and accomplishments of the Society for the Preservation of New England Antiquities and calls for a shift of the preservation movement from local historical societies to larger regional and national groups, among which he notes SPENA, the Association for the Preservation of Virginia Antiquities, the American Scenic and Historic Preservation Society, and the Archeology Institute of America's School of American Research, in Santa Fe.

4. Weinberg, "Historic Preservation," 82-152.

5. DNM April 27, 1887; John Kessell, *The Missions of New Mexico Since 1776* (Albuquerque: University of New Mexico Press, 1980), 23-24, 50-53; Boyd C. Pratt, ed., "Directory of Historic New Mexico Architects," typescript at Zimmerman Library, University of New Mexico, 1988, 76.

6. DNM April 20, 1893.

7. Archeology Institute of America, "Third Annual Report of the Managing Committee of the School of American Archeology 1910" (Santa Fe: SAA, 1910) 3, 21, 25; Peter Harrison, "Carlos Vierra: His Role and Influence on the Maya," in Peter Briggs, ed., *The Maya Image in the Western World,* exhibit catalogue (Albuquerque: University of New Mexico, 1986), 21-28; "Rito de los Frijoles, Ceremonial Cave and Kiva" file, MNM-PA.

8. *Acts of the Legislative Assembly* (Santa Fe: New Mexican Printing Co., 1909), 4-7; Jesse Nusbaum to Edgar Hewett, January 1, 1914, box 41, Nusbaum folder, MNM- H; Letter to Dear Sir [outlining work accomplished on the Palace and arguments for further funding from upcoming state legislative session], February 1, 1912, box 23, folder 4, MNM-H. As far as I have been able to determine, no formal plan for the restoration of the Palace of the Governors was prepared, but the goals and methods of that restoration are described in Archeology Institute, "Third Annual Report"; Archeology Institute, "Second Annual Report . . . School of American Research 1908-09," 178; Archeology Institute, "Fourth Annual Report . . . School of American Research 1910-11," 42. See also Michael F. Weber, "The Problem of Preservation [of the Palace]," EP 80(3) (1974): 39-41; the comprehensive collection of photographs of the Palace at the MNM-PA; Jesse L. Nusbaum, affidavit, January 7, 1913, MNM-H; Jess Nusbaum to Edgar Hewett, December 18, 1909, and January 1, 1914, box 41, Nusbaum folder MNM-H; "Links Historic Past with Living Present," EP 1(2) (December 1913): 6.

9. Archeology Institute, "Second Annual Report," 180; "Restoration of the Palace," EP 1(1) (November 1913): 5.

10. Sylvanus G. Morley, "The Most Selfish Thing for Santa Fe," undated broadside, probably 1912, MNM-WL; "Civic Improvement/The Topic Last Night," DNM August 28, 1912.

11. Santa Fe City Plan, undated typescript, probably 1912, signed by six planning commission members, under subheading "Ancient Streets and Structures," MNM-WL; Frederick L. Olmsted [Jr.] to H. H. Dorman, July 7, 1913, MNM-WL.

12. "Notes of Interest on City Planning," DNM March 5, 1912, p. 3.

13. John Kessell, *Missions,* 27-28; Beatrice Chauvenet, *John Gaw Meem: Pioneer in Historic Preservation* (Santa Fe: Museum of New Mexico Press, 1985); Society for the Restoration and Preservation of New Mexican Missions, "Imperilled Monuments of Early American History" (n.p.: author, 1925), UNM-M, box 2, file 11; "This report made up, March 5, 1935 . . .," unsigned typescript, UNM-M, box 2, file 16.

14. Edgar Hewett to Wm. P. McPhee, September 26, 1924, UNM-M, box 1, file 19; William P. McPhee to Edgar L. Hewett, September 29, 1924, UNM-M, box 2, Lewis Riley Correspondence file; Lisa Mausolf, "McPhee, Colorado; A 20th Century Lumber Company Town," in Gregory D. Kendrick, ed., *The River of Sorrows: The History of the Lower Dolores River Valley* (Denver: National Park Service Rocky Mountain Regional Office, c. 1982), 59-70; Malcolm Ebright, *The Tierra Amarilla Land Grant* (Santa Fe: Center for Land Grant Studies, 1980), ix-xii, 1-27; Victor Westfall, *Mercedes Reales: Hispanic Land Grants of the Upper Rio Grande Region* (Albuquerque: University of New Mexico Press, 1983), 127-31, 224-33.

15. Bainbridge Bunting, *John Gaw Meem: Southwest Architect* (Albuquerque: University of New Mexico Press, 1983).

16. Vincent Scully, *Pueblo: Mountain Village Dance* (New York: Viking Press, 1975), 249, 251.

17. On the early work and disputes, see L.A. Riley, "Repairs to the Old Mission at Acoma," EP 18(1) (January 1, 1925): 2-9; B. A. Reuter to John Meem, September 12, 1926, UNM-M; Juan Louis Haskey to Meem and McCormick, February 4, 1928, UNM-M, box 2, file 11. The quote is from B. A. Reuter to John Meem, October 6, 1926, and undated addendum to same letter, UNM-M, box 2, file 12.

18. John Meem, "Report of Preliminary Trip to Acoma," September 17, 1924, typescript, UNM-M, box 2, file 12.

19. Quote from B. A. Reuter, addendum to letter to John Meem, October 6, 1926, UNM-M, box 2, file 12. See also B. A. Reuter, letters to John Meem, October 6, 7, 1926, and undated letter, c. October 10, 1926, UNM-M, box 2, file 12. "Acomas" uncapitalized in original letter.

20. See Van Dorn Hooker, "To Hard Plaster or Not?," NMA (September-October 1977): 11-16; Jean-Louis Bourgeois and Carollee Pelos, *Spectacular Vernacular: The Adobe Tradition* (New York: Aperture, 1989), 166-174.

21. Chauvenet, *John Gaw Meem,* 28; B. A. Reuter to John Meem, November 10, 1926, UNM-M, box 2, file 12; John Meem to Anne Evans, November 16, 1926, UNM-M, box 2, file 12; B. A. Reuter, "Restoration of Acoma Mission," EP 22(4) (January 22, 1927): 82.

22. John Meem, office memorandum, May 25, 1927; John Meem to Mary Colter, June 3, 1927; Santa Fe Transportation Company, "Santa Fe and the Indian-Detour to Have Largest and Finest Harvey Hotel," Bulletin number 9 (August 8, 1927); all "Correspondence 55-La Fonda Addition" file, UNM-M.

23. Meem, "Report of Preliminary Trip"; John Meem to Anne Evans, June 10, 1926, UNM-M; John Meem to B. A. Reuter, September 13, 1926, UNM-M, box 2, file 12; Reuter, "Restoration of Acoma," 85-87. John Meem to Anne Evans, April 22, 1927; John Meem to B. A. Reuter, July 6, 1927; B. A. Reuter to John Meem, August 1, 1927; John Meem to Anne Evans, August 25, 1927; B. A. Reuter, untitled report on 1927 work at Acoma, c. January 1928; all UNM-M, box 2, file 11. On the thickness of the roofs of the Acoma towers, see

Edward S. Curtis, photograph of north tower of the Acoma mission, c. 1904, MNM-PA, #143699; Historic American Building Survey, "San Esteban del Rey Mission, Sheet 16, Bell Tower Details," April 5, 1934, measured drawing, Library of Congress.

24. John Meem to Anne Evans, November 16, 1926, UNM-M, box 2, file 12; Reuter, "Restoration of Acoma," 82-83; B. A. Reuter to John Meem, August 1, 1927, UNM-M, box 2, file 11.

25. John Meem to Miss W. W. Wheelwright, July 11, 1929, UNM-M, box 2, file 16.

26. Historic Santa Fe Foundation, *Old Santa Fe Today,* 3rd ed. (Albuquerque: University of New Mexico Press for the foundation, 1982), 81-82; Sherry C. Smith, "Simple Dignity: The Architecture and Furniture of William Penhallow Henderson," EP 93(2) (Winter 1987): 30-35; Christopher Wilson, "The Santa Fe, New Mexico Plaza: An Architectural and Cultural History, 1610-1921" (University Microfilms, 1982), 213-14, 246-47, contains useful photos but misattributes Sena remodeling to John Meem; "Towns, Santa Fe, Secular Buildings, Sena Plaza" folders, MNM-PA.

27. *Old Santa Fe Today,* 65-66; "Towns, Santa Fe, de la Peña House" folders, MNM-PA; for Applegate biography, see Ina Sizer Cassidy, "Arts and Artists . . .," *New Mexico Magazine* (June 1934).

28. Amelia Hollenback to John Gaw Meem, October 28, 1930, Hollenback House, Project #148 file, UNM-M; Bainbridge Bunting, *John Gaw Meem,* 138-42.

29. Memo on "Old Woodwork Available," apparently from Hollenback to Meem, July 21, 1932, UNM-M; Hollenback to Meem, October 28, 1930, 1, UNM-M; "Schedule of Ceilings," and Meem to Hollenback, March 5, 1931, UNM-M; Bunting, *John Gaw Meem,* 139; Lonn Taylor and Dessa Bokides, *New Mexico Furniture, 1600-1940: The Origins, Survival and Revival of Furniture Making in the Hispanic Southwest* (Santa Fe: Museum of New Mexico Press, 1987), 65-69, 153; interview with Mary Jean Cook in Hollenback house, September 21, 1991.

30. Hollenback to Meem, October 28, 1930, UNM-M. See also Hollenback House, site plan, November 13, 1930, Meem to Hollenback March 5, 1931, and Hollenback to Meem, October 29, 1950, all UNM-M.

31. Meem to Hollenback, August 13, 1931, UNM-M.

32. "Trips from Santa Fe Proposed by Mary Wheelwright and Mrs. Lindon Smith," RAC-RF, III 2 Z, box 42, Western Trip 1926 folder.

33. Mrs. Gerald [Ina Sizer] Cassidy, "The Old Santa Fe Association," manuscript, c. 1955, BL-CF, carton 8; I. S. Cassidy, "Santa Feans Hot, Cold on Maintaining Plan," DNM July 19, 1956, p. 1; Bunting, *John Gaw Meem,* 20-21; Chauvenet, *John Gaw Meem,* 94-95; "Santa Fe Style," DNM February 23, 1956, 4; John G. Meem to Paul J. Vollmer, January 10, 1957, BL-CF, 67/1p.

34. Chauvenet, *John Gaw Meem,* 94; Bunting, *John Gaw Meem,* 17-20; original drawings and files are in UNM-M.

35. Wallace, "Visiting the Past," 76-77; Raymond B. Fosdick, *John D. Rockefeller, Jr.: A Portrait* (New York: Harper and Brothers, 1956), 293-95, 301; "Some Aspects of Historical Preservation," JSAH 35(4) (December 1976): 264; Carl R. Lounsbury, "Beaux-Arts Ideals and Colonial Reality: The Reconstruction of Williamsburg's Capitol, 1928-1934," JSAH 49(4) (December 1990): 373-89.

36. John D. Rockefeller, Jr., to Jesse Nusbaum, April 21, 1931, and Nusbaum to Rockefeller, December 11, 1931, both in RAC-OMR, III 2 E, box 17, folder 172; David J. Saylor, *Jackson Hole, Wyoming: In the Shadow of the Tetons* (Norman: University of Oklahoma Press, 1970), 173-204.

37. Hosmer, *Persistence*, 232-74; Weinberg, "Historic Preservation," 201-3; William S. Worley, *J. C. Nichols and the Shaping of Kansas City* (Columbia: University of Missouri Press, 1990), 17-36, 129-37; David Gebhard, "The Community as Client: Architectural Review in America," *Architecture California* 12(1) (August 1990): 3-8; Margaret Crawford, "Bertram Goodhue, Walter Douglas and Tyrone, New Mexico," *Journal of Architectural Education* 42(4) (Summer 1989): 25-33; Robin E. Datel, "Southern Regionalism and Historic Preservation in Charleston, South Carolina, 1920-1940," *Journal of Historical Geography* 16(2) (1990): 197-215; Robert M. Lillibridge, "Historic American Communities: Their Role and Potential," *Journal of the American Institute of Planners* 19 (Summer 1953): 131-38, and (Fall 1953): 219-26; Carl Feiss, "Historic Town Keeping," JSAH 15(4) (December 1956): 2-6.

38. Warranty Deed, Santa Fe Estates, Inc., to C. O. and Mabel Marie Erwin, filed November 10, 1954, Santa Fe County Court House; Harland Bartholomew and Associates, *Comprehensive City Plan, Santa Fe* (Saint Louis: author, 1947); C. Mott Wooley, "Memorandum in Support of Plaintiffs' Motion for Partial Summary Judgement," 1989, filed in the case of *Locke O. Theis and Lee Theis vs. George Kwei and Gloria Y. C. Kwei*, no. SF-88-2213(C), First Judicial District Court, County of Santa Fe, State of New Mexico (dispute over the meaning of style covenants in the Catalina Addition).

39. "Centerline Will Open Unusual Store Today," DNM October 30, 1955, p. 13A; interview with John Conron, November 17, 1991; Vera D. Hahn, "New Mexico Gadfly: John Conron," *American Home* 73(3) (March 1970): 33.

40. "No Utopia But . . .," editorial, DNM January 6, 1956, p. 4; letters to the editor, DNM March 28, May 24, April 16, 1956, all p. 4; Oliver La Farge columns, DNM March 11, April 8, July 29, October 28, 1956, all p. 4. See also appendix and its sources.

41. "A Time For Action," editorial, DNM February 10, 1956, p. 4; "Duke Planner Invited to Give Views on Architectural Plan," DNM February 23, 1956, p. 1; "Murphy Plugs For Return to Santa Fe Style," DNM March 4, 1956, p. 1; "Santa Fe Style," editorial, DNM February 23, 1956, p. 4; "Planning Board Nixes Architectural Controls," DNM July 27, 1956, p. 1.

42. "Funeral Rites For La Farge . . .," DNM August 5, 1963; "Santa Fean for All Seasons," DNM December 11, 1977, p. 8; "La Farge, A Renaissance Man," DNM December 3, 1978;

Jerome H. Rosenberg, "Anthropology as Art in Oliver La Farge . . .," *Journal of American Culture* 4(4) (Winter 1981): 27-33.

43. Old Santa Fe Association: "Citizens Demand Save Santa Fe Action," DNM August 8, 1956, p. 1; John Meem to Ina Cassidy, November 19, 1956, BL-CF, 67/1p; "Old Santa Fe Association Elects Slate of Officers," DNM July 2, 1957, p. 1; "Public Planning Forum Set," DNM August 5, 1956, p. 1; W. Thetford LeViness, "Santa Fe's Historic Sites Facing Destruction," *New York Times* October 21, 1956; "Ina Sizer Cassidy," *Women in New Mexico,* exhibit catalogue (Albuquerque: Museum of Albuquerque, 1976).

44. Membership list for Old Santa Fe Association, undated but probably about 1956, judging from the other materials in the file, BL-CF; interview with Concha Ortiz y Pino de Kleven, March 10, 1990. In an attempt to trace architectural preferences, I compiled a list of twenty-three Spanish-American individuals and couples who were organizers of the Fiesta or the Sociedad Folklórica, published authors, or political leaders, which overlapped in most cases. I established their places of residence from city directories for 1928, 1934, 1938, 1944, and 1949. Of the eleven residences I located, one is in the late Territorial style, one Italinate, and four are Bungalow style. Mrs. Cleofas Jaramillo built a 1920s Spanish Colonial Revival house at 142 Griffin; Fabiola C. de Baca (Gilbert) moved into a Pueblo-Spanish Revival house at 501 San Antonio in the early 1930s; Joseph M. Montoya and Fabian Chávez, Sr., moved into Territorial Revival houses in the early 1940s at 208 Callecita and 712 Acequia Madre, respectively; and Nina Otero Warren and Anita Bergere shared the 1870 officers' house at 135 Grant from 1928 to 1948, which was remodeled in the Pueblo-Spanish style, probably during their residence.

45. Quotes from Ordinance no. 1957-18, City of Santa Fe, sections 3.A, 7.F. Ordinance also published in DNM October 25, 1957, p. 12. Although the ordinance describes both the "Old" and the "Recent" Santa Fe styles (sections 3.a and 3.b), it only formally mandates the Old Santa Fe style (section 7.f). In practice both types were allowed. On the drafting and content of the ordinance, see Philip Higgins, "Architectural Plan Offered to Chamber," DNM March 4, 1957, p. 1; "Special Meeting Set for Study Proposed Architectural Curbs," DNM May 31, 1957, p. 1; "Here Are Recommendations for Architectural Controls," DNM March 31, 1957, p. 7. On LaFarge and Charleston, South Carolina contract, see Datel, "Southern Regionalism," 209. LaFarge and Von Horvath received advice on the ordinance from Meem and the planning commission chair, architect A. R. Millington, while City Attorney Samuel Z. Montoya insisted that the guidelines be made more specific to better withstand legal challenges

46. "'Historical' Ordinance Hit by Design Council," DNM October 25, 1957; "Historical Zone Plan Gets Support, Open Forum Slated," DNM October 27, 1957, p. 1; John Conron, letter to the editor, DNM October 30, 1957, p. 4; David Gebhard, "Eclecticism, Democracy, and Santa Fe," *Roswell Museum Bulletin* 4(4) (Fall 1956); Oliver La Farge column, DNM October 27, 1957, p. 4.

47. "Historic Zoning Ordinance Debated," and editorial, DNM October 29, 1957, pp. 1, 4; "Santa Fe Adopts Law to Retain Its Pueblo-Spanish Architecture," *New York Times,* November 3, 1957, p. 1; "Meeting Indicates Architectural Plan for City is Favored," DNM April 12, 1957, p. 1; Oliver La Farge column, DNM April 7, 1957, p. 4; "Santa Fe Weighs Keeping Pueblo Style," *New York Times,* July 21, 1957. On the New Mexico Supreme Court's validation of the ordinance, see Robert L. Montague, "Santa Fe Victorious . . .," *Historic Preservation* 16(5) (September-October 1964): 174-77.

48. John B. Jackson, letter to the editor, DNM November 6, 1957, pp. 4, 12; John P. Conron, "An Architectural Control Ordinance for Santa Fe? No!," NMA 2(11/12) (November-December, 1960): 12, 15-16.

49. "Conversations in Santa Fe with Lewis Mumford," NMA 4(11/12) (November-December 1962): 7-9, continued in 5(1/2, 3/4, 5) (January-June, 1963).

50. "Renehan Structure Now Renamed Plaza Building," DNM January 20, 1947; Oliver La Farge column, DNM June 3, 1956, p. 4; Bainbridge Bunting, "The Santa Fe Plaza," *Symposia,* 1 (4) (September 1996) quotes Meem 1966 plan at length; John G. Meem, "Phase II: Santa Fe Plaza Renewal Project," typescript, April 22, 1970, UNM-M, General Files, Correspondence F file; Chauvenet, *John Gaw Meem,* 97, 99; Bunting, *John Gaw Meem,* 20.

51. Irene von Horvath, "An Architectural Control Ordinance for Santa Fe? Yes!," NMA 2(11/12) (November-December 1960): 13-14; Santa Fe Railway, "Old Santa Fe and Roundabout," 1923 booklet, E. Boyd Collection, SRCA, box 9, folder 194; Santa Fe Chamber of Commerce, "Points of Interest in Santa Fe . . .," c. 1935 map broadside, author's collection.

52. Oliver La Farge and Irene von Horvath, "Excerpt From City Planning Commission, Committee on Preservation of the Santa Fe Character, October 4, 1956, Addendum to Report of August 30, 1956," UNM-B, box 6, folder 8n. The 1956 report is also summarized in "Six Structures in Danger," DNM August 28, 1960, p. 10. Historic Santa Fe Foundation, "Map of Historic Buildings and Sites of Santa Fe, 1962," brochure, UNM-B box 6, folder 8e; "Map . . . 1962"; Historic Santa Fe Foundation, *Old Santa Fe Today* (other editions 1966, 1972, 1991; Albuquerque: University of New Mexico Press for the foundation, 1982); "The Historic Santa Fe Foundation," membership brochure, c. 1991, author's collection.

53. John Gaw Meem, letter to editor, DNM December 10, 1967; C. M. Chavez, letter to editor, DNM March 25, 1969; Richard Polese, "Ortiz Compound . . .," *Santa Fe News,* April 13, 1967, p. 1; "A New Hotel on the Scene," editorial, DNM January 16, 1973; Barbara Snow, ed., "Preservation and Urban Renewal: Is Coexistence Possible?," special issue, *Antiquities* (October, 1963); John T. Midyette, III, "How about Urbane Urbanism," NMA 10(1/2) (January-February 1968): 17-19; Mrs. (illegible) Ortiz to Old Santa Fe Association, March 28, 1967, NMRC, E. Boyd Collection, box 9, folder 146; John Crenshaw, "Old Santa Fe Group . . .," DNM March 27, 1967; Janet Berenda, "History + Progress = A Happy Truce," DNM March 9, 1969, pp. C1-2.

54. John MacGregor, "Old Padre Gallegos House . . .," DNM January 1, 1967, Pasatiempo section; John Gaw Meem, "Houses Held Reflections of History," DNM Centennial-Fiesta Edition, September, 1949, section 3, pp. 2, 13; "Restoration of Delgado House . . .," DNM November 4, 1969, p. 1; "Delgado House restored . . .," DNM March 15, 1970, p. D1; Bradley Kidder, "The Delgado House, Santa Fe, N.M.," *Symposia* (April 1970): 18-19.

55. Jim Maldonado, "Historic Styles Group . . .," DNM December 14, 1972, p. A2; "Planners Disapprove Demolition," DNM December 22, 1972, p. 1; Bob Storey, "Tully Fund Aid Asked," DNM January 14, 1973; "Money to Save Tully House," editorial, DNM January 16, 1973; John Meem to William Federici, February 6, 1974, UNM-M, General Files; "Fund Raising Drive . . .," DNM March 24, 1974, p. 4.

56. Calvin Trillin, "U.S. Journal: Santa Fe, N.M., Thy Neighbor's Roof," *New Yorker* (March 29, 1982): 124-27; City of Santa Fe, "Architectural Design Review Guidelines," January 1982; City of Santa Fe, "Resolution No. 88, Providing Guidelines to the Historic Styles Ordinance . . .," October 27, 1982; "Article 29, H District Ordinance, Unofficial Compilation . . .," typescript, November 26, 1982; City of Santa Fe, "Ordinance No. 69, 1983, Establishing A Historic Review District . . ."; City of Santa Fe, "Bill No. 8, 1983, Establishing the Don Gaspar Area Historic District . . ."

57. Interview with Jack Gaffney, November, 1983; Kathy Haq, "Developer Sees Historic Corner . . .," AJ August 19, 1986, "Journal North" section, p. 1; David L. Bell, "Blah Factor . . .," DNM May 18, 1983. Gaffney was tragically killed in a street scuffle in the summer of 1984.

58. In addition to the sources noted for the tables in the appendix, this paragraph draws on Pannell, Kerr, and Foster, "Trends in the Hotel Industry, New Mexico," superseded by New Mexico Hotel and Motel Association, "Rocky Mountain Lodging Report, New Mexico Edition," monthly reports 1986-1993, housed at the Data Center, Anderson School of Management, University of New Mexico.

59. David Bell, ". . . First Interstate Plaza," AJ March 2, 1983, "Journal North," section, p. E5; Terrell, "'Ugly' Vandal Steps up Attacks . . .," SFR May 7, 1983, p. 7; Beth Morgan, "Downtown Bank . . .," DNM April, 12, 1983, p. A1; "A Complex Concept," editorial, DNM December 19, 1982; "Board Approves . . .," AJ April 26, 1983, p. B1; "Panel May Want . . .," DNM April 12, 1983, p. A2; Beth Morgan, "The Architect 'Ought to Be Horsewhipped,'" DNM May 1, 1983; Robert Storey, "Project Builders . . .," DNM May 1, 1983; Howard Houghton, "Interstate Plaza," AJ December 22, 1982, "Journal North" section, p. I4.

60. "A New Santa Fe Hotel," NMA 25(3) (May-June 1983): 12-13; "Hotel to Follow Same Style as La Fonda," AJ July 6, 1983, "Journal North" section, p. E1; interview with John Hayes, April 7, 1986.

61. John Conron, "Old and New Architecture . . . Design Relationships," NMA 20(3) (May-June 1978): 10-14, reprinted in National Trust for Historic Preservation, *Old & New Architecture, Design Relationship* (Washington, DC: Preservation Press, 1980); Harry Moul et

al., *Design & Preservation in Santa Fe* (Santa Fe: City of Albuquerque, 1977), portions reprinted in NMA (September-October 1978); City of Santa Fe, *The Business Capitol District Handbook* (Santa Fe: author, 1986).

62. Lynn Beebe, "Standards for Evaluating Structures within Registered Historic Districts" (Washington, DC: Heritage Conservation and Recreation Service, National Park Service, 1979); *National Register Bulletin 15: How to Apply the National Register Criteria for Evaluation* (Washington, DC: National Park Service, n.d., c. 1985). In the mid-1980s, buildings previously labeled "intrusions" were reclassified with the more neutral "non-contributing." See also Catherine W. Bishir, "Yuppies, Bubbas, and the Politics of Culture," in Thomas Carter and Bernard L. Herman, eds., *Perspectives in Vernacular Architecture, III* (Columbia: University of Missouri Press, 1989), 8-15.

63. W. Brown Morton III and Gary L. Hume, *The Secretary of Interior's Standards for Historic Preservation Projects* (Washington, DC: Heritage Conservation and Recreation Service, 1979); Technical Preservation Service, *Interpreting the Secretary of Interior's Standards for Rehabilitation* (Washington, DC: U.S. Government Printing Office, 1985); interview with George Pearl, November 26, 1991.

64. Biddle Duke, "Looks Aren't Everything, Preservationists Declare," DNM December 8, 1991, p. B1+; editorial, DNM December 16, 1991.

65. Bunting, *John Gaw Meem,* 162; Santa Fe Library file, MNM-PA; David Bell, "Clark Says Design . . .," AJ February 22, 1984, "Journal North" section, p. E6; interview with Thomas Chavez, December 12, 1991; interview with Laban Wingert, December 12, 1991; Steve Terrell, "Building That Prompted Controls Will Be Razed," AJ July 30, 1986, "Journal North" section.

66. Our Lady of Guadalupe files, MNM-PA; George Kubler, *The Religious Architecture of New Mexico* (1940; reprint, Albuquerque: University of New Mexico Press, 1972), 101-2, 124-25.

67. "Six Structures in Danger," DNM August 28, 1960, p. 10; George Pearl interview; interview with Victor Johnson, December 10, 1991; interview with Gabriel Palmer, December 16, 1991.

68. Historic Guadalupe Foundation, "Stylistic Intentions for the Sanctuario de Guadalupe," typescript, 1991, in author's files.

69. Daniel D. Arreola, "Mexican American Housescapes," *Geographical Review,* 1988, 299-315.

70. Interviews with Jose N. Trujillo, 1988-91.

71. Beverly Spears, "Santa Fe's Westside/Guadalupe Historic District: Hispanic Vernacular Versus Pueblo Revival," NMA 31 (5/6) (September 1990): 9-13; Amy Shelhammer, Robert Sullivan, and Chris Wilson, "Santa Fe's Westside Neighborhood," typescript, School of Architecture, University of New Mexico, 1990. Although the proportion of Hispanics in the old Westside neighborhood fell from 76 to 61 percent during the 1980s, the city remains

375

highly integrated, with no neighborhood being less than one-quarter Hispanic or one-quarter Anglo; U.S. Department of Commerce, *1980 Census of Population and Housing*, "New Mexico, Neighborhood Statistics," Table P-1, Area 35-106; U.S. Department of Commerce, *1990 Census of Population and Housing*, "Characteristics for Census Tracts and Block Number Areas, Santa Fe New Mexico," 1990 CPH-3-297, Table 8. Although the neighborhood and tract boundaries do not match exactly, neighborhood 14, "Historic Westside," in 1980 correlates roughly to tract 7 in 1990. See also U.S. Department of Commerce, *1970 Census of Housing*, "Block Statistics, Select Areas of New Mexico," HC93-155.

72. City of Santa Fe, "Bill no. 9, 1983, Establishing a Westside-Guadalupe Historic District . . .," pp. 1, 4; Peter Eichstaedt, "Recommendations for Westside . . .," DNM April 9, 1982, p. A3; Spears, "Santa Fe's Westside," 9.

Chapter 8

1. David Gebhard, "The Myth and Power of Place: Hispanic Revivalism in America," in PSRA 152-56, (quote) 152; Virginia L. Grattan, *Mary Colter: Builder upon the Red Earth* (Flagstaff, AZ: Northland Press, 1980), 40-42; Lloyd and June Englebrecht, *Henry C. Trost, Architect of the Southwest,* (El Paso: El Paso Public Library Association, 1981); "The House of Herbert Clark Hoover," *House Beautiful* 51 (1) (January 1922): 22-23; Rexford Newcomb, "Santa Fe, The Historic and Modern," *Western Architect* (January 1924): plates 1 and 2 (Franciscan Hotel) p. 4-6, 16 plates; David Gebhard, "R. M. Schindler in New Mexico—1915," NMA 7(1/2) (January-February 1965): 15-21.

2. John Dewey, "Americanism and Localism," *Dial* 68 (June 1920): 684-88; "On Hating the Provinces," *Nation* 111 (November 17, 1920): 550; Lewis Mumford, "The Theory and Practice of Regionalism," *Sociological Review* 20(1, 2) (1928): 18-33, 131-41; Howard W. Odem and Harvey Estill Moore, *American Regionalism: A Cultural-Historical Approach to National Integration* (New York: Henry Holt and Company, 1938); Thomas Hart Benton, "What's Holding Back American Art?" *Saturday Review* 34 (December 15, 1951): 9-14+; Wanda Corn, *Grant Wood: The Regionalist Vision* (New Haven: Yale University Press, 1983); Liane Lefaivre and Alexander Tzonis, "Lewis Mumford's Regionalism," *Design Book Review* 19 (Winter 1991): 20-23.

3. Alexander Tzonis and Liane Lefaivre, "The Grid and the Pathway: An Introduction to the Work of Dimitris and Susana Antonakakis . . .," *Architecture in Greece* 15 (1981): 164-78; Kenneth Frampton, "Critical Regionalism," in Claire Downey, ed., *The American Dream* (Atlanta: Georgia Tech and ASC/AIA, 1983), 38-43.

4. Suzanne Forrest, *The Preservation of the Village: New Mexico's Hispanics and the New Deal* (Albuquerque: University of New Mexico Press, 1989), especially foreword (by John R. Van Ness), preface, and chap. 9.

5. Allen Tate, "Regionalism and Sectionalism," *New Republic* 69 (December 23, 1931):

158-61; John Crowe Ransom, "The Aesthetic of Regionalism," *American Review* 2 (January 1934): 290-310; "The Boom in Regionalism," *Saturday Review* 10 (April 7, 1934): 60; Joseph E. Baker and Paul Robert Beath, "Regionalism: Pro and Con," *Saturday Review* 15 (November 28, 1936): 3-4+; Henry D. Sedgwick, "The Importance of the Provincial," *North American Review* 243 (June 1937): 372-82; Richard J. Neutra, "Regionalism in Architecture," *Plus* 2 (February 1939): 22-23; Henry Nash Smith, "The Southwest: An Introduction," *Saturday Review of Literature* 25 (May 16, 1942): 5-6; Erika Doss, *Benton, Pollock, and the Politics of Modernism* (Chicago: University of Chicago Press, 1991). Antiregional prejudices have remained pervasive in American intellectual circles since the decline of regionalism about 1940. The book you are reading, for instance, was denied support by the National Endowment for the Humanities three times. Typical of the comments made by the academics who reviewed the proposal for the NEH were: "Seems too regional & parochial, without national implications for NEH," and "of limited (local) interest/significance, although offers potential of raising critical issues of broader concern." I considered including an appendix of my correspondence with the NEH on this issue under the title, "WARNING: National Endowment for the Humanities fellowship review panels have determined that this subject may be of only local interest."

6. Albert H. Good, *Park and Recreation Structures* (Washington, DC: National Park Service, 1938); C. W. Short and R. Stanley Brown, *Public Buildings . . . Constructed . . . with the Assistance of the Public Works Administration* (Washington, DC: U.S. Government Printing Office (?), 1939).

7. John Gaw Meem, speech delivered at AIA Annual Conference, San Antonio, 1931, quoted in Bainbridge Bunting, *John Gaw Meem: Southwest Architect* (Albuquerque: University of New Mexico Press, 1983): 23-24.

8. John Gaw Meem, "Old Forms for New Buildings," *American Architect* 145 (1934): 10-21, (quotes) 10, 11, 20. While Meem is more of a traditionalist than many, his attempts to reconcile tradition and modernity place him in the group described as New Traditionalists by Richard Striner, "Art Deco: Polemics and Synthesis," *Winterthur Portfolio* 25(1) (Spring 1990): 21-34.

9. Meem, "Old Forms," 13, 14.

10. Meem moved between a formal Beaux Arts approach in his civic commissions and the more informal American residential design tradition. His civic buildings have a hierarchical, often symmetrical organization of space and circulation clearly derived from the Beaux Arts. In major projects such as the Santa Fe city hall, and the library and administration buildings at the University of New Mexico, however, Meem supplied an element of picturesque irregularity by projecting one wing a bit farther than the other, or by varying the detailing from one wing to the next. Meem houses, by contrast, have rambling asymmetric plans that hug the ground and open to outdoor living spaces, much like the West Coast houses of

Wright, Neutra, Harris, and Wurster. Not only did Meem wrap his houses around gardens and porches, but he often widened his portals into outdoor rooms, equipped with fireplaces and built-in benches, and oriented to landscape views or direct sunlight. Bunting, *John Gaw Meem*; Jonathan Lane, "The Period House in the Nineteen-Twenties," JSAH 20(4) (December 1961): 169-78.

11. Quote from Sylvanus G. Morley, "Keeping a City Old," *Santa Fe Trail* 1(2) (August 1913): 95. For Nusbaum photos, see for example Ortiz and De Vargas Street files, MNM-PA. On the Vierra competition entry: Sylvanus Griswold Morley, "Santa Fe Architecture," *Old Santa Fe* 2(3) (January 1915): 295, plate 8. On the Pond house, see Bunting, *John Gaw Meem*, 40. See also Corinne P. Sze, "The Gustave Baumann House," *Bulletin of the Historic Santa Fe Foundation* 19(1) (June 1991): 1-9.

12. Bunting, *John Gaw Meem*, 18, 130-33, 135, 138; Carolyn Street Austin et al., "Gordon F. Street," in Boyd C. Pratt, *Directory of Historic New Mexico Architects*, typescript, 1988, in Zimmerman Library, University of New Mexico; W. G. Turley, "Map of the City of Santa Fe," 1933, MNM, showing Harrington Junior High; John Street, interview, January 3, 1992; Kestutis Germanius, interview, January 4, 1992. It may be impossible to determine the relative contributions of Meem and Street to the Territorial Revival, because while Meem's career is thoroughly documented in the archive that bears his name at the University of New Mexico, the only significant source on Street is the two-page biographical sketch by his children, cited above.

13. Austin, "Gordon F. Street"; Bunting, *John Gaw Meem*, 51; Short and Brown, *Public Buildings*, 29, 64, 226; Peter D. Paul and Boyd Pratt, *New Mexico's Capitols*, typescript, c. 1990, 42, in author's files.

14. Bunting, *John Gaw Meem*, 86-87; Chris Wilson, "A Unique Opportunity: John Gaw Meem and the Design of the Colorado Springs Fine Arts Center," in Colorado Springs Fine Arts Center: A History . . . (Colorado Springs: Colorado Springs Fine Arts Center, 1986), 26-42; Boyd C. Pratt, "A Brief History of the Practice of Architecture in New Mexico," NMA (November-December 1989), 8-13; interview with John Conron, November 17, 1991; Kenneth S. Clark and Jan Dodson Barnhart, "W. C. Kruger," in Pratt, *Directory of Historic New Mexico Architects*; interview with Bernabe Romero, July 25, 1992. Meem would continue to design magnificent houses and to work as the University of New Mexico's architect into the 1960s and as an avid preservationist into the 1970s, but he received no state government project after Kruger's emergence in private practice. If Meem moved in wealthy social circles and combined inspired design with the personal resources to keep his office operating through lean times, Kruger succeeded primarily by cultivating political connections. The quality of work from his office varied as the firm's designers changed over the years.

15. Paul and Pratt, *New Mexico Capitols*, 33-49; S. R. DeBoer, "Preliminary Plan for Proposed Building Group for New Mexico State House," typescript, 1934, Public Works file, Hockenhull

Collection, NMRC; Will Harrison, "Kruger Drawing Plans for Capitol," unidentified newspaper clipping, Kruger file, Pratt Collection, Meem Archives, University of New Mexico.

16. George Clayton Pearl, "Philosophy and Buildings," *New Mexico Architect* (January, 1960): 20-25; Don Schlegel, "Trends in Modern Architecture," *New Mexico Architect* (April 1961): 18-21; Edna H. Bergman, "The Fate of Architectural Theory in Albuquerque," (master's thesis, University of New Mexico, 1978); interview with George Pearl, October 1982; interview with Don Schlegel, October 1982; Christopher Wilson, "Regionalism Redefined: The Impact of Modernism in New Mexico," MASS 1 (1983): 16-21.

17. Talbot F. Hamlin, "What Makes It America: Architecture in the Southwest and West," *Pencil Points* 20 (December 1939): 762-76; Hugh Morrison, "After the International Style— What?" *Architectural Forum* 72(4) (1940): 345-47; *Domestic Architecture of the San Francisco Bay Region* exhibit catalogue (San Francisco: San Francisco Museum of Art, 1949); Pietro Belluschi, "The Meaning of Regionalism in Architecture," *Architectural Record* 118 (December 1955): 131-39; V. K. Thompson, "The West in Architecture," *Western Architect and Engineer* 218(3) (1959): 17-21; Sally Woodbridge, "The Great Northwest Revival," *Progressive Architecture* 55(8) (1974): 46-63.

18. Lewis Mumford, *The Urban Prospect,* 1968, quoted and summarized in Lefaivre and Tzonis, "Mumford's Regionalism," 22-23.

19. David Gebhard, "Traveling Exhibit . . .," *New Mexico Architect* (May-June 1959): 11-14.

20. Architects Associated, *The New Mexico State Capitol 1963-1980* (Santa Fe: author, 1962); Bainbridge Bunting, "A New Capitol for New Mexico," NMA 5(1/2) (January-February 1963): 13-17. It might be objected that my assessment of the capitol master plan is overly generous, considering that the American landscape is strewn with similar urban malls of this era that are used primarily by vagrants, if by anyone at all. Indeed it is impossible in retrospect to say how successful this project would have been if developed. What I find commendable is its attempts to address social and regional issues.

21. Architects Associated, *New Mexico State Capitol,* 41; Bunting, "Capitol," 16; "Plans Unveiled," DNM September 20, 1962; "General Plan for Capitol Approved," DNM September 21, 1962.

22. "SF Architect Firm Chosen . . .," DNM May 17, 1963; "Architect Gets Go-Ahead . . .," AJ August 2, 1963; "Design for New Capitol . . .," DNM December 13, 1963.

23. Romero interview; "Kruger Asserts Design . . . ," AJ December 20, 1963, p. E2.

24. Jim Colegrove, "Capitol Drawing Produced," DNM January 12, 1964, p. 1; "The Unveiling," editorial, DNM January 12, 1964, p. 4; John G. Meem, "Let's Keep Our Heritage," DNM January 12, 1964, Pasatiempo section, p. 1+; "Citizens Voice Protest . . .," DNM January 14, 1964, pp. 1-2; letters to the editor, DNM January 15-22, 1963, p. 4+.

25. "The Ancient City Finds Its Strength," editorial, DNM March 1, 1963, p. 4; "Revised Capitol Building . . .," AJ March 18, 1964, p. 4. See also "Stake Driving Ceremony . . .," pro-

gram, June 18, 1964, MNM-VF; "Serenity Belies Stormy History," DNM December 8, 1966, p. C9; "Kruger Has Designed . . .," DNM December 8, 1966, p. C6.

26. David Gebhard, "The New Mexico State Capitol," NMA 7(11/12) (November-December 1965): 9-10; Conron interview; Paul and Pratt, *New Mexico Capitols,* 52-53.

27. John W. McHugh, "The Santa Fe Opera," NMA 7(9/10) (September- October 1965): 17-23; Elizabeth C. Munro, "New Look in Santa Fe," *Opera News* 30(1) (September 25, 1965): 14-16.

28. Antoine Predock, "La Luz," NMA 11(7/8) (July-August 1969); interview with Antoine Predock, November 1, 1982; Wilson, "Regionalism Redefined," 16-21.

29. Predock, "La Luz," 7-12; "La Luz," *Architectural Record* (mid-May 1970): 92-93.

30. Untitled (auto?) biographical sketch of Peter van Dresser, three-page typescript, 1978, file 170, van Dresser Collection, NMRC, (quotes) 1. See also additional items in files 170 and 182, van Dresser Collection.

31. Peter van Dresser, "Rootstock for a New Regionalism," *Landscape* 10 (Fall 1961): 11-14; Peter van Dresser, *Development on a Human Scale: Potentials for Ecologically Guided Growth in Northern New Mexico* (New York: Praeger Publishers, 1972).

32. Jeffrey Cook, "The Varied and Early Solar Energy Application of Northern New Mexico," *AIA Journal* 62(2) (1974): 37-42; Peter van Dresser, *Homegrown Sundwellings* (Santa Fe: The Lightening Tree, 1977); William Lumpkins, *Casa del Sol: Your Guide to Passive Solar House Design* (Santa Fe: Santa Fe Publishing Company, 1981); William Lumpkins, *La Casa Adobe,* rev. ed. (Santa Fe: Ancient City Press, 1986); David Butwin, "New Trail to Santa Fe" *Saturday Review of Literature* 54 (July 3, 1971): 35-36; Laurence Veysey, *The Communal Experience: Anarchist and Mystical Communities in Twentieth Century America* (Chicago: University of Chicago Press, 1973); Jerry Williams, ed., *New Mexico in Maps* (Albuquerque: University of New Mexico Press, 1986), 316-18.

33. Cook, "Solar Energy Application," (quote) 40; "A Breakaway House That's Heated By the Sun," *House and Garden* 142 (August 1972): 46-49.

34. In addition to the sources cited in the preceding and succeeding notes, see also *Adobe News* (later *Adobe Today,* then *Solar Earthbuilder International*) magazine, 1974 to 1987; *Traditions Southwest* (later *Adobe Journal*), 1987 to 1995; Ruth Eaton, trans., Jean Dethier, ed., *Down to Earth: Mud Architecture . . .,* (London: Thames and Judson, 1981).

35. Lumpkins, *La Casa Adobe;* "Breakaway House"; "Two-story Greenhouse . . .for This Santa Fe Adobe," *Sunset* 158 (May 1977): 146-48; "A House Heated Solely by the Sun," *House and Garden* 151 (October 1979): 176-79+; Tom Yee, "A Modern Adobe," *House and Garden* 152 (May 1980): 194-97; Madeleine Wells and Jane Williamson, *So You Want to See a Solar Building? A Tour Guide for Northern New Mexico* (Santa Fe: New Mexico Solar Energy Association, c. 1981). For a biography of Lumpkins, see Lumpkins, *Casa del Sol,* 11-12, 90, back cover; Lumpkins, *La Casa Adobe,* v-viii, back cover. In retirement from architecture in the late 1980s, Lumpkins, who had painted much of his life, emerged as a highly regarded abstract expressionism.

380

36. Cook, "Solar Energy Application"; interview with Edward Mazria, January 14, 1992; Edward Mazria, *The Passive Solar Energy Book* (Emmaus, Pa.: Rodale Press, 1979).

37. Mazria interview; interview with Blain Young, September 1989; interview with real estate agent who wished to remain anonymous, 1991; *Classic* (Santa Fe Properties, Winter/Spring 1990/1991): 8, 12.

38. Jane Jacobs, *The Life and Death of Great American Cities* (New York: Random House, 1962); Robert Venturi, *Complexity and Contradiction in Architecture* (New York: Museum of Modern Art, 1966); Robert Venturi, Denise Scott Brown, and Steven Izenour, *Learning From Las Vegas: The Forgotten Symbolism of Architectural Form* (Cambridge, MA: MIT Press, 1972); Grahame Shane, "Contextualism," *Architectural Design* 46(11) (November 1976): 676-79; Charles Jencks, *Late Modern Architecture* (New York: Rizzoli, 1980).

39. Elaine Greene, "A Passion for Purity," *House and Garden* 155 (November 1983): 160-69; Christine Mather and Sharon Woods, *Santa Fe Style* (New York: Rizzoli, 1986), 178-81; Anna Dooling, "Tin Roofs Sparkle with Classic Style," AJ September 29, 1987, "Journal North" section, p. 6.

40. Young interview; interview with Beverly Spears, September 1989; Beverly Spears, *American Adobes: Rural Houses of Northern New Mexico* (Albuquerque: University of New Mexico Press, 1986).

41. Mather and Woods, *Santa Fe Style*; "Publisher Profiles," *Design Book Review* 18 (Spring 1990): 21, 31.

42. Mather and Woods, *Santa Fe Style*, 40, 21, 143.

43. Six untitled half-hour episodes about Santa Fe, producer/director Richard Morash, host Steve Thomas, PBS/WGBH, *This Old House*, 1990. The Thomas-Leyva exchange occurs near the end of episode three.

44. Paul Goldberger, "Speaking the Language of Desert and Mountain," *New York Times*, January 28, 1990, pp. H37-38.

45. Paul Horgan, "Preface to an Unwritten Book [on the Passing of Sectionalism]," *The Yale Review* 65(3) (March 1976): 321-35, (quote) 329.

46. Quotes from Antoine Predock, "Housing—Five Different Stories," *MASS* 2 (Summer 1984): 6-7; Predock interview.

47. Goldberger, "Speaking the Language"; V. B. Price, "Antoine Predock, FAIA," *Artspace* 12(1) (Winter 1987-88): 70-78; Sylvia Lavin, "Power to Heal: Antoine Predock Considers the Nature of Architecture," *Elle Decor* 1(5) (June/July 1990): 80-89.

48. David Dillon, "Hotel and Resorts Complete the Fantasy World," *Dallas Morning News*, February 24, 1991, p. C1, and "Disney Boss Likes to Hire Stars of Architecture," *Dallas Morning News*, February 24, 1991, p. C8; Suzanne Stephens, "That's Entertainment," *Architectural Record* (August, 1990): 72-79; Ross Miller, "Euro Disneyland and the Image of America," *Progressive Architecture* (October 1990): 92-95; Phillip Arcidi, "American Exotica," *Progressive Architecture* (October 1990): 92-95.

49. Antoine Predock, quoted in Shaun Duncliffe, "Hotel Designs for the Imagination," *Hotel Spec,* no date, in author's files.

50. Tzonis and Lefaivre, "The Grid," 176, 172.

51. Frampton, "Critical Regionalism," 42, 39.

52. Kenneth Frampton, "Toward a Critical Regionalism," in Hal Foster, ed., *The Anti-Aesthetic: Essays on Postmodern Culture* (Port Townsend, WA: Bay Press, 1983), 26, 27. Such is Frampton's antipathy for "cardboard scenographic populism" that he banishes ornament and overt symbolism and instead champions a glorified structural expressionism, which he calls the "tectonic" (27-28). Like the modernists, Frampton needlessly suppresses the symbolic and psychological dimension of architecture. While symbolism in place of a deeper regionalism is a sham, it does not follow that symbolism as a part of a comprehensive regionalism need also be anathema. There is no reason that those traditional forms and ornaments, colors, and materials familiar to local residents should not be employed to reflect local historical continuity and distinctiveness. The use of adobe-colored stucco in Santa Fe, for instance, is a powerful symbol of community.

53. Frampton, "Toward a Critical Regionalism," 25-28; Joel Garreau, *Edge City: Life on the New Frontier* (New York: Doubleday, 1988).

54. *Smoke Signals: West Alameda Compound Quarterly Newsletter* 1 (Autumn 1990); "The Commons on the Alameda," booklet, 1991, in author's files; Randi Hoffman, "Co-Housing: Neighborhoods by Design," in "The Goodlife," supplement to *Crosswinds* (c. May 1992); interview with Don Altshuler, Lynnwood Brown, Paula Baker, and Courteney Mathey, July 1992.

55. Christopher Alexander, Sara Ishikawa, Murray Silverstein, *A Pattern Language* (New York: Oxford University Press, 1977).

56. Kathryn McCamant and Charles Durrett, *Cohousing: A Contemporary Approach to Housing Ourselves* (Berkeley: Habitat Press/Ten Speed Press, 1988); Clare Cooper Marcus, review of *Cohousing, Design Book Review* 19 (Winter 1991): 59-60. See also Serge Chermayeff and Alexander Tzonis, *Shape of Community* (Middlesex, England: Penguin Books, 1971); Delores Hayden, *Redesigning America: The Future of Housing, Work and Family Life* (New York: W.W. Norton, 1984); Clare Cooper Marcus and Wendy Sarkissian, *Housing as if People Mattered* (Berkeley: University of California Press, 1986). Regardless of its significant social contribution, the relative cost of joining The Commons and its high Santa Fe style design may lead some to dismiss it as just another sign of the gentrification of the west side. If The Commons had also tried to break new ground in affordable housing and architectural style, it probably would have failed by diluting its focus. (The 1963 capitol master plan, to take a similar example, may have failed in part because the style of its mesa wall buildings kept Meem and the traditionalist from supporting its program of public plazas and courtyards.) It remains for others to combine the compound community idea with a greater emphasis on owner-built sweat equity, creative low-cost financing, straw-bale construction, and so forth, to create better affordable housing.

Conclusion

1. "Not Wanted," editorial, DNM March 6, 1942; *Socorro Chieftan* editorial, reprinted in AJ April 20, 1942. See also "A Patriotic Duty," editorial DNM, March 9, 1942; "Social Effects, Aliens and Concentration Camps" [newspaper clipping book], 7-18, NMRC. "Among" capitalized in original of last quote.

2. "Social Effects"; John J. Culley, "The Santa Fe Internment Camp and the Justice Department Program for Enemy Aliens," in Roger Daniels et al., eds., *Japanese Americans: From Relocation to Redress* (Salt Lake City: University of Utah Press, 1986); Edward and Donna Brett, "Santa Fe's Shameful 'Jap Trap'," SFR February 15, 1984, p. 11; Sharon Niederman, "The Years of 'Los Japos,'" SFR July 10, 1991, pp. 17-19; Toshio Hirano, *A Sketch of My Life: The Autobiography of the Reverend Toshio Hirano* (n.p.: Hirano family, c. 1982); Michi Weglyn, *Years of Infamy: The Untold Story of America's Concentration Camps* (New York: Morrow Quill, 1976).

3. "The Good Life: Guide to Healthy, Environmentally-Conscious Living" supplement to *Crosswinds* (c. May 1992); Tamar Stieber, "Permaculture," AJ September 6, 1992, pp. F1, 3; "Saving Santa Fe" (an in-depth week-long series), DNM October 3-10, 1993. This debate has been most sustained in the pages of the *Santa Fe Reporter* and *Crosswinds*.

4. William H. McNeill, "Mythistory, or Truth, History, and Historians," *American Historical Review* 91 (1) (February 1986): 1-10, (quote) 4; Paul Ricoeur, *History and Truth* (Evanston, IL: Northwestern University Press, 1965), 283.

5. "Artists Object, Statue is Forfeited; Mrs. Austin, Applegate Protest," DNM, October 12, 1927; and subsequent articles through October 19, 1927.

6. Oliver La Farge, "10-Year-Old La Farge Story Clears Obelisk," DNM November 5, 1967.

7. Webb Young, letter to John Meem, November 23, 1959, UNM-M, box 1, "OSFA: City Affairs 1960" file; Myra Ellen Jenkins, "Archivist Opposes Plans to Change Santa Fe Plaza," DNM October 1, 1967, "Pasatiempo" section, p. 1; Jim Danneskiold, "Hispanic Group . . .," AJ March 8, 1989, "Journal North" section; Dorsey Griffith, "Old Monument Focus of New Debate," DNM April 12, 1989, p. 1; Orlando Romero, "The Plaza Statue," SFR April 12, 1989, p. 7; Kelly Richmond, "Statue Designs . . .," DNM March 20, 1990.

8. Interview with Luis Jiménez, February 27, 1992; Jim Danneskiold, "Angry Commissioner . . .," AJ September 27, 1989; Frank V. Ortiz, "Editorial on Statue . . .," DNM August 22, 1990, MNM-VF.

9. Kelly Richmond, "Panel Decides . . .," DNM August 14, 1990; Jim Danneskiold, "Peralta Statue . . .," AJ August 14, 1990, "Journal North" section; "City Deserves Better," editorial, AJ August 18, 1990; Thomas E. Chávez, Orlando Romero, "Letters to Journal North," AJ August 25, 1990; Nancy Baca, "Arts Jury . . .," AJ July 13, 1991, "Journal North" section.

10. Bill Hume, "Bronze Onate Retraces Journey," AJ February 9, 1992, p. B3; Marc Simmons, "The Onate Statue," SFR April 29, 1992, p. 24.

11. Patrick Nagatani, *Nuclear Enchantment* (Albuquerque: University of New Mexico Press,

383

1991). See also "Bravo 20 National Park, A Proposal," in Richard Misrach, *Bravo 20: The Bombing of the American West* (Baltimore: Johns Hopkins University Press, 1990).

12. This section has been informed by the following works: Ricoeur, *History and Truth*; Lewis Mumford, *Technics and Civilization* (1934; reprint, New York: Harcourt Brace Jovanovich, 1963); Henry Glassie, "Meaningful Things and Appropriate Myths: The Artifact's Place in American Studies," *Prospectus* 3 (1973); T. J. Jackson Lears, "The Concept of Cultural Hegemony: Problems and Possibilities," *American Historical Review* 90(3) (June 1986): 567-93; Wendell Berry, "The Futility of Global Thinking," *Harper's Magazine* 279(1672) (September 1989): 16-22.

13. Rina Swentzell holds a master's of architecture and a doctorate in American studies. Although she remains active in the religious and cultural life of Santa Clara, she lives in a passive solar adobe house with picturesque mountain views, which she built with her husband on the west edge of Santa Fe. Pertinent publications by Swentzell include "An Architectural History of Santa Clara Pueblo" (master's of architecture thesis, University of New Mexico, 1976); "An Understated Sacredness," MASS (Journal of the School of Architecture and Planning, University of New Mexico) 3 (Fall 1985): 24-25; "Bupingeh: The Pueblo Plaza," EP 94(2) (Winter 1988): 14-19; "Pueblo Space, Form and Mythology," in PSRA, 23-30; "Conflicting Landscape Values: The Santa Clara Pueblo and Day School," *Places* 7(1) (Fall 1990): 18-27; "Santa Clara Pueblo: A Changing Community," in Boyd C. Pratt and Chris Wilson, eds., *The Architecture and Cultural Landscape of North Central New Mexico* (Santa Fe: New Mexico Historic Preservation Division, 1991). On Swentzell, see Jim Sagel, "Architect Sees Pueblos Losing Focus," AJ March 11, 1987, "Journal North" section. See also Alfonso Ortiz, *The Tewa World: Space, Time, Being, and Becoming in a Pueblo Society* (Chicago: University of Chicago Press, 1969); Peter Nabokov and Robert Easton, *Native American Architecture* (New York: Oxford University Press, 1989), 348-409, 419-20.

14. Swentzell, "Pueblo Space," 23.

15. Swentzell, "Bugingeh," 16, italics added; Swentzell, "Changing Community," 16. On 1990 census, see chap. 7, n. 71.

16. John Dewey, "Americanism and Localism," *Dial* 68 (June 1920): 684-88.

Appendix

1. For 1790, see Janie Louise Aragon, "People of Santa Fe in the 1790's," *Aztlán* 7 (3) (Fall 1976): 391-417. For 1850-80, see for Spanish and non-Spanish surname proportions: Deena J. González, "The Widowed Women of Santa Fe: Assessment on the Lives of an Unmarried Population, 1850-1880," in Ellen C. DuBois and Vicki L. Ruiz, eds., *Unequal Sisters: A Multicultural Reader in U.S. Women's History* (New York: Routledge, 1990), 39. For 1850 to 1990, see Department of Commerce, *Census of Population,* (Washington, DC: U.S. Government Printing Office, various dates): 1850, p. 994; 1860, p. 570; 1870, p. 206; 1880,

p. 200; 1890, p. 242; 1900, p. 274; 1910, p. 166; 1920, p. 529; 1930, pp. 53-4; 1940, p. 700; 1950, p. 31-10; 1960, p. 33-9; 1970, p. 33-15, 169; 1980, p. 33-8, 12; 1990, New Mexico tables 5, 15.

2. Over 90 percent of gross receipts and employment in the county occur in the city of Santa Fe. This table is based primarily on U.S. Department of Commerce, *Decennial Census of Population,* 1930-1990, "Employment by Industry Groups," New Mexico, county tables, found, respectively, in 1930, vol. III, pt. 2, p. 247; 1940, vol. 2, p. 992; 1950, table 31-155; 1960, table 33-127; 1970, table 33-214; 1980, table 33-200; 1990, Summary Tape File 3A, New Mexico, Santa Fe County, Occupation, Industry. Additional information was drawn from: U.S. Department of Commerce, *County Business Patterns, First Quarter, 1948; First Quarter 1959; 1970; 1980; 1990* (Washington, DC: U.S. Government Printing Office 1949, 1961, c. 1972, 1982, 1992); New Mexico Taxation and Revenue Department, "Analysis of Gross Receipts Tax by SIC," bound computer print-outs for 1982, 1990, 1992 at Data Center, School of Business, University of New Mexico, Albuquerque; Southwest Planning and Marketing, *Santa Fe Arts Impact Study* (Santa Fe: author, 1993). Tourism and travel expenditures and employment are notoriously difficult to estimate, because all of the sectors of the economy in which tourists are active (restaurants, service stations, apparel purchases, lodgings, etc.) are also patronized by local residents. To estimate the tourism economy, I compared 1990 gross receipts in Santa Fe with Roswell, New Mexico, a similar regional service center with a population of 43,187. Roswell has little state government or tourism economy (although the fourth largest city in the state, it is not among the top ten in lodging rooms). While Roswell is the primary shopping town within a 100-mile radius, Santa Fe loses a significant portion of its potential retail trade to Albuquerque, 60 miles distant. Per capita lodging gross receipts in Santa Fe were more than seven times those in Roswell, and retail sales were more than double. Based on this, I have attributed 90 percent of lodging employment from *County Business Statistics* and 60 percent of retail sales employment from the decennial census to tourism. Because tourism was more seasonal in earlier years, I have reduced the allocation of retail employment to tourism by 5 percent each decade: to 55 percent in 1980, 50 percent in 1970, and so forth, down to 30 percent in 1920. I have also assumed that 10 percent of manufacturing employment has been of goods such as jewelry and furniture, made for tourist consumption. I have also attempted to estimate the number of people making most of their income from the production of crafts and arts, primarily for the tourist market. Because most are self-employed (selling their goods on consignment, at annual arts fairs, under the Palace of the Governors portal, etc.), they do not show up in business employment statistics. (The *1987 Census of Retail Trade* makes the first tentative attempt to track these "Nonemployer Statistics.") I have reinterpreted the *Santa Fe Arts Impact Study.* To prepare for this survey of artists living in Santa Fe County, the authors compiled a list of 3,154 artists from thirty-two membership and mailing lists from arts and arts fair organizations, government arts agencies, cultural groups, art gal-

385

leries, the telephone book, and so forth, and by advertizing in the mass media. While the authors estimate a total of 6,600 artists in the county, I believe it is unlikely that large numbers of artists making a living from their work would have been omitted from their list, and therefore I estimate 3,500 artists in the county. Of the 1,172 artists who responded to the survey, 25 percent reported annual sales of over $20,000 (who I assume made the majority of their income from their work), and another 16.5 percent reported sales of between $10,000 and $20,000 (two-thirds of whom I assume were supported primarily by their work). Applying these percentages to my estimate of 3,500 artists yields a total of 1,257 people employed more than half-time in the arts. As this represents 4.5 people for each art gallery and Indian goods store listed in the phone book, I have multiplied the number of such stores in previous years by 4.5 and added the separate listings for artists to arrive at very rough estimate of artists in those earlier years: 455 in 1980, 200 in 1970, 132 in 1960, 107 in 1950, 102 in 1940, 101 in 1930, 18 in 1920.

3. *Complete Business Directory of New Mexico* (Santa Fe: New Mexican Publishing Co., 1882); *Corry's New Mexico Gazetteer and Business Directory* (Topeka: George Crane, 1892); *Business Directory, Arizona and New Mexico for 1897* (Las Vegas, NM: Daily Examiner, 1897); *New Mexico Business Directories, 1903-4, 1907-8.* 1911, 1921 (Denver: Gazetter Publishing, 1903, 1907, 1911, 1921); *Santa Fe City Directories, 1930-31, 1940, 1951* (El Paso: Hudsepth Directory Company, 1930, 1940,1951); *Telephone Directories for Santa Fe, 1960, 1970, 1980* (n.p.: Mountain States Telephone and Telegraph Company, 1960, 1970, 1980); *Santa Fe Yellow Pages* (n.p.: US West Direct, 1992). The number of lodging rooms was calculated based on the sources above and on floor plans for representative New Mexican historic hotels; "Santa Fe" (New York: Sanborn Map Company, 1882; 1886; 1890; 1898; 1902; 1908; 1913; 1921; 1930; 1951), multiple sheets of insurance maps for each year, UNM-MG; "Santa Fe Hotels," clippings file, Southwest Room, New Mexico State Library, Santa Fe; *Arizona New Mexico Tour Book* (Heathrow, FL: American Automobile Association, 1992); interview with Phil Kithill (director, New Mexico Hotel Motel Association), October 19, 1993. Where listings appear under two headings in a directory (for both Indian Goods and Art Galleries, for instance), I have divided them equally between headings.

Illustration Credits

Abbreviations

KSHS	Kansas State Historical Society, Topeka
MA	Meem Archives, Center for Southwest Research, Zimmerman Library, University of New Mexico, Albuquerque
MNM	Photo Archives, History Museum, Museum of New Mexico, Santa Fe
PP	Patricia Pollock
RR	Robert Reck
SARC	State Archives and Record Center, Santa Fe
SAR-MNM	School of American Research Collections, Photo Archives, History Museum, Museum of New Mexico, Santa Fe
CW	Chris Wilson

387

Illustrations are reproduced by permission and appear courtesy of:

PP. 14-15. MNM # 61561

P. 16. MNM # 10173

P. 17. MNM # 10171

PP. 18-19. MNM # 60326

1. Universal City Studios, © 1987

2. Chicago Historical Society

3. MNM # 65038

4. Peter Nabakov and Robert Easton, *Native American Architecture,* © 1989

5. Reader's Digest Association, Inc., *Reader's Digest Mysteries of Ancient Americas,* © 1986

6. MNM # 16096

7. MNM # 11125

8. Library of Congress, Washington D.C., # LC-USZA1-1150

9. MNM # 15030

10. The British Library, London

11. Wilson Hurley, Dr. and Mrs. Albert Simms, and the School of American Research, Santa Fe

12. MNM # 10170

13. PP

14. MNM # 28472

15. MNM # 11075

16. MNM # 10110

17. PP

18. Cartographic Branch, National Archives, Suitland, Maryland

19. MNM # 61561

20. MNM # 10685

21. SAR-MNM # 15844

22. MNM # 29086

23. MNM # 10713

24. SAR-MNM # 15847

25. MNM # 15145

26. MNM # 127377

27. MNM # 10005

28. SAR-MNM # 15854

29. MNM # 11252

30. U.S. Army Signal Corp Collection in MNM # 9099

31. SAR-MNM # 15376

32. Library of Congress, Washington, D.C., #517666

33. MNM # 10763

34. MNM # 14758

35. MNM # 10778

36. MNM # 139208

37. MNM # 10016

38. MNM # 56846

39. MNM # 10392

40. MNM # 10639

41. MNM # 10728

42. MNM # 87442

43. New Mexico Bureau of Immigration, *Illustrated New Mexico,* 1885

44. MNM # 21043

45. New York Historical Society, photographic copy by Leland Roth

46. J.W. and D.B. Shepp, *Shepp's World's Fair Photographed,* 1893, MNM # 99695

47. J.W. and D.B. Shepp, *Shepp's World's Fair Photographed,* 1893, MNM # 99694

48. Advertising/Creative Services, The Atchison, Topeka and Santa Fe Railway Company

49. MNM # 49212

50. David Francis, *The Universal Exposition of 1904*, 1904, MNM # 99693

51. MNM # 61366

52. MNM # 81967

53. Jack Parsons

54. RR

55. CW

56. CW

57. RR

58. MNM # 55540

59. CW

60. CW

61. CW

62. CW

63. Eva Cockcroft and Sam Leyba

64. Eva Cockcroft and Sam Leyba

65. CW

66. RR

PP. 106-107. MNM # 118249

PP. 108-109. MNM # 67890

67. MNM # 61662

68. MNM # 61669

69. MNM # 61379

70. MNM # 23100

71. MNM # 81918

72. MNM # 28087

73. MNM # 10541

74. MNM # 10544

75. MNM # 61445

76. Colorado Historical Society, Denver, # 34165

77. MNM # 6783

78. MNM # 46782

79. MNM # 60335

80. MNM # 60254

81. MNM # 38336

82. MNM # 22970

83. MNM # 6741

84. MNM # 31539

389

85. MNM # 31538

86. MNM # 390

87. MNM # 50912

88. MNM # 122896

89. MNM # 23103

90. PP

91. La Fonda Files, Meem Collection, MA

92. MNM # 10662

93. MNM # 51386

94. MNM # 51927

95. MNM # 67890

96. MNM # 91637

97. MNM # 135233

98. MNM # 69247

99. MNM # 9928

100. MNM # 132819

101. Elizabeth Martinez and Paul Groth

102. Luis Jiménez, 1993

103. Harry Fonseca, 1982

104. Nora Naranjo-Morse, 1987

105. Harry Fonseca, 1990

106. Mark Nohl and Davis Mather Folk Art Gallery, 141 Lincoln Avenue, Santa Fe 87501

107. Santa Fe Country Furniture Store, 1708 Cerrillos Road, Santa Fe 87505

108. CW

109. Lewis E. Thompson Productions, P.O. Box 152, Santa Fe 87504

110. Anita Rodríguez and Handsel Gallery, Santa Fe

111. Anita Rodríguez and Handsel Gallery, Santa Fe

112. Miguel Gandert, © 1995

113. Loomis Collection, SARC, # 21895

114. SAR-MNM # 15819

115. MNM # 11001

116. MNM # 14091

117. MNM # 51674

118. Pettibone Company, *Lodge Supplies for Knights of Pythias,* Cincinnati, about 1900, MNM # 157454

119. MNM # 139021

120. MNM # 7271

121. MNM # 7875

122. MNM # 52848

123. MNM # 52575

124. MNM # 52785

125. MNM # 52421

126. Department of Development Collection, SARC, # 2294

127. MNM # 57833

128. MNM # 13692

129. MNM # 117941

130. MNM # 10885

131. MNM # 52470

132. MNM # 132200

133. MNM # 118249

134. MNM # 41301

135. MNM # 22689

136. MNM # 117680

137. MNM # 135050

138. MNM # 135044

139. KSHS, # 4/D-4.31

140. MNM # 110864

141. KSHS, # 4/D-4.11

142. MNM # 143101

143. KSHS, # 4/D-4.08

144. CW

145. MNM # 13967

146. MNM # 46777

147. author's collection

148. MNM # 143698

149. MA

150. MA

151. MNM # 10690

152. MNM # 7864

153. Abbie Caplin Winterrowd

154. MNM # 16547

155. MNM # 61509

156. MNM # 51186

157. MNM # 15335

158. MNM # 29013

159. MA and © 1993 by the Trustees of the Ansel Adams Publishing Rights Trust

160. MA

161. Colonial Williamsburg Foundation, Virginia, # 91-TE6-825, 35s

162. MNM # 56414

163. John Conron

164. PP

165. MNM # 29076

166. MNM # 106739

167. CW

168. MNM # 43396

169. CW

170. CW

171. CW

172. MNM # 117155

173. CW

174. MNM # 117125

175. CW

176. CW

177. CW

178. CW

179. PP after earlier plans by Sattler, Sprick and Hesse

180. CW

181. CW

182. author's collection

183. MNM # 19646

184. MNM # 95327

185. MA, and Laura Gilpin Collection, Amon Carter Museum, Fort Worth © 1981

186. MNM # 51304

187. MA, and © 1993 by the Trustees of the Ansel Adams Publishing Rights Trust

188. CW

189. MNM # 51417

190. MNM # 56409

191. John Conron

192. John Conron

193. Kruger Collection, MA

194. MNM # 161280

195. CW

196. CW

197. CW

198. CW

199. Russ Ball and Edward Mazria

200. CW

201. MNM # 117146

202. Michael Tincher, © 1991

203. © Timothy Hursley

204. Christopher Mead

205. Courteney Mathey

206. CW

207. Department of Special Collections, University Research Library, UCLA

208. CW

209. MNM # 90294

210. Luis Jiménez

211. CW

212. CW

213. CW

214. Patrick Nagatani

215. Rina Swentzell

Suggested Reading

Alexander, Christopher, Sara Isikawa, and Murry Silverstein. *A Pattern Language.* New York: Oxford University Press, 1977.

Anaya , Rudolfo A., ed. *Voces: An Anthology of Nuevo Mexicano Writers.* Albuquerque: University of New Mexico Press, 1987.

——, and Francisco Lomeli, eds. *Aztlán: Essays on the Chicano Homeland.* Albuquerque: Academia/El Norte Publications, 1989.

Anzaldúa, Gloria. *Borderlands/La Frontera: The New Mestiza.* San Francisco: spinsters/aunt lute, 1987.

Barrera, Mario. *Race and Class in the Southwest: A Theory of Racial Inequity.* Notre Dame: Notre Dame University Press, 1979.

Bogart, Michele. *Public Sculpture and the Civic Ideal in New York City, 1890-1930.* Chicago: University of Chicago Press, 1989.

Briggs, Charles L. *The Wood Carvers of Córdova, New Mexico: Social Dimensions of an Artistic "Revival."* 1980, rpt. Albuquerque: University of New Mexico Press, 1989.

Bunting, Bainbridge. *Early Architecture of New Mexico.* Albuquerque: University of New Mexico Press, 1976.

——. *John Gaw Meem: Southwest Architect.* Albuquerque: University of New Mexico Press, 1983.

Carnes, Mark C. *Secret Ritual and Manhood in Victorian America.* New Haven: Yale University Press, 1989.

Campa, Arthur. *Hispanic Culture in the Southwest.* Norman: University of Oklahoma Press, 1979.

Chauvenet, Beatrice. *Hewett and Friends: A Biography of Santa Fe's Vibrant Era.* Santa Fe: Museum of New Mexico Press, 1983.

Chavez, Angelico. *My Penitente Land: Reflections on Spanish New Mexico.* Albuquerque: University of New Mexico Press, 1974.

Chavez, John R. *The Lost Land: The Chicano Image of the Southwest.* Albuquerque: University of New Mexico Press, 1984.

Clifford, James. *The Predicament of Culture: Twentieth-Century Ethnography, Literature, and Art.* Cambridge: Harvard University Press, 1988.

Cordova, Gilberto Benito. *The 3 1/2 Cultures of Española*. Albuquerque: El Norte Publications/Academia, 1990.

DeBouzek, Jeanette and Diana Reyna. "Gathering Up Again: Fiesta in Santa Fe." Video, 1992.

deBuys, William. *Enchantment and Exploitation: The Life and Hard Times of a New Mexico Mountain Range*. Albuquerque: University of New Mexico Press, 1985.

Dening, Greg. *Mr Bligh's Bad Language: Passion, Power and Theatre on the Bounty*. Cambridge: Cambridge University Press, 1992.

Dorst, John. *The Written Suburb: An American Site, An Ethnographic Dilemma*. Philadelphia: University of Pennsylvania Press, 1989.

Doss, Erika, *Benton, Pollock, and the Politics of Modernism*. Chicago: University of Chicago Press, 1991.

Espinosa, Aurelio M. *The Folklore of Spain in the American Southwest*. Norman, Oklahoma: University of Oklahoma Press, 1985.

Forrest, Suzanne. *The Preservation of the Village: New Mexico's Hispanics and the New Deal*. Albuquerque: University of New Mexico Press, 1989.

Garcia, Mario T. *Mexican Americans: Leadership, Ideology and Identity, 1930-1960*. New Haven: Yale University Press, 1989.

Gill, Sam D. *Mother Earth: An American Story*. Chicago: University of Chicago Press, 1987.

Glassberg, David. *American Historical Pageantry: The Uses of Tradition in the Early Twentieth Century*. Chapel Hill: University of North Carolina Press, 1990.

Gómez-Peña, Guillermo. *Warrior for Gringostroika*. St. Paul, Minnesota: Greywolf Press, 1993.

Gonzáles, Felipe. "The Political Construction of Latino Nomenclature in Twentieth Century New Mexico." *American Journal of the Southwest* 35/ 2 (Summer 1993): 158-85.

Grimes, Ronald. *Symbol and Conquest: Public Ritual and Drama in Santa Fe, N.M.* Ithaca: Cornell University Press, 1976.

Gutiérrez, Ramón A. *When Jesus Came the Corn Mothers Went Away: Marriage, Sexuality, and Power in New Mexico, 1500-1846*. Stanford: Stanford University Press, 1991.

Hall, Edward T. *An Anthropology of Everyday Life: An Autobiography*. New York: Doubleday, 1992.

——. *Beyond Culture*. Garden City, New York: Anchor/Doubleday, 1976.

Hall, Thomas D. *Social Change in the Southwest, 1350-1880*. Lawrence: University Press of Kansas, 1989.

Hobsbawm, Eric, and Terence Ranger eds. *The Invention of Tradition*. Cambridge: Cambridge University Press, 1983.

Horsman, Reginald. *Race and Manifest Destiny: The Origins of American Racial Anglo-Saxonism*. Cambridge: Harvard University Press, 1981.

Journal of the Southwest 32/4 (Winter 1990). [Issue devoted to tourism in the region].

Keefe, Susan E. and Amado M. Padilla. *Chicano Ethnicity*. Albuquerque: University of New Mexico Press, 1987.

Kessell, John L. *The Missions of New Mexico Since 1776*. Albuquerque: University of New Mexico Press, 1980.

Koller, James et al., eds. *Coyote's Journal*. Berkeley: Wingbow, 1982.

La Farge, Oliver. *The Man with the Calabash Pipe*. Boston: Houghton Mifflin, 1966.

———. *Santa Fe: The Autobiography of a Southwestern Town*. Norman: University of Oklahoma Press, 1959.

Lears, T.J. Jackson. *No Place of Grace: Anti-modernism and the Transformation of American Culture*. New York: Pantheon, 1981.

Limerick, Patricia Nelson. *The Legacy of Conquest: The Unbroken Past of the American West*. New York: W. W. Norton, 1987.

Lowenthal, David. *The Past is a Foreign Country*. Cambridge: Cambridge University Press, 1985.

McCamant, Kathryn, and Charles Durrett. *Cohousing: A Contemporary Approach to Housing Ourselves*. Berkeley: Habitat Press/Ten Speed Press, 1988.

McCannell, Dean. *The Tourist: A New Theory of the Leisure Class*. New York: Shocken Books, 1976.

———. "Reconstructed Ethnicity: Tourism and Cultural Identity in the Third World." *Annals of Tourism Research* 11/3 (1984).

McLuhan, T. C. *Dream Tracks: The Railroad and the American Indian 1890-1930*. New York: Harry N. Abrahams, 1985.

Man on Fire/El Hombre en Llamas: Luis Jiménez. Albuquerque: Albuquerque Museum, 1994.

Markovich, Nicholas C., Wolgang F.E. Preiser, and Fred G. Strum eds. *Pueblo Style and Regional Architecture*. New York: Van Nostrand Reinhold, 1990.

Mather, Christine and Sharon Woods. *Santa Fe Style*. New York: Rizzoli, 1986.

Mazria, Edward. *The Passive Solar Energy Book*. Emmaus, Pa.: Rodale Press, 1979.

Meinig, D. W. *The Shaping of America, Volume 2, Continental America, 1800-1867*. New Haven: Yale University Press, 1993.

Mumford, Lewis. *Technics and Civilization*. 1934, rpt. New York: Harcourt Brace Jovanovich, 1963.

Nabokov, Peter and Robert Easton. *Native American Architecture*. New York: Oxford University Press, 1989.

Nagatani, Patrick. *Nuclear Enchantment*. Albuquerque: University of New Mexico Press, 1991.

Naranjo-Morse, Nora. *Mud Women: Poems From the Clay*. Tucson: University of Arizona Press, 1992.

Nichols, John. *The Milagro Beanfield War*. New York: Holt, Rinehart and Winston, 1974.

Nobel, David ed. *Santa Fe: History of an Ancient City*. Santa Fe: School of American Research, 1988.

Ortiz, Alfonso *The Tewa World: Space, Time, Being, and Becoming in a Pueblo Society*. Chicago: University of Chicago Press, 1969.

Padilla, Genaro. *My History, Not Yours: The Formation of Mexican American Autobiography*. Madison: University of Wisconsin Press, 1993.

Pierce, Donna ed., *!Vivan Las Fiestas!* Santa Fe: Museum of New Mexico Press, 1985.

Rodríguez, Sylvia. "Art, Tourism, and Race Relations in Taos: Toward a Sociology of the Art Colony." *Journal of Anthropological Research* 45/ 1 (Spring 1989): 77- 100.

——, "Ethnic Reconstruction in Taos." *Journal of the Southwest* 3 2/4 (Winter 1990): 541-55.

Robertson, Edna, and Sarah Nestor. *Artists of Canyons and Caminos: Santa Fe, the Early Years.* Salt Lake City: Gibbs M. Smith, 1982.

Roscoe, Will. *The Zuni Man-Woman.* Albuquerque: University of New Mexico Press, 1991.

Rudnick, Lois Palken. *Mabel Dodge Luhan: New Woman, New Worlds.* Albuquerque: University of New Mexico Press, 1984.

Said, Edward. *Orientalism.* New York: Vintage Books/Random House, 1979.

Schöler, Bo. *Coyote Was Here: Essays on Contemporary Native American Literary and Political Mobilization. The Dolphin* 9 (April 1984).

Sheppard, Carl D. *Creator of the Santa Fe Style: Isaac Hamilton Rapp.* Albuquerque; University of New Mexico Press, 1988.

——, *The Saint Francis Murals of Santa Fe.* Santa Fe: Sunstone Press, 1989.

Spears, Beverly. *American Adobes: Rural Houses of Northern New Mexico.* Albuquerque: University of New Mexico Press, 1986.

Starr, Kevin. *Inventing the Dream: California Through the Progressive Era.* New York: Oxford University Press, 1985.

Swentzell, Rina. "Pueblo Space, Form and Mythology." in Nicholas C. Markovich et al. eds. *Pueblo Style and Regional Architecture.* New York: Van Nostrand Reinhold, 1990

——, "Conflicting Landscape Values: The Santa Clara Pueblo and Day School." *Places* 7/ 1 (Fall 1990): 18- 27.

Taylor, Lonn, and Dessa Bokides. *New Mexican Furniture, 1600-1940.* Santa Fe: Museum of New Mexico Press, 1987.

van Dresser, Peter. *Development on a Human Scale: Potentials for Ecologically Guided Growth in Northern New Mexico.* New York: Praeger Publishers, 1972.

Weigle, Marta, and Kyle Fiore. *Santa Fe and Taos: The Writer's Era, 1916-1941.* Santa Fe: Ancient City Press, 1982.

——, and Peter White, *The Lore of New Mexico.* Albuquerque: University of New Mexico Press, 1988.

Whisnant, David E. *All That is Native and Fine: The Politics of Culture in an American Region.* Chapel Hill: University of North Carolina Press, 1983.

397

INDEX

398

399

Gaastra, T. Charles, 138, 140, 281

Gaffney, Jack, 262–63, 298

Garcia House, floor plan, **13**

GAR. *See* Grand Army of the Republic

Gebhard, David, 257, 290

genízaros, 29–31, 42–43, 155, 336n.21

gentrification, 269–73

Gilpin, William, 49

Goldberg, Paul, 300–301

Gold's Old Curio Shop, **81,** 234

Gonzales, Felipe, 162, 355n.1

Gothic cathedrals, 56–58, **59**

Governor's Palace. *See* Palace of the Governors

Grand Army of the Republic (fraternal organization), 185

"grand carnival." *See* Pasatiempo

Greek Revival style, 54. *See also* Territorial Revival style

Haozous, Bob, 316, 318–19

Harper's Weekly, 80

Harris, Harwell Hamilton, modern regionalist, 285

Hartley, Marsden, 141

Henderson, William P., 143, 244–45, 281

Hendrickson, A. C. *See* Rapp, Rapp and Hendrickson

hermanitos. See manitos

Hewett, Edgar Lee, 115, 141, **194,** 250, 353n.60; establishes Museum of New Mexico, 117–21, 349n.20; and Fine Arts Museum, 131–35; and Palace of the Governors, 125, 128; and Plan of 1912, 121

hijos de la iglesia (children of the church), 31, 42–43

Hispanics, 152, 162–64, 359n.32, 360n.35.

See also Chicanos; *españoles;* Hispanos; Latinos; Mexican-Americans; Spanish-Americans; triculturalism

Hispanos, 74, 149, 155, 256, 357n.18. *See also* cultural purity; Hispanics; triculturalism

historical amnesia: overcoming, 313–15, 318–22, 324–29; and public monuments, 315–18; and tourism, 311–13, 322–24. *See also* cultural purity; "Scrape" approach

historic preservation, 233, 260–62, 322. *See also* design control; restoration

Historic Santa Fe Foundation, 260–62

Historic Sketches of New Mexico (Prince), 74

Hollenback, Amelia, house of, **97,** 246–50

Hollis, Pat, 288

Horgan, Paul, 153, 301

Hotel Santa Fe. *See* hotels

hotels: Clair, 69, **70,** 75–76, 331 table ; El Dorado, 264; El Navajo, 275; El Ortiz, **114;** Franciscan, 275, 279; Inn at Loretto, 297; La Fonda, **101,** 138–40, 242–43, 265, 279; Palace, 65, 71, 81; Santa Fe (Euro Disneyland), 303–4

house museums, 233

Howling Coyote. *See* Coyote

hybridization, cultural and racial, 169–80, 312. *See also* Anglo-Saxons; coyotes; *mestizos*

Hysterical Pageant, 212–13, 216–17, 219–20, 225

Illustrated New Mexico, 81–82

Ina Sizer and Gerald Cassidy House, 143–44, **145**

incorporation, the new economic panacea, 75–76

"The Indian Next to You" (La Farge), 222–23

Indians. *See* Pueblo Indians

403

404

405

407

408

409

410